The Human Tradition in American History

CHARLES W. CALHOUN
Series Editor
Department of History, East Carolina University

The nineteenth-century English author Thomas Carlyle once remarked that "the history of the world is but the biography of great men." This approach to the study of the human past had existed for centuries before Carlyle wrote, and it continued to hold sway among many scholars well into the twentieth century. In more recent times, however, historians have recognized and examined the impact of large, seemingly impersonal forces in the evolution of human history—social and economic developments such as industrialization and urbanization as well as political movements such as nationalism, militarism, and socialism. Yet even as modern scholars seek to explain these wider currents, they have come more and more to realize that such phenomena represent the composite result of countless actions and decisions by untold numbers of individual actors. On another occasion, Carlyle said that "history is the essence of innumerable biographies." In this conception of the past, Carlyle came closer to modern notions that see the lives of all kinds of people, high and low, powerful and weak, known and unknown, as part of the mosaic of human history, each contributing in a large or small way to the unfolding of the human tradition.

This latter idea forms the foundation for this series of books on the human tradition in American history. Each volume is devoted to a particular period or topic in American history and each consists of minibiographies of persons whose lives shed light on that period or topic. Well-known figures are not altogether absent, but more often the chapters explore a variety of individuals who may be less conspicuous but whose stories, nonetheless, offer us a window on some aspect of the nation's past.

By bringing the study of history down to the level of the individual, these sketches reveal not only the diversity of the American people and the complexity of their interaction but also some of the commonalities of sentiment and experience that Americans have shared in the evolution of their culture. Our hope is that these explorations of the lives of "real people" will give readers a deeper understanding of the human tradition in American history.

THE HUMAN TRADITION IN
COLONIAL AMERICA

Pocahontas (Matoaka). An engraving by Simon Van de Passe, London,
1616. *Courtesy of the National Portrait Gallery, Smithsonian Institution,
Washington, DC*

THE HUMAN TRADITION IN COLONIAL AMERICA

No. 1
The Human Tradition in American History

Edited by

Ian K. Steele
and
Nancy L. Rhoden

A Scholarly Resources Inc. Imprint
Wilmington, Delaware

Scholarly Resources Inc.
104 Greenhill Avenue
Wilmington, DE 19805-1897

Library of Congress Cataloging-in-Publication Data

The human tradition in colonial America / edited by Ian K. Steele
and Nancy L. Rhoden.
    p. cm. — (The human tradition in American history ; no. 1)
    Includes bibliographical references and index.
    ISBN 0-8420-2697-5 (cloth : alk. paper). — ISBN 0-8420-2700-9
(pbk. : alk. paper)
    1. United States—History—Colonial period, ca. 1600–1775—
Biography. I. Steele, Ian Kenneth. II. Rhoden, Nancy L. (Nancy
Lee), 1965– . III. Series.
E187.5.H88 1999
973.2'092'2—dc21   98-33247
[B]   CIP

For Our Spouses

Love transforms life as wondrously
as life transforms matter

About the Editors

NANCY L. RHODEN, whose Ph.D. is from Princeton University, teaches early American and English history at the University of Southern Indiana. She is the author of *Revolutionary Anglicanism: The Colonial Church of England Clergy during the American Revolution (1999)* and co-editor of *The Human Tradition in the American Revolution* (forthcoming).

IAN K. STEELE, whose Ph.D. is from the University of London, teaches British Atlantic and American colonial history at the University of Western Ontario. His best-known books are *The English Atlantic, 1675–1740: An Exploration of Communication and Community* (1986), *Betrayals: Fort William Henry and the "Massacre"* (1993), and *Warpaths: Invasions of North America* (1994). He is co-editor of *The Human Tradition in the American Revolution* (forthcoming).

I believe in aristocracy, though—if that is the right word, and if a democrat may use it. Not an aristocracy of power, based upon rank and influence, but an aristocracy of the sensitive, the considerate, and the plucky. Its members are to be found in all nations and classes, and all through the ages, and there is a secret understanding between them when they meet. They represent the true human tradition, the one permanent victory of our queer race over cruelty and chaos. Thousands of them perish in obscurity, a few are great names. They are sensitive for others as well as for themselves, they are considerate without being fussy, their pluck is not swankiness but the power to endure, and they can take a joke.

—E. M. Forster, *Two Cheers for Democracy* (1951)

Contents

Introduction: Meeting Colonial Americans, *xiii*
    IAN K. STEELE

1
Alvar Núñez Cabeza de Vaca: Conquistador and Sojourner, *1*
    PETER STERN

2
Squanto: Last of the Patuxet, *21*
    NEAL SALISBURY

3
Gabriel Sagard: A Franciscan among the Huron, *37*
    CORNELIUS J. JAENEN

4
Anne Hutchinson, the Puritan Patriarchs, and the Power
of the Spirit, *49*
    MARILYN WESTERKAMP

5
In Search of Pocahontas, *71*
    KATHLEEN BROWN

6
Daniel Clocker's Adventure: From Servant to Freeholder, *97*
    LOIS GREEN CARR

7
John Cotton Jr.: Wayward Puritan Minister? *119*
    SHEILA MCINTYRE

8
Isabel Montour: Cultural Broker on the Frontiers of New York
and Pennsylvania, *141*
    JON PARMENTER

9

Caspar Wistar: German-American Entrepreneur and
Cultural Broker, *161*
ROSALIND J. BEILER

10

Lewis Morris Jr.: British American Officeholder, *181*
MICHAEL WATSON

11

Pierre Pouchot: A French Soldier Views America, *197*
BRIAN L. DUNNIGAN

12

George Whitefield: Transatlantic Revivalist, *217*
NANCY L. RHODEN

13

Samson Occom: Mohegan Leader and Cultural Broker, *237*
MARGARET CONNELL SZASZ

14

Susannah Johnson: Captive, *257*
IAN K. STEELE

15

Bryan Sheehan: Servant, Soldier, Fisherman, *273*
MARGARET KELLOW

16

Olaudah Equiano: An African in Slavery and Freedom, *291*
ROBERT J. ALLISON

Index, *305*

Introduction
Meeting Colonial Americans

Ian K. Steele

Why has it been difficult for students of history to meet ordinary colonial Americans? In the rush to share the results of hundreds of intriguing scholarly books that analyze general trends and meanings in colonial American history, textbooks allow little room for biography. Ordinary colonial Americans did not usually leave enough evidence to allow a detailed reconstruction of their lives. There is also widespread suspicion that the biographical is somehow subversive. Although such work is an excellent way to navigate through the increasingly daunting requirement to explore all possible aspects of any historical subject, apprenticing historians are still discouraged from writing biographies, on the grounds that these are too narrow and distorting. Meeting individuals often dissolves stereotypes and sweeping generalizations. It seems fair to ask whether history is distorted more by biographies or by easy generalizations.

Colonial history has never lacked names to be learned, together with a sentence or two on their "significance." A handful of the prominent and powerful, whose blatant self-advertisings have become major sources for colonial historians, have managed to attract too much attention for too long. Self-important Captain John Smith has been able to impose his version of the founding of Virginia in Powhatan territory. Cotton Mather, prolific author and angst-ridden inheritor of Puritan leadership in Massachusetts, has long represented New England Puritanism in crisis; his wayward uncle, John Cotton Jr., affords a rather different perspective. Benjamin Franklin has successfully projected his own sanitized autobiography as our most familiar portrait of a colonial American: a frugal youth preoccupied with self-improvement who became an inventive and upwardly mobile businessman, accepting traditional morality for practical reasons, though secular enough to regard wasted opportunity as the only grievous sin.* Daniel Clocker or Caspar Wistar provides a less extravagant but more plausible success story.

*Mitchell Robert Breitwieser, *Cotton Mather and Benjamin Franklin: The Price of Representative Personality* (New York, 1984).

Although Franklin may prove irresistible to educators anxious to encourage us to seek "the American dream," his hallowed status also owes much to his being an elderly Founding Father of the Republic. Franklin has too easily become the most accessible and representative colonial American. Are those traditional "colonial heroes," the explorers and revolutionaries, chosen to encourage readers to believe that anyone can achieve anything, without noticing that these exemplars were all privileged and powerful male Caucasians? The "common sort" who paddled the canoes are the kind of people we will meet in these pages. However, it would be equally biased to exclude all of the prominent figures from our gathering of early Americans.

E. M. Forster provides the title for this volume when he invites us to seek a new "aristocracy of the sensitive, the considerate, and the plucky," who, he felt, "represent the true human tradition, the one permanent victory of our queer race over cruelty and chaos." The humble, the tolerant, and the peaceable are usually given even less space in our histories than they receive in our news; the self-advertising, the violent, and the domineering always seem to attract undue attention. By largely avoiding the best-known colonial Americans, those who possessed economic and political power and are too readily presented as the "makers" of history, we come to see a rather different world. Rather than making history, most of these people simply endured it. Heroics were less about power and the accomplishment of memorable deeds than about the more widespread preoccupation with survival.

The people gathered here, each of them introduced by a scholarly interpreter, have been "invited" because they are varied and intriguing. They are not particularly representative, partly because they have left some form of record. Born and raised in places as different as Spain, Patuxet, and Iboland, they lived in economies and disease environments as different as New England fisheries, Chesapeake Bay plantations, and the Native American villages of sixteenth-century Texas. Most were not contemporaries, but George Whitefield and Samson Occom met, and Olaudah Equiano heard Whitefield preach. All are presented here in birth order, with birth dates ranging over two-and-one-half centuries, from about 1490 to 1745. How many of the numerous differences among these people can be associated with larger changes occurring in those centuries? Native American communities were stronger, in both absolute and relative terms, in the days of Squanto and Pocahontas than in the time of Madame Montour and Occom. The intensity of the Protestant Reformation was more sectarian in the time of Anne Hutchinson than in that of Whitefield. The rivalry between Britain and France as world powers increasingly affected those living in early America, culminating between 1754 and 1763, as the lives of Pierre Pouchot, Susannah Johnson, and Bryan Sheehan illustrate.

The search for Forster's special kind of aristocrat has focused on those who reached out to others unlike themselves, those who took risks in crossing cultural frontiers, and those who interpreted strangers for their own people. These intermediaries take us well beyond those valuable, though obvious, comparisons of Spanish, English, and French meetings with Apalachee, Powhatan, and Huron. Not only do our witnesses provide precious evidence about cultures that they encountered, but they also reveal those aspects of their own societies that were taken for granted and recorded only when making comparisons with other societies. To varying degrees, the majority of our guests ventured across the boundaries between their native communities and other worlds, becoming "cultural brokers."

Caspar Wistar brokered between German migrants and the English society they entered. Alvar Núñez Cabeza de Vaca, Gabriel Sagard, Pouchot, and Johnson all lived with Native Americans for a time and, sooner or later, offered influential explanations of those communities to their European countrymen. Squanto, Pocahontas, and Occom made spectacular entries into the English world and aided in formal and informal negotiations between these communities. Isabel Montour, a *métisse* (of mixed French and Indian ancestry), lived between her Indian and European heritages and reminds us that history is about people rather than about unalloyed cultures. Some, like John Cotton Jr., brokered between their immediate face-to-face communities and their region. Others were instrumental in strengthening the broader Atlantic communities of which the colonies were part. Migrants all provided conscious and unconscious connections with their homelands. Whitefield and Occom were significant in a thoroughly transatlantic religious revival. Lewis Morris Jr. and Pouchot were effective and adaptable royal office-holders. People who learned, adjusted, and explored life between communities are every bit as revealing as those unyielding souls who championed their own European, colonial, or Native American cultures and offered only domination or defiance to others. The people whom you meet here inhabited an early American new world that was very multicultural.

Fourteen of our sixteen guests were migrants, either forced or voluntary, who shared in the repeopling of early modern North America. Several accounts suggest a wide range of motives, some pushing people from their homelands, and others drawing migrants with dreams of opportunities in North America. Did they prosper by their migration? Three showed marked improvement in material well-being: Cabeza de Vaca, Clocker, and Wistar. Cabeza de Vaca's bizarre adventures eventually led to a Spanish imperial governorship, but they may also have ensured that he would promptly be deposed, imprisoned, and disgraced. Clocker rose from indentured servitude to become a substantial landowner, and Wistar was a German immigrant who prospered in a variety of ways. However, striking material advancement was not an automatic result of living in colonial North America. Bryan Sheehan's miserable life showed both barriers and foolish choices, and Olaudah Equiano's adventures and evident successes cannot be tested against the life he might have led had he not been enslaved at age eleven. A few were born into various degrees of privilege, including Anne Hutchinson, John Cotton Jr., and Lewis Morris Jr. Hutchinson undertook one voluntary religious exile and was forced into another, Cotton was an embarrassment to his calling, and Morris failed to match his father's achievements.

Although we learn about the family life of only a few of our guests, family was not only the basic unit of the communities into which they all were born but also a powerful value. Was a thriving family a significant indicator of personal success? In what ways did their perception of family differ from ours? Susannah Johnson celebrated her large extended family and remembered, with enthusiasm, her remarriage after four years of widowhood. The loss of eight of her fourteen children in infancy was much worse than infant mortality rates in her native New England, though not unlike those in Clocker's Maryland. A large family could be celebrated in the rude sufficiencies of the New England and Maryland frontiers, but it was one of the reasons why Sheehan had left his Irish community. Wistar raised his status by marrying into a Pennsylvania Quaker founding family. The wealthy Morris proved successful enough to pass prosperity on to all of his four sons. Extended family was a source of worth and essential diplomatic information for Madame Montour and of pride for Occom. In contrast, Squanto lost all of his people through disease, and Pocahontas lost hers through marriage to John Rolfe. Marriages across societies, such as those of Pocahontas and Equiano, not only were possible but evidently were also accepted by English associates.

Adult migrants far from their own parents often display a powerful attachment to their own nuclear families. Migrants can value family highly without thereby incurring responsibilities to their own absent parents, and they can benefit directly from teaching the importance of family to their children. Nuclear family ties are initially strengthened by isolation from old friends and communities. Migrating individuals might use marriage as a way to join the new community and to demonstrate personal maturity and success. Johnson and Occom showed another sense of family by displaying considerable interest in their ancestors. In the seemingly eternal tension between self and community, were those who left personal accounts likely to be more individualistic than their siblings and neighbors who left no such records? Whose commitment to family was likely to be stronger?

We can meet only those who have left behind enough evidence— in diaries, journals, letters, printed accounts of their adventures, or court records—and then only if a modern scholar is interested in introducing them to us by portraying their lives in some detail. The kinds of evidence surviving certainly affect what we can learn about colonial Americans. Diaries and journals are preferred sources, for they reveal immediate private reflections on events described. Perhaps not coincidentally, the only diaries or journals that survive from our group are those of the clergymen, Occom and Whitefield. Memoirs and recollections, reconstructed years after the events described, are our main sources for Cabeza de Vaca, Sagard, Pouchot, Johnson, and Equiano. These accounts may have been derived from journals subsequently lost, but the accounts had allowed their authors to reshape their remembrances to serve various conscious or unconscious purposes. Letters, court records, or even printed attacks by enemies have provided essential, if sometimes quite biased, evidence with which to reconstruct several lives. The reader should appreciate the strengths and weaknesses of the central sources for each of these biographies as well as the self-fashioning possibilities of some records.

Meeting individuals almost always means suspending, challenging, or destroying stereotypes about groups of people previously unknown. Before we generalize about colonial Americans, let us meet some for more than just a moment. Our guests are worth knowing not only in their own right but also for what they can tell us about the particular world that they inhabited. We may have many questions to ask them about race, gender, class, God, self, empire, migration, social mobility, and culture. What mattered more and what mattered less to them than it does to us? Should these people be appreciated for their contributions to their own communities, or should we evaluate them according to their success in anticipating what has come to matter in our world? Are we trying to understand them or trying to make them understand us? Our gathering will be a great success if, after meeting these people, we find it more difficult to generalize about race, class, ethnicity, or gender in colonial America.

1

Alvar Núñez Cabeza de Vaca
Conquistador and Sojourner

Peter Stern

A Spanish nobleman who understood the traditional attitudes and the methods of expansion into new territory by private investment and royal blessing, Alvar Núñez Cabeza de Vaca (c. 1490–c. 1557) came to La Florida with all the advantages and limitations of a privileged officeholder without any experience in the Americas. He offered his explanation for the failure of the expedition and for his own role in what he regarded as the crucial decisions. How did his account of Spanish cannibalism fit with his readers' assumptions? Failure of the treasure-seeking expedition left him stranded, a stranger seeking survival in Native American communities. His reception was noteworthy, as was his adaptability. His role as intertribal merchant suggests a continuing enthusiasm for tradeable local resources amid chronic belligerence among these Native American communities. If Cabeza de Vaca could prosper as a wandering healer among Native Americans, was his little party of survivors somehow free of the microbes that made Europeans the bearers of death for so many Native Americans? His gratitude and understanding made him very sympathetic to his hosts. Nonetheless, Cabeza de Vaca called his life with Native Americans "a melancholy and wretched captivity." His subsequent appointment as colonial governor suggests that the Spanish authorities found his views acceptable. What do his difficulties with Spanish settlers in his province, and with royal officialdom, suggest about the contest between policies and practices in the Spanish Empire at this time?

Peter Stern is a Latin American specialist at the University of Massachusetts, Amherst, and the author of numerous articles on Spanish borderland history.

A lvar Núñez Cabeza de Vaca was a conquistador, one of an audacious breed of men who embarked from Spain to win their fortunes in the New World that Christopher Columbus had discovered only thirty-five years before. Shipwrecked on the coast of Texas, nearly naked, starving, and freezing, he and a small group of companions set out to find their way back to friendly Spanish territory in Mexico. They walked for nearly three thousand miles through what is today west Texas, New Mexico, and Sonora, meeting many Indian tribes along the way and becoming healers and medicine men. They were the first Europeans to reach the valley of the Río Grande, and they ultimately brought tragedy to the peoples who lived in the Southwest. Their journey produced the first "captivity narrative" in the Americas and the first written account of the Southwest of the United States. Above all, Cabeza de Vaca was a man of his time—bold and courageous, but also greedy, narrow-minded, and prejudiced.

Alvar Núñez Cabeza de Vaca was born in the Spanish city of Jerez de la Frontera around 1490, although the exact year is uncertain. His surname, Cabeza de Vaca, literally means "head of a cow"; and although this sounds absurd to us today, it actually represented a great honor for his family. During the Reconquista, the seven-hundred-year-long struggle of the Christians to push the Moors (a generic term that the Spaniards used for all Muslims in Iberia, whether they were Berbers or Arabs) out of Spain, the Christian army reached the Sierra Morena north of Seville in 1212. The Moors held all the mountain passes, and the Spanish army was stymied. But a peasant offered to show the Spanish king an unguarded mountain pass that would allow the Christians to attack their enemies from the rear. The peasant marked the pass with the skull of a cow, and the Christian army was able to surprise the Muslims and defeat them. After the battle, King Sancho ennobled the peasant, who was an ancestor of Alvar Núñez, and gave him and his descendants the title Cabeza de Vaca.

In 1492, Columbus sailed westward, in search of the Great Khan of the Indies, and discovered a new world instead. But by 1519 bright hopes for that New World had turned to despair. The Spaniards, eager to find gold, had used the native peoples of the Caribbean for slave labor, abused and maltreated them, and had unknowingly passed on to them many of the common diseases of Europe—measles, smallpox, mumps, and even the common cold—to which the Indians had no immunity or resistance. Within the space of thirty years, the native population of the Caribbean had been reduced to a tiny fraction of its numbers in 1492. Spanish greed and, more important, European microbes had created a wasteland out of paradise.

In 1521 everything changed again. In that year, Hernándo Cortés, with a few hundred men, completed his conquest of the empire of the Aztecs, making the Spaniards lords of all Mexico and fabulously rich. Adventurous young Spanish men eagerly sailed for the New World in the hopes of enlisting in another great venture, the next Mexico.

Young Cabeza de Vaca was born into a household of adventurers; his grandfather had taken part in the conquest of the Canary Islands, far out in the Atlantic Ocean. Cabeza de Vaca grew up listening to the stories and songs of the Guanche servants in his grandfather's household; the Guanches, natives of the Canaries, had been enslaved by Spanish conquistadores. In 1511, when he was twenty-one, he sailed as part of an expedition sent by King Ferdinand to Italy, where Pope Julius II was fighting French invaders. Cabeza de Vaca fought in battles at Bologna and Ravenna, and was rewarded for his bravery by being promoted to the rank of *alférez*, or ensign. When he returned to Spain in 1513, he was made a steward in the household of the Duke of Medina Sidonia. As a steward, or *camarero*, he was both household manager and soldier; he helped to put down an internal revolt of *comuneros* in Spain and was again promoted for bravery. Cabeza de Vaca went on to fight the French again in Navarre, earning for himself more honors and the reputation of a man of courage and dedication. Serving in the household of a royal duke, he may well have met conquistadores returning from their campaigns in America.

Little is known about the next years of Cabeza de Vaca's life. He married, although the records of his marriage have been lost. In 1527 he joined Pánfilo de Narváez's expedition to the West Indies to conquer an unknown land called La Florida. Narváez was an experienced conquistador, a veteran of fighting in both the Caribbean and Mexico, which makes his subsequent follies harder to comprehend. Cabeza de Vaca was made treasurer of the expedition, a key position requiring a great deal of trust, as the treasurer collected the king's *diezmo*, or royal tenth of any gold or other treasure found by this *entrada*, or military incursion. In order to carry out this task, Cabeza de Vaca was also made provost marshal, in charge of military discipline for the expedition. To ensure his loyalty, he posted a bond of two thousand pieces of gold before leaving Spain.

Narváez sailed in June 1527 with five ships and six hundred men (accompanied by at least ten wives). Horses and dogs were loaded onto the ships as transportation and offensive weapons of war; cattle and pigs would provide meat "on the hoof" in Florida. Five Franciscan monks went along to convert the Indians whom the Spaniards were sure to encounter. The trip to the Caribbean took two months, and the journey was an awful one. Crammed into tiny, leaking wooden ships and fed a monotonous diet of biscuit, with a little wine, meat, salt fish, and olive oil, many of the men were sick of the whole business by the time the fleet reached the island of Hispaniola (today the Dominican Republic and Haiti). One hundred and twenty deserted as soon as the ships reached port. Narváez managed to pick up a few men in Cuba, his last stop before the mainland, to replace those who had already fled. Bad weather kept the fleet in Cuba for the entire winter and part of the spring, but on April 12, 1528, the ships of the Narváez expedition reached the southwest coast of Florida, landing at what is today Tampa Bay.

By the spring of 1528, Florida had already been visited by the expeditions of Juan Ponce de León and four other conquistadors. Thanks to the cruel way in which the Spaniards treated the natives, seizing them as slaves and torturing them to obtain gold, the Indians of Florida were very wary of the strangers. When Narváez's ships anchored in a beautiful bay, they could see over the dunes huge mounds of oyster shells and, beyond them, an Indian village.

Their first contacts with the Indians were not very promising. An emissary of Narváez was rowed ashore to assure the Indian chief, or cacique, of the Spaniards' good intentions. The chief gave the man a gift of venison and fish, but when the emissary left, the entire village fled into the forest. The rest of the Spaniards went ashore to find that the Indians had left behind nothing—in particular, no food. But they did find a gold rattle in one hut. This discovery excited them enormously; they reasoned that if the Indians could give an infant a rattle made of gold, then surely they must have huge quantities of the precious metal.

The party raised the flag, and Narváez took possession of the land in the name of the king of Spain. He then read aloud the *requerimiento*—a long statement that informed the Indians that they were now subjects of the Crown and, furthermore, that they were to be baptized Christians and give up their "heathen" ways. (The reading of the *requerimiento* was a legal necessity, but, as one historian wryly noted, it was sometimes read out of arrow shot of the natives.) That there were no Indians in sight to hear this proclamation mattered not at all—the forms had been observed, and from that moment the natives had to obey all Spanish civil or religious laws. If they did not, they could be legally enslaved and sold. Thus the Spaniards dealt with the natives of their new land of Florida. The rest of the day was spent in getting the horses ashore; of the eighty horses with which the Spaniards had left Cuba, only forty-two were still alive by the time the ships reached Florida.

The next day was Easter Sunday. The Franciscans held Mass for the entire expedition, but the solemn occasion was marred when a party of Indians approached the Spaniards and angrily gestured at them to go away. On Monday, the serious business of exploration began. Governor Narváez took forty men, including Cabeza de Vaca, off to the north to see if they could find more people and, of course, more gold. They ran across a few Indians, whom they immediately made prisoners, and showed them some ears of corn, asking in sign language where more were to be found. The Indians took them to a village where corn was growing. The Spaniards found a few more bits of gold among the natives; and, when asked about this metal, the Indians pointed to the north, saying "Apalachen." The Spaniards and the Indians could not understand one another, but the former chose to convince themselves that this "Apalachen" was where more precious gold was to be found.

This incident exemplifies a common occurrence in relations between the Spaniards and the Indians of the Americas. The Europeans, always convinced that gold would be found in great quantities just around the next bend, were ready to read the presence of precious metals into the most innocent of statements by the Indians. In fact, small amounts of gold could be found in West Florida and Georgia and were collected by the Apalachee Indians— the "Apalachen" to whom the natives around Tampa Bay, who were Timucan, were referring. But there was no gold where they were at the moment, nor much in the way of food. There was an urgent need for them to move on or starve to death because, to the Spaniards, there was nothing edible growing in the flats of northwest Florida.

Governor Narváez held a council with some of his trusted men, including Cabeza de Vaca. Narváez proposed that the expedition march inland, following the coast, in search of a great bay that all of his pilots insisted was just a short distance away. The Spaniards had no idea that they were almost two thousand miles from Mexico; they assumed that it was just a few days' sail until they reached friendly territory again, at Pánuco (today's Tampico). In the meantime, the ships would sail up the coast directly to this great harbor. Cabeza de Vaca argued against splitting up the party:

> It seemed to me, I answered, that under no circumstances should we forsake the ships before they rested in a secure harbor which we controlled; that the pilots, after all, disagreed among themselves on every particular and did not so much as know where we then were; that we would be deprived of our horses in case we needed them; that we could anticipate no satisfactory communication with the Indians, having no interpreter, as we entered an unknown country; and that we did not have supplies to sustain a march we knew not where. . . . I concluded that we had better re-embark and look for a harbor and soil better suited to settle, since what we had so far seen was the most desert and poor that had ever been discovered in that region.[1]

But the majority accepted the pilots' declaration that they were just ten to fifteen leagues (about twenty-five to forty miles) from Mexico, and the governor agreed with them. Narváez turned to Cabeza de Vaca and proposed that, since he seemed to be afraid of marching inland, he should go with the ships and establish a settlement in case the flotilla reached a harbor before the column. Cabeza de Vaca felt insulted by this suggestion and refused. That night the governor came to him once more, this time with less scorn in his voice, and asked him to reconsider; he needed someone whom he could trust to go with the ships. Once again, Cabeza de Vaca refused. He was determined to share the dangers with the rest of the men.

On May 1, three hundred men and forty horses set out for the interior. Each man's rations consisted of two pounds of biscuit and one-half pound of bacon, all of the food left to the expedition. Swamps and creeks constantly hampered their march; they saw no villages, no tilled fields, and no other people. After two weeks, they came to a river, which they crossed on makeshift rafts constructed on the spot. On the other side they encountered a band of several hundred Indians, who made menacing gestures with their weapons. The Spaniards seized a few as hostages; the captured Indians led the party to a village, where the corn stood ripe in the fields for harvesting. The ravenous Spaniards immediately stripped the fields of the entire crop.

A few days later the party crossed the Suwanee River; entering another village, they found once again that the natives had fled at the sight of them. Finally, on June 25, they reached their goal, the village of Apalachee. Cabeza de Vaca was ordered to take fifty men and nine horses and storm the town. The Spaniards had marched for weeks and suffered privations in order to conquer a new Indian empire like that of the Aztecs. Instead, in Cabeza de Vaca's words, "We found a large stand of corn ready to pick, and a lot more already dried and stored; also many deerskins, and, with them, some small, poor-quality shawls woven of thread. The women partially cover their nakedness with such garments. We also noted the bowls they grind corn in. . . . The village consisted of forty low, small thatch houses set up in sheltered places for protection from the frequent storms. It was surrounded by dense woods and many little lakes, into which numerous big trees had fallen to become effective obstructions."[2] This, then, was the mighty Apalachee that they had sought for so long! There were no gold, no jewels, no mighty palaces, and no empire. They had been seeking a phantom kingdom.

There were only women and children in the village. While the Spaniards were milling about, the native men returned and began shooting arrows at the Europeans, killing one horse. They then fled, but came back two hours later and asked for a truce. Narváez agreed, but seized the cacique as hostage (a tactic that Cortés had used in dealing with Emperor Moctezuma in Mexico). The Indians responded by attacking the Spaniards the next morning. Over the next few days, the Indians ambushed them several more times, attacking and retreating so quickly that the Spaniards could not respond effectively to these guerrilla tactics.

Narváez and his men stayed in the village for almost a month. Several reconnaissance trips showed that the surrounding country-side was sparsely populated and difficult to traverse because of the swamps, woods, and lakes. The natives indicated that Apalachee was the biggest town in the area; to the north the villages were smaller and more scattered, and in the interior were only immense forests and lakes, with no precious metals or powerful native king-doms. The Indians were telling the Spaniards the absolute truth: there were no Mexicos in the forests of northern Florida and south-ern Georgia. The Spaniards were disappointed, ready to quit and return home: "Taking everything into consideration—the poverty of the land and unfavorable reports of the people . . . the constant guer-rilla tactics of the Indians, wounding our people and horses with impunity from the cover of the lakes whenever they went for water . . . we decided to strike for the sea."[3] Cabeza de Vaca then wrote at length about the natives' skill at warfare, which he could not help but admire: "All the Indians which we had seen so far in Florida had been archers. They loomed big and naked and from a distance looked like giants. They were handsomely proportioned, lean, agile, and strong. Their bows were as thick as an arm, six or seven feet long, accurate at 200 paces."[4] The Spaniards' steel armor could not deflect the Indians' arrows; Cabeza de Vaca swore that he had seen an arrow buried half a foot in a poplar trunk. (While fight-ing the Aztecs, the Spaniards had observed how their steel breast-plates were penetrated by native arrows and had switched to the quilted cotton armor that the Indians wore.)

The Spanish, marching to the Gulf of Mexico, passed through a big town (Aute) that had already been deserted and burnt by its inhabitants; the Indians, however, had left behind corn, beans, and squash, which the starving Spaniards seized and devoured. By the time the party reached Apalachee Bay, many were sick, including Governor Narváez. Cabeza de Vaca, although slightly wounded in an Indian ambush, took sixty men to try to find a harbor. For several days they marched over salt flats and sand dunes, eating oysters from the bay, but found no secure landing spot and no sign of the ships. The whole expedition was in a desperate plight, and dissen-sion broke out among the men; the expedition's horsemen plotted to abandon the rest of the weak, sick, and starving party and strike out for Mexico on their own. They were dissuaded from this shameful act, but the fact remained that the fleet was nowhere to be seen, and most of the party was in terrible condition (more than forty died from hunger and disease), stranded on a bleak shore and menaced by hostile Indians. The desperate expedition then decided to build boats and try to make it to Mexico by sea, although no one knew how to navigate.

Somehow the Spaniards managed to build five boats out of materials that they found on the shore or had with them, and on September 22, 1528, the two hundred and forty-seven surviving men of the Narváez expedition, which had set out to conquer the territory of Florida for the king of Spain, cast off on their voyage of desperation. For weeks the leaky crafts, crammed with too many men, slowly made their way to the north and west, constantly running aground on the sandbars and shallows of the coastal waters. Once they encountered some Indians in canoes, who fled from the strange, bearded skeletons. The party went ashore at a small village, which was abandoned, and ate up the dried mullet that they found there. They also seized the native canoes and used them to reinforce their boats.

Onward they sailed, occasionally spotting a distant canoe. After a month had passed, they found shelter on a small island, where they huddled for six days as a terrible storm lashed the Gulf of Mexico. They had no fresh water with them; some of the men became so desperate that they drank salt water and died in agonies of thirst. Finally, the Spaniards reached the end of their rope: "Rather than succumb right there, we commended our souls to God, and put forth into the perilous sea as the storm still raged."[5] They headed in the direction where they had seen a solitary canoe, rounded a point of land, and found themselves in a great bay (Pensacola Bay).

Here their luck seemed to change for the better; they came across a large Indian settlement, where the inhabitants were friendly and invited the starving Spaniards to eat and drink. They gave the Europeans water and fish; the cacique invited the governor into his hut. Narváez responded with courtesy, presenting the chief with some parched corn. But that night the Indians turned hostile and fell upon the men. Narváez was hurt, and several men killed; most of the rest clambered aboard one of the boats and pulled out to sea. Cabeza de Vaca and fifty men stood on the beach to cover their comrades' retreat. Three times during the night the Indians attacked, but were driven back. At dawn, Cabeza de Vaca burned the Indians' canoes, and he and the remainder of his men reembarked on their boat.

When the party reached what is now Mobile Bay, they encountered a fleet of Indian canoes, and once again relations between the Spaniards and the Indians turned hostile. After some Spaniards and a black slave went ashore with the Indians for water, they were never seen again; the Spaniards then seized some Indian chiefs in retaliation. Finally, the bedraggled flotilla reached a mighty river, clearly the Mississippi. Here the expedition literally broke up; the boats started to drift apart in the strong current, and Governor Narváez's craft, with the strongest and fittest men, began to row ahead of the rest. Cabeza de Vaca yelled for them to throw him a rope, but Narváez shouted back that each man must make for home as best he could. Narváez was clearly abandoning the remnants of his expedition; neither he nor his men were ever seen again. On November 6, 1528, Cabeza de Vaca's boat ran aground on an island (Galveston Island), and he and his surviving handful of explorers were marooned.

It is from this point onward that the tale of Alvar Núñez Cabeza de Vaca fundamentally changes. Until his shipwreck, he had been a conquistador; he had come, along with other Spaniards, to conquer and to take from the native people what was not his. But on Galveston Island, he became a supplicant, asking others (the Karankawa Indians) to save his life. The Indians on the island reacted to Cabeza de Vaca and his men with sympathy, giving them food and water in return for a few bells and beads that the Spaniards had with them. When the Spaniards tried to relaunch their craft, a wave swamped it and three men drowned. As they had put their clothing on board, the survivors were now naked as well as cold and hungry. The Indians actually began to weep when they found out what had happened, a sympathetic reaction that the Europeans had never seen before: "The Indians, understanding our full plight, sat down and lamented for half an hour so loudly they could have been heard a long way off. It was amazing to see these wild, untaught savages howling like brutes in compassion for us."[6] Cabeza de Vaca asked the Indians to take his party to their village. Some of the veterans of Mexico warned that they would all be sacrificed, but necessity made them accompany the Indians to their settlement. The Spaniards huddled together, fearing their imminent death as the Indians danced in celebration, but the night passed, and the men relaxed as it became apparent that no such fate awaited them.

The Spaniards called the island on which they were marooned *la isla malhadada*—the island of doom—and it and the Texas coastal plain nearby were to be their home for the next six years. One last attempt to relaunch their boat ended in failure. Cabeza de Vaca later wrote: "With most of us naked and the weather discouraging walking or swimming across rivers and coves—also with no food supply or even anything to carry one in—we resigned ourselves to remaining where we were for the winter."[7] The Spaniards decided that four of their most robust men should try walking to Pánuco (which they believed was nearby) to report their presence and bring back rescuers. These four set out and were never seen again.

"Within a few days of the departure of the four Christians," wrote Cabeza de Vaca, "the weather turned so cold and stormy that the Indians could not pull up roots; their cane contraptions for catching fish yielded nothing; and the huts being open, our men began to die."[8] Many of the Spaniards died from exposure; a few marooned on the mainland nearby were reduced to cannibalism as their comrades died—a practice that profoundly disturbed the Indians. Cabeza de Vaca reported that "five Christians quartered on the coast came to the extremity of eating each other. Only the body of the last one, whom nobody was left to eat, was found unconsumed. . . . The Indians were so shocked at this cannibalism that, if they had seen it sometime earlier, they surely would have killed every one of us."[9]

Cabeza de Vaca reported in his narrative that of the ninety Spaniards who had survived the shipwreck of the various boats on the island and the nearby mainland, only sixteen were alive "in a very short while." Then, as happened so often when Europeans and Native Americans met in the New World, the Indians began to die; they came down with "a disease of the bowels," possibly dysentery caught from the soldiers. Some of the Indian survivors came to kill the Spaniards, blaming them for the many deaths, but one Indian stopped them, ascribing to the foreigners the power of sorcery.

Eventually, Cabeza de Vaca began to act as a trader and go-between among the various tribes (mostly Karankawa and Attakapa Indians) who lived on the island and the nearby mainland. His travels as a trader took him deep into Texas (some scholars believe that he got as far as Oklahoma). Cabeza de Vaca, tiring of his lowly status as a laborer, described his own metamorphosis:

> I set to contriving how I might transfer to the forest-dwellers, who looked more propitious. My solution was to turn to trade. . . . The various Indians would beg me to go from one quarter to another for things they needed; their incessant hostilities made it impossible for them to travel cross-country or make any exchanges. But as a neutral merchant I went into the interior as far as I pleased. . . .

> My principal wares were cones and other pieces of sea-snail, conchs used for cutting, sea-beads and a fruit like a bean [mesquite] which the Indians value very highly, using it for a medicine and for a ritual beverage in their dances and festivals. This sort of thing I carried inland. By barter I got and brought back to the coast skins, red ochre which they rub on their faces, hard canes for arrows, flint for arrowheads, with sinews and cement to attach them, and tassels of deer hair which they dye red.

> This occupation suited me; I could travel where I wished, was not obliged to work, and was not a slave. Wherever I went, the Indians treated me honorably and gave me food, because they liked my commodities. They were glad to see me when I came and delighted

to be brought what they wanted. I became well known; those who did not know me personally knew me by reputation and sought my acquaintance. This served my main purpose, which all the while was to determine an eventual road out.[10]

Cabeza de Vaca must have acquired enough fluency in the native languages to facilitate his work as neutral go-between and trader.

He and several of the other Spaniards also became, almost involuntarily, medicine men to the Indians: "The islanders wanted to make physicians of us without examination or a review of diplomas. Their method of cure is to blow on the sick, [with] the breath and the laying-on of hands supposedly casting out the infirmity." Cabeza de Vaca and the other Spaniards blessed the sick people, blew upon them, and recited a Pater Noster and Ave Maria over them. When the patients got well, they ascribed their miraculous recovery to the "magic" of the Spaniards, and in this way Cabeza de Vaca and his companions acquired a reputation as healers. "In consequence," he wrote later, "the Indians treated us kindly. They deprived themselves of food to give to us, and presented us skins and other tokens of gratitude."[11] Cabeza de Vaca and his companions scoffed at the natives' belief in their healing powers and initially refused to practice their "medicine," but the Indians withheld food from them until they finally yielded. He does not say what happened when their "patients" did not recover, but he admitted that the Spaniards were occasionally nervous about failing to work their miracles.

Meanwhile, about a dozen other Spaniards lived with various Karankawa bands along the coast. The survivors later called themselves slaves of the Indians, but they were not captives. The Indians, tired of feeding loafers, sometimes drove out the Europeans, and they wandered until they found a new band with whom to live. Andrés Dorantes wrote years later that "they were treated as slaves, and used more cruelly than by a Moor, naked and barefoot on a coast that burns like fire in summer . . . and since they were *hidalgos* [gentlemen] and men of standing and new to such life it was necessary to have patience as great as their labors."[12] However, a famous colonial chronicler noted wryly: "Those Indians, in whose company these few Christians were, tired of giving them [food] to eat, as always happens when the guest stays longer than the host wishes and in particular if they have not been invited nor contribute anything."[13] These *hidalgos* had few skills to offer to the well-being of the Indian tribes, and so were reduced to fetching water and wood and digging roots for their hosts, and they were sometimes taunted and abused. They thought of themselves as slaves of the Indians and dreamed continually of escape.

Finally, there were only a few Spaniards left alive, scattered among the various bands of the coast; and in the summer of 1534, Cabeza de Vaca was joined by Andrés Dorantes, Alonso del Castillo Maldonado, and Estevánico, or Esteban, a Moorish slave belonging to Dorantes. In September or October they conferred on how best to escape and headed west. Thus began the quartet's epic journey.

We begin to see in Cabeza de Vaca's *Relación* a change in attitude toward the Indians. Until this point, he had nearly always been at the mercy of Indian bands, often in peril of his life, and his writing about them is either contemptuous or detached. From this point onward, in his manuscript (written eight years later), he began to refer to the natives with sympathy, even warmth. Cabeza de Vaca was undergoing a remarkable conversion, from haughty conquistador to sympathetic and engaged observer. Almost immediately, the Spaniards began to assume their role as healers: "The very evening of our arrival [the day they decided to escape the coast], some Indians came to Castillo, begging him to cure them of terrible headaches. When he made the sign of the Cross over them and commended them to God, they instantly said that all pain had vanished."[14] The Indians rewarded the party with venison and some tuna cacti (a type of prickly pear).

Now other Indians began to approach the men, bringing them sick people whom they begged the Spaniards to cure. The men made the sign of the Cross and prayed over the afflicted. While it always seemed to work, Castillo, for one, was afraid that they would fail and the Indians' admiration would turn deadly. When a call came for help from an Indian camp, the Spaniards arrived to find a man without a pulse, apparently dead. Still, they prayed for his recovery; that night, Indians returned to tell the Spaniards that the "dead" man had indeed recovered! Now all four began to practice healing; said Cabeza de Vaca, "We all came to be physicians." The Indians believed that the strangers were "truly sons of the sun," as they began to call the Europeans. The quartet lived with one band of natives, the Avavares, for eight months. Cabeza de Vaca became the boldest and most adventurous in trying to cure anything: "With no exceptions, every patient told us he had been made well. Confidence in our ministrations as infallible extended to a belief that none could die while we remained among them."[15]

Cabeza de Vaca's writing was often anthropologically descriptive, as he related how the Indians he encountered lived their material and spiritual lives. The Avavares, for instance, among whom the Spaniards had dwelt so long, were not especially prosperous. All went naked, covering themselves with deerskins only at night. The Indians had no corn, acorns, or pecans. They had little fish either, and so they were hungry most of the time; only when the prickly pears ripened did the Indians have enough to eat. When the Spaniards passed from the land of the Avavares to that of the Maliacones on the coast, their privations were even more acute. Cabeza de Vaca's narrative refutes the idea, widely held in popular contemporary culture, that America was an absolute Eden when the Europeans arrived. In nontemperate, arid zones such as west Texas and many other parts of the West, geography, climate, and the scarcity of water made for a harsh environment in which hunger often afflicted Native Americans.

In fact, Cabeza de Vaca related that "all these tribes are warlike, and have as much strategy for protection against enemies as if they had been reared in Italy in continual feuds. . . . All these nations, when they have personal enmities and are not related, assassinate at night, waylay, and inflict gross atrocities on each other." Yet he also praised their physical endurance: "I believe that these people see and hear better and have keener senses in general than any in the world. They know great hunger, thirst, and cold, as if they were made for enduring these more than other men, by habit and nature."[16]

Within weeks after starting their trek, Cabeza de Vaca and his companions were accompanied by a large retinue of Indians as they traveled from one village to the next, still in search of other Europeans. To avoid the Indians of the coast, they turned north and west. After wandering along the Colorado, Pecos, and Peñasco Rivers, they turned south and crossed the Río Grande at El Paso, but again turned northwest and headed into what is today New Mexico. News of their coming went before them, and large crowds of natives turned out to greet them: "Since the Indians all through the region talked only of the wonders which God our Lord worked through us, individuals sought us from many parts in hopes of healing."[17] But the Spaniards were disturbed by a new phenomenon: "Those who accompanied us plundered our hospitable new hosts and ransacked their huts, leaving nothing. We watched this with deep concern, but were in no position to do anything about it; so for the present had to bear it until such time as we might gain greater authority. Those who lost their possessions, seeing our dejection, tried to console us. They said they were so honored to have us that their property was well bestowed—and that they would get repaid by others farther on, who were very rich."[18]

Cabeza de Vaca's attitude toward the people of the region had turned from fear and dislike to admiration and sympathy, but he also started to think once again like a conquistador. He began to speculate about returning some day with authority to rule over the natives, and to behave like an explorer, turning to the north, toward the distant mountains, to see what lay in the interior of the country.

One day, as the party continued to travel westward toward distant mountains, they encountered two women who were carrying heavy packs. The women offered the Spaniards some cornmeal; the four had not seen maize since they had left Florida years before. A few days and a few villages onward, they were presented with some more gifts: a copper rattle and some cotton shawls. Where did these things come from? The Indians pointed to the north, where, they said, strange people lived; almost certainly they were referring to the Pueblo Indians of northern New Mexico, although metals such as copper were rare among Native Americans.

Finally, the Spaniards and their enormous retinue of Indians descended into the valley of the Río Grande. By now their companions no longer looted each village as they entered it; rather, the natives offered the newcomers all that they possessed. The four continued to bless and "heal" the sick Indians; indeed, Cabeza de Vaca described how he performed an operation in the "mountain country," opening up a man's chest with a flint knife and extracting an arrowhead from an old wound. The patient survived; and, as Cabeza de Vaca wrote, "This cure so inflated our fame all over the region that we could control whatever the inhabitants cherished."[19]

The Spaniards and their retinue continued journeying westward, telling the natives that they wished to go where the sun sets. They reached the land of the Cow People, so called because the Indians there were skilled buffalo hunters. In what is now New Mexico, in the Río Grande Valley, the natives lived in huts of mud and cane, raised cotton and wove cloth from it, and cultivated corn, beans, and squash. In one town of the Pima Indians, the party was presented with six hundred deer hearts as food and gifts.

All flocked to the famous healers to be cured of their illnesses. Cabeza de Vaca and his companions spoke of their God and Christian faith to the masses as well, although with little effect. The Indians were convinced that the visitors came from Heaven. To better maintain their authority over the Indians, the Spaniards gradually stopped communicating with them and made Esteban the Moor their intermediary.

One day, probably in early January 1536, when they were in the country of the Opata Indians in what is now Sonora, in northwest Mexico, Castillo saw a native wearing around his neck a sword-belt buckle; stitched next to it was a horseshoe nail. "We asked the Indian what it was. He said it came from Heaven. But who had brought it? He and the Indian with him said that some bearded men like us had come to that river from Heaven, with horses, lances, and swords, and had lanced two natives."[20] Casually, the Spaniards asked what had become of the men from Heaven. They had traveled across the water, came the reply. "We gave many thanks to God our

Lord," wrote Cabeza de Vaca. "Having almost despaired of finding Christians again, we could hardly restrain our excitement."[21] Now the party began to travel more quickly, and each day they heard more tales of these strangers.

They hurried through an empty land, the natives having fled to the mountains in fear of Spanish soldiers clearly on a slaving expedition from Mexico. "With heavy hearts we looked out over the lavishly watered, fertile, and beautiful land, now abandoned and burned, the people thin and weak, scattering or hiding in fright."[22] By this time, Cabeza de Vaca, treasurer of an expedition to conquer La Florida, had made an inner journey as well as a physical one, from arrogance to compassion, from conquistador to emissary of peace. When he had first set foot in America, his purpose was to loot and enslave; now he was intent upon stopping his fellow countrymen from doing so. In his *Relación* to the Spanish king, he remarked that the only certain way to bring the Indians to Christianity and subjection to the Crown was through kindness.

The day of meeting arrived at last; in late January 1536, near the Río Sinaloa in Mexico, Cabeza de Vaca and Esteban encountered a party of four mounted Spaniards, who stared at the bearded vagabonds in astonishment. Curiously, Cabeza de Vaca said little about the momentous, long-deferred reunion: "We gave thanks to God our Lord for choosing to bring us out of such a melancholy and wretched captivity. The joy we felt can only be conjectured in terms of the time, suffering, and peril we had endured in that land."[23] Diego de Alcáraz commanded the slave-hunting party. Cabeza de Vaca asked for a certificate stating the year, day, and month in which he had at last encountered his countrymen.

Within a few days, after Dorantes and Castillo had joined Cabeza de Vaca and Esteban, along with six hundred Indians who accompanied them, the quartet found themselves at odds with the Spaniards under Alcáraz. These men wanted to make slaves of all the Indians, but Cabeza de Vaca and his companions argued with Alcáraz and ordered the Indians to return home. The Indians insisted that it was their obligation first to deliver Cabeza de Vaca and his party into the hands of other tribes, as custom demanded, which aroused the jealousy of the Spanish slavers:

> Alcáraz bade his interpreter tell the Indians that we were members of his race who had long been lost; that his group were the lords of the land who must be obeyed and served, while we were inconsequential. The Indians paid no attention to this. Conferring among themselves, they replied that the Christians lied: We had come from the sunrise, they from the sunset; we healed the sick, they killed the sound; we came naked and barefoot, they were clothed, horsed, and lanced; we coveted nothing but gave whatever

we were given, while they robbed whomever they found and bestowed nothing on anyone.[24]

To the last, said Cabeza de Vaca, he could not convince the Indians that he and his companions were of the same people as the Christian slavers, but he did induce them to return to their homes. The slavers sent the quartet under escort to Culiacán, in Sinaloa, the nearest Spanish settlement, where the *alcalde*, or mayor, tried to convince the four that the greatest service they could do the Indians was to persuade them to come out of hiding and settle down as farmers under Spanish "guidance."

Cabeza de Vaca and his companions finally reached Mexico City in the summer of 1536 to a tumultuous welcome. They had walked about twenty-eight hundred miles from the coast of Texas, and had been out of touch with other Europeans for almost nine years. Viceroy Antonio de Mendoza was interested in sending the Spaniards back into the wilderness to bring the barbarian Indians (in his words) to submission, but Cabeza de Vaca was intent upon returning to Spain to seek an audience with the king. He had two goals in mind: to persuade the monarch that kindness and charity, rather than enslavement, would ultimately bring more native souls to God and Spanish authority; and to get himself named governor of Florida.

In this effort he failed, for Charles I had already named Hernando De Soto as the new governor. Although Cabeza de Vaca talked with De Soto before he left for the West Indies, that gentleman repeated every mistake of Pánfilo de Narváez and more besides, by alienating an already suspicious and fearful people and enslaving and killing the Indians of Florida and Alabama, until he died of fever in 1542. The only difference between De Soto's expedition and that of Narváez is that a few hundred Spaniards from the De Soto *entrada* managed to reach Pánuco, empty-handed and in rags, four years after leaving Havana.

Cabeza de Vaca continued to follow his dreams of glory in America; named governor of the province of Río de la Plata (now Argentina), he tried to put into effect his rather advanced ideas about treating the native peoples of the interior with respect and fairness. For this, he lost his office and was arrested and imprisoned by Spanish settlers and royal officials whom he had alienated. The settlers hated him because he had forbidden concubinage between Spaniards and unwilling Indian women, seized for that purpose by conquistadores. The royal officials who complained about him to the king resented his curbs on their abuse of the powers of taxation. In 1546 he was seized by rebellious Spaniards in Asunción (today the capital of Paraguay) and sent back to Spain in chains. He spent years arguing his case before the Council of the Indies, but in vain; the entrenched power of rapacious conquistadores, power-hungry missionaries, and corrupt royal officials was too strong to resist. In 1551 the Council ruled against him, stripped him of his royal offices, and banished him from the Indies for life. From this point on, the historical sources are unclear. One story has him dying penniless; another states that the king gave him a pension. He apparently died sometime around 1559.

His Spanish companions in the great trek fared better. Both Castillo and Dorantes married wealthy widows and lived prosperously in Mexico. Esteban the Moor came to a bad end: sent back to the far north by Viceroy Mendoza along with a Franciscan monk to report on the natives, he collected an escort of Indians as in the old days, forging far ahead of the missionary in his eagerness to be the first discoverer of the pueblos of the Río Grande. But Esteban became overconfident and self-important, demanding that each village furnish him with turquoises and women. When he arrived at Háwikuh Pueblo in the Zuñi country, the Indians there killed him. Fray Marcos, the Franciscan, turned back. When he returned to Mexico City, he embellished his story, telling the viceroy that he had seen from afar the Seven Cities of Cíbola, fabulous cities of gold. The Spaniards mounted a huge expedition, headed by Francisco de Coronado, to conquer these kingdoms. Even though Coronado failed in his objective, the long road to occupation and bitterness for the Pueblo Indians of New Mexico had begun.

Alvar Núñez Cabeza de Vaca was very nearly unique in the bloody annals of Spain's "encounter" with the New World. He was a rare conquistador, and one of a mere handful of Spaniards, who believed that the way of the conqueror was morally wrong and practically inefficient. He came to these beliefs through a remarkable empathetic transformation wrought from hardship, hunger, fear, and pain. He discovered a common humanity between Europeans and Native Americans, and for these beliefs he ultimately sacrificed his own career. The thousands-mile trek of Cabeza de Vaca wrought a bridge between two peoples—an ephemeral one that, once it was sundered by the human follies of ignorance and greed, could never be rebuilt.

Notes

1. Alvar Núñez Cabeza de Vaca, *Cabeza de Vaca's Adventures in the Unknown Interior of America*, trans. and annotated by Cyclone Covey, with a new Epilogue by William T. Pilkington (New York, 1961), 33–34.

2. Ibid., 39.

3. Ibid., 41.

4. Ibid., 42.

5. Ibid., 48.
6. Ibid., 57–58.
7. Ibid., 59.
8. Ibid., 60.
9. Ibid.
10. Ibid., 66–67.
11. Ibid., 64–65.
12. Carl Ortwin Sauer, *Sixteenth-Century North America: The Land and People as Seen by Europeans* (Berkeley, CA, 1971), 111.
13. Gonzalo Fernández de Oviedo y Valdés, *Historia general y natural de las Indias*, book 35 (Madrid, 1851–1855), as quoted in Sauer, 111–12.
14. Cabeza de Vaca, *Cabeza de Vaca's Adventures*, 85.
15. Ibid., 89.
16. Ibid., 96–97.
17. Ibid., 88.
18. Ibid., 103.
19. Ibid., 110.
20. Ibid., 122.
21. Ibid.
22. Ibid., 123.
23. Ibid., 125.
24. Ibid., 128.

Suggested Readings

Two primary source narratives were written after the journey of Alvar Núñez Cabeza de Vaca and his companions. Cabeza de Vaca himself wrote the *Relación y comentarios del Gobernador Alvar Núñez Cabeza de Vaca de lo acaescido en las dos jornadas que hizo a las Indias*, published in 1542. Many editions in Spanish have appeared under the title *Naufragios y comentarios*. A number of English translations have been made of the *Relación*; the most widely read is *Cabeza de Vaca's Adventures in the Unknown Interior of America*, trans. and annotated by Cyclone Covey (New York, 1961).

The three survivors—Cabeza de Vaca, Dorantes, and Castillo—also presented a joint report in 1537 to the Audiencia of Santo Domingo. This report, principally made by Dorantes, was excerpted and condensed by the historian Gonzalo Fernández de Oviedo y Valdés in book 35 of his *Historia general y natural de las Indias*, partially published in 1535 and 1547, but not published in a full edition until 1851–1855 in Madrid.

The secondary literature on Cabeza de Vaca's journey is immense. Fanny Bandelier, along with her husband Adolph, not only translated Cabeza de Vaca's account but also retraced the route of his party through Texas and the Southwest. The result was published as *The Journey of Alvar Núñez Cabeza de Vaca and His Companions from Florida to the Pacific, 1528–1536* (New York, 1905). In 1940, Cleve Hallenbeck made his own calculation of the

Spaniards' route across the Southwest, published as Cleve Hallenbeck, *Alvar Núñez Cabeza de Vaca: The Journey and Route of the First European to Cross the Continent of North America, 1534–1536* (Port Washington, NY, 1940).

Two noteworthy scholarly examinations are Carl Ortwin Sauer, *Sixteenth-Century North America: The Land and People as Seen by Europeans* (Berkeley, CA, 1971); and David A. Howard, *Conquistador in Chains: Cabeza de Vaca and the Indians of the Americas* (Tuscaloosa, AL, 1997). Donald E. Chipman, "In Search of Cabeza de Vaca's Route across Texas: An Historiographical Survey," *Southwestern Historical Quarterly* 91, no. 2 (1987): 127–48, is a review of the many attempts (including one made by James Michener in the novel *Texas*) to retrace the party's journey.

If in recent decades historians have overlooked Cabeza de Vaca in their pursuit of more cutting-edge topics, literary scholars have more than made up the difference. The number of articles examining Cabeza de Vaca's *Relación*, even in English, is impressive. Among the most interesting are Rolena Adorno, "The Discursive Encounter of Spain and America: The Authority of Eyewitness Testimony in the Writing of History," *William and Mary Quarterly* 49 (1992): 210–28; idem, "Peaceful Conquest and Law in the *Relación* (Account) of Alvar Núñez Cabeza de Vaca," in *Coded Encounters: Writing, Gender, and Ethnicity in Colonial Latin America*, ed. Francisco Javier Cevallos-Candau et al. (Amherst, MA, 1994), 75–86; idem, "The Negotiation of Fear in Cabeza de Vaca's *Naufragio*," *Representations* 33 (1991): 163–99; Juan Francisco Maura, "Truth versus Fiction in the Autobiographical Accounts by the Chroniclers of Exploration," *Monographic Review / Revista Monográfica* 9 (1993): 28–53; Jacqueline C. Nanfito, "Cabeza de Vaca's *Naufragio y comentarios:* The Journey Motif in the Chronicle of the Indies," *Revista de Estudios Hispánicos* (Puerto Rico) 21 (1994): 179–87; Lee H. Dowling, "Story vs. Discourse in the Chronicle of the Indies: Cabeza de Vaca's *Relación*," *Hispanic Journal* 5, no. 2 (Spring 1984): 89–99; and Mary M. Gaylord, "Spain's Renaissance Conquests and the Retroping of History," *Journal of Hispanic Philology* 16, no. 2 (Winter 1992): 125–36.

2

Squanto
Last of the Patuxet

Neal Salisbury

Squanto (d. 1622) is one Native American of the early colonial period whose name is familiar; he is known primarily because the Pilgrims and their historians have found him useful. A Native American who spoke English and taught newly arrived colonists to plant corn was not only providential, but he also easily became part of an idealized Thanksgiving tableau of Native Americans inviting and justifying the Pilgrim presence in Patuxet. As we learn more of Squanto's story, he emerges as a clever and adaptable captive and refugee who finds a momentary role in Pilgrim settlement and Wampanoag survival. It may have been because he was a captive elsewhere that Squanto survived the spread of a disease that destroyed his village of Patuxet. That epidemic made the Wampanoag particularly interested in the Pilgrims' survival, and made Squanto valuable to both communities. The treaty that he helped arrange lasted nearly half a century, in part because it was the sole legitimacy for Pilgrim landownership; the Pilgrims never had a charter. Tempted to extract more than was thought appropriate from his position as broker between these societies, Squanto effectively destroyed his own position.

Neal Salisbury is a leading expert on relations between Native Americans and Europeans in colonial New England, the author of *Manitou and Providence: Indians, Europeans, and the Making of New England, 1500–1643* (1982), and a longtime student of Squanto's life. He teaches colonial and American Indian history at Smith College, Northampton, Massachusetts.

An earlier version of this essay appeared in David Sweet and Gary B. Nash, eds., *Survival and Struggle in Colonial America* (Berkeley, CA, 1981), 228-46. Copyright © 1981 by The Regents of the University of California. I am grateful to the University of California Press for permission to publish this modified version.

An enduring American legend tells of a lone Indian named Squanto, who rescued the Pilgrims from the wilderness by teaching them how to plant corn and introducing them to friendly Native Americans. In so doing, the legend implies, he symbolically brought about the union of the English colonizers and the American land. Although recent events and scholarship have undermined such self-serving representations of early Indian-white relations, Squanto's story retains significance. For when placed in its historic and cultural contexts, it reveals the range of qualities called forth among Native Americans during the early colonization of New England.

As befits a mythic hero, the time and circumstances of Squanto's birth are unknown. His birth date can only be inferred from what the sources say and do not say. The firsthand descriptions of him, written between 1618 and his death in 1622, do not suggest that he was strikingly young or old at that time. All we can safely conclude is that he was probably in his twenties or thirties when he was forcibly taken to Europe in 1614.

Although Squanto's early years are obscured by a lack of direct evidence, we know something of the cultural milieu that prepared him for his unexpected and remarkable career. Squanto, or Tisquantum, was a Wampanoag Indian from the village of Patuxet. Patuxet maintained close ties with the other Wampanoags around Plymouth Bay, on Cape Cod, on the islands of Martha's Vineyard, and westward to the principal Wampanoag community on Narragansett Bay. The Wampanoag spoke Massachusett, a language they shared with the Massachusett and Pawtucket Indians to the north. The differences between Massachusett and other languages spoken by Native Americans in what is now southern New England were minimal, so that the Wampanoag could communicate with Indians throughout this region. Like other coastal villages south of the Saco River, Patuxet was positioned to allow its inhabitants to grow crops, exploit marine resources, and have easy access to wild plants and animals. In accordance with the sexual division of labor maintained by virtually all eastern North American Indians, Squanto's major activities would have been hunting game and certain kinds of fishing. The women at Patuxet, on the other hand, were in charge of farming, the gathering of wild plants and shellfish, and the preparation of all foods. Squanto would also have fashioned a wide variety of tools and other items and participated in the intensely ritualized world of trade, diplomacy, religious ceremonies, recreation, warfare, and political decision making that constituted public life in Patuxet.

The training of young men in precontact southern New England was designed to prepare them for that world. Among the

Wampanoag, Plymouth leader Edward Winslow wrote: "A man is not accounted a man till he do some notable act or show forth such courage and resolution as becometh his place."[1] A Dutch official from New Netherland noted that young Wampanoag men were left alone in the forest for an entire winter. On returning to his people in the spring, a candidate was expected to imbibe and vomit bitter poisonous herbs for several days. At the conclusion of his ordeal, he was brought before the entire community, "and if he has been able to stand it all well, and if he is fat and sleek, a wife is given to him."[2]

As a result of such testing, young Wampanoags learned not only how to survive but also how to develop the capacities to withstand the most severe physical and psychological trials. The result was a personality type that Europeans came to characterize as stoic, the supreme manifestation of which was the absolute expressionlessness of prisoners under torture. Although the specific content of such training did little to prepare Squanto for his later experiences in Málaga, London, or Newfoundland, it imparted a sense of psychological independence and prepared him for adapting to the most demanding environments and situations.

Wampanoag men such as Squanto also exercised their independence in making political judgments and decisions. As elsewhere in southern New England, a Wampanoag political leader, or sachem, was drawn from one of a select group of families. The sachems distributed garden plots to families and exercised certain judicial prerogatives. They also represented their community on diplomatic and ceremonial occasions. But a sachem's power was derived directly from the members of the community. To secure economic and political support he needed leadership ability as well as a family name. Community members could oblige a faltering sachem to share the office with a relative or to step down altogether. Moreover, major political decisions were reached through a consensus in meetings attended by all adult males. Squanto came from a world, then, where politics was a constant and integral component of a man's life.

Squanto was even better prepared for his unusual career if, as seems probable, he was a *pniese* (elite warrior and sachem's counselor) in his community. In preparation for this position, young men were chosen in childhood and underwent unusually rigorous diets and training. The purpose of this preparation was not simply to fortify them and develop their courage but also to enable them to call upon and visualize Hobbamock, a deity capable of inflicting great harm and even death on those whom he did not favor. Hobbamock appeared in many forms to "the chiefest and most judicious amongst them," in Winslow's words, "though all of them strive to attain to that hellish height of honor."[3] It is clear that those who succeeded in the vision quest had developed the mental self-discipline demanded of all Indians to an extraordinary degree. By calling on Hobbamock, the *pnieses* protected themselves and those near them in battle and frightened their opponents. They were universally respected not only for their access to Hobbamock and for their courage and judgment but also for their moral uprightness. Because of his psychological fortitude, his particularly astute grasp of Indian politics and protocol, and his continued sense of duty to his community even after its demise, it is quite likely that Squanto was a *pniese*.

The few recorded observations of Patuxet during Squanto's early years show that it was a very different place from the "wilderness" that the Plymouth colonists later described. Both Samuel de Champlain in 1605 and 1606 and John Smith in 1614 noted that most of the coast between Massachusetts and Plymouth Bays was under cultivation. The colonists were told, probably by Squanto himself, that in Plymouth Bay "in former time hath lived about 2,000 Indians."[4] The total Wampanoag population in 1615 was probably about twenty thousand, most of whom were concentrated in village communities ranging in size from five hundred to fifteen hundred individuals. Squanto's homeland, then, was far more densely settled before the English arrived than afterward.

Although no one could have known it at the time, Squanto was born at a turning point in the history of his people and his region. For a century, Europeans had been trading and skirmishing with, and sometimes kidnapping, Native Americans along the coast. At the time of Squanto's birth, however, these activities had not been extended south of Canada on a regular basis. Occasional visits from European explorers and traders and the Native Americans' own well-established exchange routes brought some iron tools and glass beads to Patuxet. But these visits were too infrequent to have induced any lasting economic or cultural changes. Unlike some fur-trading Indians to the north, the Wampanoag had not become dependent on European trade items for their survival.

The turn of the century marked an intensification of French and English interest in New England's resources. The differing economic goals of the colonizers from the two countries gave rise to differing attitudes and policies toward the region's Native Americans. The French were concerned primarily with furs. Following Champlain's explorations of the New England coast in 1605 and 1606, French traders using his descriptions and maps began to visit annually and to cultivate an extensive trade as far south as Cape Cod. Their goals encouraged the maintenance of friendly relations with coastal Indian communities and even the development of broad regional ties among the native peoples.

For the English, however, furs were at best a useful by-product of more pressing interests. Beginning with Bartholomew Gosnold's expedition in 1602, they showed a preference for extracting resources such as fish and sassafras that did not require the cooperation of native communities. Moreover, they thought in long-range terms of making Indian land available to English farmers, a goal that virtually guaranteed eventual conflict with Native Americans. The English cultivated Indian allies only to gain their assistance in establishing colonies, and English methods were generally more coercive than those of the French. Nearly every English expedition from Gosnold's to that of the *Mayflower* generated hostility with Native Americans. By 1610, taking captured Indians to England had become commonplace. Would-be colonizers such as Sir Ferdinando Gorges hoped to impress their captives with the superiority of English culture, to learn as much as they could about the lay of the land, and to use them as mediators with local Indians. They also displayed their captives prominently in order to attract financial and public support in England for their projected colonies.

John Smith, the former Virginia leader, witnessed the results of the competition between the two colonial strategies when he explored the coast from the Penobscot River to Cape Cod in 1614. Smith found that he had arrived at the end of an active trading season. Aside from one Englishman's cozy monopoly at the mouth of the Pemaquid River, all of the ships were French. The better-endowed region north of the Pemaquid had yielded 25,000 skins that year, and Smith judged the south capable of producing as many as 6,000 to 7,000 annually. He himself had retrieved 1,300 pelts, mostly beaver, in the wake of the French departure. He also found that all the Indians in the area he visited were friendly with one another through three loose regional alliances. Ostensibly formed to resist incursions from the Micmac in eastern Canada, the friendship chain had an economic function as well, for Smith noted that some primarily horticultural Indians in southern New England traded corn to Abenaki hunting groups farther north. In return, the horticulturalists obtained some of the Abenaki's supply of European trade goods. Though only minimally developed by 1614, this trade was already fostering a specialized division of labor among France's clients in New England.

The extent of Wampanoag participation in the corn trade is unknown, but Squanto and his people were producing substantial surpluses of furs by the time of Smith's visit in 1614 and had gained at least some acquaintance with the Europeans. From the visits of Champlain, Smith, and the traders, Squanto had learned something of European approaches to trade, diplomacy, and military conflict and had witnessed some of their technological accomplishments. But the regularized trade was less than a decade old. The ease with which groups of Patuxet men were manipulated by Smith and his officer, Thomas Hunt, in 1614 suggests that they had not developed the wariness toward Europeans, particularly the English, of the more experienced Indians to the north.

Squanto's life reached a sudden and dramatic turning point with Hunt's visit. Smith had returned to England, leaving Hunt in charge of his fishing crew to complete the catch and carry it to Málaga, Spain. Before departing, Hunt stopped at Patuxet. Using his association with Smith, who had left on friendly terms, he lured aboard his ship about twenty natives, including Squanto. Quickly rounding Cape Cod, he drew off seven more Indians from Nauset and then turned east for Málaga. Hunt's action marked the English as an enemy of all the Wampanoags. Referring to southeastern New England, Gorges said that Hunt's action had resulted in "a warre now new begunne betweene the inhabitants of those parts and us," while Smith condemned Hunt for moving the Indians to "hate against our Nation, as well as to cause my proceedings to be more difficult."[5]

Native outrage at Hunt's action was reinforced by the near-simultaneous return of an earlier Wampanoag captive, Epenow, a sachem of Capawack, on Martha's Vineyard. Epenow had been seized three years earlier and taken to Gorges's house in England. On constant public display, he learned English well and impressed Gorges and others as "a goodly man of brave aspect, stout and sober in his demeanour."[6] Thus his fabricated tales of gold on Martha's Vineyard were eagerly seized upon; and in 1614, Gorges commissioned a voyage under Nicholas Hobson, accompanied by Epenow as a guide. Epenow had apparently planned his escape all along, but the news of Hunt's deed hardened his desire for revenge. As the ship drew near his island, Epenow escaped under a cover of arrows from the shore. A fierce battle ensued with heavy casualties on both sides. Among the injured was Hobson himself, who returned to England empty-handed. Epenow thereafter constituted one source of the anti-English sentiment that the Plymouth colonists would encounter six years later.

Meanwhile, Squanto and his fellow captives reached Málaga, where Hunt tried to sell them as slaves. A few had already been sold when, according to Gorges, "the Friers of those parts took the rest from them and kept them to be instructed in the Christian faith."[7] What happened to Squanto over the next three years is not clear. Particularly intriguing are questions about the extent and influence of his Catholic instruction and the means by which, in William Bradford's words, "he got away for England."[8] We know only that by

1617 he was residing in the London home of John Slany, treasurer of the Newfoundland Company, where he learned, or at least improved, his English and his understanding of colonial goals. In the following year, he went to Newfoundland itself, presumably at Slany's instigation. Here for the second time he met Thomas Dermer, an officer with Smith in 1614 who now worked for Gorges. Dermer was so impressed with Squanto's tales of Patuxet that he took him back to England to meet Gorges. Although the strategy of employing captive Indians as guides had backfired several times, Gorges was ready to try again. He saw in Squanto the key to countering French domination of the New England fur trade and to reestablishing England's reputation among the Indians. For his part, Squanto knew, as had earlier captives, how to tell Gorges what he wanted to hear in order to be returned home. In March 1619 he and Dermer were bound for New England.

Moving in the circles he did, Squanto undoubtedly knew something of the epidemic that had ravaged New England, including Patuxet, during his absence. A Gorges expedition under Richard Vines had witnessed what Vines called simply "the plague" at Sagadahoc in 1616 in reporting on its effects. Most notable was the immunity of the English; while most of the Indians were dying, Vines and his party "lay in the Cabbins with those people, [and] not one of them ever felt their heads to ake."[9] This immunity and the 75-to-90 percent depopulation among the Indians make it clear that a virgin-soil epidemic of European origin had been planted in New England's isolated disease environment. Although the specific instigator cannot be identified because of the frequency with which Europeans were visiting New England, it is noteworthy that the stricken zone, as reported by Dermer in 1619, was the coast from the Penobscot to Cape Cod—precisely the area encompassing the loose coalition of Indian groups engaged in trade with the French and one another. At its southern extremity the epidemic spread among the Wampanoags, including those at Pokanoket, located at the head of Narragansett Bay. But the sickness did not affect the Wampanoags' Narragansett rivals on the western side of the bay who traded with the Dutch in New Netherland. This pattern suggests that the epidemic was of French origin.

Squanto found his hometown of Patuxet completely vacated. Most of its inhabitants had died, and the survivors had fled inland to other villages. He surely noticed, as did others, the undergrowth that had overtaken the formerly cultivated fields and the vast numbers of unburied dead whose "bones and skulls," in one Englishman's words, "made such a spectacle . . . it seemed to me a new found Golgotha."[10] The depopulation was so great that the Narragansetts were able to force the weakened Wampanoags at

Pokanoket to abandon their position at the head of Narragansett Bay and to retain only the eastern shore.

The Narragansetts' avoidance of the epidemic gave them a greater advantage than that derived from numbers alone. In the view of their stricken neighbors, the Narragansetts' good health reflected their faithful sacrifices to the deity, Cautantowwit. The ritual worlds and belief systems of the Wampanoags who survived, however, had been badly shaken by the epidemic. The usual practice of gathering with the powwow (medicine man) in a sick person's wigwam could only have helped spread the disease more rapidly. With even their powwows succumbing, the Wampanoags could only conclude that their deities had aligned against them. Being unable to observe the proper burial rituals, the survivors also had to fear the retribution of the dead. Their momentary fear that they had lost touch with sources of spiritual power to which others had access would be a critical factor in facilitating Squanto's later political success.

As Dermer's expedition traveled overland from Patuxet in the summer of 1619, Squanto's presence and diplomatic skill enabled the English to break through the antagonism toward them and to make friendly contacts at Nemasket (near Middleboro) and Pokanoket (near Bristol, Rhode Island). For once an Indian captive had performed as Gorges had hoped. But as Dermer returned to his ship and prepared to sail around Cape Cod, Squanto took his leave to search for surviving Patuxet Wampanoags. On his own, Dermer was unable to persuade the Indians at Monomoy (now Pleasant Harbor) of his good intentions. He was captured and barely succeeded in escaping. After a seemingly cordial meeting on Martha's Vineyard with Epenow, the former Gorges captive, Dermer was attacked off Long Island and again managed to escape. Returning to New England in the summer of 1620, he was captured by his newly made friends at Pokanoket and Nemasket, and released only after Squanto interceded on his behalf. Dermer, with Squanto, then proceeded to Martha's Vineyard, where they were attacked by Epenow and his followers. Most of the crew was killed this time, while the luckless captain escaped with fourteen wounds and died later in Virginia. Squanto was again made a captive, this time of his fellow Wampanoags.

In a letter written after his release at Nemasket, Dermer attributed his reception there to the Wampanoags' renewed desire for revenge. He noted that another English crew had just visited the area, invited some Indians on board their ship, and then shot them down without provocation. The incident could only have revived the Indians' suspicions of the English that had prevailed before Squanto's return. These suspicions were now focused on Squanto himself, as Dermer's accomplice, and led to his being turned over to Massasoit, or Ousamequin, the leading Wampanoag sachem, based at Pokanoket. Here, Squanto remained until he was ransomed by the Plymouth colonists in March 1621.

In the autumn of 1620, the Wampanoag homeland was vastly different from a decade earlier when French traders had begun to frequent it regularly. Fewer than 10 percent of its 20,000 former inhabitants were still living, and they were now consolidated into a few tiny communities. The region was vulnerable, as never before, to exploitation by outsiders. Pokanoket and its sachem, Massasoit, had been subjected to a humiliating tributary relationship with the Narragansett, who were emerging as the most important political force in New England because of their size and their control of Indian-European trade links east of Long Island. Moreover, the decimated Indians could no longer count on the fur trade as a means of compensating for other weaknesses. Always limited in both the quality and quantity of its fur resources, the region's loss of most of its hunters now made it an unprofitable stop for traders.

Although he was their captive, Squanto was able to capitalize on Pokanoket's despair. "He told Massasoit what wonders he had seen in England," according to a future settler, "and that if he could make [the] English his friends then Enemies that were too strong for him would be constrained to bow to him."[11] He did not have to wait long to be proved right. In December 1620, less than six months after Dermer's departure, word reached Pokanoket that a shipload of English colonists had established a permanent settlement at Patuxet.

Like the other Puritans who later settled New England, the group at Plymouth (for so they renamed Patuxet) were motivated by a combination of religious and economic motives that shaped their attitudes toward Native Americans. Their persecution by the Church of England and their self-imposed exile to the Netherlands had only sharpened their desire to practice their exclusionary, intolerant separatism without external interference. While seeking literally to distance themselves from English ecclesiastical authorities, the settlers were endeavoring to reinforce their English identities. They had abandoned their Dutch haven for fear that their children would become assimilated there. Finally, though ostensibly migrating to fish and trade for furs, the colonists actually sought land to improve themselves materially and, they supposed, spiritually. Neither very rich nor very poor, most were small farmers and artisans who sought to escape the shortage of land and inflated prices that threatened their tenuous economic independence. Although Plymouth lacked the sense of divine mission of the later nonseparatist Puritan colonies, its goals of religious and ethnic exclusivity and its desire for land had clear implications for its relations with the Wampanoag and other native peoples.

These implications were apparent in Plymouth's early policies and attitudes toward the Indians. In a major promotional pamphlet published in 1622, Robert Cushman restated what had already become a familiar justification for dispossessing Native Americans of their lands: "Their land is spacious and void, and there are few and do but run over the grass, as do also the foxes and wild beasts. They are not industrious, neither have art, science, skill, or faculty to use either the land or the commodities of it, but all spoils or rots, and is marred for want of manuring, gathering, ordering, etc. As the ancient patriarchs therefore removed from straiter places into more roomy . . . so is it lawful now to take a land which none useth, and make use of it."[12] Cushman's statement was consistent with the emerging European doctrine of *vacuum domicilium*, by which "civil" states were entitled to the uncultivated lands of those in a "natural" state. Although Plymouth's own "civility" was formalized by the hastily contrived Mayflower Compact, its financial backers had anticipated its need for more than an abstract principle to press its claim—among its own people as well as among any natives whom they might encounter. Accordingly, they had hired Miles Standish, a soldier of fortune fresh from the Dutch wars, to organize the colony militarily. It was Standish who would shape Plymouth's Indian policy during its first generation.

Standish began to execute this policy even before the *Mayflower* arrived at Patuxet. Landing first at Cape Cod, the settlers aroused hostilities by ransacking Indian graves, houses, and grain stores. At Patuxet they also stirred suspicions during the first four months of their stay. But their own situation grew desperate during their first New England winter. They lost half their numbers to starvation and disease and were ill prepared for the approaching planting season. In this condition, they could no longer expect to alleviate their shortages through pilferage with impunity. The impasse was broken one day in March 1621 by the appearance of Samoset, an Abenaki sachem from the Pemaquid River community that had been trading with the English for more than a decade. Samoset learned of the needs and intentions of the colony and returned a few days later with Squanto.

The Wampanoags had been watching the Plymouth group throughout the winter. With Samoset and the newly useful Squanto offering advice and experience, they concluded that the time was ripe to befriend the settlers instead of maintaining a hostile distance. Such an alliance would enable them to break the grip of the Narragansetts, whose haughty demeanor stung even more than that of the English. Nevertheless, the decision was not to be taken lightly. William Bradford wrote that the Indians did first "curse and execrate them with their conjurations" before approaching the settlers.[13] But this description betrays his fear of witchcraft as it was understood by Europeans, rather than his comprehension of Indian rituals. More likely, the Wampanoags were ritually purging themselves of their hostilities toward the English.

Samoset and Squanto arranged the meeting between the Wampanoags and Plymouth colonists that resulted in their historic treaty, in which each side agreed to aid the other in the event of attack by a third party, to disarm during their meetings with each other, and to return any tools stolen from the other side. In addition to these reciprocal agreements, however, several others were weighted against the natives. Massasoit, the sachem at Pokanoket, was to see that his tributaries observed the terms; the Indians were to turn over for punishment any of their people suspected of assaulting any English persons (but no English settlers could be tried by Indians); and, the treaty concluded, "King James would esteem of him [Massasoit] as his friend and ally."[14] The colonists' understanding of this last honor was made explicit by Plymouth's Nathaniel Morton, who wrote that Massasoit, by the treaty, "acknowledged himself content to become the subject of our sovereign lord the King aforesaid, his heirs and successors, and gave unto them all the lands adjacent to them and theirs forever."[15] Morton made clear that among themselves the English did not regard the treaty as one of alliance and friendship between equals, but rather as one of submission by one party to the domination of the other, according to the assumptions of *vacuum domicilium*.

For the Wampanoags, however, the meaning of a political relationship was conveyed in the ritual exchange of speeches and gifts, not in written clauses or unwritten understandings based on concepts such as sovereignty that were alien to them. From their standpoint, the English were preferable to the Narragansett because they demanded less tribute and homage while offering more gifts and autonomy and better protection.

The treaty also brought a change in status for Squanto. In return for his services, the Wampanoags now freed him to become guide, interpreter, and diplomat for the colony. Thus, he finally returned to his home at Patuxet, a move that had, as we shall see, more than sentimental significance. Among his first services was the securing of corn seed and instruction in its planting, including the use of fish as fertilizer.

Squanto also enabled Plymouth to strengthen its political position in the surrounding area. He helped secure peace with some Wampanoag communities on Cape Cod and guided an expedition to Massachusetts Bay. His kidnapping by anti-English Wampanoags at Nemasket and subsequent rescue by a heavily armed Plymouth force speaks compellingly of his importance to the colony. Moreover, this incident led to a new treaty, engineered in part by Squanto, with all the Indian groups of Massachusetts Bay to the tip of Cape Cod, including even Epenow and his community. By establishing a tributary system with the surrounding Indian bands, Plymouth was filling the political vacuum left by the epidemic and creating a dependable network of corn suppliers and buffers against overland attack. In so doing, however, Plymouth incurred the resentment of the Narragansett by depriving them of tributaries just when Dutch traders were expanding their activities in the bay. In January 1622 the Narragansett conveyed their displeasure by sending colony leaders a snakeskin filled with arrows. On Squanto's advice, Plymouth's leaders returned the skin filled with powder and shot. The Narragansett sachem, Canonicus, refused to accept this counterchallenge, in effect thus acknowledging the colony's presence and political importance.

However effective it appeared, Plymouth's system of Indian diplomacy was fraught with tensions that nearly destroyed it. A Pokanoket *pniese*, Hobbamock (named for the powerful spirit), became a second adviser to Plymouth in the summer of 1621. Whether the English thought that Hobbamock would merely assist Squanto or would serve to check him is unclear. In any event, Squanto was no longer the only link between the colony and the Indians; indeed, being from Pokanoket, Hobbamock had certain advantages over him. As one whose very life depended on the colony's need for him, Squanto had to act decisively to check this threat to his position. His most potent weapon was the mutual distrust and fear still lingering between English and Indians; his most pressing need was for a power base so that he could extricate himself from his position of colonial dependency. Accordingly, he began maneuvering on his own.

Squanto had been acting independently for several months before being discovered by the English in March 1622. As reconstructed by Edward Winslow: "His course was to persuade the Indians [that] he could lead us to peace or war at his pleasure, and would oft threaten the Indians, sending them word in a private manner we were intended shortly to kill them, that thereby he might get gifts to himself, to work their peace; so that whereas divers [people] were wont to rely on Massasoit for protection, and resort to his abode, now they began to leave him and seek after Tisquantum [Squanto]."[16] In short, he sought to establish himself as an independent native political leader. At the same time, he endeavored to weaken Pokanoket's influence on Plymouth by provoking armed conflict between the two allies. He circulated a rumor that

Massasoit was conspiring with the Narragansett and Massachusett Indians to wipe out the colony. The English quickly verified the continued loyalty of Pokanoket but, though angry at Squanto, were afraid to dispense with him. Instead, they protected him from Massasoit's revenge, which brought tensions into the Pokanoket-Plymouth relationship that were finally assuaged only when Squanto died later in the year.

In seeking to establish his independence of Plymouth, Squanto was struggling for more than his survival. As Winslow put it, he sought "honor, which he loved as his life and preferred before his peace."[17] What did honor mean to Squanto? For one thing, of course, it meant revenge against Pokanoket, not only for threatening his position at Plymouth but also for his earlier captivity. But it meant more than that. Squanto appears, in a short period of time, to have gained substantial influence among Wampanoags loyal to Massasoit. Winslow indicated, unknowingly and in passing, the probable key to this success. The news of Massasoit's alleged treachery against Plymouth was brought, he said, by "an Indian of Tisquantum's family."[18] Contrary to the Plymouth sources (all of which were concerned with establishing the colony's unblemished title to the land around Plymouth Bay), there were certainly a few dozen Patuxet survivors of the epidemic at Pokanoket, Nemasket, and elsewhere. Although Squanto undoubtedly sought the loyalty and tribute of others, it was to these relatives and friends that he would primarily have appealed. The honor that he sought was a reconstituted Patuxet community placed under his own leadership and located near its traditional home.

Squanto's hopes were shattered when his plot collapsed. With Massasoit seeking his life, he had, in Bradford's words, "to stick close to the English, and never durst go from them till he dies."[19] Squanto's isolation from other Indians and his dependence on the colonists help to explain their willingness to protect him. In July, Squanto again engineered an important breakthrough for Plymouth by accompanying an expedition to Monomoy, where suspicion of all Europeans persisted. The Wampanoags here had attacked Champlain's party in 1606 and Dermer's in 1619. Standish's men had taken some of their corn during a stop at Cape Cod in November 1620. Now, as Winslow phrased it, "by Tisquantum's means better persuaded, they left their jealousy, and traded with them."[20] Monomoy's leaders agreed to turn over eight hogsheads of corn and beans to the English. But as the expedition prepared to depart, Squanto "fell sick of an Indian fever, bleeding much at the nose (which the Indians take for a symptom of [impending] death) and within a few days died there."[21]

By the time of Squanto's death, the Plymouth colony had gained the foothold it had sought for two and one-half years. The expedition to Monomoy marked the establishment of firm relations with the last Wampanoag community to withhold loyalty. Although the colony was now feeding itself, the collection of corn remained a symbolic means of affirming the tributary relationships that bound Wampanoag communities to the English. These accomplishments would have been infinitely more difficult, if not impossible, without Squanto's aid. But it is questionable whether his contributions after the summer of 1622 would have been as critical. Thereafter, the colony's principal dealings were with the hostile Massachusett and Narragansett Indians beyond Patuxet's immediate environs. Moreover, the world in which Squanto had flourished was vanishing. A rationalized wampum trade had begun to transform Indian-European relations in southern New England. And the end of the decade would bring a mighty upsurge in English colonization that would surround and dwarf Plymouth. Within the restrictions imposed by his dependence on Plymouth's protection, Squanto would have adapted to these changes, but his knowledge and skills would no longer have been unique nor his services indispensable.

Notes

1. Edward Winslow, "Good Newes from New England," in *Chronicles of the Pilgrim Fathers*, ed. Alexander Young (Boston, 1841), 363.

2. Isaack de Rasieres to Samuel Bloomaert, c. 1628, in Sydney V. James Jr., ed., *Three Visitors to Early Plymouth* (Plymouth, MA, 1963), 79.

3. Winslow, "Good Newes," 357.

4. Emmanuel Altham to Sir Edward Altham, September [?] 1623, in James, *Three Visitors*, 29.

5. James Phinney Baxter, ed., *Sir Ferdinando Gorges and His Province of Maine*, 3 vols. (Boston, 1890), 2:211; Edward Arber, ed., *Travels and Works of Captain John Smith*, 2 vols., 2d ed. (Edinburgh, 1910), 1:219.

6. Baxter, *Gorges*, 2:20–21.

7. Ibid., 1:210.

8. William Bradford, *Of Plymouth Plantation*, ed. Samuel Eliot Morison (New York, 1967), 81.

9. Baxter, *Gorges*, 2:19.

10. Thomas Morton, *New English Canaan*, ed. Charles Francis Adams Jr. (Boston, 1883), 132–33.

11. Phineas Pratt, "A Declaration of the Affairs of the English People that First Inhabited New England," *Massachusetts Historical Society Collections*, 4th ser., 4 (1858): 485.

12. Dwight B. Heath, ed., *A Journal of the Pilgrims at Plymouth*, orig. title *Mourt's Relation* [1622] (New York, 1963), 91–92.

13. Bradford, *Of Plymouth Plantation*, 84.

14. Heath, *Journal*, 57.

15. Nathaniel Morton, *New Englands Memoriall* [1669], ed. Howard J. Hall (New York, 1937), 24.

16. Winslow, "Good Newes," 289.

17. Ibid., 289–90.

18. Ibid., 287.
19. Bradford, *Of Plymouth Plantation*, 99.
20. Winslow, "Good Newes," 301.
21. Bradford, *Of Plymouth Plantation*, 114.

Suggested Readings

I have treated fully the context within which Squanto lived and acted in *Manitou and Providence: Indians, Europeans, and the Making of New England, 1500–1643* (New York, 1982). For additional information on native peoples and cultures in southern New England and surrounding regions, see Bruce G. Trigger, ed., *Northeast*, vol. 15 of *Handbook of North American Indians*, general ed. William C. Sturtevant (Washington, DC, 1978). For perspectives on the larger history of Native Americans in the colonial era, see Bruce G. Trigger and William R. Swagerty, "Entertaining Strangers: North America in the Sixteenth Century," and Neal Salisbury, "Native People and European Settlers in Eastern North America, 1600–1783," both in *The Cambridge History of the Native Peoples of the Americas*, vol. 1, *North America*, ed. Bruce G. Trigger and Wilcomb E. Washburn (Cambridge, England, 1996), pt. 1, 325–98, 399–460; Francis Jennings, *The Invasion of America: Indians, Colonialism, and the Cant of Conquest* (Chapel Hill, NC, 1975); and Ian K. Steele, *Warpaths: Invasions of North America* (New York, 1994). On epidemic disease and depopulation among Native Americans, see Alfred W. Crosby, *The Columbian Exchange: Biological and Cultural Consequences of 1492* (Westport, CT, 1972); and Russell Thornton, *American Indian Holocaust and Survival: A Population History since 1492* (Norman, OK, 1987).

3

Gabriel Sagard
A Franciscan among the Huron

Cornelius J. Jaenen

Brother Gabriel Sagard (c. 1580–c. 1636) spent ten months working as a Franciscan missionary among the Iroquoian-speaking Huron
people of what is now Ontario. His wide-ranging curiosity and relative
tolerance for alien customs make him a witness of enduring interest.
Why would the Huron permit Sagard's extended visit and how would the
mission lodge he helped build at Caragouha, with its latched door and
fenced garden, appear to them? Was there value in maintaining a
certain aloofness for Europeans such as Sagard and Cabeza de Vaca,
who were competing as shamans in Native American societies? How
would the reason for writing *Le grand voyage du pays des Hurons*
influence Sagard's "remembrance" of events and his views of the Huron
as potential Christians? Our first three witnesses are very different (a
soldier, a captive, and a priest) but invite comparisons among Spanish,
English, and French initial interactions with Native Americans.

Cornelius Jaenen, emeritus professor of history at the University of
Ottawa, has published a number of books on New France, including
*Friend and Foe: Aspects of French-Amerindian Cultural Contact in the
Sixteenth and Seventeenth Centuries* (1976) and *The French Régime
in the Upper Country of Canada during the Seventeenth Century*
(1996).

Gabriel Sagard, a brother of the Franciscan order of Récollets of
the religious province of Saint-Denis in France, sometimes
dignified as the first religious historian of New France, labored as a
missionary in the villages of the Huron confederacy near Georgian
Bay, on the eastern shore of Lake Huron, in 1623–24. Neither the
date of his birth nor the date of his death is known. Also, little is
found about his origins or education, although he appears to have
been a member of the Récollet order by 1604. His writings would
seem to indicate that, although quite observant and literate, he had
not benefited from advanced classical studies. His religious order

placed more emphasis on piety and charity than on erudition.

Who were these first sandal-shod missionaries, clad in their gray, rough-homespun hooded cloaks, who appeared in the "upper country" of Canada (New France), the central region of present-day Ontario, early in the seventeenth century? History has not been particularly kind to them, the more spectacular and controversial enterprises of the wealthy Jesuits having overshadowed their pioneering work in Canada, Acadia, and Newfoundland. Bishop François de Laval, who arrived in Canada in 1659, was a fervent supporter of the Jesuits, and he did his utmost to suppress or restrict Récollet activities in the nascent colony. The Franciscans had been founded by Francis of Assisi (Giovanni di Bernardone) and were officially recognized by the Roman Catholic Church at the Lateran Council in 1215. From the beginning, there were internal debates because of their literal observance of the ideal of apostolic poverty as practiced in the primitive Church. These discussions culminated in a reformation of the order in 1517, which set off another series of returns to the so-called strict observance of poverty, especially among the Récollets in France after 1592. They were never without opponents, in other words, within the Church.

Sagard affirmed that he had entered the Récollet monastery at Metz, had been transferred to the Grand Duchy of Luxembourg, and, in 1614, was appointed secretary to the provincial of the Récollets of Saint-Denis, Jacques Garnier de Chapouin. It was there that Samuel de Champlain's recruiting agent, the comptroller of the saltworks at Brouage, came seeking missionaries for Canada. Champlain, as lieutenant of the fur trade monopolists and the viceroys of New France, had decided that permanent missionaries were required to serve the religious needs of the few merchants (many of them Protestants) and the small number of colonists as well as to begin the conversion of the aboriginal inhabitants with whom French trading activities were developing. He had initially asked for Récollets from the province of Aquitaine, who ministered in his hometown of Brouage, but he had to settle for Récollets from Saint-Denis in 1615.

The papal nuncio in Paris granted the Récollets verbal permission to begin their evangelical labors in Canada, but it was not until March 20, 1618, that their mission was officially recognized by the Holy See and that papal "faculties and privileges" and a royal patent of Louis XIII were granted. Rome sought to impose its direct control over all foreign missions, as Pope Gregory XIV created the Sacred Congregation for the Propagation of the Faith (Propaganda Fide) on June 22, 1622. All these events greatly affected the work and views of Brother Sagard.

He was not among the first contingent of his confrères bound for

Québec and the interior missions in 1615. These early missionaries concluded by 1621 that the small colony was in dire straits because of the abuses connected with the unregulated fur trade, brandy trafficking, and threats posed by foreign interlopers. Moreover, their missionary efforts among the nomadic Algonquian peoples proved unfruitful; and even among the hinterland Huron and Petun peoples, who were sedentary agriculturalists, the Récollets had little success. This failure appears to have been the result of their traditional European mission strategy. They believed that it was necessary to "civilize," or impose a French mode of life and beliefs, prior to attempting to convert and assimilate their hearers. To this end, they established a "seminary," or boarding school, near Québec for Algonquian youths, but they were unable to persuade most of their pupils to submit to the rigid discipline, daily routine, and the curriculum for any length of time.

Such was the state of affairs in the colony in 1623, when Brother Sagard was assigned to accompany Father Nicolas Viel to the mission field. They left Paris on March 18, begging food and lodging as they proceeded on foot to Dieppe, where they arrived just a few hours before the departure of a vessel bound for the "newfound-lands." The ship first proceeded southward from Normandy toward La Rochelle to take on a load of salt, barely escaped being captured by Dutch pirates, and then got stranded on a sandbar near Brouage during low tide. The stormy ocean crossing brought them first to Gaspé, a fishing entrepôt frequented by Bretons, Normans, and Basques, where they boarded the pinnace *La Madeleine*, bound for Tadoussac at the mouth of the Saguenay River. Tadoussac at this time was still an important summer trading rendezvous for nomadic Montagnais bands. Sagard and his companion finally reached Québec on board another pinnace, *La Réalle*, on June 29. There were no more than five families at Champlain's habitation, so they decided to push onward as quickly as possible to the mouth of the Richelieu River to link up with a Huron trading party who were preparing to return to their homeland in the region between Georgian Bay and Lake Simcoe. From Cap de la Victoire, Sagard accompanied Nicolas Viel and Father Joseph Le Caron, who had established the first Huron mission at the village of Caragouha in 1615. The Huron mission had strategic importance for both the fur trade and the missions, because it gave access to the traditional trade routes and the interior tribes of the Great Lakes Basin. The Huron were located on the northern limit of corn culture and there-fore were the intermediaries in the exchanges between southern Iroquoian agricultural peoples and northern, nomadic Algonquian hunting bands.

Sagard and his companions left for the country of the Huron on

August 2 and did not reach their destination at Ossassane until August 20. The arduous trip through rapids and over portages impressed Sagard, but like his travel companions he had to submit to taunts and humiliations from time to time from the seasoned Huron canoemen. He described the experience as a trial of his faith and patience. In addition to the natural dangers in the waterways, he had to endure "the stench that these dirty disagreeable fellows emit," the arduous portages over treacherous bogs, around rocky outcroppings, and through "dark thick woods," "countless swarms of mosquitoes and midges," and the fruitless efforts to swallow the pasty corn dishes "so dirtily and badly cooked." Later he would discover the delicate wild parsnips and wild garlic that abounded in the woods. In spite of the hardships, he concluded that his Huron canoemen were examples of patience, cheerfulness, and courage: "I found more good in them than I had imagined."*

No comfortable headquarters with domestics awaited them upon arrival. On the contrary, the Récollet mission was characterized by a certain instability and a lack of sufficient financial resources. Although eighteen missionaries came to Canada, and another three from Acadia tried to join them at Québec, there were never more than four of them active in the Huron country at a time. Two Récollets were captured by Anglo-Huguenots led by the Kirke brothers in the Gulf of St. Lawrence in 1627. The Duke of Ventadour, upon being appointed viceroy of the colony, encouraged the Jesuits to move into the Huron mission alongside the pioneer missionaries.

At Caragouha, Sagard and his companions set to work building a rough-hewn lodge, not wishing to accept the generous offer to share the hospitality of a native longhouse and its numerous inhabitants. The erection of this building was an occasion for the Récollets to earn respect as intercessors. The region had been subject to heavy and incessant rains, so the Huron asked the missionaries to cause the rain to cease. After a night of prayer, the Récollets were delighted to see that the rain had stopped so work could proceed. This apparent miracle, which greatly impressed the Huron, became a problem later when the missionaries were called upon to intervene in numerous natural events, often with little success. Sagard was impressed when "the good savages," as he called them, all worked together to erect the lodge, which consisted of two modest rooms—a chapel and living quarters. A bark door was kept closed with a bit of cord, he informs us, "for fear of thievish hands." The little kitchen

*All quotations herein are translations by the author from Gabriel Sagard, *Histoire du Canada et voyages que les Frères Mineurs Récollets y ont faict pour la conversion des Infidèles*, 4 vols. (Paris, 1636.)

garden planted nearby was fenced off by stakes to keep out the children, "who for the most part seek only to do mischief." The episode was characteristic of the humble beginnings of the mission to the Huron.

True to their historic apostolic pattern of evangelism, the Récollets visited the various villages scattered in clearings in the heavily wooded countryside. On these itinerant missions they suffered from hunger and cold, but deemed themselves "unworthy servants" privileged to bear these crosses. Sagard also recorded that many came to their modest dwelling to learn about the new religion, while others came mainly to steal some small object. It appears that Sagard took notes at that time for an intended publication and began to compile a French-Huron dictionary, although he had acquired very little knowledge of these Iroquoian languages.

Sagard's brief experience among the Huron peoples did not convince him that much success awaited their labors. He wrote that "we obtain few true conversions among our Native people; the day of grace has not yet arrived here." There was no mention of any overt or concerted opposition to Catholic evangelization at this time. The Huron practice of never contradicting guests and never discrediting novel ideas presented the Récollets with little opportunity to evaluate the effects of their preaching. Sagard concluded that their greatest success had been in the number of infants and dying adults baptized, an admission of the effects of epidemics introduced by European intrusion. Employing the same arguments given by early medieval missionaries, Sagard insisted that it was better in most cases to delay baptism until the hour of death in order to prevent converts from falling into apostasy. He knew that the few children to whom a brief education had been given, at the Récollet monastery near Québec, had lapsed into their traditional beliefs and ways once they returned to their families.

In the spring of 1624, Sagard started down to Québec with the Huron fur brigade with the intention of picking up supplies for the mission. They arrived on July 16, and sometime later Sagard received an order from Polycarp du Fay, his provincial superior, to return to France. The reasons for this recall remain obscure, but it did fit the Récollet pattern of constant rotation of missionaries. By returning to France at this time, he avoided the capture of Québec by an Anglo-Huguenot expedition, which resulted in the Récollets being sent to Plymouth on English vessels, whence they made their way to Dover, crossed the Channel over to Calais, and walked barefoot to Paris, according to Sagard.

Back in France, he undertook publication of an account of his experiences and observations in Canada. Although he had lost the notes concerning the time between his departure from Dieppe and his arrival in the country of the Huron, he was able to recall the main events and include them as a second chapter in his account of the ten months spent in the Upper Country. This work was *Le grand voyage du pays des Hurons*, published in Paris in 1632. A third chapter was devoted to an overview of the settlement of Québec, followed by two chapters describing the journey up the northern canoe route to the Great Lakes Basin by way of the Ottawa and Mattawa Rivers, Lake Nipissing, and the French River to Lake Huron. The seventeen remaining chapters were an unsophisticated ethnographic account of Huron mores, festivals, marriage and burial customs, occupations, recreation, and witchcraft. His willingness to accept diabolical apparitions, satanic spells, and stories of monstrous creatures was not an unusual reaction to new environments in the early seventeenth century.

One of the cultural legacies of the Middle Ages was the belief in the existence of wild hairy men, primitive forest dwellers, cruel cannibals who lived in the unexplored and uncultivated regions of the world, such as newly "discovered" America. This concept goes a long way toward explaining some early missionary views that Canada was a land that had produced "little more than thorns since the earliest centuries," and that Huron souls were burdened with all the evils that a land long abandoned to Satan could produce. The extreme cold of its winters rendered the country sterile, incapable of producing bread and wine for the Eucharist, while the extreme heat of its summers was a foretaste of Hell itself. Here was a region where the healing rays of the sun could scarcely penetrate its deep dark forests and where swamps exhaled noxious vapors. It was truly a wilderness and a land of darkness, both naturally and spiritually.

On the other hand, Sagard's willingness to entertain the view that the native peoples were intelligent and creative, that they were capable of adopting the Catholic religion and European civility, and that they were tolerant to the point of not persecuting those who adhered to different spiritual concepts was remarkable for the times. He opposed the Protestant concept of the total depravity of humanity and believed that Huron souls were "good ground" by nature for the Gospel that he and his companions freely preached. Franciscan religious utopianism, which effectively balanced their environmental pessimism, was rooted in thirteenth-century Catholic mysticism and apocalypticism that had prophesied a restoration of the Church to its apostolic purity, the conversion of the heathen nations, followed by the millennium. The Récollets were among those who saw in the "discovery" of America and its indigenous peoples the revelation of the remainder of God's children and the possible advent of universal Christian dominion.

In 1632, Sagard published his *Dictionnaire de la langue*

huronne, which was not a dictionary but rather a brief French-Huron vocabulary. Sagard commented that the language was in a state of rapid evolution. There was no mention of the fact that he might be dealing with several different Huron dialects. The document is not without value, but it was obviously not the work of Sagard. He merely set down information gathered from interpreters and especially from the notes of his coreligionist, Father Joseph Le Caron. There was a publication problem inasmuch as the printing presses could not reproduce the symbols employed by the missionaries to transcribe Huron consonants and vowels.

In 1636 an enlarged version of his voyage appeared in Paris under the title *Histoire du Canada et voyages que les Frères Mineurs Récollets y ont faict pour la Conversion des Infidèles*. By this time, the Jesuits had replaced the Récollets in the Huron mission. Furthermore, Governor Jean de Lauson of the Company of New France (Hundred Associates) that had been organized under Louis XIII's first minister, Cardinal Richelieu, to administer, colonize, and exploit the resources of the colony, adamantly opposed the resumption of the Récollet mission in 1635. The new edition of Sagard's work was substantially enlarged to highlight and justify their pioneer work in the colony from 1615 to 1629. Sagard hoped that his book would document the legitimacy of a Récollet mission in the colony through a direct appeal to Pope Urban VIII. His provincial superior did order Governor Lauson to restore the Récollets to their rights and property, but the latter paid no attention to the directive. Additional firsthand information on colonial developments found in this history cannot be attributed to Sagard. Numerous important documents were included, such as Sagard's letter of recall, a conversation with two Iroquois captives, and Father Le Caron's visit to the Iroquoian-speaking confederacy of the Neutrals in southern Ontario. The editor, probably a Récollet who had no personal experience of the Canadian mission, used some of the information in the Jesuit *Relations* as well as in the colony's first secular history, Marc Lescarbot's *Histoire de la Nouvelle France* (1609), and in Samuel de Champlain's *Voyages et descouvertes faites en la Nouvelle France depuis l'année 1615* (1627) to fill in many details.

This amplified edition of Sagard's earlier work must be seen in the context of the Récollets' frustration at seeing their pioneer missionary efforts in Canada taken over completely and exclusively by the Jesuits. The anti-Jesuit bias of *Histoire du Canada* induced the unidentified editor to change the name of the Récollet residence at Québec, recorded by Sagard and other primary sources as Saint-Charles, to Notre-Dame-des-Anges in order to make it appear that the superior of the Jesuits, Father Jérôme Lalemant, had usurped even the name of the Récollet residence.

Brother Sagard, in contrast to the Jesuit chroniclers who were inundating the reading public in France with their *Relations*, was less interested in the political and economic context of colonization than in the daily labors of a poor itinerant missionary. His *Grand voyage* had little to say about the haphazard administration of New France by merchant associations, the problems generated by the fur trade monopoly, the behavior of the few colonists, the natural resources of the country, and the possible future development of the colony. Indeed, upon his return to France, apart from his role in the two aforementioned publications, he seemed most interested in attacking the Jesuit monopoly on mission work and the supposed threats posed by the presence of Protestant merchants, traders, artisans, and sailors in the colony. The Jesuit *Relations* he defined as instruments "to proclaim their virtues" and propaganda pieces designed to recruit funds and religious vocations. To the viceroy, the Duke of Montmorency, he complained that the Protestants "sing their psalms of Marot in the presence of the Natives who come to trade during the celebration of Mass." The complaints of the Récollets did not go unheard, because in 1627 it became clear that the Edict of Nantes, which had granted limited toleration to metropolitan Protestants (Huguenots or Calvinists) in 1598, had no application in New France. All public display of Protestantism was strictly prohibited, and permanent residence in the colony was restricted to "natural-born French Catholics."

What remains of special interest to present-day readers are Sagard's descriptions of Huron life, customs, and beliefs as filtered through his own Eurocentric cultural, religious, and philosophical views. We learn almost as much about European mores and prejudices, and native reactions to missionary intrusion, as we do about the Huron themselves. In matters of religion, Sagard found that they had some concepts of a Creator, of benign and malevolent spirits, of an afterlife, and of the efficacy of prayers and sacrifices. The missionaries could build on these elements. On the other hand, he was convinced that the Huron were under satanic domination and were deluded by their shamans. The "festival of the dead," or periodic feast when the bones of the deceased were carefully prepared for reburial in a common grave, impressed Sagard to the point of observing that while it signified that in life, as in death, they should live in unity and harmony, "so in fact they do live." As he thought on the licentiousness of most fur traders and the avarice of the merchants, he could not refrain from exclaiming that "in this respect they [the Huron] surpass the piety of Christians." This open-mindedness, so uncharacteristic of his age and profession, came from the simplicity and altruism of his particular community. In his mind, the chief obstacles to the propagation of the faith were nonpracticing Catholics, Protestants, and native shamans.

With kindness, devotion, and perseverance, Sagard believed that one hundred thousand souls in the Canadian hinterland could be won for Jesus Christ, the treasure that he and his coreligionists sought. Generous and hospitable peoples welcomed them, and there was no question of martyrdom among them because they left all persons to their own beliefs. Indifference to the preaching of the Gospel was an obstacle that Sagard apprehended. He deplored the attitudes of so many of his countrymen, irreligious persons for whom treasure consisted only of "quantities of furs, from various species of terrestrial and amphibious animals."

In spite of the hardships faced in the mission, Sagard had many positive things to say about his Huron hosts. In describing their marriage customs, he adopted the official view that their premarital sexual relations were wickedness and prostitution. Nevertheless, he proceeded to describe the courtship and trial cohabitation leading to permanent alliances, praise the stability of their marriages, and commend the loving care that they bestowed on their children. He failed to understand the matrilineal and matrilocal nature of their social organization, and therefore he associated their family structure with the fact that "the children of such marriages cannot be vouched for as legitimate." The permissive upbringing of the children also distressed him. But the chief annoyance was the "continual importunity and requests to marry us." Whatever the Huron reaction to his affirmations of patriarchy and celibacy, if these were ever transmitted over the language barrier, he appears to have been adopted into the family of his host, Oonchiarey. Adoption was the ultimate sign of confidence and trust, because as a member of the clan he gained access to the deliberations of his hosts and could participate in some decision making.

Sagard's sojourn in Huron country was not sufficiently long to enable him to discern the pattern of village, tribal, and confederacy councils, or to understand the roles of various "chiefs," matrons, and shamans. He noted their fear of a raid by the neighboring Attiwondaronk or Neutral nation to the south, from whom they obtained tobacco, as well as their perpetual apprehension of attack by the Iroquois Five Nations, chief rivals in the fur trade. Native warfare he described as "nothing but surprises and treachery," deploring the practice of scalping, the subjecting of some captives to platform torture, and the occasional cannibalism that marked victory celebrations. On the positive side, he admired their habit of taking dried food with them on war parties, suggesting that Europeans would do well to "cultivate the same frugality" in order to avoid ravaging the regions they invaded.

During the winter of 1623–24, he was able to observe the

activities of the Huron when agriculture, trading, and warfare were not pursued. There was much feasting, accompanied by frenzied dancing and loud singing, and prolonged gambling contests that sometimes pitted village against village. The women and girls were occupied in weaving fishing nets and baskets, making snowshoes, war clubs, and suits of wooden armor. The men took up ice fishing and made and mended canoes. Their industry and communal harmony prompted him to observe that "if they were Christians these would be families among whom God would take pleasure to dwell."

Europeans were, in Sagard's view, still culturally greatly superior to the aboriginal peoples of Canada. Nevertheless, there were some aspects of native culture that were commendable. He was interested in the music of the Huron, in spite of a comment in *Histoire du Canada* about their "dances, songs, and other ridiculous ceremonies." In the *Grand voyage*, he had said that "their usual singing is quite disagreeable," but went on to report that at one of their feasts they "were singing all together, then alternately, a song so sweet and pleasing that I was quite amazed and carried away with admiration." The Récollets were deeply appreciative of the role that music played in sacred ceremonies, and therefore they began composing carols and chants using tunes familiar to Huron ears.

Sagard was a devout lay brother given to self-mortification and drawing moral lessons from his insightful observations of nature and native life. He did not fail to note the Huron attribution of spiritual qualities to natural objects and phenomena. In a real sense he followed in the footsteps of Francis of Assisi inasmuch as he had great respect for the plants, birds, and animals, upon which he never failed to comment. He inquired specifically about the roots and plants with medicinal properties that the Huron used to cure illnesses. He took time to decribe the gambols of a couple of bear cubs, and he made a pet of a young muskrat that he fed reeds and couch grass gathered along the way. Before leaving for France, Sagard gave the chief canoeman who had brought him down to Québec from the Huron country a special gift—a cat to take back to his country as a rarity unknown to them. He was assured that it would do good service in keeping down the mice that attacked their corn stores.

The last documentary evidence of his activities in France is a request of October 1638 for a transfer to the Cordelier community, and a Récollet counterclaim, the outcome of which remains unknown. Was Sagard unhappy within his religious community? We do not know, nor is there any record that he ever attained the priesthood. Of all the missionaries of early New France who left important writings, Sagard stands out as the individual about whom we have the least information concerning origins, education, and metropolitan career. Jesuit historian Lucien Campeau, not known for his indulgence of critics of his society, regards Sagard's *Grand voyage* as an outstanding work that can be relied upon, although the polemics inserted into the *Histoire du Canada* should not be attributed to Sagard's pen.

Suggested Readings

Primary Sources

Edict du Roy pour l'establissement de la Compagnie de la Nouvelle France. Paris, 1633.

Grande Viaggio nel paese degli Uroni (1623–1624) di Gabriel Sagard. Milan, 1972.

LeClercq, Chrestien. *Premier établissement de la Foy dans la Nouvelle France*. Paris, 1691.

Lefebre, Hyacinthe. *Histoire chronologique de la province des Récollets de Paris*. Paris, 1677.

Ouellet, Réal, and Jack Warwick, eds. *Le grand voyage du pays des Hurons*. Montreal, 1990.

———. *Le grand voyage du pays des Hurons, situé vers la mer douce, ès derniers confins de la Nouvelle France, dite Canada*. 2 vols. Paris, 1632.

Sagard, Gabriel. *Dictionnaire de la langue huronne, Nécessaire à ceux qui n'ont l'intelligence d'icelle*. Paris, 1632.

———. *Histoire du Canada et voyages que les Frères Mineurs Récollets y ont faict pour la Conversion des Infidèles*. 4 vols. Paris, 1636.

Wrong, G. M., ed. *The Long Journey to the Country of the Hurons*. Toronto, 1939.

Secondary Sources

Dubé, Pauline. *Les Frères insoumis ou "l'ombre d'un clocher."* Montreal, 1995.

Glacken, Clarence J. *Traces on the Rhodian Shore: Nature and Culture in Western Thought from Ancient Times to the End of the Eighteenth Century*. Berkeley, CA, 1967.

Heidenreich, Conrad. *Huronia: A History and Geography of the Huron Indians, 1600–1650*. Toronto, 1971.

Hodgen, Margaret. *Early Anthropology in the Sixteenth and Seventeenth Centuries*. Philadelphia, 1964.

Jaenen, Cornelius J. *The French Regime in the Upper Country of Canada during the Seventeenth Century*. Toronto, 1996.

———. *Friend and Foe: Aspects of French-Amerindian Cultural Contact in the Sixteenth and Seventeenth Centuries*. New York, 1976.

————. *The Role of the Church in New France.* Toronto, 1976.

Phelan, John L. *The Millennial Kingdom of the Franciscans in the New World.* Berkeley, CA, 1970.

Trigger, Bruce G. *The Children of Aataentsic: A History of the Huron People to 1660.* Montreal and Kingston, 1976.

————. *Natives and Newcomers: Canada's "Heroic Age" Reconsidered.* Montreal and Kingston, 1985.

Articles

Jaenen, Cornelius J. "France's America and Amerindians: Image and Reality." *History of European Ideas* 6 (1985): 405–20.

Rioux, Jean de La Croix. "Sagard, Gabriel." *Dictionary of Canadian Biography,* 14 vols. to date (Toronto, 1966–), 1:590–92.

Warwick, Jack. "Humanisme chrétien et bons sauvages." *XVIIe Siècle,* no. 97 (1972): 25–49.

————. "Le Grand Voyage du pays des Hurons." *Dictionnaire des oeuvres littéraires du Québec,* 6 vols. (Montreal, 1978), 1:296–99.

4

Anne Hutchinson, the Puritan Patriarchs, and the Power of the Spirit

Marilyn Westerkamp

Anne Hutchinson's life (1591–1643) reveals the possibilities and limitations of a woman's spiritual leadership in Puritan New England. Anne's family allowed her to gain a private religious education, and her husband had the resources and temperament to allow her to follow a religious quest to Massachusetts. Patriarchal authority—in home, parish, or court—did not initially try to prevent Anne's powerful service to her religious community; she was a full member of the church, and her talents were useful in strengthening that community. Puritanism had only recently changed from a religion protesting Anglican authority in England to a church trying to maintain authority in New England. Was Puritanism clear on the role of earthly authority in salvation, or did the banishment of Roger Williams and Anne Hutchinson represent the banishment of alternative views equally characteristic of Puritanism? In God's name, Puritans already had a long history of defying magistrates and ministers. Charismatic Anne Hutchinson attracted the support of powerful Puritans of both genders who challenged the religious and political leadership of the young colony. She even inspired civil disobedience. Did the magistrates' actions reflect Puritan attitudes concerning the proper role of women in society, or was the appeal to patriarchy a sign of the weakness of the case that John Winthrop was trying to make? With the emigration, banishment, or recantation of Hutchinsonians, would Puritanism, as practiced, be narrower and more patriarchal after 1637 than it had been before?

Marilyn Westerkamp has published authoritatively on colonial American religious history, including *Triumph of the Laity: Scots-Irish Piety and the Great Awakening, 1625–1760* (1987). She teaches American colonial, religious, and women's history at the University of California, Santa Cruz.

In November 1637, Anne Hutchinson was banished from the colony of Massachusetts Bay. The sentence concluded her two-day trial before the General Court and resolved the most serious crisis that had threatened the colony during its first decade. The importance of the trial was reflected in the number and rank of people involved, including most of the colony's officials: the governor, deputy governor, magistrates, and local representatives from the towns. Additionally, many of the clergy attended and demonstrated, through their testimony, a vested interest in the outcome. This trial has long fascinated historians, for it seems less an equitable trial of justice than a ritual performance acted out so that Massachusetts leaders could do what they had already decided to do: namely, rid themselves of Hutchinson. In other words, the government brought her to trial to justify and ensure her forced departure. The magistrates had many grievances. She socialized with persons who had challenged the government, and she had assumed a leadership role not proper to women. These were relatively minor complaints that she easily discounted in court. Of a more serious nature, however, she was charged with sedition against the colony's ministers, a charge more difficult to prove because the evidence was initially so controversial. More serious still was the suggestion of blasphemy involving false claims about her relationship with God, but this question remained unresolved. The final exchange of the trial said it all. When Hutchinson asked, "I desire to know wherefore I am banished?" she was silenced. "Say no more, the court knows wherefore and is satisfied."[1]

The hostility surrounding Hutchinson at that moment starkly contrasted with the vast popularity she had enjoyed as a religious leader only eighteen months before. Intellectually gifted and personally charismatic, she had welcomed many to her home for private prayer and study. Her guests included men as well as women; many were among the highest leaders in the colony. Between sixty and eighty persons came weekly to hear her expound upon the week's sermons and advise them in their spiritual journeys, and she had, according to leading minister John Cotton, greatly helped many women of the town. "I doubt not but some of you [women] have also received much good from the Conference of this our Sister and by your Converse with her: and from her it may be you have received help in your spiritual Estates."[2] Yet by November, she seemed almost friendless and powerless as she fought for her freedom, her own beliefs, and her status as a spiritual leader called by God. Who was this woman who attracted so many disciples? And why did government officials of this colony less than eight years old, a colony in the wilderness, find it necessary to throw her out?

Anne Marbury Hutchinson lived during an era of rising Puritan power, a time when the Puritan movement was growing in both numerical size and political strength. Puritans can best be described as religious reformers who hoped to "purify" the Protestant Church of England of all vestiges of Roman Catholicism. About fifteen years after Martin Luther had ignited the Protestant Reformation on the European continent, the English church had declared itself separate from Rome. For twenty-five years, religious insecurity, even chaos, ensued under the disjointed reigns of the barely Protestant Henry VIII, the devoted reformer child-king Edward VI, and the equally resolute Roman Catholic Mary. Upon Mary's death in 1558, the church, under the guidance of Queen Elizabeth, began to follow a middle road between closeted Roman Catholics and the somewhat more open Puritans who struggled to further the work of reformation. Puritans wanted to eliminate all formal church rituals, judging such practices man-made and therefore artificial. These included prayers read from books, patterns of gestures and signs, and any aspect of community worship whose words and actions were explicitly fixed by the institution. Puritans also rejected extraneous unscriptural elements such as graven images (statues, pictures, stained glass), candles, vestments, and holy day celebrations. Additionally, Puritans rejected the hierarchy of the Anglican Church as unbiblical. They denied that bishops had any scriptural right to authority over congregations or ministers, finding instead that the early church communities of the New Testament deferred to the congregation as the primary seat of authority. They complained that the Anglican clergy frequently lacked erudition, or even moral respectability. Puritans called for a return to clerical accountability, to godly conduct, and to the plain preaching and plain worship outlined in the Scriptures. By the end of the sixteenth century, Puritan reformers had united themselves in a formidable religious and political coalition driven by a spiritual authority lodged in Puritans' intense relationship with God.

Like most Reformed Protestants of this era, Puritans were followers of John Calvin's theology. They believed in the total depravity of humanity, the inability of people to save themselves, and the gracious mercy of God in lifting a few chosen, or the elect, out of their evil pathways and bringing them to salvation. The atonement of Christ, through his Crucifixion, was a miracle, and the elect were able to accept Christ's love in faith through the intervention of divine grace, a grace that was irresistible. In other words, God empowered those few elect to have faith; the rest were left to the terrifying punishment they so justly deserved. Puritans believed that, from the beginning of time, all individuals had been predestined to either salvation or damnation. They knew that their destiny had been decided by God's arbitrary will, and no amount of virtuous acts or evildoing could change a believer's ultimate fate. Oddly enough, this lesson did not destroy hope or create anarchic pleasure-seeking. Instead, most Puritans, who were generally convinced of the real potential for their own salvation, struggled to convince themselves and others that they were indeed among the elect. At some points, they were afflicted with great anxiety; at others, they were filled with the supreme joy of divine assurance in a salvation that no person could destroy, because it was, in fact, effected by God.

Dissatisfied with the spiritual "emptiness" of Anglican services led by uninspired pastors, many felt justified in turning to private religious meetings to satisfy their spiritual cravings. Laypersons gathered weekly, sometimes more frequently, to pray, study, and preach. They discovered among themselves the piety, inspiration, and even knowledge absent on Sundays. They followed personal moral regimens of labor, rest, and carefully prescribed pleasures. They also recommended to each other reliable, reformed ministers known for their learning, personal piety, and spiritual guidance. All persons were required to educate themselves, pray, study, and follow Christ; and while they might enjoy the assistance of sympathetic clerics and one another, the spiritual quest was a lonely one, traveled by the individual in direct relationship with God. Then God offered grace, the soul was transformed, and salvation was realized.

Anne Marbury was born in 1591, the second of thirteen children. Her childhood was spent in the Puritan stronghold of Lincolnshire, East Anglia. Her parents, Bridget Dryden and Francis Marbury, were among the lesser gentry in England. As a girl, Anne Marbury would not have been formally educated, but from what is known about her parents, it might safely be supposed that she was well educated by them. Bridget Dryden was connected to a well-placed family network that would produce the poet laureate John Dryden in 1631. Francis Marbury seems to have been an obstreperous clergyman and a published theological writer who was deeply committed to the value of education. Ordained a deacon in 1578, Francis Marbury was, within a year, summoned before the London Consistory Court. There he publicly accused the bishops of ordaining unfit men and was therefore imprisoned. Seven years later, he was curate and schoolmaster in the town of Alford. Although he complained in 1590 that he had been silenced and deprived of his living, within four years he was preaching again, and silenced again. The primary charges centered on his outspoken criticism of the clergy, especially his call for better-educated ministers. In 1605 about three hundred pastors were removed from their congregations in an effort to stop the rising Puritan tide. Since Marbury had confined his comments to clerical standards of learning and avoided other criticisms of the Church of England's structure, theology, and practice, his infractions were deemed comparatively minor, and he was advanced in this period of a scarcity of clergy. He moved his family to London in 1605, and held a series of respectable pulpits and livings there until his death in 1611.

At twenty-one, Anne Marbury married William Hutchinson, a successful merchant living in her hometown—Alford, England. There the Hutchinsons prospered for twenty-two years, and during those years Anne bore fourteen children, all but two of whom survived into adulthood. Very little is known about the Hutchinsons during this central period of their lives. Alford seems to have been a good choice for business as William's trade increased with his family, and his reputation and status rose accordingly. But it was also a good choice for a clergyman's daughter who was deeply interested in the affairs of the soul and who embraced the cultural critique and spiritual intensity of the Lincolnshire Puritan community. Some twenty miles south, in the larger city of Boston, St. Botolph's Church was pastored by the renowned John Cotton. Although the Hutchinsons could travel there only occasionally, Anne found his preaching so inspiring that she attended his services whenever the long journey could be made. It is difficult to ascertain whether this was Anne's or William's desire. If the Hutchinsons' New England years fairly reflected their marriage, William pursued his economic and political callings while Anne attended to the spiritual side. Although a believer himself—William would become a member of the congregation after he had arrived in Massachusetts—he left religious leadership to his wife. In any case, Cotton so impressed Anne with his theological understanding and his experience of grace that she and her family followed him to New England and joined his congregation there.

After King Charles I ascended the throne in 1625, the Church of England became more committed to its bishops and its formalistic rituals, and the troubles of Puritans increased. More and more laypersons were fined or imprisoned for refusing to attend church services or to pay their tithes to support the ministers. Clergymen sympathetic to Puritanism were defrocked, deprived of their livings, and imprisoned because they refused to perform the sacraments or read prayers from the church's official prayer book, challenged the authority of bishops, or openly criticized the Anglican magisterium. In response to Charles's heightened efforts to control, if not eradicate, the Puritan influence, a group of merchants and investors looked toward colonization as the best way to escape the intensified persecutions. Others judged that the increased decadence within the Church of England warned of the impending Apocalypse foretold in Revelation. Seeing themselves as the saved remnant of the New Israel, many Puritans followed an impulse to escape divine vengeance upon England and build a godly commonwealth according to scriptural precepts.

On April 7, 1630, under the sponsorship, though beyond the control, of King Charles, some seven hundred settlers embarked for New England. During the next six years, the region would absorb hundreds, often thousands, of immigrants annually. These were not adventurers seeking great fortunes, but husbands and wives with their children, relatives, and servants planning to build a permanent colony. For most of the 1630s and 1640s, Massachusetts Bay would be led by John Winthrop, a man of affluence and influence in East Anglia, a man with the knowledge and mental strength to serve as the founding governor of the colony. He moved the primary settlement from the exposed Salem to the relatively sheltered seaport that they would call Boston. He divided the original settlers into seven different companies, or towns, assigned them land, and then organized colonists to build shelters and gather food while he negotiated with the native peoples for land and food supplies. He ordered, at his own expense, additional (and necessary) food stores for the winter. Within a year, owing largely to the dedication of the people and the guidance of Winthrop, the colony of Massachusetts was economically self-sufficient.

It would be difficult to overestimate the importance of religion in the New England world, not only in the lives and hearts of individuals but also in the very construction of the government. The colony's magistrates and ministers agreed with Winthrop's description of the experimental settlement as a "City on a Hill," a shining example to the rest of the world, a godly colony privileged by God and therefore strictly obligated to operate according to divine law. They envisioned their society as the New Israel and structured their churches and their government according to biblical guidelines. While their legal system conformed to the English common law, their criminal code was based upon Leviticus, the third book of the Old Testament. This religious worldview was not merely evident in legal codes, but it had also been internalized by every committed Puritan believer.

The Hutchinson crisis cannot possibly be understood apart from the deeply religious nature of the colony and its English inhabitants. Every town organized its own church and called its own pastor, and there were literally dozens of ministers available. Some of the best and the brightest clerical stars made their way to New England. People met for religious services on Sunday mornings and evenings, and, in response to popular requests, weekday lectures were delivered. Although individuals had to apply to become members of the church, demonstrating their election by means of godly behavior and personal testimony, almost all of the colonists joined their congregations. Some congregants took notes during sermons; many kept personal journals to track their own spiritual progress. Additionally, laypersons continued to hold private prayer meetings where they pored over sermons, clarified difficult points, studied theological texts, and shared with others the experiences of their souls and their hopes for salvation. That Anne Hutchinson held private meetings in her home was not in any way odd or disruptive, particularly since she originally invited only women to share a space in which they could speak freely, ask questions, and reveal the work of the Spirit in their lives. One of the more revealing omissions in the original Hutchinson record is the absence of any official concern about, or even acknowledgment of, these early gatherings. Historians have not even determined precisely when the meetings began. Magistrates and ministers became concerned about her work only after the weekly attendance had reached sixty to eighty persons, and only after her disciples' criticism of the Bay Colony's ministers became public.

Hutchinson's influence over more than sixty persons, in a town of perhaps six hundred, threatened the social and cultural foundations of this society. Puritan leaders envisioned themselves as patriarchs in the biblical sense. Old Testament patriarchs and kings became role models, and their recorded wisdom, reinforced by the Apostle Paul's pronouncements in the Epistles, guided Puritans toward an orderly society. While some few were called to exercise power as magistrates and ministers, and many more as husbands and fathers, most men, and certainly all women, were called to subject themselves to the rule of others. In the Bible, Puritans found a clearly ordered family system that arranged all persons into hierarchical pairs: master over servant, parent over child, husband over wife. Of course, religion did not serve alone; secular authorities, including English tradition and the common law, also reinforced patriarchal structures. In most ways, Anne Hutchinson's life mirrored that of her peers. Her years in England had been spent as the daughter of a minister, wife of a small merchant, and mother of fourteen children. Her labors were domestic; her status was defined by the legal construct of coverture, which placed a wife under the "cover" of her husband and denied her any civil standing.

Apart from explicit legal restrictions, women were as active as men in defining the traditions that constructed their lives, sometimes accepting customs and at other times transforming practices within their own sphere. The housewife, by virtue of her skills and experience, controlled the domestic economy. Moreover, women produced not only food and clothing but also children; and in the birthing chamber, women controlled a women-only space. The politics of reproduction and midwifery reflected the power located and contested within the household, and it is not surprising to find that Anne Hutchinson had gained a reputation as a skilled midwife. When describing Hutchinson's early success among Boston women, Winthrop looked toward her proficiency in the birthing chamber: "Being a woman very helpful in the times of child-birth, and other occasions of bodily infirmities, and well furnished with means for those purposes, she easily insinuated herself into the affections of many."[3] In the early seventeenth century, Puritan men were generally content to allow women such domestic authority. But when an Anne Hutchinson grew too strong, or actually confronted the male leadership, governors could (and did) retreat with security into the customs, laws, and biblical texts that established absolute male control and female subservience. With haphazard logic but consistent politics, ministers and magistrates found extensive justification for the patriarchy that served their own interests so well.

In 1634, Anne Hutchinson had landed in Boston, one year after John Cotton was established as the teacher of the Boston congregation. There she found a colony scarcely four years old and a town that was little more than a village with great ambitions. As Boston had only five hundred inhabitants, the Hutchinsons significantly increased the population. Their entourage numbered twenty-five persons: the couple, their eleven children, a daughter-in-law, two spinster cousins, a sister, a brother, a sister-in-law, and at least six servants. Additionally, William's wealth and substance earned him immediate recognition. At a time when social and geographic place mattered deeply, the Hutchinsons were assigned a house lot directly across from Governor Winthrop, and William was allotted six hundred acres, a clear acknowledgment of his rank, since he was a merchant, not a farmer. He represented Boston at the General Court and served in town and church leadership roles as the head of a family that added twenty-five people to the town and fourteen members to the congregation. As the wife of a prominent merchant, Anne would have found a respectable position among Boston's matrons. Beyond this, her healing gifts established some early authority, but her biblical knowledge and theological sophistication also were soon greatly admired. Such skills and abilities increased her reputation independently of William, but her rise to prominence, and ultimate downfall, inexorably tied her husband's stature to her own.

For a while there were no problems. In the same month that the Hutchinsons joined the church, John Wilson sailed for England to try, for a third and final time, to persuade his wife to come to Massachusetts. People had been quite clear about this matter. It was a scandal that Wilson was here without his family; and if his wife still refused to sail, he should remain in England. In Wilson's absence, Cotton served as the sole pastor, and Hutchinson probably instituted her private religious meetings. Her superior intellect and charisma made her a natural leader, and she quickly moved beyond explicating his sermons to preaching her own. At some point, women began to bring their husbands, and soon Hutchinson was holding two weekly meetings, one for women only and one for both women and men. Her enemies estimated a general attendance of sixty to eighty persons, an estimate that is supported by the large number of men who would be disciplined by the government for their subversive activities as Hutchinsonians. In 1635, Wilson, with his wife, returned to Massachusetts and the pulpit at the Boston Church; so, too, did the hot-tempered minister John Wheelwright, Hutchinson's brother-in-law, arrive. These two rigid, uncompromising personalities would become key performers as the controversy took hold, and the presence and activities of each one would stir his rival to greater exertions in the cause of truth.

Trouble when it first arose concerned neither of those men but Cotton's dissatisfaction with the theology of his colleagues, including Wilson. Anne Hutchinson and her followers agreed with Cotton's opinion and promoted his views, but the early (and private) dispute occupied Cotton and a few ministers. One theological issue involved the relationship between human effort and salvation. The Calvinist principles of predestination and election placed salvation completely in the hands of God. Believers could have no responsibility for their salvation because they had no ability to effect it. Grace extended to the elect transformed their thoughts and actions, and such saints became recognizable through their sanctified, or godly, behavior.

Cotton and the Hutchinsonians emphasized God's free, unconditional offer of divine grace and thus stressed the futility of human action and the value of an absolute, passive dependence upon an all-powerful God. While most New England ministers did not deny the twin truths of predestination and election, they thought that undue emphasis upon these two principles might lead to irreligion and anarchy. They understood the anxiety of believers desperate for some sign of their salvation and emphasized the hope that lay in the evidence of sanctification. Moreover, many promoted an idea that the potential saint could prepare for grace. Although acknowledging that human effort had no impact upon God, ministers encouraged people to study Scripture, attend services, watch their conduct, and pray so that they would be ready to receive divine grace. Such efforts may have kept believers from feeling desperate and lost, but Cotton found in this "preparationism" disturbing hints of salvation through works—earning your way into Heaven. Because Cotton enjoyed a gentle, conciliatory personality, he might well have been able to resolve quietly his differences with those colleagues had not

Hutchinson and her followers become involved. In her meetings she had apparently condemned those who preached sanctification and preparationism, which challenged most ministers, and her disciples expressed those misgivings publicly and aggressively.

A second dispute involved the question of the union of the Holy Spirit with the saint. While most theologians rejected outright any idea of a persistent divine presence within the soul, Cotton embraced a belief in the indwelling of the Spirit, although he did not mean that any divine properties were communicated or granted to the believer. This question was not merely academic. Here was lodged the center of Hutchinson's charisma. She spoke and preached out of an authority that came not from a university education or a congregation's call (of course, women could not be called to ordination), but from the authority of the Spirit within. One disciple described her as "a Woman that Preaches better Gospel than any of your black-coats that have been at the Ninniversity, a Woman of another kind of spirit, who hath had many Revelations of things to come, and . . . I had rather hear such a one that speaks from the mere motion of the spirit, without any study at all, than any of your learned Scholars, although they may be fuller of Scripture."[4]

In 1636, in response to the continuing strife, Puritan authorities held conferences, one in October and a second in December. Ostensibly, the clergy met to discuss their disagreements with Cotton, Wheelwright, and Hutchinson. How extraordinary that Hutchinson, a layperson and a woman, would attend such a conference! This reveals much about the situation in Massachusetts. The problem was not with Cotton questioning the preaching of other clergy, but with Hutchinson doing so. It might be argued that by bringing her to what was essentially a clerical conference, the clergy acknowledged her leadership. While they certainly denied her any legitimate claim to such a role, their actions unconsciously confirmed the strength of her spiritual authority. Any person suspected of heretical views, particularly a laywoman, could have been dealt with privately, but Hutchinson had so many followers that she had become a public figure. However, they could not afford to deal with her publicly because they might lose. At this point she was quite powerful; she had the support of Cotton, three magistrates, several deputies to the General Court, the majority of the congregation of the Boston Church, including the two lay elders, and the current governor of the colony, Henry Vane. Even if they did succeed in bringing her to trial and banishment, an open confrontation risked the immediate emigration of those leaders, including Cotton. Winthrop hoped to retain as many leaders as possible. Eventually, Hutchinson would be brought to public trial twice, before the state and before the church. But at this time the clergy seemed more interested in buttressing their own position, perhaps by persuading her to accept their arguments and their authority. Consequently, they chose a peculiar public-private meeting: a private conversation that could be reported publicly. John Cotton remembered the first conference as fairly successful at achieving a common theological understanding, but the events of that autumn and the following year demonstrated that a final confrontation had merely been delayed.

A series of public confrontations began in the last months of 1636. Since these were the actions of men, Hutchinson was not directly involved. However, both the clergy and magistrates would later work on the assumption that Hutchinson was privately directing the charge. Boston's Hutchinsonians challenged the authority of Wilson by calling John Wheelwright as a third minister to the Boston Church; the effort was derailed by a small minority led by Winthrop, who invoked a technical rule that a pastoral call must be unanimous. Wilson then delivered a sermon on the sadly divided condition of the churches, pointing to the rise of new, dangerous opinions and further irritating his congregation. The General Court called for a "Day of Fasting" to pray for reconciliation, and Cotton invited Wheelwright to preach. He delivered an outrageous sermon that revived the theological controversy, attacked the concept of the fast itself, and argued that any who strove to do God's work were hypocrites pretending to salvation through their own merits. Encouraged by Wheelwright's sermon, the Hutchinsonians took their struggle into the outlying towns, heckling preachers, irritating their congregations, and refusing to serve in the militia organized to fight the Pequot, a local Indian nation, because the militia's chaplain was John Wilson.

The Hutchinsonians may have dominated Boston, but their influence ended there. When the General Court met in March, a strong anti-Hutchinson coalition was evident. They approved Wilson's sermon, charged Wheelwright with sedition, and refused to consider petitions filed by Wheelwright's supporters. At Winthrop's recommendation, they moved the June elections to Newtown, effectively disenfranchising most Bostonians because they could not travel so far. At the June session, before petitions for Wheelwright could be read, Winthrop's faction called for elections, and the new majority elected Winthrop as governor and threw the two Boston magistrates and Henry Vane out of office. Boston in turn elected Vane and Hutchinsonian William Coddington as its two deputies. The honor guard refused to escort Winthrop into Boston, but this was merely a last show of defiance. The tide had turned, and Winthrop spent the rest of the summer dismantling the coalition and preparing for Anne Hutchinson's trial.

Concerned about the possible arrival of new Hutchinson recruits, the General Court enacted a law ordering that no strangers could stay in Massachusetts more than three weeks without the explicit permission of the magistrates. They also passed a resolution that condemned lay efforts to dispute doctrine with the preacher. Of greatest importance, the court forbade Hutchinson's meetings: "That though women might meet (some few together) to pray and edify one another; yet such a set assembly (as was then in practice at Boston), where sixty or more did meet every week, and one woman (in a prophetical way, by resolving questions of doctrine, and expounding Scripture) took upon her the whole exercise, was agreed to be disorderly, and without rule."[5] The magistrates and clergy then called yet another conference, without Hutchinson, to address Cotton's opinions and create a theological consensus. They identified eighty-two errors and nine unsavory phrases, many involving the connections between human effort and divine grace. Some errors, however, concerned the nature of faith and revelation, hinting in official documents, for the first time, of a hidden but primary issue at the heart of the crisis.

Once an intellectual compromise had been reached, Winthrop dealt with the Hutchinsonians. Henry Vane had already left the colony disillusioned, as had several leading merchants and their families. Wheelwright was summoned, convicted of sedition, and banished, and leading Hutchinsonian men were questioned and, depending on their answers, were forgiven, disarmed, disfranchised, fined, and/or banished. Only then, on November 7, could Mistress Hutchinson, "the head of all this faction . . . the breeder and nourisher of all these distempers . . . a woman of haughty and fierce carriage, of a nimble wit and active spirit," be brought safely to trial.[6] And even with all his pretrial maneuvers, Winthrop further shored up his strength by holding the meeting of the General Court in Newtown, that is, outside Boston.

Because Hutchinson's trial could end in her banishment, she could only be tried by the General Court. It was neither a criminal court moderated by a justice nor a supreme court with a panel of justices but rather the entire colonial government of governor, magistrates, and town representatives. While usually functioning as a legislature, the General Court did serve as the highest judiciary in the colony. In this incredible confrontation with the amassed political authority of the colony, Hutchinson revealed her formidable intellectual prowess. For one and one-half days she ran circles around her opponents. They quoted Scripture; she quoted back. They interpreted a verse against her; she responded with an alternative text. Winthrop began with a lengthy, condemnatory, rather frightening speech accusing her of disturbances, errors, and discord;

he then demanded a response. She replied that she could not answer charges until she knew precisely what they were. She put Winthrop immediately on the defensive, for he had very few specific charges, and those he did have were supported only by hearsay.

He first said that she broke the Fifth Commandment—Honor thy father and thy mother—because she countenanced those who had signed the Wheelwright petitions and challenged the authority of the General Court, that is, their parents. She responded that she might entertain persons as children of God without approving their transgression. After a quick verbal thrust and parry, a frustrated Winthrop asserted that she did adhere to the petitioners' cause, she did endeavor to promote their faction, and thus she dishonored the magistrates, who stood as her parents, breaking the Fifth Commandment. Further, the Court did "not mean to discourse with those of your sex."[7] Undoubtedly, Winthrop hoped to silence her, and perhaps calm the uneasiness of the General Court, by dismissing the right and ability of a woman to hold, maintain, and debate a dissenting opinion. However, such flourishes did not change the fact that debates with this woman continued.

Winthrop moved on to her private meetings. The Scriptures clearly forbade women to teach publicly, but, answered Hutchinson, her home was not public, and the Bible taught the duty of elder women to instruct younger ones. When questioned about men attending these meetings, she insisted that at mixed ones only the men spoke, and Winthrop had no evidence to countermand her assertion. When Winthrop refused to acknowledge that her biblical citations provided a rule for her leadership, she asked whether she must "shew my name written therein?" In a second outburst of frustrated authority, Winthrop announced that the meetings must end because he said so. "We are your judges, and not you ours and we must compel you to it."[8] She agreed to accept the court's order.

However, her acquiescence did not satisfy the magistrates. They wanted her gone, for, as Deputy Governor Thomas Dudley complained during the trial, three years before the colony had been at peace, but from the moment that Hutchinson arrived, she had ignited great disturbances. Knowing that she was the primary problem, they sought weightier charges in order to banish her, and so they turned to her criticism of the clergy. If she had argued that the clergy were not preaching the true pathway to salvation, she implied that the colony's spiritual guides were beneath the regard of an ordinary congregant. The clergy believed, and the magistrates agreed, that such a view had to be curtailed and condemned, but Winthrop had to prove that Hutchinson had delivered such derogatory opinions. Initially, the magistrates' complaints sounded like hearsay and rumor. Magistrates had certainly heard the uncomplimentary opinions held by some Hutchinsonians about certain clergymen, but the magistrates had apparently never heard Hutchinson herself utter any such statements. Nor could they expect her followers to testify against her. Instead, Dudley and Winthrop opened a third fruitless dialogue, accusing Hutchinson of making statements that she then denied. Finally, cleric Hugh Peters, who hoped that he and other ministers "may not be thought to come as informers against the gentlewoman," proceeded to inform against her.[9] At the December conference, Peters reported, Hutchinson had discounted their abilities and spirituality. She had said that they preached a Covenant of Works, that is, salvation through human endeavor, and so argued that they were not true ministers of the Gospel. Several clerics testified to their own memory of her statements, providing corroboration for each other's accounts. Hutchinson challenged her clerical accusers, at one point asking John Wilson for the notes that he took at the conference. The day ended with yet another standoff.

On the following morning, Hutchinson brilliantly redirected and enlivened the proceedings by demanding that those clergymen testifying against her swear an oath. In this request, she invoked standard legal procedure. She had read Wilson's notes and she asserted that she remembered the conversations differently. This obvious affront to the clergymen's veracity ignited a self-righteous defense of the reliability and sincerity of the ministers, but doubt had been raised, and the clergy proved reluctant to swear, lending credence to Hutchinson's challenges. She then asked that three witnesses be called. Although supporter John Coggeshall was frightened into silence, and church elder Thomas Leverett proved able to utter only three sentences before he was rebuffed by Winthrop, a third witness delivered his troubling testimony in full. John Cotton had not wanted to testify, but his own memory of the conference agreed with Hutchinson's account. He regretted that he and his colleagues should be compared, but he did recall mild disagreements, and the difference was not then "so ill taken as it is [now] and our brethren did say also that they would not so easily believe reports as they had done and withall mentioned that they would speak no more of it, some of them did; and afterwards some of them did say they were less satisfied than before." He also asserted that he "did not find her saying they were under a covenant of works, nor that she said they did preach a covenant of works."[10]

By this point, the trial was proving a disaster for Winthrop. Hutchinson had responded to the initial charges with skill and finesse. She outmaneuvered her opponents in scriptural argument and then graciously agreed to their demands. The later, more serious charge of sedition against the ministry held great promise, but it had to be substantiated with ministers' reports of a private conference held a year before. Just as the momentum seemed strongest, Hutchinson derailed the prosecution with the reasonable demand for sworn testimony, underlining the weakness of the prosecution's evidence. In the midst of the procedural discussion, three witnesses challenged the clerical version of the conference; and, while two were easily silenced, Cotton's personal authority and prestige demanded the court's attention. Winthrop was running out of arguments. Hoping to invoke the law to legitimate proceeding against Hutchinson, Winthrop found that she could use the trial to expose him and his government.

Hutchinson chose this moment to proclaim her vision. Turning to her own spiritual conversion, she told the court of her early religious experiences: her doubts, her ultimate dependence upon God, and God's response to her pleas. She granted that she had become "more choice" in selecting a minister, for God had led her to distinguish the voices of truth.

> MR. NOWELL: How do you know that that was the spirit?
> MRS. H.: How did Abraham know that it was God that bid him offer his son, being a breach of the sixth commandment?
> DEP. GOV.: By an immediate voice.
> MRS. H.: So to me by an immediate revelation.
> DEP. GOV.: How! an immediate revelation.
> MRS. H.: By the voice of his own spirit to my soul.[11]

Pouncing upon her testimony, Winthrop and other accusers pursued this question of revelation. They believed that any claim to a miraculous revelation was blasphemy, for the age of miracles had long passed. By the end of the proceedings, the overwhelming majority of the court would agree with Winthrop's disingenuous conclusion: "Pass by all that hath been said formerly and her own speeches have been ground enough for us to proceed upon."[12]

Had she really condemned herself? The examination continued long after her extraordinary claim, and new witnesses testified to previous prophetic declarations. Still, this testimony produced not an immediate censure but a prolonged debate upon the nature of revelation itself. In the Puritan mind, claiming revelation was not necessarily blasphemy. When asked to denounce her, Cotton refused, and instead began a protracted, abstract discourse upon the two types of revelation: the miraculous and the providential. A miraculous, direct revelation would represent a delusion; however, any believer might recognize and interpret a special Providence, or symbolic revelation communicated through the workings of nature. He could not judge her without further clarification, and while Hutchinson expressed her conviction in a special Providence, her opponents accused her of prophesying the miraculous. Another stalemate threatened. At this point, the court returned to earlier charges, and three ministers did testify under oath. This testimony satisfied those members of the court who believed that she was dangerous, but hesitated to pass judgment without following proper legal procedures. With satisfied consciences, the General Court avoided the labyrinth of proving blasphemy and, resting comfortably with sedition, banished Anne Hutchinson.

Many historians have judged Hutchinson weak in proclaiming her revelations. Surely a woman who displayed such intelligence during her trial knew better than to open this door. However, the moment might also be seen as one of exceptional strength. She began by warning, "Now if you do condemn me for speaking what in my conscience I know to be truth I must commit myself unto the Lord."[13] She seemed to revel in her prophetic moment, as the court remained riveted upon her words. The leadership wanted, indeed needed, these revelations discounted, and several witnesses tried, without much success. More than providing evidence against her, Hutchinson's claims of direct revelation seem to have frightened Winthrop. He revealed this anxiety in his own analysis:

> Mistress *Hutchinson* having thus freely and fully discovered herself, the Court and all the rest of the Assembly . . . did observe a special providence of God, that . . . her own mouth should deliver her into the power of the Court, as guilty of that which all suspected her for, but were not furnished with proof sufficient to proceed against her, for here she hath manifested, that her opinions and practise have been the cause of all our disturbances, & that she walked by such a rule as cannot stand with the peace of any State; for such bottomless revelations . . . if they be allowed in one thing, must be admitted a rule in all things; for they being above reason and Scripture, they are not subject to control.[14]

Long suspected of charisma grounded in her prophetic revelations, Hutchinson undermined the authority of secular and sacred leaders with her own spiritual power. At last she had openly claimed her own spiritual authority, for which her opponents were profoundly grateful, but they remained unable to convince many people, including Cotton, that her pronouncements were blasphemous. Winthrop and the clergy returned to charges of sedition and procedural rules of evidence, winning her banishment with the agreement of all but three participants. Winthrop must indeed have been satisfied.

Following this trial, the Hutchinsonian community divided. Some acknowledged their fault and remained in Massachusetts; some followed Wheelwright to a new colony in what would become

New Hampshire; others, including the Hutchinson family, settled in Rhode Island. Because she was sentenced at the beginning of winter, the court extended a questionable mercy, permitting Hutchinson to remain in the colony until the spring but demanding that she live in the home of an unsympathetic clergyman. While many of her followers, including her husband and her young children, moved on to Rhode Island, Hutchinson became the unhappy focus of extensive clerical counsel. Supposedly in the interest of her conviction, repentance, and ultimate salvation, ministers engaged in an intellectual barrage that explored esoteric questions and doctrines that had been raised in neither of the 1636 conferences nor in her examination before the General Court. All of this material would be brought forward to her final examinations before the church.

A congregation had authority solely over its members, and the only sentences that a congregation could pass against a member were admonition, suspension from membership, or excommunication. A church trial such as this one usually represented the last efforts of a community to bring one of its errant members back into the fold; all of those penalties, including excommunication, were meant to sound an alarm and recall the lost saint to godliness. In moving to such examinations at this point, the community was working completely backwards. Generally, a church member might be dealt with by her church, but if she proved unrepentant to the point of excommunication, and her sins were egregious, she might then be charged before the government. To be fair, ministers may not have wanted to risk a church trial until this point. Hutchinson might well have survived unscathed, since the majority of the Boston Church members were her followers. Bringing her to a church trial after her banishment had been ordered would be quite after the fact. Was this merely a vindictive clergy seeking further revenge? What did the clergy hope to accomplish?

Of course, the Boston Church, in March 1638, had been chastised and transformed. Many Hutchinsonians were simply no longer in Boston, while others had acquiesced to the government's demands. Thus, a new Boston Church considered charges against Hutchinson. The examination explored her beliefs concerning the soul's immortality, the body's resurrection, and the union of the individual spirit to Christ—questions that she only began to explore at the insistence of the clergy that winter. As Hutchinson repeatedly noted, none of these questions had been asked before. However, by pushing her to assert opinions on complex questions that she had not much considered, the clergy might evoke heretical statements that no knowledgeable theologian would uphold. As predicted, her accusers were dissatisfied with her responses, and the congregation ordered John Cotton to deliver the sentence of admonition, because she respected him so highly. Unsaid, but of great importance to the other clergy, was the fact that delivering this admonition would fix Cotton's alignment with the majority position. A week later, Hutchinson again appeared before the church, acknowledging errors of extravagant expressions. She also tried to accept responsibility for her errors and to confess that she had slighted the ministers, but her sincerity was challenged. She was repenting only those errors discovered after November and left untouched the questions raised at her November trial. Her failure to address those issues was a mutual one; her examiners did not want to revisit a primary focus of continued disagreement. The theological issues were murky, her continued adherence to her revelations troubling, but, fortunately for her accusers, her "insincerity" made her a liar. Because she had troubled the church with errors, upheld her revelations, and had "made a Lye," she was excommunicated. She left the congregation for the last time accompanied by one person, her longtime follower Mary Dyer.

Anne Hutchinson then joined her family in Rhode Island. William served in the leadership of the new community, and the two grew frustrated at the bickering among the residents. After William died in 1642, Hutchinson and her seven younger children moved to Long Island where, in August 1643, she and six of the seven children were killed by Indians. In this violent end, some New Englanders found the divine vindication of Winthrop's work and judgment. "I never heard that the Indians in those parts did ever before this, commit the like outrage upon any one family, or families, and therefore God's hand is the more apparently seen herein, to pick out this woeful woman, to make her and those belonging to her, an unheard of heavy example of their cruelty above all others."[15]

Looking back over those three years during the first decade's settlement, the Hutchinsonians represented many threats to the governing elite. Personally, Winthrop had lost support among Boston's leadership and his premier position, sitting as deputy under twenty-two-year-old Governor Vane. The Hutchinsonian crisis also involved competition between Boston and the outlying towns that would support Winthrop against his own community. The theological differences were problematic, though initially resolvable, since both sides agreed that divine grace was freely granted, human effort had no impact upon salvation, and sanctified behavior was evidence of election. The involvement of the laity in the debates, and its criticism of the standing clergy, exacerbated the situation as people on each side, both clerical and lay, began to oversimplify issues and stereotype their opponents.

Still, the Hutchinsonian crisis involved more than politics, social conflict, and theological disputes. Under both of the trials and all of the accounts ran a current of male fury at the audacity of a woman to challenge the patriarchal magisterium. At her November trial, magistrates grieved that in leading these private meetings she was stepping outside her prescribed role. Winthrop would later say that she was more husband than wife, and he described William as "a man of very mild temper and weak parts, and wholly guided by his wife."[16] Additionally, extremely vindictive, misogynist comments followed the childbirth tragedies experienced by Mary Dyer and Anne Hutchinson. Dyer's deformed child was stillborn in October 1637, while Hutchinson was reported to have given birth to some thirty monsters in Rhode Island. "And see how the wisdom of God fitted this judgement to her sin every way, for look as [Hutchinson] had vented misshapen opinions, so she must bring forth deformed monsters." Both Dyer's and Hutchinson's deformed infants were seen as judgments: clear, harsh expressions of divine displeasure. Thomas Weld asserted that "God himself was pleased to step in . . . as clearly as if he had pointed with his finger, in causing the two fomenting women in the time of the height of the Opinions to produce out of their wombs, as before they had out of their brains, such monstrous births as no Chronicle (I think) hardly ever recorded."[17] These were punishments tied to, or perhaps growing out of, their corrupt femaleness. Weld seemed to say that she was a disgusting woman, an unwomanly woman. She could not even give birth.

Overall, it really is not surprising that the Puritan ministers and magistrates, committed as they were to their own patriarchal authority, would do everything possible to destroy her. She was a powerful woman who had attracted a significant community of female followers, and her example as a religious leader could have brought women to question their own acceptance of a subordinate domestic role. Her punishment certainly served as a deterrent to any other woman who might step outside the household. What is astonishing, however, is the trouble that she caused. If this truly had been an unbending patriarchal society, if Puritans truly felt that women had no authority and no power, they would not have worried about her. Rather than simply ignore her, or quietly censure her in church, the leadership brought her into clerical conferences and banished her from the colony, but not before further destroying her credibility through excommunication. Obviously, women could have power in this society in one of the colony's most important arenas—religion. Anne Hutchinson heard the voice of the Holy Spirit and said so. That is, she believed that God spoke through her, and so did many Bostonians. To women and men of influence, she spoke as a prophet.

Seventeenth-century Massachusetts was a paradoxical society

that embraced an intense, personal spirituality and yet valued an ordered hierarchy as outlined in the Bible. People embraced the voice of the Holy Spirit, for it offered personal assurance of salvation and privileged community efforts to establish an exemplary biblical commonwealth. Still, Puritan leaders knew that God did not respect earthly inequalities of wealth, class, education, and gender. They knew that the ignorant, the poor, and women could be touched by the Spirit, and they did not want to share their civil or spiritual power with any women. The charismatic Hutchinson, whose experience of the Holy Spirit was revealed in prophetic speeches, undermined the established secular and sacred authority. An intellectually powerful woman who criticized clergymen represented a threat to order at many levels. During the state trial, Anne Hutchinson successfully countered biblical arguments and acceded to all demands that she cease public activity, yet she was still dangerous to the leaders. Even in silence, a woman claiming an authority from God that was recognized by the majority of her community represented a threat to the standing order. A woman who received revelations from God was under no civil or clerical control. In the end, although the ostensible cause for her banishment was sedition, the primary factors that drove her accusers were her leadership of women and men, her claims to prophetic revelations, and the challenge that these threats represented to their own magistracy and patriarchal power.

Notes

1. "Examination of Mrs. Hutchinson at the Court at Newtown," 1637, in David D. Hall, ed., *The Antinomian Controversy, 1636–1638: A Documentary History* (Middletown, CT, 1968), 348. The spelling in all quotations has been modernized.

2. "A Report of the Trial of Mrs. Anne Hutchinson before the Church in Boston," 1638, in Hall, ed., *Antinomian Controversy*, 370.

3. John Winthrop, *A Short Story of the Rise, reign, and ruine of the Antinomians, Familists & Libertines* (1644), in Hall, ed., *Antinomian Controversy*, 263.

4. Edward Johnson, *Wonder Working Providence of Sions Saviour in New England, 1628–1651* (1659; facsimile reprint, New York, 1974), 96.

5. John Winthrop, *Winthrop's Journal "History of New England," 1630–1649*, ed. James Kendall Hosmer (New York, 1908), 1:234.

6. Winthrop, *Short Story*, 262–63.

7. "Examination of Mrs. Hutchinson," 314.

8. Winthrop, *Short Story*, 269; "Examination of Mrs. Hutchinson," 316.

9. "Examination of Mrs. Hutchinson," 319.

10. Ibid., 332–37

11. Ibid., 336–37. This exchange is also summarized in Winthrop, *Short Story*, 273–74.

12. "Examination of Mrs. Hutchinson," 345.

13. Ibid., 337.
14. Winthrop, *Short Story*, 274.
15. Thomas Weld, "Preface" to Winthrop, *Short Story*, 218.
16. Winthrop, *Journal*, 1:299.
17. Weld, "Preface" to Winthrop, *Short Story*, 214. From the extraordinarily graphic descriptions provided by Winthrop, medical historians believe that Dyer's child was afflicted with severe spina bifida, while Hutchinson, possibly in menopause, expelled a hydatidiform mole.

Suggested Readings

Barker-Benfield, Ben. "Anne Hutchinson and the Puritan Attitude toward Women," *Feminist Studies* 1 (1972): 65–96. An outstanding interpretive essay analyzing the nature of Puritan religious culture in conflict with the society's commitment to patriarchal order.

Battis, Emery. *Saints and Sectaries: Anne Hutchinson and the Antinomian Controversy in the Massachusetts Bay Colony.* Chapel Hill, NC, 1962. Battis's psychological portrait of Hutchinson is grounded more on speculation than evidence, and the psychoanalytic theory he applies does not fit well with the evidence that does exist. However, his reconstruction of Hutchinson's male supporters is quite detailed and helpful.

Erikson, Kai T. *Wayward Puritans: A Study in the Sociology of Deviance,* 33–107. New York, 1966. An exploration of the nature of deviance through a historical study of three incidents in the early history of Massachusetts: the persecution of Quakers, 1656–1665; the Salem witch trials, 1692–1693; and the Hutchinsonian controversy.

Gura, Philip F. *A Glimpse of Sion's Glory: Puritan Radicalism in New England,* 237–75. Middletown, CT, 1984. A detailed discussion of Puritan dissent in New England that includes a rewarding chapter on Hutchinson.

Hall, David D., ed. *The Antinomian Controversy, 1636–1638: A Documentary History.* Middletown, CT, 1968. Contains most of the key historical documents, including two independent accounts of the examination before the General Court. The first can be found in John Winthrop's *Short Story of the Rise, reign, and ruine of the Antinomians, Familists & Libertines.* The second account, "Examination of Mrs. Anne Hutchinson at the Court at Newtown," is an anonymous and less hostile transcription. The original document is now lost, but it was once appended by Thomas Hutchinson, Hutchinson's great-great-grandson, to his *History of the Colony and Province of Massachusetts Bay* (Boston, 1767).

Johnson, Edward. *Wonder Working Providence of Sions Saviour in New England, 1628–1651.* 1659; facsimile reprint, New York,

1974. A history of Massachusetts during its founding decades.

Koehler, Lyle. "The Case of the American Jezebels: Anne Hutchinson and Female Agitation during the Years of the Antinomian Turmoil, 1636–1640." *William and Mary Quarterly* 31 (1974): 55–78. An engaging essay examining Hutchinson and her female followers as forerunners to feminism.

Lang, Amy Shrager. *Prophetic Woman: Anne Hutchinson and the Problem of Dissent in the Literature of New England.* Berkeley, CA, 1987. A literary study looking at the history of Hutchinson's experience and its impact on nineteenth-century American literature.

Morgan, Edmund S. *The Puritan Dilemma: The Story of John Winthrop,* 134–54. Boston, 1958. A readable biography of Winthrop with a good, descriptive chapter on the Hutchinsonian crisis.

Norton, Mary Beth. *Founding Mothers and Fathers: Gendered Power and the Forming of American Society.* New York, 1996. A detailed analysis of gender politics in New England during its first fifty years that includes a chapter devoted to Hutchinson called "Husband, Preacher, Magistrate," 359–99.

Rutman, Darrett B. *Winthrop's Boston: Portrait of a Puritan, 1630–1649,* 135–63. New York, 1965. An excellent monograph on the first two decades of Boston's history, incorporating a fine chapter on the Hutchinsonian crisis and its relation to city and colony politics.

Westerkamp, Marilyn J. "Anne Hutchinson, Sectarian Mysticism, and the Puritan Order." *Church History* 59 (1990): 482–96. Places Hutchinson within the context of English Puritanism and argues for the importance of gender in understanding the conflict.

Williams, Selma R. *Divine Rebel: The Life of Anne Marbury Hutchinson.* New York, 1981. An extremely readable biography, studying Hutchinson in the context of English Puritan culture.

Winthrop, John. *Winthrop's Journal "History of New England," 1630–1649,* ed. James Kendall Hosmer. 2 vols. New York, 1908.

5

In Search of Pocahontas

Kathleen Brown

Pocahontas (c. 1596–1617), the most widely known Native American woman, proves not to be known very well after all. Kathleen Brown invites us to join in sifting and weighing the secondhand and fragmentary evidence about Pocahontas's life. Captain John Smith's self-serving accounts of Pocahontas are at once essential and highly suspect. In addition to offering her own measured judgments on the sources, Brown leaves the reader free to consider several alternative readings.

In the first months of 1617, Pocahontas and Squanto were both in London; the two are not known to have met, but their stories bear some comparison. Both facilitated the peaceful coexistence between English settlers and Native American powers. Both became suspect in their own communities for doing so. Pocahontas became a Christian, married into the English community, and bore a son, Thomas. As the daughter of Powhatan, a powerful chieftain, and as the Christian wife of John Rolfe, an English gentleman, Pocahontas was given a "gentlewoman's" status and tried to behave accordingly (*see* frontispiece); Squanto was a refugee trying to find his way home. Pocahontas contracted a fatal respiratory ailment while visiting England; Squanto's community was destroyed by a European disease carried to New England. The uneasy "peace of Pocahontas" ended with a Powhatan surprise attack of March 1622, in which her widower was among the 350 persons killed. Thomas would return to a different Virginia and later serve as the militia commander who defended Fort James against his mother's people.

Have both Pocahontas and Squanto been celebrated in American history not so much because they reached beyond their own communities, but because their doing so could be construed as evidence that English settlers were welcome in the land that they then confiscated?

Kathleen Brown, who teaches at the University of Pennsylvania, is an authority on the history of gender and race in colonial Virginia. She is author of *Good Wives, Nasty Wenches, and Anxious Patriarchs: Gender, Race, and Power in Colonial Virginia* (1996).

> Powhatan . . . sent his Daughter,
> a child of tenne yeares old, which not only for
> feature, countenance, and proportion,
> much exceedeth any of the rest of his
> people, but for wit, and spirit, the only
> Nonpariel [*sic*] of his Country.[1]

John Smith's description of Pocahontas in 1608 marks the beginning of one of the most powerful and enduring legends about the founding of the British colonies in North America. For nearly four centuries, the story of the Indian princess who showed compassion for the English settlers at Jamestown has inspired paintings, music, poetry, plays, and historical scholarship. In the 1990s, Pocahontas made her debut as a character in a Disney movie, which was accompanied by a line of children's toys. In these latter-day incarnations, Pocahontas is not the ten-year-old girl who captivated the crusty Captain Smith, but a mature, sexually attractive beauty whose feelings for Smith blossom into a mutual romance.

Just who was Pocahontas, and why is her story so important to us? Part of her appeal, both for those who knew her in Virginia nearly four hundred years ago and for us today, undoubtedly is the mystery surrounding her. Having left no firsthand written account of her life, her motives, and her feelings, Pocahontas is historically at the mercy of people like John Smith, who did leave extensive written accounts, and of generations of historians, whose speculations have helped to construct her legend. Everyone connected with Pocahontas in the seventeenth century wanted a piece of her for themselves. Her father Powhatan, John Smith, John Rolfe, Ralph Hamor, the Virginia Company, and the English Crown all had their own versions of who she should be. Later, Pocahontas's image was seized by Euro-Americans telling stories about their beginnings on the North American continent. Much of the interest in the Indian girl whom John Smith described as peerless, the "Nonpareil" of her country, thus derives from the adaptability of her life story to serve the needs of others.

The main source of our fascination with Pocahontas, however, is very likely her brief, action-packed life. She lived probably only twenty years, yet in that short space of time she served as an emissary for her people, witnessed an important agreement between her father and the leader of the English settlers, was kidnapped, became a religious convert, learned an entirely new language fluently, entered a culturally mixed marriage, bore a child, crossed an ocean, and visited the court of an English king and queen. Pocahontas was a central player not just in the culture of her birth, as might have been the case for any other precocious or well-born Indian or English woman, but also in the strange world of Anglo-Indian conflict and exchange at a time when the rules of such encounters were not yet established. All of the significant events in her short life took place within the framework of this cultural meeting and conflict; all took place within the span of a single decade, from 1607, when she was approximately ten years old, until her death in England in 1617. Hers was an extraordinary life, lived at an extraordinary time in the history of the Atlantic world.

This essay reexamines the evidence for Pocahontas's unusual life. The emphasis in most accounts has been on her relationships with John Smith and John Rolfe, the two Englishmen who did so much to change her life and create her historical identity. Very little attention has been given to her relationships with other Indian people, including her father, or with other children, for instance, the young English boys at Jamestown. After an attempt to assess all these relationships through close readings of the most reliable texts about Pocahontas, some counterfactual questions about her role in early Atlantic and early American history are raised.

Like all other accounts of Pocahontas's life, this one remains constrained by the lack of evidence from Pocahontas herself. Thus, this essay still relies on the written evidence supplied by Smith and Rolfe. By necessity, Pocahontas's relationships with the men who wrote about her become part of her story.

Daughter of Powhatan

Pocahontas's world changed forever in April 1607 when three English ships sponsored by the Virginia Company touched land at the base of the Chesapeake Bay. Repulsed by an Indian attack, the ships continued upriver to what the English would call Jamestown Island, a protected and easily navigable location that seemed ideal for a fort. Initially, the English planned to use Jamestown as a base for mining and trade. They soon discovered that there was little gold to be mined and that the Indians in the region were not willing to labor as their counterparts in Mexico had for the Spanish. After several years of widespread disease and high mortality, a few of the pioneers also realized that Jamestown was possibly the most unhealthy place they could have settled.

Although the English described the countryside surrounding Jamestown as "uninhabited" or "virgin," they could not have been more wrong. Several thousand Algonquian-speaking Indians, including the Powhatans, had lived in the region for thousands of years. Their subtle and complex uses of the land included agriculture but left different marks upon the landscape from those familiar to the English. Indians did not regard land as property in the way the English did, a fact that only encouraged the Virginia Company to claim the territory as its own. Despite their denigration of the Indians for naked savagery, sexual immorality, and laziness, the English settlers who survived the first years in Jamestown owed these native peoples their lives. Although they were technologically more sophisticated than the Indians, the settlers simply did not have enough supplies to last through the winter, nor could they manage to grow enough wheat or corn to make up the difference. Without the Indian corn procured through trade and plunder, the English would have starved.

Chief among those wrangling for corn to feed the hungry residents of Jamestown was the savvy adventurer John Smith. Born of the yeomanry rather than the gentry, Smith felt that his social superiors never gave him the credit he deserved for his leadership as president of Jamestown. Until 1617, Smith and his successors negotiated, threatened, and skirmished with Powhatan, the dominant *werowance* (district chief) of the region. Since the 1590s, perhaps in reaction to previous contact with Europeans, Powhatan had been strengthening and adding to his tributary chiefdom until it included over half a dozen tribes and several thousand people. By the time that John Smith arrived in 1607, Powhatan was without question the most powerful Indian in the region and the one who controlled the largest supplies of corn.

Powhatan was Pocahontas's father. He was probably already elderly when she was born in 1596 or 1597. As was customary for powerful *werowances*, Powhatan had fathered children by several different women, a practice that strengthened his hold over his paramount chiefdom. Pocahontas could thus count dozens of half brothers and sisters living throughout the area, many of them considerably older than she. The identity of Pocahontas's mother remains a mystery. If she was anything like Powhatan's other wives, she was young and among the most beautiful women of her tribe before her marriage. She might have spent a few years living at the paramount chief's house until she had borne a child. At that point, she would either have returned to her own people or, if she was a great favorite, remained near Powhatan's court so that the *werowance* could enjoy the company of his wife and daughter.

The first written evidence of Pocahontas's existence is John Smith's mention of her in his *True Relation*, a letter describing his adventures in Virginia that was published in 1608 without his permission or knowledge. Brief though the mention may be, it is a potentially rich and relatively reliable source of information about the young Indian girl. Historians have generally considered *True Relation* to be the most informal and least embellished of Smith's several publications on his adventures in Virginia. It is also the only commentary on Pocahontas published before she became known in England as the "Nonpareil" of Virginia.

The occasion for Pocahontas's appearance in Smith's letter was her father Powhatan's attempt to secure the release of over two dozen Paspahegh Indian prisoners being held by Smith at Jamestown. Smith had seized the Indian men allegedly to retaliate against Indian theft and harassment of the English settlement. He subsequently tortured several of the captives to gain information about Powhatan's plans to ambush Jamestown. He had also refused to exchange the prisoners either for an English boy whom Powhatan had been holding as a hostage or for the stolen tools and supplies that the paramount chief had recently returned to him.

Smith introduced Pocahontas into his narrative in the context of this political chess game with her father: "Powhatan, understanding we detained certaine Salvages, sent his Daughter, a child of tenne yeares old, which not only for feature, countenance, and proportion, much exceedeth any of the rest of his people, but for wit, and spirit, the only Nonpariel of his Country." Accompanying Pocahontas to Jamestown was Powhatan's "trustie messenger," Rawhunt, whose "subtill wit," "crafty understanding," and "deformitie of person" presented a striking contrast to the young Indian girl. The messenger, who probably also served as a translator, explained Powhatan's purpose in sending his daughter to meet with Smith: "He with a long circumstance told mee how well Powhatan loved and respected mee, and in that I should not doubt any way of his kindnesse, he had sent his child, which he most esteemed, to see me." Lest the point be lost on the Englishman, Powhatan had sent "a Deere and bread besides for a present."[2]

According to Smith, Pocahontas functioned as both an emissary for her father and a token of his goodwill. Unlike the boy hostage whom the English gave to Powhatan as a pledge of their good word, Pocahontas was not being exchanged for peace or the release of men. Nor was she a gift, like the venison and corn bread given to Smith. Rather, she seems to have been sent by her father to soften up the tough Englishman. Perhaps knowing that Smith would find his daughter's wit and beauty appealing, Powhatan sent her to the English settlement to convince the leader of Jamestown of the Indians' affection and good faith.

Throughout the brief appearance recorded in Smith's *True Relation*, Pocahontas behaved more like an adult than a little girl. Smith believed that she had been instructed by her father not to take "notice at all of the Indeans that had beene prisoners," an order she seems to have obeyed dutifully until the relatives of the captive men arrived to negotiate for their release. Rather than freeing the men individually and reuniting them with the kin who had come for them, however, Smith released the prisoners as a group, placing them in the custody of the young girl as a way of acknowledging her "fathers kindnesse in sending her." In a special effort to please Pocahontas, Smith gave her "such trifles as contented her, to tel that we had used the Paspaheyans very kindly in so releasing them."[3]

What can Smith's first account of Virginia tell us about the young Pocahontas? In the pages of the *True Relation*, Pocahontas is a self-possessed, self-disciplined ten-year-old, capable of charming the deeply suspicious Smith and carrying out her father's orders. Her charisma was such that it crossed cultural boundaries, earning her a special place in her father's heart and captivating Smith, who found her without peer among the Algonquian Indians. What the document fails to tell us is also interesting. Smith made no mention of a previous relationship with Pocahontas, yet his impassioned declaration of her superiority to all other Indians suggests an acquaintance deeper than this brief meeting. It is possible that Powhatan chose to send Pocahontas to resolve the conflict over the Indian prisoners because the Englishman and his daughter had already met (Smith would later claim this in a subsequent publication about Virginia). Ultimately, to get a sense of Pocahontas's personality beyond the narrow depiction in Smith's first text on Virginia, we must turn to other sources.

References to the youthful Pocahontas appeared in two other published accounts in 1612, four years after Smith first wrote about her in *True Relation*. In both of these texts, Pocahontas was portrayed as an energetic and lovable girl who moved easily between the world of her own people and that of the English. Indeed, one gets the impression from these two accounts that Pocahontas herself was an important bridge between the two cultures.

William Strachey's *Historie of Travell into Virginia Britania*, completed in 1612, offered a detailed account of the English encounter with Virginia Algonquians that borrowed heavily from Smith, the main authority about the region's Indians. Strachey had been in Virginia since 1609, when Pocahontas was about twelve years old, but had not finished his history until she was close to fifteen. Thus, much of Strachey's information about Pocahontas's childhood probably came from other settlers. He noted, for example, that she had been accustomed to visiting the fort at Jamestown "in tymes past." He also used her as an illustration of the freedom that Indian boys and girls enjoyed before they reached puberty, recalling that Pocahontas had been known to "gett the boyes forth with her into the market place and make them wheele, falling on their hands and turning their heeles upwardes, whome she would follow, and wheele so her self naked as she was all the Fort over." Lest the respectable English reader get the wrong impression about Indian women's modesty, Strachey observed that upon turning twelve, Indian girls began wearing aprons "before their bellies" and became "very sham-fac'd to be seene bare."[4]

Strachey's description of Pocahontas organizing the Jamestown boys to do cartwheels around the fort and then joining in the fun herself provides a vivid example of the "wit" and "spirit" that Smith found so delightful. We can imagine a group of pale Jamestown boys, overdressed in wool, being goaded into turning cartwheels by a brown-skinned Indian girl, scantily dressed by European standards, whose acrobatic skills probably put them to shame. What Strachey manages to capture in this anecdote (which no other author save Smith evokes) is Pocahontas's energy and zest for life. She stood out among Powhatan's children not simply because she visited the English at their fort, but also because she seemed unfazed by the cultural distance between the two groups. At least for a time, Pocahontas found that crossing cultural boundaries involved little stress or sorrow. Leadership skills, athleticism, and perhaps not a little charisma made it possible for this prepubescent Indian girl to make a group of English boys do her bidding. Strachey's account thus lends credence to Smith's claims in 1608 about Pocahontas's unique charms.

Strachey offered one other tidbit of information about Pocahontas that no other writer thought to mention. After observing that Indians typically were given several names, including an "affectionate Title" usually chosen by their mothers, he presented the example of Pocahontas, who was known to the English by the pet name given to her by her father. Strachey speculated that "Pochahuntas" might mean "Little-wanton," a term which in the seventeenth century implied mischievous, willful, or promiscuous behavior. That Powhatan could have chosen such a label for his favorite daughter is not only suggestive of Pocahontas's personality, but it also reveals a great deal about Indian culture. Imagining a young Elizabeth I, known in later life as the Virgin Queen, being affectionately called "little strumpet" or "wild thing" by her father Henry VIII, is a helpful device for highlighting the differences between the two cultures' attitudes toward female personality and sexuality. What Powhatan might have considered a humorous reference to Pocahontas's affectionate, energetic, and uninhibited manner, an English king could only have seen as shameful or undesirable.[5]

Strachey's discussions of the youthful Pocahontas reveal a great deal about seventeenth-century Algonquian attitudes toward rearing girls. Although Pocahontas was very likely born with her open, risk-taking, adventuresome personality, nothing in her upbringing had repressed that spirit or energy. In the fragments of information that remain, we glimpse a girl who felt comfortable crossing the boundaries of gender and culture to cavort with English boys and enchant men of her father's generation. Coming from a society in which little girls were paid little mind, Strachey's contemporaries might have been amazed to discover that Algonquians in Virginia tolerated, perhaps even encouraged, such qualities in the young daughter of Powhatan. Indeed, to the degree that little girls are still seen as relatively insignificant members of society, readers in the present day might also find this extraordinary.

Pocahontas appeared in another text published in 1612. Smith's *Map of Virginia*, a guide to the land and its resources, contained a brief list of Indian vocabulary in which Pocahontas made a cameo appearance. Amid the Indian words for communicating hunger, geographic location, and elapsed time, Smith included the following sentence: "Bid Pokahontas bring hither two little Baskets, and I wil give her white beads to make her a chaine."[6] By the time this phrase appeared in print, it was already outdated, as Pocahontas would have been at least fifteen years old, well beyond the age of childhood antics around the fort. Yet Smith would not have known this fact from personal experience, having left Virginia in 1609 after suffering a severe injury. In his mind, Pocahontas remained perpetually childish, ready to do favors for him in exchange for pretty trinkets. Pocahontas's perpetual youthfulness in Smith's guide to Virginia captured the initial promise of Anglo-Indian relations in the region and of his own rising fortunes in the colony.

Rescuer of John Smith

The incident for which Pocahontas is best known is her alleged rescue of Smith in December 1607, just seconds before Indian executioners would have dashed out his brains with their clubs. Although Smith claimed that this dramatic rescue occurred before he met with Pocahontas in Jamestown in 1608 to discuss the fate of the Indian prisoners, curiously he had failed to write about the incident until 1624, seven years after her death in England. None of the accounts published before 1624 by Smith, or any of the Jamestown chroniclers who borrowed from him, made any mention of a dramatic rescue. In light of Smith's knack for self-promotion and his ceaseless efforts to be appreciated by his superiors in London, many historians wonder whether the rescue actually took place. It seems highly unlikely that the boastful Smith could have managed to remain silent about this incident for seventeen years. Some scholars have hypothesized that in 1624, two years after the Indian attack upon English settlements that led to the dissolution of the Virginia Company, Smith was hoping to restore his reputation as a brave and effective opponent of the Powhatan Indians. He may also have been trying to capitalize on Pocahontas's posthumous popularity in England by exaggerating the length and intimacy of their relationship. Yet another point against believing Smith's revised version of the story is that, in several previous accounts of his adventures around the globe, he claimed to have been rescued from certain death by beautiful young women.

Despite these grounds for skepticism, Smith's 1624 account of the 1607 rescue by Pocahontas is difficult to dismiss altogether. Indeed, there are several reasons for taking the account seriously. First, although Smith could have added Pocahontas to the tale for effect, the basic outline of the captivity story remained the same through several retellings. Second, what Smith described in 1624 as a rescue from execution bears some similarity to Indian adoption rituals in the northeast. Third, as already noted, his 1608 letter describing his meeting with Pocahontas leaves open the possibility that they had already met and developed a friendship. Fourth, in light of Pocahontas's relationship with her father and the respect accorded to her by other Indian people, it is reasonable to think that she might have participated actively in an important event such as a tribal adoption. Finally, and perhaps most compellingly, Smith's accounts of his relationship with Powhatan, including those written soon after the alleged near-death experience, suggest that Powhatan had begun to treat the Englishman like a kinsman, much as he might have done if Smith had been adopted by the Powhatans.

The basic outline of Smith's captivity story remained consistent throughout several retellings. In *True Relation* (1608), *Proceedings of the English Colonie in Virginia* (1612), and *Generall Historie of Virginia* (1624), Smith recounted the tale of an English scouting mission gone awry. Having divided his men into two groups to reconnoiter better the upper James River and search for food, he returned to the canoes to find himself ambushed. All of his companions were slain, but Smith, who used his Indian guide as a human shield, managed to escape the barrage of arrows with only a minor wound to his leg. The fact that Powhatan's warriors, whose aim was otherwise deadly accurate, fell short of injuring Smith with nearly thirty arrows suggests that Powhatan wanted Smith brought to him alive. Taken back to Powhatan, Smith was imprisoned and fed huge quantities of food, which made him suspect that he was being fattened up to be eaten, a fate he had probably read of in Spanish accounts of the New World. In all three versions of the tale, Smith claimed that he charmed and entertained his captors with stories of European technology and the majesty of King James.

Where the versions part company is in Smith's addition in 1624 of a near-death scene. In the 1608 account, his own charm and growing friendship with Opechancanough, brother of Powhatan, resulted in his kind reception by the paramount chief, who had apparently already decided that Smith would be set free. In the 1624 rendition, however, Smith's favor with Powhatan resulted from Pocahontas's timely intervention. After being urged to wash his hands and eat abundantly, Smith witnessed a "long consultation" that resulted in "two great stones" being "brought before Powhatan." While Indian men and women seized Smith to lay his head on one of the stones, Pocahontas begged for his life. Just as he was about to be clubbed to death, the daughter of Powhatan "got his head in her armes, and laid her owne upon his to save him from death."[7] This poignant display of affection, according to Smith, persuaded Powhatan to let Smith live to serve him and his daughter.

Smith's account of his rescue by Pocahontas has many credible features as well as many curious ones. It was not unheard of for Indians elsewhere in eastern North America symbolically to "kill" an individual whom they planned to adopt, nor would it have been inappropriate for a woman to be involved in incorporating the adoptee. Pocahontas would have been a bit young for this role, but her status as a favorite daughter of Powhatan and her precocious character may have made up for her youth. Powhatan's decree that Smith be spared to manufacture tools and trinkets for him and his daughter is consistent with other Indian adoption practices. What little we know of Powhatan's view of the newly arrived English settlers and his subsequent efforts to deal with their presence also fits with an interpretation of this story as an adoption. Powhatan initially pursued an incorporative rather than a defensive strategy with the English, attempting to strike advantageous bargains for the corn that he knew they needed and reminding them of their dependence upon him. Following the near-death ritual, Powhatan referred to Smith as a son and a *werowance*, a likely outcome of a tribal adoption. It is plausible, in light of these consistencies with Indian practice, to interpret Smith's story as mistaking an adoption ritual for an interrupted execution.

What does not make sense about the 1624 version of Smith's captivity is why he might have omitted it from both his 1607 letter and his 1612 *Proceedings*. Was he embarrassed about being saved by a ten-year-old girl? Did he feel that the rescue made him appear less rather than more heroic? Had he not yet fabricated the event? It is also hard to fathom Pocahontas's motive for wanting to adopt a man who would have been a total stranger to her. Perhaps she found the hirsute and solidly built Smith intriguing and exotic looking. If she had taken a liking to him and played an active role in his adoption, performing what he believed to be a rescue, it is not surprising that he would describe her a few months later as the

"Nonpareil" of her country.

The 1624 *Generall Historie* contained several other new or embellished references to Pocahontas that had not appeared in Smith's previous publications. He recounted one incident in which the young girl attempted to ease the fears of a group of Englishmen who had come to visit her father. Soon after the arrival of the second supply ship in the early autumn of 1608, Smith journeyed to the Pamunkey River with four companions to present Powhatan with gifts and royal regalia sent by King James. Anxious about the danger of an ambush, Smith waited to receive a reply from the *werowance* about the most suitable site for a coronation. While the Englishmen waited, they were entertained by Pocahontas, who calmed the edgy captain by "willing him to kill her if any hurt were intended."[8] The addition of this new reference to Pocahontas, which was missing from the 1612 version of the story, might have reflected Smith's desire in 1624 to portray himself as an intimate friend of the by-then famous Indian princess.

Smith's claim that "Pocahontas and her women" entertained the Englishmen with a "Virginia Maske" was also new to the 1624 account. In England, a masque was a theatrical performance that included music, pageantry, costumes, and dancing. Smith's use of the term to describe an Indian entertainment both commented on the similarities between the two cultures and highlighted the great differences between the allegedly civilized English and the reputedly savage Virginia Indians. Although Smith had described the masque in detail in 1612, he had neither called it by that name nor linked it to Pocahontas. He attributed it instead to Powhatan's women, a sexual inference reinforced by his description of the event. The Indian performers were thirty young women, he noted, "naked . . . onely covered behind and before with a few greene leaves, their bodies all painted." Wearing animal skins and carrying tools and weapons, the women proceeded to sing and dance in a fashion that Smith found strange. Following the masque, they invited Smith and his men back to their lodgings where they "tormented him . . . with crowding, pressing, and hanging about him, most tediously crying, Love you not me?"[9] In all likelihood, the women were offering sexual hospitality to the men, as was customary during the visits of honored guests and foreign diplomats.

Upon retelling the story in 1624 to include Pocahontas, Smith left her role in the masque and the sexual hospitality that followed ambiguous. He noted her presence before the masque began but then failed to mention her again. This could possibly reflect the fact that Pocahontas was not among the performers. In September 1608 she was probably still a girl on the verge of sexual maturity. It is doubtful that she would have been old enough to be among those crowding around Smith and demanding his love. Smith simply may have added her to the story in 1624 without stopping to consider whether she was too young to have participated in the masque.

Smith wrote of one other incident in the 1624 *Historie* that demonstrated the Indian girl's special affection and loyalty to the English captain. He had previously mentioned this incident briefly in his 1612 *Proceedings*, but the 1624 version was much more elaborate. The fact that this story was not newly introduced in 1624 makes it somewhat less suspicious than Smith's other attempts to connect his name to that of Pocahontas.

During the icy winter of 1608-09, Smith traveled to Powhatan's winter camp to negotiate with him for corn. The two men wrangled over whether the corn was a gift to keep the English from starving or tribute to keep them from attacking. Powhatan reluctantly agreed to give Smith the provisions he needed but then disappeared from the camp, leaving Smith and his men to load the corn on their barges and pick their way through the frozen river back to Jamestown. While they waited for the high tide to float their boats from the frozen ground, Smith was warned by Pocahontas that her father was planning a surprise attack: "For Pocahontas his dearest jewell and daughter, in that darke night came through the irksome woods, and told our Captaine great cheare should be sent us by and by: but Powhatan and all the power he could make, would after come kill us all, if they that brought it could not kill us with our owne weapons when we were at supper. Therefore if we would live shee wished us presently to bee gone."[10] According to Smith, Pocahontas delivered the warning with great emotion, yet she remained capable of thinking logically about her relationship with the father whom she had betrayed: "Such things as shee delighted in, he [Smith] would have given her: but with the teares running downe her cheekes, shee said shee durst not be seene to have any: for if Powhatan should know it, she were but dead, and so shee ranne away by her selfe as she came."[11]

Can Smith's account of this warning from Pocahontas be trusted as evidence of her affection for her father's enemies? Smith's failure to describe this incident in detail in 1612 casts some doubt on the exact language of the warning and Pocahontas's state of mind. The alert reader cannot help but be suspicious of Smith's decision to quote Pocahontas at length only after she was no longer alive to contradict him. As in the case of the alleged rescue, it is tempting to dismiss this story entirely as the fabrication of the publicity-hungry John Smith.

Smith's brief mention of the incident in 1612, however, makes it more likely that Pocahontas did warn the Englishman of impending danger. If we compare the 1624 depictions of the young Pocahontas with Smith's earliest description of her in 1608, moreover, interesting continuities and contrasts emerge that strengthen the possibility that Smith's story contains a grain of truth. In both accounts, for instance, Powhatan's power over his young daughter is apparent. In Smith's 1608 account of his first meeting with the girl, Pocahontas was a dutiful daughter who carried out her father's orders. One year after making Smith's acquaintance, according to his 1624 account, she had betrayed Powhatan and was fearful of the consequences. In both accounts, there is also evidence of Smith's desire to please the young girl with presents. Whereas in 1608, Pocahontas openly accepted gifts from the Englishman, in 1609 she feared that gifts would mark her as a traitor to her people, who had come to view the English as enemies.

The warning scene in the 1624 *Generall Historie* illustrates the transformation of Pocahontas's role as a cultural go-between. In the short year since her meeting with Smith as her father's emissary, Pocahontas has been transformed from an official representative who travels by day, escorted by her father's messenger, to a shadowy figure who enters the woods alone at night. In sharp contrast to her triumphant return to her father in 1608 with the newly released prisoners, in 1609 she runs, crying and alone, through the dark woods after delivering her warning to Smith. Only twelve or thirteen years old, Pocahontas has already lost her innocence. She is caught between her loyalty to two men who have become enemies. As a consequence, she no longer fits as seamlessly or as unselfconsciously into her own culture.

Wife

Pocahontas's loss of cultural innocence was accompanied by her coming to sexual maturity. Once she was no longer a little girl doing cartwheels around the English fort, she became a potential pawn in the political game being played by her father, John Smith, and the subsequent leaders of Jamestown. Feminist scholars have described the social usefulness of sexually mature women as occurring through "the traffic in women" conducted by fathers, brothers, and husbands. By exchanging women in marriage, men form social bonds with other men, thereby turning enemies and competitors into allies. Ultimately, this traffic in women helps to bind men together to form the foundations of society. Both patrilineal European and matrilineal Native American societies engaged in marriage customs that could be interpreted as an exchange of women among men, but it was unclear when the English settled Jamestown whether a traffic in women would eventually bind Englishman and Indian together into one society.

The first evidence of Pocahontas approaching marriageable age comes in 1612, the year William Strachey reported that she was "now marryed to a pryvate Captayne called Kocoum some 2 yeares synce."[12] Strachey's report suggested that Powhatan had chosen to marry his daughter to a high-ranking Algonquian-speaking Indian, perhaps with an eye toward strengthening his ability to resist the English settlers. If Strachey was correct, Pocahontas married when she was thirteen or fourteen years old, a year or two after donning the modest aprons of a sexually mature woman. Assuming that her courtship and marriage were similar to those of other young Indian women, Pocahontas might have received gifts of poultry, fish, venison, bear meat, fruits, and berries from her prospective husband. This was the traditional way to convince a woman and her father that a man was a good hunter, capable of providing a wife with food throughout the year. As a very young woman, just entering puberty, Pocahontas would probably have needed her father's permission to marry. As the favorite daughter of the paramount chief, moreover, her marriage would have been politically important to the future of the Powhatan people. Curiously, Strachey was the only Jamestown chronicler to mention this marriage. If Pocahontas's first husband really was an Indian, he died soon after they were wed or the marriage was annulled, for he is never mentioned again in any subsequent publication on Virginia.

In the same year that Strachey reported Pocahontas's marriage to Kocoum, John Smith boasted in his *Proceedings* that he could have married Powhatan's daughter himself:

> Some propheticall spirit calculated hee had the Salvages in such subjection, hee would have made himselfe a king, by marrying Pocahontas, Powhatans daughter. It is true she was the very nomparell [sic] of his kingdome, and at most not past 13 or 14 yeares of age. Very oft shee came to our fort, with what shee could get for Captaine Smith, that ever loved and used all the Countrie well, but her especially he ever much respected: and she so well requited it [by warning him of an ambush by Powhatan]. . . . But her marriage could no way have intitled him by any right to the kingdome, nor was it ever suspected hee had ever such a thought, or more regarded her, or any of them, than in honest reason, and discreation he might. If he would he might have married her, or have done what him listed [what he wanted].[13]

Smith purposely repeated gossip about his relationship with Pocahontas to refute charges that he had been attempting to make himself the king of Virginia. He also minimized both her political usefulness to him and his interest in marrying her, although he suggested that she would have been available to him as either a wife or a lover had he wanted her. Like his previous references to Pocahontas, Smith's speculations about a possible marriage reveal his underlying respect for Powhatan's daughter. But his tone had changed significantly now that Pocahontas had become a woman. Reports of her frequently visiting the fort combined with Smith's own claim that he could "have done what him listed" to create an impression of Pocahontas's vulnerability to the desires of Englishmen. In seventeenth-century England, a woman who allowed herself to become vulnerable to sexual exploitation risked losing her respectability. That Pocahontas did not become his wife or his concubine had little to do with her own will, as Smith saw it, but instead reflected the integrity and "discreation" of John Smith.

Two years after Strachey's and Smith's comments on Pocahontas's marital status, Ralph Hamor published *A True Discourse of the Present State of Virginia,* an account of the settlement that detailed Pocahontas's central role in the conflict between the English and the Powhatans. According to Hamor, Pocahontas was in the midst of a three-month stay at Patawomeck in the spring of 1613, conducting some business for her father and visiting with friends, when English Captain Samuel Argall arrived at this northern Virginia location. Hamor claimed that Pocahontas's purpose was to "exchange some of her fathers commodities" with her Patawomeck friends, which suggests that her father still trusted her to act as his representative. If she had been married, in all likelihood her husband was now dead or they were divorced, making it possible for her to stay in Patawomeck for such a long period of time. Hamor described Pocahontas as "desirous to renue hir familiaritie with the English," "delighting to see them" and "fearefull perhaps to be surprised."[14] Despite trepidations, she did not hesitate to visit the English captain, although clearly she no longer felt as carefree among his people as she had in her youth.

When he heard of her impending visit, Argall concocted a plan to kidnap her, hoping eventually to ransom her for the Englishmen being held prisoner by Powhatan as well as for weapons and tools recently stolen from Jamestown. Enlisting the help of two Patawomeck Indians, Iopassus and his wife, by promising them a copper kettle and some other goods, Argall schemed to lure Pocahontas to his ship, where he would hold her prisoner until her father met English demands. The plan called for Iopassus's wife to express interest in going aboard the English ship. Iopassus, in turn, would pretend to refuse her request, until she became tearful. At that point, Iopassus would relent and persuade Pocahontas, the only other woman present, to accompany his wife.

After an evening of fine entertainment and a night spent in the gunner's room of Argall's ship, Pocahontas became "most possessed with feare, and desire of returne." She awoke the sleeping Iopassus, requesting that they leave the ship immediately, only to be informed that she was now a hostage. Upon receiving the news, she "began to be exceeding pensive, and discontented," until gradually, "with extraordinary curteous usage," she seemed to accept her predicament with patience and resignation.[15] The ship returned to Jamestown, where Argall dispatched a messenger to inform Powhatan of his daughter's captivity and the terms of the ransom.

Powhatan's reaction to the news of the kidnapping was somewhat curious. Smith and Hamor claimed that he made no response for three months while he sought advice from his councillors, a claim that at least one historian finds doubtful. When at last he did respond, he returned the seven captive Englishmen along with broken and unserviceable muskets. Deeming this inadequate, the English once again gave Powhatan an ultimatum for the return of the other weapons he held. This time, several months elapsed without any response from the paramount chief.

By March 1614 the English had become impatient and decided to travel to Powhatan's village with Pocahontas in tow. Adding insult to injury, several of the men previously ransomed had run away from the English settlement to return to their Indian captors. Sir Thomas Dale's plan was to force Powhatan either to fight for his daughter or to return the goods and men demanded by the English. When news reached Powhatan's village that the English had brought Pocahontas with them, two of Powhatan's sons asked to see their half sister to determine whether her captors had been treating her well. Pleased with what they learned about her condition, at least according to Hamor, or possibly even more determined to rescue her, the two brothers left the ship declaring their willingness to redeem Pocahontas and negotiate a permanent peace with the English.

At least one English chronicler reported that the long months of captivity had taken their toll on Pocahontas, leading her to doubt her father's affection for her. Dale claimed that when she initially went ashore near her father's village, Pocahontas "would not talke to any of them scarce to them of the best sort, and to them onely, that if her father had loved her, he would not value her lesse then olde swords, peeces [firearms], or axes: wherefore she would stil dwel with the English men, who loved her."[16] Dale's recollection of Pocahontas's words were undoubtedly self-serving, yet it does resonate with what we call today the "Stockholm syndrome," in which a hostage identifies with the needs, political agenda, and interests of her or his captors. After spending nearly a year living among the English, Pocahontas would likely have begun to question her father's handling of the situation and to see the world in the way the English did. Her refusal to talk to her own people, except to complain about her father's failure to ransom her, hints at the resentment that she might have felt at continuing to be a pawn in the conflict between the two groups.

Although bitter feelings toward the father whom she believed had abandoned her may have accounted for much of Pocahontas's growing sympathy for her captors, several other factors also played a role. First, while she waited to be ransomed, Dale seized the opportunity to instruct her in the principles of Christianity. According to the Reverend Alexander Whitaker, who probably carried out much of the actual instruction, Pocahontas "openly renounced her countrey Idolatry, confessed the faith of Jesus Christ, and was baptised; which thing Sir Thomas Dale had laboured along time to ground in her."[17] Dale, who clearly saw Pocahontas's conversion as a political coup, was quick to point out that "she desired" to be baptized. "Were it but the gayning of this one soule," he wrote, "I will thinke my time, toile, and present stay well spent."[18] Taken together, Whitaker's and Dale's comments suggest that Pocahontas was under considerable pressure to make them feel that their time was "well spent." Cut off from her father and her people, she would have found it increasingly difficult to resist such pressures as the months of her captivity wore on.

One of the most tangible ways to display Pocahontas's conversion to Christianity and to imprint her new identity even more deeply was to transform her outer appearance to that of a respectable Englishwoman. Sometime after her kidnapping, the daughter of Powhatan relinquished her deerskin aprons and beads for the confining petticoats, bodice, and overskirts that comprised a genteel Englishwoman's outfit. For this to take place, Pocahontas would undoubtedly have been turned over to one of the small number of Englishwomen in Jamestown for advice and assistance in wearing her new clothing. Perhaps even more than being able to recite prayers and the catechism, this transformation of her appearance offered compelling evidence of what the English hoped to accomplish with their allegedly uncivilized neighbors if given a chance.

Forming affective ties with particular Englishmen was yet another factor influencing Pocahontas's views of her captors and their culture. Hamor, Dale, and Whitaker all noted that, even before the English went on the offensive and brought Pocahontas to Powhatan's village to press for their ransom demands, she had fallen in love with John Rolfe, a member of the lower gentry who was then twenty-eight years old. All three chroniclers noted that Rolfe's interest in marrying Pocahontas resulted not only from his admiration for her, but also from his love of the Virginia plantation and his interest in furthering his experiments with tobacco. Both of these projects were likely to benefit from a peaceful alliance with the neighboring Indians who had grown the plant for hundreds of years. In addition, Rolfe believed that by becoming Pocahontas's husband, he could secure her soul for Christianity, a victory that would ultimately be for her own good. Although he denied that his marriage to Pocahontas was grounded in "the unbridled desire of carnall affection," a sinful passion that would have reminded many English adventurers of the excesses of the Spanish conquistadores, Rolfe did admit to enjoying the company of the woman "to whom my hartie and best thoughts are, and have a long time bin so intangled, and inthralled in so intricate a laborinth, that I was even awearied to unwinde my selfe thereout."[19] What Pocahontas saw in Rolfe is less well documented, although as a hostage bereft of contact with family and friends for an entire year, she could easily have become emotionally dependent on the attentions of an "inthralled" Englishman. What we do know is that she was willing to renounce or displace much of her heritage and identity to marry him according to English standards. Dale recounted that her baptism took place before the wedding, most likely accompanied by her adoption of the name Rebecca.

Pocahontas's previous participation in Smith's adoption may have made her more receptive to efforts to acculturate her to English ways. If she believed that her marriage to Rolfe was somehow equivalent to Smith's incorporation into Powhatan society, she may have been more willing to cooperate with English attempts to transform her. Valuing reciprocity and balance, as any Powhatan Indian would have, Pocahontas might have found it easier to accept her fate if she viewed it as but one of many cultural exchanges within the larger context of Anglo-Indian relations.

The final factor to consider in assessing the impact of Pocahontas's year of captivity is her age. Only sixteen or seventeen when she was taken hostage, Pocahontas faced a barrage of pressures to participate in her own cultural transformation. The people who wished to change her were not total strangers, moreover, but from a culture she had known since the age of ten. That few Indian women could claim as much firsthand knowledge of the English as Pocahontas does not negate the impact of her youth. Being a seasoned veteran of the Anglo-Indian conflict in Virginia did not exempt her from the emotional trials and tribulations of being a young adult.

One cannot help but wonder if Pocahontas would have been as quick to judge her father as unloving and her English captors as her friends if she had been able to read what they wrote about her. Unlike John Smith, who had described the young girl as the "Nonpareil" of Virginia, John Rolfe wrote of his wife-to-be as "one whose education hath bin rude, her manners barbarous, her generation accursed."[20] Hamor repeated Rolfe's words in his account of Virginia, using

Pocahontas's barbarous state before her marriage as evidence of Rolfe's character and commitment to the Virginia settlement. In these descriptions, Pocahontas was no longer the self-possessed girl capable of charming wary Englishmen, but merely a savage indebted to the English for the gifts of Christianity and civility. The main attractions that she held for her husband-to-be and his advisers were the political capital they could reap from the marriage and the prosperity that might flow from an alliance with Powhatan.

News of Pocahontas's impending union with John Rolfe reached her father at about the same time that Thomas Dale presented Powhatan with one last ultimatum: He would allow Powhatan's people to resume their spring planting and give them additional time to decide how best to satisfy the English demands, but if a final agreement between the two groups was not reached by harvesttime, the English would "returne againe and destroy and take away all their corne, burne all the houses upon that river, leave not a fishing *Weere* [net trap] standing, nor a *Canoa* [canoe] in any creeke therabout, and destroy and kill as many of them as we could."21 Meanwhile, Pocahontas had told her brothers of her plan to marry Rolfe, and they had, in turn, told Powhatan that his favorite daughter was about to become the wife of an Englishman. According to Hamor, Powhatan signified that he found the match "acceptable" by giving his "sudden consent thereunto."22 Dale similarly noted the paramount chief's "approbation" of his daughter's union with Rolfe.23 The threat of an imminent attack and the long separation from his favorite daughter may have made Powhatan think that agreeing to the marriage was the only means of securing his daughter's safety and his people's future happiness, but "approbation" is probably too strong a word to describe Powhatan's acquiescence in the first official Anglo-Indian marriage in Virginia.

Pocahontas's wedding took place in the chapel in Jamestown on April 5, 1614, less than a year after she was kidnapped. Dale, Whitaker, Pocahontas's two brothers, and Opachisco, an old uncle who acted as her father's deputy, attended the ceremony. Powhatan did not travel to Jamestown to see his daughter married. Soon after the event, he vowed never again to set foot on an English plantation, perhaps fearing that he, too, might be the victim of kidnapping. As Hamor explained it, the union between Pocahontas and Rolfe accomplished what seven years of theft, murder, destruction, gifts, and negotiation could not: "ever since [the wedding] we have had friendly commerce and trade, not onely with *Powhatan* himselfe, but also with his subjects round about us."24 The exchange of Pocahontas from Powhatan to Rolfe, however grudgingly conceded by the paramount chief, had effectively brought about an end to the undeclared war between the men of both groups.

The "Peace of Pocahontas," as the temporary cessation of hostilities came to be known by the English, seemed to hold such promise that Dale attempted to arrange another marriage between a daughter of Powhatan and an Englishman. Six weeks after the Rolfe-Pocahontas wedding, he sent Ralph Hamor, accompanied by a former boy hostage as his interpreter, to visit Powhatan. According to Hamor, the paramount chief asked first after Thomas Dale, whom he referred to as his brother, and then after Pocahontas and his "unknowne sonne" John Rolfe. Hamor's reply, intended to set the stage for the request of another daughter, probably struck Powhatan as rude; Pocahontas was "so well content that she would not change her life to returne and live with him," Hamor claimed, to which Powhatan "laughed heartily, and said he was very glad of it."[25] Hamor then asked to be allowed to return to Jamestown with Powhatan's youngest daughter, a girl not yet twelve years old, so that she could become the wife of Dale and further cement the bond of love between the two peoples. Almost as an afterthought, Hamor mentioned Pocahontas's desire to see her sister. Powhatan refused Hamor's request respectfully and firmly, informing him that the girl was already married to a nearby *werowance*. Hamor's offer of beads, copper, and hatchets would not budge him; the chief informed the Englishman that he wished to retain the ability to see this beloved daughter, something he could not do if she went to live among the English.

We have very little direct evidence of Pocahontas's daily life in Virginia after her marriage to Rolfe, other than this plaintive secondhand request to see her sister. Dressed in Englishwomen's clothes, she likely experienced Virginia completely differently from the way she had as a young woman clad in moccasins and unconstricting deerskin aprons. Heat, dusty earth, and the need to make long treks through the woods raised nearly impossible obstacles to travel for a woman whose dress limited her physical mobility. Being the Indian wife of an Englishman and a recent convert to Christianity also made Pocahontas unusually vulnerable to scrutiny, not only by her English neighbors but also even by her own husband. From all accounts, she bore these changes in her life with a grace and poise that impressed those who met her. Thomas Dale, in particular, praised her for "liv[ing] civilly and lovingly" with Rolfe. So confident was Dale in her ability to act the part of the respectable English lady that when he made plans in 1614 to return to England in 1616, he had already decided that "she will goe into England with me."[26] It is clear from the historical record that most English people were happy with Pocahontas's transformation. What remains unknown is how Pocahontas herself felt about her new life as the wife of an Englishman.

Mother and Transatlantic Traveler

Sometime during 1615 or early 1616, Pocahontas gave birth to Thomas, her only known child. Thomas's birth was in many ways an auspicious event. The grandson of the paramount chief and the son of a prominent English settler, the younger Rolfe was well situated to make a life for himself in Virginia and to bring the Indians and the English closer together. Events conspired to keep him from his rich bicultural heritage, however. Dale's plan to return to England triumphantly with Pocahontas and Rolfe, with Thomas in tow, which finally came about in 1616, resulted in Pocahontas's son being raised as an Englishman, with only a secondhand knowledge of his mother's culture.

Unfortunately, we have few details of Thomas's birth. He was born to a mother whose people were reputed to give birth with little pain, yet she had, by the time he arrived, already been acculturated to many English ways. We have no way of knowing whether she had the assistance of other Indian women when she went into labor, or whether she was compelled, even during the most intense phase of pain, to continue her performance of Englishness. Whatever her experiences of the birth itself, Pocahontas prepared to travel with her son to his father's homeland.

It is possible only to speculate about the complex set of feelings that Pocahontas must have had as she sailed to England in the spring of 1616. English ships had announced the presence of the settlers off the Virginia coast in 1607. An English ship had carried away her friend, John Smith. It was aboard an English ship, moreover, that Pocahontas ultimately lost her freedom and began her cultural journey away from her father's people. Nothing in her own experiences of canoe travel on Virginia's rivers could have prepared her for the size and scale of an English ship and the duration of the journey. That she was also probably still nursing her son could only have added to the physical and emotional strain of the Atlantic crossing.

The ship arrived in Plymouth, England, in June 1616, carrying Pocahontas, Rolfe, their son, and ten or twelve Indian people, including Uttamatomakkin, Powhatan's councillor. Upon reaching London, Pocahontas and her retinue began a whirl of social activity. Many of the expenses of clothing, entertainment, and hobnobbing with London society were absorbed by the Virginia Company, which hoped to use Pocahontas's transformation to respectable Christian womanhood as an advertisement for investors. Although it is not clear whether Pocahontas brought significant new investment to the Company, she certainly gave its experiment in Virginia great publicity. Her grace and ease at social events impressed her genteel hosts, eventually earning her an invitation to the Twelfth Night masque in January 1617. Company investor John Chamberlain noted in his diary that "the Virginian woman, Poca-hontas, with her father-counsaillor, hath ben with the King and graciously used, and both she and her assistant well placed at the maske."[27] To be well placed at a masque performed for the king was to be given seating saved for a privileged favorite.

By inviting them to the masque, however, James I may have been treating Pocahontas and Uttamatomakkin to a special send-off. According to Chamberlain, plans had already been made for their return voyage to Virginia, much against Pocahontas's will. Either she or her son was already ill, or she was simply enjoying life in London too much to go back to her marginal and isolated place in the Jamestown settlement.

Some time before she left London, Pocahontas sat for a portrait that has become the basis for all the images we have of her at present. It reveals a well-dressed and genteel, if not aristocratic, woman whose collar, hat, and coat were all somewhat androgynous, as was the fashion among London gentlewomen during the late 1610s. Eyes that seem slightly almond shaped offer a clue that the subject might not be a typical Englishwoman, along with extra shading of the face in engravings of the portrait to indicate a ruddy complexion. Only the label clearly identifies the subject as Pocahontas, alias Matoaka, daughter of Powhatan. Of the near-complete transformation of the Powhatan woman suggested in the portrait, John Chamberlain commented snidely, "Here is a fine picture of no fayre Lady and yet with her tricking up and high stile and titles you might thincke her and her worshipfull husband to be somebody."[28] Better than a more persuasively English likeness, the engraving of Pocahontas reflected the Virginia Company's invest-ment in her gentility, representing her as an Indian indebted to the English for the gift of civility.

Pocahontas herself might have depicted the debt differently. Although we have only John Smith's 1624 version of his meeting with her during the final weeks of her stay, it suggests that she had finally become embittered about the way that English people cava-lierly put aside their promises and their obligations. Angered that Smith had not visited her during the whole of her stay in London, after having not seen her for eight years, Pocahontas refused at first to speak to him. Smith's initial and somewhat predictable reaction to her silence was mortification; apparently he feared that her unwillingness to speak might somehow reflect badly upon him, since he had attested to her fluency in English. When she did speak, according to Smith, it was to upbraid him for his rudeness and to remind him "of what courtesies shee had done."[29] She also reminded Smith that he had betrayed his promise to share with Powhatan all that he had and failed to live up to his obligations as Powhatan's adopted son.

Smith's version of his final interview with Pocahontas ended with their conflict over what to call each other. To Smith's dismay, the daughter of Powhatan insisted on calling him Father, despite his supposedly modest demurrals that he could never be a father to a king's daughter. Pocahontas reminded Smith that in Virginia he had been fearless (one senses that Smith embellished his account here) and questioned his fear of being called Father now that they were in England. She informed him that she still planned to call him Father and expected him to call her Child, "and so I will bee for ever and ever your Countrieman."[30]

Having lost her close affectionate bond with her Indian father as a consequence of her conversion to Englishness, Pocahontas aggressively claimed paternal affection and protection from the one man who behaved as bravely as herself when confronted with a strange new culture. Although Smith's version of this final interview was undoubtedly engineered to emphasize his own heroic qualities, her anger, her "well set countenance," and her demands upon him are all consistent with the responses of a woman who had not only lost her innocence through her interaction with the English but had also finally lost her faith in the Englishman for whom she had taken the greatest risks.[31]

By the time the winds were right for Dale's ship to return to Virginia, both Pocahontas and her son were too ill to travel. Left behind in Gravesend, she succumbed to a respiratory ailment in March 1617. She was probably just twenty years old when she died, yet during her short life she had been part of one of the most significant interactions in the Atlantic world. Changing her name, converting to Christianity, marrying an Englishman, bearing a biracial child, and crossing an ocean—all of these decisions, including those over which she had little choice, reflected her fearlessness about crossing cultural boundaries. Had she lived longer, perhaps there would have been less bloodshed in Virginia and more intermarriage. Perhaps, instead of killing Indians to gain access to land, a creative leader with the surname Rolfe might have crafted a more just policy for cooperative Indian and English land use. In light of her final conversation with Smith, however, one has to consider that Pocahontas's sense of betrayal might finally have tipped the scales, sending her back across the cultural frontier to rejoin her people.

Notes

1. John Smith, *A True Relation of Such Occurrences and Accidents of Noate as Hath Hapned in Virginia*, 1608, in *The Complete Works of Captain John Smith, 1580–1631*, ed. Philip L. Barbour, 3 vols. (Chapel Hill, NC, 1986), 1:93.

2. Ibid.

3. Ibid., 1:95. Smith's *Proceedings of the English Colonie in Virginia*, 1612, in *Complete Works*, 1:220–21, tells essentially the same story with more emphasis on Pocahontas's position as her father's favorite and on Smith's efforts to please her.

4. William Strachey, *The Historie of Travell into Virginia Britiania* (London, 1612), 62, 72.

5. Ibid., 113.

6. John Smith, *A Map of Virginia*, 1612, in *Complete Works*, 1:139.

7. John Smith, *The Generall Historie of Virginia*, 1624, in *Complete Works*, 2:151.

8. Ibid., 182–83.

9. Ibid., 183.

10. Ibid., 198.

11. Ibid., 199.

12. Strachey, *Historie of Travell*, 62.

13. Smith, *Proceedings*, in *Complete Works*, 1:274.

14. Ralph Hamor, *A True Discourse of the Present State of Virginia* (London, 1615; reprint ed., Richmond, VA, 1957), 4.

15. Ibid., 6.

16. Ibid., 53–54, Letter of Sir Thomas Dale.

17. Ibid., 59–60, Letter of Alexander Whitaker.

18. Ibid., 55, Letter of Sir Thomas Dale.

19. Ibid., 63, Letter of John Rolfe.

20. Ibid., 64.

21. Hamor, *True Discourse*, 10.

22. Ibid., 11.

23. Letter of Sir Thomas Dale, in *True Discourse*, 56.

24. Hamor, ibid., 11.

25. Ibid., 40.

26. Letter of Sir Thomas Dale, in *True Discourse*, 55.

27. John Chamberlain, *The Letters of John Chamberlain*, ed. Norman Egbert McClure, 2 vols. (Philadelphia, 1939), 2:50.

28. Ibid., 56–57.

29. Smith, *Generall Historie*, in *Complete Works*, 2:261.

30. Ibid.

31. Ibid.

Suggested Readings

Barbour, Philip. *Pocahontas and Her World*. Boston, 1970.

Hamor, Ralph. *A True Discourse of the Present State of Virginia*. London, 1615; reprint ed., Richmond, VA, 1957.

LeMay, J. A. Leo. *Did Pocahontas Save Captain John Smith?* Athens, GA, 1992.

Mossiker, Frances. *Pocahontas: The Life and Legend*. New York, 1976.

Robertson, Karen. "Pocahontas at the Masque," *Signs* 21 (Spring 1996): 551–83.

Smith, John. *The Complete Works of Captain John Smith, 1580–1631*, ed. Philip L. Barbour. 3 vols. Chapel Hill, NC, 1986.

Tilton, Robert. *Pocahontas: The Evolution of an American Narrative*. New York, 1994.

6

Daniel Clocker's Adventure
From Servant to Freeholder

Lois Green Carr

Daniel Clocker (1619?–1676) is an early American success. As a poor and illiterate young man, he came to newly founded Maryland and became head of a family, a landowner, and even an officeholder. In gauging the wisdom of Clocker's migration, Lois Green Carr measures his life against that of other poor people in both his native and adopted lands. By carefully comparing Daniel and his wife, Mary, with other immigrants, farmers, and householders of seventeenth-century Maryland, Carr gives us many insights into daily life on a frontier farm. Daniel's life may have been hard and simple, but he was fortunate. Having survived "seasoning," he prospered as a farmer and carpenter, but he seemed most at risk when accepting appointments that might be seen as marks of his success. English political convulsions not only affected Daniel and Mary directly, disrupting the entire colony and pro-viding excuses for incursions by brigands, but also offered opportunities to buy land and even to become a "Millitary Officer." Having chosen what proved to be the losing side in English politics, he never held a major post again, although he and his wife did escape direct retribution. Daniel may have felt restored in status by being named an executor of the will of a prominent officeholder in 1661, but he would end his life deeply in debt to the heir.

Lois Green Carr is the historian with Historic St. Mary's City Commission and adjunct professor of history at the University of Maryland at College Park. She has authored and coauthored numerous books and articles on the colonial Chesapeake region, including *Robert Cole's World: Agriculture and Society in Early Maryland* (1991).

In 1636 a young Englishman named Daniel Clocker arrived in Maryland, just two years after its first settlement. He began life there as a servant bound to Thomas Cornwaleys, one of the colony's Catholic leaders. Once Clocker's time of service was up, he worked for himself. He married, acquired land, raised a family, and died forty years after his arrival—a respected official in the government of St. Mary's City, the provincial capital.

Why did he come? Was the decision risky? What were his expectations? What was his new life like? And can he be thought of as a typical early Maryland settler?

We know nothing certain about Daniel Clocker before his arrival in Maryland, but he was probably born in Cumberland County in the north of England. His grandfather probably was Gosper Clocker, denoted "duchman," who had arrived in the area in the late 1560s as part of a small colony of Germans imported to work in newly opened copper mines. The register for Crosthwaite Parish marriages in Cumberland shows that Gosper was wed to Mabel Bulfill in 1568, and there are numerous references in the registers and other local records to Clockers from that time on. Probably Daniel was the son born to Hans and Bridgid Clocker of Parkside in Crosthwaite Parish and baptized on May 30, 1619. The Daniel who came to Maryland had an older brother John, and the baptismal register shows that Daniel, son of Hans, did also.

The Cumberland and Westmorland area (now known as Cumbria) is a rugged country of mountains, lakes, and fells. In the seventeenth century it was part of a border region considered savage by outsiders. To make a living, people mined and quarried, grazed sheep and cattle on the mountain pastures, and raised grains in the valleys, although on soils poor in comparison to those of southern England.

Daniel Clocker may have grown up in a family that combined mining with some self-sufficent husbandry, a common combination in the north, but he evidently left Cumberland to seek his fortune. In early seventeenth-century England, many Englishmen were on the move, often from the countryside to towns and ultimately to major urban centers. For a century, population had been growing, and opportunities to work were becoming scarce, with increasing unemployment and underemployment. In the north, furthermore, grain harvests could be meager; and in the more inaccessible mountain parts, the 1620s saw several years of famine. The particulars of how Daniel made up his mind to try his luck elsewhere, we do not know, but by 1636 he had reached a port—probably London—from which emigrants were sailing to the New World. He had a kinsman in London, Jasper (that is, Gosper) Clocker—possibly the youngest child of Gosper and Mabel—who lived in St. Botolph Without Aldgate Parish.

Little is known about the ways in which emigrants learned of opportunities to sail for America, especially at an early date. Daniel probably did not have America, much less Maryland, in mind when he left Cumberland, but he may well have been seeking adventure.

The Proprietor of Maryland, Lord Baltimore, published a series of pamphlets advertising his colony and its opportunities, but Clocker, who could not write his name, may not have been able to read; and, in any case, such literature was aimed at investors, not servants. Most news came to people by word of mouth. Perhaps Daniel looked for work as a laborer at the waterfront and heard talk of a ship sailing to "Virginia," as the whole Chesapeake region was then known. Or he may have worked at an inn where he overheard the conversation of travelers or where he caught the attention of a merchant looking for laborers for the colonies. The only facts we have are that, in 1636, Clocker arrived in Maryland; he had come to a barely established New World settlement where tobacco was quickly becoming a profitable product for export; and he became an indentured servant to Captain Thomas Cornwaleys, one of the major investors and first leaders of the new Province of Maryland.

Indentured servitude was the chief mechanism for transporting poor people in need of work across the ocean to the English North American colonies. In the seventeenth-century Chesapeake, 70 to 80 percent of immigrants came this way. Most were young men; the sex ratio was six men to one woman in the 1630s and three to one by midcentury and after. Passage cost about £6 sterling, which the servant repaid to his master by four or more years of labor. During these years, the master provided shelter, food, clothing, and medical care, and, when the servant's time was up, gave him or her freedom dues. In early Maryland, these dues were a new set of clothes, three barrels of Indian corn, and (for men) an axe and a hoe. The corn would feed the former servant for a year, with seed for the next year's crop. The axe and hoe were the basic tools needed for raising corn to eat and tobacco to sell. In all, here was food and equipment for making a start. The master, by that time, had received the several years of labor he needed to profit from the export of tobacco to a European market. In theory, at least, the indenture system benefited both the master and his servant.

The form of indenture that Lord Baltimore published in a recruiting pamphlet also specified fifty acres of land as a part of freedom dues, but Maryland records make clear that what was intended was a warrant for fifty acres. A warrant enabled its owner to locate a piece of land and pay for a survey and patent. Thus, land was not free, but it was inexpensive compared to the price of freehold land in England, where the great majority of people owned none. Because the master was due a one-hundred-acre warrant for paying the transportation costs of the servant, he was in effect giving his former servant one-half. It appears however, either that many indentures did not have such a clause or that many masters simply ignored it. Lord Baltimore soon found it expedient to reduce the warrant for a settler's transportation to fifty acres and would himself grant a fifty-acre warrant to any former servant who applied for it.

Lord Baltimore offered his settlers two lures. First was the land, which he granted to anyone who paid his own way or that of another. The use of "headrights" in return for land benefited the proprietor as well as the recipient, since it brought in settlers. Second, Maryland was to be a Catholic refuge, where Catholics would be free of the English penal laws that forced them to worship in secret, fined them for not taking Communion in the Church of England, and prevented them from holding public office. The Proprietor was not trying to create a Catholic colony; he knew that this would be impossible. A Protestant king of a Protestant country would never grant a charter to a Proprietor who would exclude Protestants. At any rate, Lord Baltimore needed all the settlers he could get, whatever their religion. What he offered was a place where all Christians could worship as they pleased; no man otherwise qualified could be excluded from public office for his religion; and no public taxes could be demanded for the support of any church.

What were the lures for Daniel Clocker? Would that we knew for sure. Was he simply hungry and without hope, basically in search of survival? Or did he believe that with hard work a better life awaited him? His later career tells us that he was not a Catholic. Indeed, religion probably did not enter into his decision, but the possibility of acquiring land once his servitude was over may have had a heady impact.

Did he consider the risks? They were greater than he probably knew. All newcomers to the Chesapeake fell ill during the first year. They had moved to a new disease environment. Although many of the illnesses were familiar, the strains of the diseases were different, and Englishmen had no immunities built up in childhood to these. In the very early years, 20 to 30 percent of new emigrants may have died in their "seasoning," the term settlers used to describe the experience in their first year. Furthermore, those who survived had life expectancies shorter than they would have had if they had stayed in England. Mean age at death for a seasoned man who arrived at age twenty was only forty-three years, and 70 percent would die before the age of fifty. Luckily for Clocker, he won this gamble. He died in his late fifties or early sixties.

Clocker arrived at Maryland's first settlement early in its third year. In March 1634, Lord Baltimore's son, Governor Leonard Calvert, had selected a beautiful spot on St. Mary's River, a small tributary of the Potomac River just above where it joins the Chesapeake Bay. Here had been a village of the Yaocomico Indians, who were ready to abandon it. They lived in fear of the fierce

Susquehannock Indians, who lived along the Susquehanna River north of the bay. The spot was ideal. Soils were excellent, fields were already cleared, and timber and fresh water were ample. The Yaocomico sold their village to Governor Calvert for trade goods, and by the time Clocker arrived, all of them had moved away.

When Clocker disembarked, the fort built in 1634 was still in use. Leonard Calvert described it as "a pallizado [palisade] of one hundred and twentie yarde square, with fower flankes [four flanks, or sides], we have mounted one peece of ordnance [a cannon], and placed six murderers [small cannon or mortars] in parts most convenient."[1] About 140 people had occupied the fort in 1634 and about 60 had arrived the next year. If we estimate that 20 percent of them had died by 1636, Clocker joined a settlement of about 160 people, mostly young servant men. Doubtless many still lived in the fort, but others had probably built cabins nearby. The settlers were growing tobacco, Indian corn, beans, and peas in the nearby fields, and some cabbages and other garden crops as well.

Lord Baltimore, who remained in England to defend his charter, had ordered that his first settlers lay out a town and expected them to build their houses there. To Europeans, towns were necessary to civilization. However, despite the Proprietor's instructions, even the cluster of settlement around the fort was about to end. The handful of major investors were eager to start developing the land that they were entitled to claim, and most other colonists were still indentured servants who would follow their masters. Lord Baltimore recognized that more incentive would be needed to develop town properties. In 1636 he ordered that for the next two years, the first adventurers, in addition to the land grants he had already offered, could have ten acres of Town Lands on the fields of St. Mary's for each person they transported. Later adventurers could have five acres per person. The investors responded, but the result was not a village. By 1641 there were about eleven houses spread out over some fifteen hundred acres, not all of it yet surveyed. Another twenty-five years would pass before even a hamlet, such as Daniel had known at home, came into being on the Town Lands.

Daniel must have blessed his good luck for arriving safely, but he undoubtedly was soon sick during his seasoning period. Probably he caught malaria early, an intermittent disease that stayed with him the rest of his life. He may also have suffered dysentery, another common ailment, or typhoid, or typhus. Once he was well, he was put to hard work. Cornwaleys had been using his servants to build the fort, erect temporary housing for settlers, and raise tobacco. Daniel doubtless helped both in the fields and on various construction projects, where he gained experience in planting and in carpentry that was to prove useful in later life.

Clocker's status as a servant was different from what he had likely experienced in England. There, boys and girls customarily left home after age fourteen to work in the households of others until they could marry and establish their own. Some were apprenticed for several years to learn a trade, but most worked as servants in husbandry on yearly contracts, giving them chances to escape harsh or incompatible masters. By contrast, in Maryland, Clocker's service to Cornwaleys was payment for his ocean passage. He began with a debt to his master. Consequently, his contracted term was much longer; and, even more important, his master could sell him without his consent. He could not choose a master. Furthermore, penalties for running away could be severe. Runaway servants—most were caught or returned on their own, if they did not perish—had to pay extra days of service for each day they were absent. Some unhappy Chesapeake indentured servants called their circumstances slavery.

Nevertheless, Maryland custom, later established in law, gave Clocker and his fellow servants important protections. They could complain to the courts if food, clothing, shelter, or medical care was insufficient, or if beatings for correction had resulted in serious injury. The courts would order masters to remedy deficiencies and forbid punishment of servants for bringing complaints. Early court records are missing that might show whether Daniel Clocker had occasion for complaint against Cornwaleys, and, if so, what the outcome was; but we know that, on the whole, the system worked. From the standpoint of colony leaders, the shortage of labor was too severe to risk developing a reputation for Maryland as a place that poor Englishmen should avoid. From the standpoint of the servant, he or she could seek redress for serious neglect or mistreatment and could look forward to being free in a society that—for several decades, at least—offered real opportunities, provided that early death did not intervene.

Living conditions were also new to Clocker. For one thing, he had to adjust to a new climate. Winters were colder and summers much hotter than in England. For another, he had to accept new foods. English settlers could not grow wheat, the staple of their diet at home. Growing wheat required plowing the ground; and in the Chesapeake, for many decades, plowing was usually impractical. The root systems of trees in forests never before cleared took too long to dig out. Settlers adopted Indian agriculture, which produced Maize, or Indian corn. They learned how to kill the trees by girdling them so that the sap could not rise. When the leaves fell off, the sun reached the ground, and laborers could then use a hoe to make hills of earth beneath the branches and plant kernels of corn. The yield was extraordinary to English eyes; the productivity per acre was twice that of wheat. Furthermore, once the land was ready, the crop was simple to produce. In about four days, and armed only with a hoe, a man could make hills and plant enough seed to feed himself for a year. He would need to spend another few days here and there, weeding until the maize was high enough to shade out competing plants, but otherwise the crop required little attention until the planter was ready to harvest it. This was in many ways an ideal food crop.

Daniel may have missed English bread and at first disliked corn bread and corn mush, or hominy. Moreover, he probably found the preparation of the kernels for making them edible an onerous task. Of necessity, in the absence of flour mills, settlers used the Indian method of preparation, soaking the kernels for several hours to soften the shell a little and then pounding them in a mortar with a pestle. After sifting, the cook used the fine grains to make bread and boiled the coarse grains for several hours to make hominy. It took ten minutes to pound a cup, and the ration per man was about four and one-half cups per day, or nearly an hour of pounding. Some settlers complained that they could not digest the bread or the hominy. However, most adjusted quickly to maize, which continued as a staple of the Maryland diet long after wheat or rye or barley became a practical alternative.

Maize has one disadvantage, however. It is not so complete in nutrients as wheat or rye or barley. It is lacking in niacin, an essential element, and a diet confined to maize brings on a debilitating disease, pellagra, with painful sores and severe gastritis. The Indians avoided this illness by supplementing their corn with beans and peas, which they grew among the corn stalks, and by hunting for meat and fish. The English did the same.

In consequence, Daniel ate some foods not so easily procured in England. In 1636 little domestic livestock was as yet on hand at St. Mary's, but deer, small mammals, and birds were abundant, oyster beds lined the shores of the St. Mary's River, and fish of many kinds were easily caught. Daniel Clocker probably had the first venison, the first oysters, the first sturgeon, perhaps the first wild duck or goose that he had ever eaten. Archaeologists working on seventeenth-century Chesapeake sites have found ample evidence of such consumption. Cornwaleys doubtless supplied all his servants from such sources, or they would have become too weak to work. Clocker may have eaten better than he ever had in England.

More than English bread, Clocker may have missed the beer and cider he was used to drinking. Barley for English beer could not easily be grown in unplowed land, and corn did not make good beer. While the settlers brought seeds for planting fruit trees, the few existing orchards in 1636 were not yet producing: peaches required three years and apple trees seven before they bore fruit. Local cider would soon be generally available, both as a beverage and as an important source of nutrition, but for the moment colonists drank water. Luckily they had abundant springs on the Town Lands and nearby.

Also different from England, and far less satisfactory than the food and drink, was the housing, and not just to servants like Clocker. Houses were made of wood and the "earthfast" framing posts were not set on foundations but put into the ground, where moisture and termites soon attacked them. Many houses were very small one-room structures with earthen floors, and probably few were more than one story high, with a loft above. In some, smoke from the fire escaped from a hole in the roof, although most house-holders probably built chimneys of wattle and daub as soon as possible. All were covered by rived clapboard siding and roofing, easily penetrated by wind and rain. Such buildings rotted quickly, requiring major repairs within about fifteen years. By contrast, English houses, put on foundations of stone or brick, constructed of timber filled in with wattle and daub, and covered with thatched roofs, were more permanent and in every way more comfortable: much warmer and drier and usually larger. However, travelers' descriptions, builders' contracts, and archaeological excavations tell us that over the whole seventeenth century, most Chesapeake settlers continued to live in such impermanent leaky structures, although as time went on, they were improved with extra rooms and occasionally a brick chimney. Such houses were built quickly and inexpensively in a labor-short society.

Furnishings for the early houses were minimal. Twenty-six colonial estate inventories from 1638 to 1642 that survive show that people slept on the floor on tickings filled with flock and used wool blankets or rugs for a covering. Masters might have sheets, but most buildings were too small and crowded to permit bedsteads, which could not be rolled away during the day. Only two inventories indicate their presence. Nor were tables or chairs usually listed; such items appear in only five inventories. People sat on chests or brought in stumps or perhaps simply squatted, and large chests doubled as beds and tables. In winter, these quarters must have been dark unless the window shutters were open, in which case the rooms were undoubtedly very cold. If Daniel Clocker lived in Cornwaleys's house, he may have been more comfortable than most settlers, but his master very likely crowded his many servants into separate housing and provided few furnishings.

Finally, Clocker had to learn a whole new system of husbandry organized around tobacco and corn. Tobacco had two characteristics that dominated all planter decisions. First, it required a great deal of land. It was a crop so demanding of nutrients that the planter had to move to new land after three years. He could grow corn on the old land for another three or four years, since the deeper root systems of corn tapped a new level of nutrients, but thereafter—in the absence of manuring, which gave tobacco smoke an unpleasant aroma and taste—the land had to lie fallow for twenty years. In any one year, the planter did not use much of his land. One worker could handle only two to three acres in tobacco plants, plus two acres in corn that custom and then law required to ensure the colony's subsistence. However, over the long term, a tobacco planter needed twenty acres per hand if he was not to deplete his land. Since he also needed land for timber and firewood and for livestock to range over, contemporaries considered fifty acres the minimum acreage for a farm.

Second, tobacco was a very labor-intensive crop, and one that required careful tending and observation nearly year-round. Work began in February with clearing and planting a small tobacco seedbed. It ended in December with packing the leaf in casks for shipping to overseas markets. In between were months of hoeing unplowed ground into hills; planting corn and transplanting tobacco seedlings; weeding, deworming, and pruning the tobacco; and cutting the crop and hanging it to dry in the tobacco barn. Clocker and his fellow servants needed to learn from their overseer how to judge when the leaf was ripe for cutting, how to hang it to ensure proper drying, and how to judge when it was ready to be stripped and packed. They hoped one day to be planters themselves, and mistakes would spoil the crop.

Taking care of livestock was a daily routine for English farmers that was missing from Clocker's new life. In Maryland, cattle and hogs ranged for their food in the forest, and planters did not stable or feed them much even in winter. To feed their cattle, planters would have had to raise corn beyond what they needed for their own subsistence, and tight schedules for hilling and planting in the spring meant that hills for more corn would mean fewer for the cash crop. Since the animals had to fend for themselves, planters fenced in their crops, not their livestock—another difference from English practices, and one that discouraged the collection of manure.

Throughout the seventeenth century, visiting Englishmen were dismayed at what seemed to them inefficiency and neglect in the Chesapeake: cattle running loose, unstabled and starving in winter; houses leaky and rotting; crops unmanured; old fields full of dead stumps and weeds and looking forsaken, although as the land renewed itself, it would produce good timber. The English farmer used oxen or horses to plow his land and fertilized it with manure from his animals, making long-term fallows unneeded. He found or made grass pasture for his cattle and, as necessary, stabled and fed them in winter. His wife or his dairymaid milked his cows and made butter and cheese, often to sell. What English critics did not understand were the constraints that faced colonists in the Chesapeake. Unlike England, land in the Chesapeake was plentiful and cheap, whereas labor was scarce and expensive. Virgin forest provided ample timber but made plowing and hence production of English grains impractical. At the same time, these woodlands supplied sufficient forage for animals nearly the year-round. A long-fallow agriculture, range-fed cattle, and earthfast clapboard houses that could be quickly constructed were efficient solutions to new circumstances.

By 1640, Clocker was free of his indenture. What were his choices then? He was a laborer in a labor-short economy, where wages were high. He could contract to serve Cornwaleys or another employer for wages. This arrangement would probably provide him with room, board, and laundry but would deprive him of much autonomy. His master would dictate his activities and have power to discipline him as a member of the household, or Clocker could persuade a planter to lease him land on which he could set up his own household and plant his own crops, perhaps paying part of his rent with labor. These circumstances would require him to supply his own housekeeping, grow his own food, and perhaps even build himself a house to live in and a tobacco barn for his crop. If he had to build housing, he would pay no rent for his land during the first year or two, but even so, the capital necessary to undertake such an arrangement was most likely not at hand for a newly freed servant, unless he could get credit from his landlord. Finally, he could use the headright that Cornwaleys owed him to take up a fifty-acre tract and become not just a householder, but a landowner. This last option was the least available as a first step. To take up land, he had to pay a surveyor and a clerk for his survey and patent. These additional costs required capital or credit that a newly freed servant usually did not have.

What Clocker decided is unknown. Probably he found another former servant to be his "mate" in establishing a tenancy on Cornwaleys's land. Besides the rent the captain charged—perhaps a third of the tobacco crop—his return was in the improvements that Clocker and his mate made in housing, fencing, and in planting and caring for the orchard always required in a lease. Once Clocker moved on, Cornwaleys could rent or sell the property at a higher price than unimproved land would bring. Such development leases, usually made for seven years, benefited both landlord and tenant in a newly settled colony.

As a freeman, Clocker was entitled to vote for a representative in the Maryland Assembly, or, if all freeman were called to attend, to cast his vote for any legislation the Assembly considered. Lord

Baltimore's charter for Maryland gave the Proprietor vast powers to create his own government and raise armies to defend his province, with of course, leadership in the hands of a few. But the charter also provided a basic protection for his settlers: he could not make laws without "the Advice, Assent, and Approbation of the Free-Men. . . . Or of the great Part of them, or of their Delegates or Deputies."2 Several times before 1650, all freemen were called to the Assembly and were permitted to vote for delegates. There were as yet no property requirements for the vote in law or custom, a situation without precedent in England. In such a small community, so isolated from its home base, the cooperation of everyone was essential. Actually, however, attending the Assembly could be time consuming and expensive, especially for poor men. Rather than attend, many freemen gave their proxies to one of the colony leaders, and, in March 1642, so did Daniel Clocker.

The next stage in Clocker's life was marriage to Mary Lawne Courtney. She had arrived in 1638, at age twenty-four, as a servant indentured to Margaret Brent, a prominent Catholic. However, Mary Lawne had not remained a servant long in this small, woman-short society. In 1639, James Courtney, a free immigrant, had purchased her time and married her. By early 1643, she was a widow with a son, Thomas, at most a year old. Sometime in 1645 or very early 1646, she married Daniel Clocker.

Marriage gave Daniel new status. He was now truly head of a family, a position that sharing with a partner, if he had had one, did not give him. As head, he was held responsible for the welfare and behavior of his wife and children and any other household members. The community expected him to keep "good order," and the law allowed him to correct any of his charges with physical punishment, provided that any stick used in a beating was no thicker than a man's finger at its thicker end. Beating even his wife was permissible. Under English common law, he owned whatever property Mary brought to the marriage and he was in a position to control the assets of her child. As a married woman, Mary could not make a contract; her husband had to act for her. On the other hand, he owed her maintenance and a share of his estate if he died before she did. Mary had had independence as a widow, but in this land three thousand miles away from any English kin, she had needed a husband more.

Still, Mary's position was not so subordinate in reality as this description would suggest. Running a household, especially once there were children and perhaps servants, was necessarily a team effort. Mary pounded the corn, a daily two-hour task just for Daniel, herself, and little Thomas, and a task that grew with the family, although eventually the children would help out. As well as keeping house and preparing meals, she gathered wild greens and berries, grew and administered medicinal herbs, raised cabbages, onions, and sweet potatoes, picked and dried apples or peaches from the orchard (once Daniel had one), and milked the cows. She watched the children when they were small and trained her daughters in housewifery as they grew older. When necessary, she assisted in the fields, perhaps watering or weeding the tobacco seedlings, or transplanting them into the hills, or hoeing weeds. All these activities contributed vitally to the family economy. A man without a wife was handicapped, unless he had a daughter old enough to take her mother's place. In this woman-short society, wives had an especially high value. If husband and wife disagreed, the husband was likely to prevail, but family peace and efficiency required many shared decisions.

The Clockers began life together in troubled times for the Maryland colony. In 1642 civil war had broken out in England between King Charles I and Parliament, and early in 1645 the conflict reached Maryland. Richard Ingle, a ship captain who had been trading in Maryland and Virginia for tobacco, used letters of marque from Parliament—authorization to seize enemy ships—to attack the St. Mary's settlement. His excuse was that Maryland Catholics supported the king, as most Catholics in England did. He took the colony completely by surprise. Governor Leonard Calvert fled to Virginia. Ingle made other leaders and at least two Jesuit priests his prisoners, and his men pillaged at will with the help of disaffected Protestant settlers. He then returned to England, taking his prisoners with him and leaving the colony without a government. Calvert did not reestablish proprietary authority until nearly two years later, with the help of mercenaries from Virginia.

Calvert left a colony with five hundred or more inhabitants; he returned to one with perhaps a hundred, fewer than had come in the first expedition in 1634. The years of his absence were later called the "time of troubles." After Ingle left, unchecked looting evidently continued for several months. Mary Courtney lost a cow during, in her words, the "time of the Plunder."[3] In search of stability, many Maryland settlers pulled up stakes and moved across the Potomac River to an as-yet unsettled part of Virginia.

The Clockers did not go, and their decision was undoubtedly wise. Once Lord Baltimore's government was reestablished, new settlers rapidly piled into Maryland, and once more it was a place where a planter could work toward success. Clocker must have continued to raise corn and tobacco, and his skills as a carpenter were in some demand. By 1650 he was ready to pay the costs of acquiring freehold land.

In 1650 and 1651, Clocker obtained 150 acres, 100 of which he patented, using his and Mary's service rights. This land on the Chesapeake Bay, about seven miles east of the Town Lands, he called Daniel Clocker's Hould. About the same time, he also purchased a 50-acre Town Land tract called St. Andrews from Margaret and Mary Brent—Mary Clocker's former mistresses—who were moving to Virginia. Daniel already may have been leasing the land from the sisters, and, if so, he must have jumped at the opportunity to buy it. The work that he and Mary had already put into building a farm there would spare them the labor of building anew.

The Clockers lived at St. Andrews for the rest of their lives. They kept Clocker's Hould but renamed it Clocker's Marsh, which suggests that the tract was more valuable for raising livestock than for growing tobacco. They may have let cattle graze there instead of trying to farm it. By 1659, Daniel had also acquired a 50-acre tract just across St. Andrews Creek, called Clark's Freehold. By that time he owned 200 acres in all, enough to provide an inheritance for several children.

By 1661 the Clockers had five living children. They are named in a gift of cattle that Clocker made to them that year. Elizabeth had been born in 1646, Daniel Jr. in 1648, and Mary in 1650. Like most mothers in preindustrial times, Mary Clocker nursed her babies, and the contraceptive effect of nursing (it was thought) meant that a new pregnancy was not so likely until the baby was weaned, shortly after his or her first birthday. Hence, children often arrived about two years apart, as Mary Clocker's did. However, during the 1650s, Mary bore only two children who were still alive in 1661, John and Catheryn. Perhaps she had become less fertile; in 1659 she was forty-five. Or she may have had miscarriages or carried to term two or three other children who died in infancy. Child mortality was very high everywhere in the seventeenth century. In Maryland, 45 to 55 percent of children born did not survive to adulthood, and most of these died before the age of four. Daniel Jr. and Mary—and Rebecca, probably on the way but not yet born when the gift was made—were to live to marry and establish their own families, but Elizabeth, John, Catheryn and perhaps several other Clocker children did not.

The Clockers raised and sold tobacco, but they also gained income from other sources. They were lucky, since an unusually substantial portion of immigrants in the late 1640s to the mid-1660s came in family groups. Unlike newly arrived servants, who would move into already established households, families needed dwelling houses, tobacco barns, and livestock. Daniel began to appear in records as "Daniel Clocker, carpenter," especially after his stepson and sons had reached the age when they could really help in the fields. Furthermore, Mary had skills as a dairymaid, an occupation confined to women, and a market grew among her new neighbors for butter and cheese when she had time to produce them. In addition, once the Clockers had well-established herds of cattle and pigs, they could sell pregnant cows and sows to households just starting out. The sale of a cow with her calf supplemented income from tobacco, adding the value of more than half a tobacco crop from the late 1640s until the mid-1650s and between one-third and one-half thereafter. And Mary was also the local midwife. A court record in 1659 shows that in one difficult case she was owed 200 pounds of tobacco, at that time nearly one-fifth of a year's crop.

What the Clockers could not do was purchase necessary manufactures locally. All such goods were imported from England, a situation that prevailed during most of the seventeenth century. There was work for carpenters to build houses, coopers to make casks for the tobacco crop, and tailors to make clothing, but other crafts did not flourish. It was simply more cost efficient for settlers to import cloth, metal and leather manufactures, and other products in return for tobacco.

Over these years, Daniel Clocker appeared in the records from time to time as a participant in community affairs and government, although the absence of the county court records limits the amount and variety of information. Appointed by the provincial court, which acted as a probate court, he appraised the estates of deceased neighbors to establish the value of their assets. This practice protected both creditors and heirs or legatees of the deceased. As early as 1648 he was a petit juror at the provincial court, and in 1653 he was part of a provincial court grand jury that investigated a murder. Clearly, he was establishing himself as a reliable neighbor and citizen.

Mary Clocker was also making her mark in the community. Ordinarily, women played no role in public affairs, but midwives were important in policing sexual misconduct. When women bore bastard children, the courts wanted to know who the father was, if only to ensure that he would support the child, who might otherwise need public relief. It was customary for the midwife to interrogate the mother while in labor as the surest route to a truthful answer. No one believed that women in the throes of childbirth and hence in danger of immediate death would dare to lie. In 1651, Mary delivered a child of Susan Warren, who swore in "the time of her delivery" that Captain William Mitchell, briefly a member of the council, had fathered the child and, early in the pregnancy, had given her a "physick" to destroy it.[4] Mary also testified that the child was born dead but had reached full term. Her testimony saved both parents from prosecution for infanticide, although not for fornication on Warren's part and adultery and attempted abortion on Mitchell's. For these offenses, the mother was whipped and Mitchell was dismissed from office and heavily fined.

Although Maryland grew rapidly during the late 1640s and 1650s, despite its collapse during Ingle's Rebellion, Lord Baltimore faced political attacks on his charter in Parliament and challenges to his authority in Maryland. Leonard Calvert's sudden death in 1647 gave him the opportunity to appoint a Protestant governor. He selected William Stone, a planter-merchant from Virginia's Eastern Shore, who had excellent contacts with Protestant merchants in London whose support the Proprietor was seeking. In addition, Lord Baltimore lured to Maryland a group of radical Protestants who were being persecuted in Virginia, promising them religious toleration. In preparation for their arrival late in 1649, he wrote, and the Maryland Assembly passed, the colony's famous Act Concerning Religion, which granted freedom of conscience in religion to all Trinitarian Christians. He hoped that this statute would serve several purposes: protect Maryland Catholics, who were a minority in his colony and about to become even more so; reassure the incoming Virginians; and make clear to Parliament, dominated by Protestant dissenters, that English Protestants of all but the most radical persuasions were welcome in Maryland.

These strategies did not prevent disaster in the 1650s. Parliamentary commissioners, sent to reduce Virginia, which had supported Charles I during the English Civil War, extended their mission to Maryland. In 1654 they ousted Stone and appointed several leaders of the radical Protestant immigration to carry on the Maryland government. Armed confrontation followed in which Stone and his men suffered total defeat. But in England, Oliver Cromwell, by then the Lord Protector, did not confirm the actions of commissioners or the government that they had established in Maryland, but recommended instead a negotiated settlement. Consequently, in 1657, Lord Baltimore regained control of his province.

These events had a major impact on Daniel Clocker. On April 24, 1655, the new Protestant government appointed him one of seven justices of the peace for St. Mary's County. Yet he was a small landholder of very humble origins who could not write his name, had no important connections, and showed no signs that he would ever be wealthy. To be sure, probably none of the others appointed met the English standard, which generally confined officeholding at this level to the landed gentry. Few Maryland settlers of the 1650s could meet English norms for pedigree, wealth, and education. Of Clocker's colleagues on the bench from 1655 to 1658, all owned substantial amounts of land, but at least two had come to Maryland as servants, and three could not write. Although at least three were merchants as well as planters, only one, the planter-merchant Captain Robert Slye, the chief justice, had considerable wealth.

In England, leaders among the gentry would have questioned

whether men not born to rule could successfully exercise authority. In Maryland, there was no alternative. Clocker and his colleagues were a mixture of people not unlike those who became justices of the peace in Maryland counties across the rest of the seventeenth century. When possible, the governor and council, who made these appointments, selected literate men of birth and/or large estate, but when they were not available, they were obliged to appoint men of lesser education and status. Despite lowly origins, such justices generally were successful in maintaining order, and were quickly replaced if they were not. Men sought the honor and the power and endeavoured to measure up to the office's requirements.

The reestablished proprietary government did not reappoint Daniel Clocker as county court justice when it issued its new county commissions early in 1658. Two years later, however, he had another chance at a high-status position when Lord Baltimore's new governor, Josias Fendall, betrayed his trust. In late February 1660, Fendall called a meeting of the Assembly, not at St. Mary's, but twenty miles away at St. Clement's Manor. This assembly seems to have declared an end to proprietary rule and tried to establish a commonwealth, with Fendall as its head. Under this regime, Daniel Clocker was made one of the "Millitary Officers."[5]

Clocker's tenure as an officer was brief. Unbeknown to members of the Assembly, who probably hoped for approval in England from Richard Cromwell's protectorate (Oliver's son and successor), Charles II was assuming the English throne. In late June, when royal authority was secure, Lord Baltimore procured from the king an order for "all Magistrats and Officers, and all other [of] his Majesties loyall Subjects" in Maryland and Virginia to assist in the reestablishment of proprietary government.[6] Fendall was at first defiant, but when the new governor, Philip Calvert, Lord Baltimore's half brother, issued the royal order, all the participants in this "pigmie Rebellion" submitted.[7] They had lost the gamble of support from England and knew that now they could only seek mercy. The governor immediately proclaimed Lord Baltimore's pardon for all but the ringleaders, and Daniel Clocker successfully made his peace with his august neighbor. Calvert even put one of Fendall's principal henchmen, John Hatch, into Clocker's custody until Hatch could find bondsmen to guarantee his appearance for trial in the provincial court.

The surviving records, for the most part, provide only snippets of information, barely enough to construct the skeleton of Daniel and Mary Clocker's lives, and one longs for something that reveals their personalities. Luckily, a court case concerning Mary Clocker provides some insight. In 1659 she was indicted, tried, and sentenced to be hanged—although later pardoned—as an accessory to the theft of

£50 worth of items from merchant Simon Overzee. The loot included kerchiefs, quoifs (coifs, or caps), gorgets (collars), and smocks, all of Flanders lace. The depositions reveal that Mary Clocker had been midwife to Mrs. Overzee, who had died in childbirth while her husband was absent from home. They conjure up a grisly picture of Mrs. Overzee lying in her coffin, while Mary Clocker, who was nursing the child, and a certain Mary Williams obtained the keys to a huge Dutch trunk and rifled it. The two women stuffed the goods under their skirts and in pillowcases and carried them home. Mary Williams's husband took fright and hid some of the loot in a tree, where two small children found it.

Each woman accused the other, but Mary Clocker appears to have done the planning. In Mary Williams's words, Mary Clocker urged "her to itt Saying hang him, If we doe not doe it wee shall never have anything for our paynes & I Mary Williams made answere how can I doe it? I have not the Keyes, and Mary Clocker replyed you are to make a pudding, goe fetch the Keys of Mr Chandler to take Spices, and then you may doe itt." She did, and they did, and yet why? They could not use or sell such finery. According to Mary Williams, when she argued this point, her accomplice answered, "Hang . . . him rather than ever hee shall have them, I will burne them, & further sayd shee would bury them in a Case in the Grownd."[8] Daniel had only shortly before enjoyed his brief honors as a justice of the peace. Perhaps Mary Clocker had allowed herself to dream that one day she would be dressed in laces. In any event, she clearly was a woman of strong personality, able to influence and lead others but subject to impulsive behavior that could cloud her judgment.

The 1660s and 1670s were at last years of peaceful growth in Maryland, and the Clockers prospered. Although Daniel never again held a major office or achieved the title "Mr.," he had clearly survived the years of turmoil with an enhanced standing in his community. He appears in the records of the provincial court more frequently than earlier, taking his turn on juries, as an appraiser of dead men's estates, and in county offices such as overseer of the highways. He stood bond for neighbors even when large sums were required.

Over these years, the Town Lands began to change. As the colony's population grew, St. Mary's needed public buildings and inns for courts and assemblies and to serve people who came to do business at the capital. At last, a small village began to emerge about a mile from the Clockers' home. In 1669, to promote this development, Governor Charles Calvert chartered St. Mary's City as an area of one mile square round and about this cluster.

The chartering of the "city" brought Clocker his last position of honor: membership on its common council. Daniel did not thereby become a magistrate again; only the aldermen were magistrates. But the councillors voted on city bylaws and participated in the yearly selection of the mayor from among the aldermen and in replacements of these officers. To be a member of the common council was a position of some responsibility.

Unfortunately, town development was slow. The economic base lay solely in the business of government. When courts and assemblies were functioning, the village of the 1670s was a very crowded place, but at other times it probably had at most eleven households. Nevertheless, the appearance of a village offered Clocker a new opportunity. He watched as Alderman Garrett Van Sweringen, the lawyer Robert Ridgely, and other innkeepers attracted customers to their ordinaries, as inns were called. He evidently had made up his mind to join them when, in 1675, he took up a city lot and built a house.

Death intervened before Clocker had brought this project to completion. He wrote his will on February 4, 1676, and was dead eight days later. If he was the son of Hans and Bridgid Clocker, then he was fifty-six years of age. Mary had died before him, and presumably so had at least three children. In his will, he mentioned only three: Daniel Clocker Jr., age about twenty-eight; Rebecca Clocker, probably age fifteen and not yet married; and Mary Clocker Watts, wife of Peter Watts. He also left two grandchildren, Peter and Mary Watts. He was luckier than most seventeenth-century immigrants—very few survived long enough to see their grandchildren.

Clocker knew that he was heavily in debt and had left instructions in his will to sell land if necessary to pay his obligations. What was left was to be divided between his son Daniel and his daughter Rebecca, who were also to share what remained of his movable property once his debts were paid. Doubtless he had given his daughter Mary her portion when she married, but he left her two children a cow each.

Clocker's assets in movable property, or personalty, came to 17,026 pounds of tobacco, or about £71 sterling. This sum was well above the £50 sterling that was the median value of personalty in Maryland probated estates at this time. In land, he possessed 230 acres—he had added 30 acres adjacent to Clark's Freehold in 1674—plus the city lot and house. The city property had to be sold to pay debts, but the assets that remained left his children well established in the yeomanry of St. Mary's County.

Clocker's inventory demonstrates the progress in material comfort that middling planters had achieved since the first days of settlement. Clocker had three bedsteads with curtains, a large table with a bench, three chairs, and two small tables. He also had bedsheets and table linens. There was even a carpet for the large table—perhaps intended for the projected ordinary—and a "smoothing" iron for pressing linen and clothes. All this equipment had been missing from the great majority of households in the 1630s, regardless of wealth or status, but by the 1670s most inventories valued at more than £50 had some or most of these items. Of course, the poor lived more primitively; and, in general, the standard of material life across all levels of colonial wealth was still lower than it was in England.

A large part of Clocker's debt had resulted from his guardianship of Anne Price. In 1661, Daniel had probably been especially gratified when Colonel John Price, a member of the council, named him one of four executors of his will. Price, an illiterate man of humble origins, had arrived in Maryland as a freeman in 1636; the two men had known each other over many years. Daniel and his considerably richer coexecutors administered the estate and acted as guardians to Anne, age about three at her father's death. Once the debts were paid, the guardians divided Price's movable estate into four parts, each taking one-quarter, mostly in livestock. In 1674, Anne married Richard Hatton, the younger brother of William Hatton, another of her guardians, and the couple at once demanded her inheritance. The time had come for Daniel to pay to Anne the share of her property that he had held for a decade. Unfortunately, a severe drought that year had had a devastating effect on livestock and seems to have decimated Anne's inheritance. When Clocker's estate was accounted early in 1677, what he owed Anne was nearly half the total of his indebtedness.

These events demonstrate one attempt to cope with a major problem in early seventeenth-century Maryland society. Kin networks were undeveloped, and life expectancy was so short that children lost their parents at an early age. Price and his wife, who had predeceased him, had no kin in the Chesapeake area to take responsibility for his orphaned daughter, and he had to rely on friends to look after her welfare. Beginning in 1663, Maryland laws began to establish procedures for protecting such children, but the oversight provided did not always supply what was needed if no kin were at hand to complain. Fortunately, Price picked responsible guardians. Clocker and his colleagues had the benefit of the estate during Anne's minority, but by law they also had to absorb any losses and return to her, either in kind or in value, the property that her father had left her. This charge they carried out. Whether, overall, any of the four enjoyed gains we do not know, but Clocker must have had losses, given the large debt to Anne that appears in his account. Sadly, both Richard and Anne were dead within a few days of Clocker. William Hatton became executor of Richard Hatton's will, guardian of his infant son, Richard, and responsible for little Richard's property and education. It was William who collected from Clocker's estate what was due to Anne. The cycle of care and risk had begun again. By contrast, the Clocker children were lucky. Thanks to their father's longevity, they escaped this cycle.

Daniel Clocker had arrived in Maryland with nothing but the willingness and capacity to work with his hands; he died a well-respected landowner who had served in a position of power, albeit briefly. Was his career typical of seventeenth-century indentured servants in Maryland, or did he have exceptional good luck?

The answer to such a question requires a carefully designed analysis of servant careers. In 1973, a study of all identifiable male servants who had entered Maryland before the end of 1642 found 275 men. Of these, 117—more than 40 percent—disappeared from the records before becoming freemen. Probably the great majority had died before completing their terms, although proof of their fate remains for only 14. Of the 158 others, 15 died, and 27 left Maryland before they had been free for ten years. Another 25 left only a fleeting reference in the records. Presumably they, too, died or moved on. Only 92 lived in Maryland for ten years or more after freedom. But of these 92, 79 to 81, or more than 90 percent, acquired land. In addition, at least 11 of the 27 known to have moved away became landowners in Virginia. There was also political opportunity. Thirty percent of these former servant landowners gained office or power, although some, like Clocker, only briefly.[9]

Clocker, then, was representative of men who arrived early in Maryland and had the physical stamina to survive a climate that was wasteful of life, especially among immigrants. For such men, opportunity was great. On the other hand, we must remember the losers. Of the 275 identified servants who left England for Maryland over the first nine years of the colony, less than 30 percent achieved ownership of land and the economic independence it brought. For at least half, their adventure ended in early death.

Nevertheless, Clocker and men like him created the landscape of early Maryland. While there were rich planters who had hundreds of acres, many servants, and eventually slaves, the typical household for several decades was headed by a man who had arrived with little or nothing but who, with hard work, a strong constitution, and some good luck, would one day acquire a plantation and a respected place in the community. These survivors had found a trade-off. In seventeenth-century Maryland, life was shorter than in England, work was harder, and the standard of material comfort was lower. What they were gaining was land and the control over their lives that ownership of land provided.

Opportunity at the bottom began to diminish in the settled parts of Maryland after the 1660s, and especially after the 1670s. Population growth and the increasing substitution of slaves for servants produced rising costs of land and labor. As a result, new-comers who had arrived without capital took increasingly longer than had Daniel Clocker to acquire land, and more and more of them died before achieving that goal. By the early eighteenth century, few former servants could look forward to more than ten-ancy unless they were willing to follow the frontier of settlement as it moved west.

In the face of these changes, Daniel Clocker's children were barely able to maintain the status that he had gained. Still, his descendants remained on his Town Land for another two hundred years. In the eighteenth century, either Clocker's grandson Daniel III or his great-grandson Daniel IV built a small house on Clark's Freehold that the family owned and occupied until his great-great-great grandson sold it in 1877. The house still stands today, a reminder of the first Daniel Clocker's achievement.

Notes

1. The *Calvert Papers*, Number Three, Maryland Historical Society, *Fund Publication* 35 (Baltimore, 1899): 21.

2. Translation of the Maryland Charter, printed in Thomas Bacon, *The Laws of Maryland* (Annapolis, 1765), and reprinted in *Maryland Manual, 1985–1986*, ed. Gregory Stiverson et al. (Annapolis, MD, 1985), 671–72.

3. William Hand Browne et al., eds. *Archives of Maryland*, 1st ser., 72 vols. (Baltimore, 1883–1972), 41:185.

4. Ibid., 10:177.

5. Ibid., 41:427.

6. Ibid., 3:394.

7. A much-quoted characterization from George Alsop, *A Character of the Province of Maryland* (London, 1666), reprinted in *Narratives of Early Maryland, 1633–1684*, ed. Clayton Colman Hall (New York, 1910), 381.

8. *Archives*, 41:211.

9. Russell R. Menard, "From Servant to Freeholder: Status, Mobility, and Property Accumulation in Seventeenth-Century Maryland," *William and Mary Quarterly* 30 (1973): 37–64.

Suggested Readings

Carr, Lois Green. "Emigration and the Standard of Living: The Seventeenth-Century Chesapeake," *Journal of Economic History* 52 (1992): 271–91.

———. "The Foundations of Social Order: Local Government in Colonial Maryland." In *Town and County: Essays on the Structure of Local Government in the American Colonies*, ed. Bruce C. Daniels, 72–110. Middletown, CT, 1978.

———. " 'The Metropolis of Maryland': A Comment on Town

Development along the Tobacco Coast," *Maryland Historical Magazine* 69 (1974): 124–45.

———. "Sources of Political Stability and Upheaval in Seventeenth-Century Maryland," *Maryland Historical Magazine* 79 (1984): 44–70.

Carr, Lois Green, Russell R. Menard, and Lorena S. Walsh. *Robert Cole's World: Agriculture and Society in Early Maryland.* Chapel Hill, NC, 1991.

Carr, Lois Green, and Lorena S. Walsh. "The Planter's Wife: The Experience of White Women in Seventeenth-Century Maryland," *William and Mary Quarterly*, 3d ser., 34 (1977): 542–71.

Horn, James. *Adapting to a New World: English Society in the Seventeenth-Century Chesapeake.* Chapel Hill, NC, 1994.

Krugler, John D. " 'With Promise of Liberty in Religion': The Catholic Lords Baltimore and Toleration in Seventeenth-Century Maryland," *Maryland Historical Magazine* 79 (1984): 21–43.

Main, Gloria L. *Tobacco Colony: Life in Early Maryland, 1650–1720.* Princeton, NJ, 1982.

Menard, Russell R. "From Servant to Freeholder: Status, Mobility, and Property Accumulation in Seventeenth-Century Maryland," *William and Mary Quarterly* 30 (1973): 37–64.

———. "Population, Economy, and Society in Seventeenth-Century Maryland," *Maryland Historical Magazine* 79 (1984): 71–92.

Menard, Russell R., and Lois Green Carr. "The Lords Baltimore and the Colonization of Maryland." In *Maryland in a Wider World*, ed. David B. Quinn. Detroit, 1982.

Morgan, Edmund S. *American Slavery—American Freedom: The Ordeal of Colonial Virginia.* New York, 1975.

Walsh, Lorena S. " 'Till Death Do Us Part': Marriage and Family in Seventeenth-Century Maryland." In *The Chesapeake in the Seventeenth Century: Essays on Anglo-American Society and Politics*, ed. Thad W. Tate and David L. Ammerman, 126–52. New York, 1979.

7

John Cotton Jr.
Wayward Puritan Minister?

Sheila McIntyre

As the son of the prominent minister who had inspired Anne Hutchinson, the talented and well-educated John Cotton Jr. (1640–1699) could hope to become a leading Massachusetts minister. A serious scandal checked his progress, but it did not destroy his marriage or entirely end his career. He was "called" to become minister to the Wampanoag of Martha's Vineyard and seems to have learned the language and preached effectively. Becoming a minister in Plymouth may have ended his near banishment, but it still left him on the margins of the Congregational New England ministry. What was Cotton's role when King Philip's War erupted between relatives of his former parishioners (the Wampanoag) and his current parishioners of Plymouth? Would there be special fervor and meaning in Cotton's conventional preaching that the war was God's punishment for the community's sinfulness?

Cotton's voluminous correspondence, and his careful nurturing of his sons' ministerial careers, may well have reflected his wish to remain connected to a more cosmopolitan world that he had lost through his own sin. By 1696, Cotton's long, if mild, rustication seemed over, but his opportunity was lost because of renewed sexual scandal. His wife, Joanna, had stayed with him through the earlier scandal, had assisted his ministries with her own talents as a healer and midwife, and had raised their seven children. Does her leaving John in 1697 indicate that the scandal was definitely a new one?

John Cotton Jr.'s final exile may seem a severe punishment for his weakness. However, it should be noted that he had never been tried in any court, had never been banned from ministering (in a religious community that left parishioners free to choose their own ministers), and had lived a full ministerial life. Did his rather gentle punishments—gentle compared to that of fellow religious leader Anne Hutchinson—indicate either that he was not regarded as a serious threat, he was treated sympathetically because he was a man, he benefited from changes in Puritanism that many denounced as decline, or some

119

combination of the above? His life seems a special invitation to rethink the easy stereotypes about Puritans.

Sheila McIntyre is an authority on colonial New England's cultural and communications history. Her essay, " 'On Whose Judgment and Integrity You May Depend': The Role of the Reliable Source in Early Colonial News," is forthcoming in *Objectivity: Four Centuries of Journalism's Most Vexing Problem*, ed. Steven Knowlton (1999). She completed her studies at Boston University and currently teaches colonial American history at Harvard University.

> Concerning m^r Cottens going into
> Mis Chittendens Chamber with good wife
> [W]right Pretending mearly to see the
> furnituer of the hous we aprehend a foolish
> Curiosity and a mater of noe good Report.[1]

In early 1662, John Cotton, a twenty-two-year-old minister in Wethersfield (Connecticut colony), was caught in a maiden's bedroom with a married woman named Mrs. Wright. Cotton had married a local girl, Joanna Rossiter, in early November 1660, and she gave birth to a son in August 1661. The General Court dispatched a committee to investigate adultery charges against Cotton. In his own defense, Cotton told the committee that he had gone into Miss Chittenden's bedroom with Mrs. Wright just to look at the furniture. To look at the furniture? Surely, the young minister must have known how dubious his excuse sounded to the revered members of the committee, which included his mentor and teacher in Hartford, Samuel Stone, and one of New England's leading clergymen, John Allen. Along with his sightseeing adventure, Cotton was found guilty of speaking "sinfull Rash unspeakabell" things against another woman in Wethersfield, Mrs. Wells. Cotton testified that Mrs. Wells was "guilty [of] licivious whorish practices," which the members found to be untrue and of a "veary high defaming [nature] Rashly spoken and in no way Proved by him." The committee members acknowledged that Cotton's role as minister worsened his sin; after all the testimony, however, they could not find enough evidence to punish Cotton for adultery. The report chastised Cotton for his behavior, and ordered him and everyone involved to "Consider them self in quiet why the allmighty Contendeth with them [and to] express them selfs Daily to keep truth and love that the Weary God of Peace may be with them."[2] John Cotton's ministerial career seemed doomed.

The Reverend John Davenport, the leading minister in New

Haven, wasted no time in adding his own opinions to the court's. Davenport, who had escaped religious persecution in London by emigrating first to Holland in 1633 and then to the English colonies in 1637, penned a scathing letter to Cotton days after the court's decision. Davenport scolded Cotton for "sinfull miscarriages" and worried that his sexual misconduct would provoke "scandal" that would "hinder the acceptance of your exercise of guifts in preaching, with men, & the blessing of it from God." Believing that Cotton's "publick acknowledgm^t [was] slight & unsatisfying," Davenport coolly reprimanded the scandalous young minister. To humiliate Cotton further, Davenport wrote how disappointed Cotton's deceased father, a friend of Davenport's, would have been: "How often have I fervently desired that as you beare boath of your father's names, so you might hold forth the virtues of Christ . . . which would have given you a double interest, in the hearts of God's people, who knew, loved, & highly honoured your blessed Father, who being dead would thus have lived in you."[3]

The ministers and congregation at Cotton's home church reacted harshly to his sexual misconduct—they excommunicated him from the church that his father had founded, Boston's First Church. On May 1, 1664, the congregation voted to excommunicate the younger Cotton for "lacivious uncleane practices with three women and his horrid lying to hide his sinne." Evidently, the church members did not believe that he was merely looking at the furniture. Adultery in early New England ranged from a modern definition (sexual intercourse with someone other than one's own wife or husband) to lesser crimes, such as sexual dalliance, keeping company, or "adulterous carriages." Therefore, in the seventeenth-century definition, "adultery" always involved a married person, but did not always involve sexual intercourse. The Boston church found Cotton guilty of one of the lesser charges ("lascivious practices"). Following his "penitential acknowledgement openly Confessing his sinnes," the gathered church welcomed back Cotton only one month later, on June 12, 1664.[4]

Surely Cotton's lineage helped the church members forgive him, especially since his remorse seemed so heartfelt. John Cotton was descended from the most powerful ministerial family in New England. His biological father was John Cotton; and, following his father's death, his mother, Sarah, married Richard Mather. Both men were members of the founding generation of dissenter exiles. The elder Cotton composed more than three thousand pages of published sermons, including the farewell sermon to John Winthrop's first fleet of emigrants in 1630 and *The Keys to the Kingdom of Heaven*, a text seminal in defining Congregational Church polity in the New World; and Richard Mather wrote the *Cambridge Platform*, which structured New England church doctrine. If the younger Cotton's sexual sinfulness were not devastating enough, he needed to look no further than to his fathers' greatness when measuring his own failure.

Cotton's career began with great promise. Like most early ministers in New England, he had attended Harvard College. Founded in 1636 to train a learned ministry, Harvard produced the vast majority of working ministers educated in the colonies, until the founding of Yale College in 1701. Following his graduation in 1657, at age seventeen, Cotton apprenticed himself to Samuel Stone, the leading minister in Hartford. Beginning in 1659, he preached in Wethersfield, where his older brother, Seaborn Cotton, had preached before him to great acclaim. Like many young graduates, Cotton spent his first years after Harvard learning how to minister, and he expected to preach at several churches before receiving a permanent invitation from a congregation. Before the sexual misconduct charges, Cotton surely believed that his apprenticeship with Stone and his successful preaching in various Connecticut towns nearly guaranteed him a pulpit either in Boston or in one of the newly settled towns in the interior. Although the repentant sinner had been readmitted as a church member promptly, the adultery charges caused most congregations to question Cotton's suitability.

With little hope of a more prestigious invitation, Cotton began his ministerial career with a band of praying Indians on Martha's Vineyard, a small island off the coast of the Massachusetts Bay Colony. Despite the bleak outlook, he embraced his calling and transformed what should have been a dismal future into successful pastoral work. His missionary work on the Vineyard saved Cotton's career and shaped the rest of his life, long after he left the island for a more settled clerical calling. When he left for Plymouth in 1667, he continued his ministry for an additional thirty years, before scandal and sexual misconduct complicated his life again in 1697. Until his death in 1699, Cotton dedicated himself to the pastoral care of godly flocks on three different frontiers of the English Atlantic empire: Martha's Vineyard, Plymouth, and Charleston, South Carolina. While Cotton may not have fulfilled the expectations of his father's friends—he certainly never presided over a prestigious congregation and never published great works of doctrine—the sexual scandal had a surprising effect on his life. Rather than destroying his career, his sins in Wethersfield prepared him for a different kind of work. Cotton retained some of the power that went with being a Cotton, but he lived with and ministered to much more ordinary people. His ability to move between worlds— metropolis and frontier, elite and ordinary, English and Indian—

contrasts with what most envisioned his future to be. This essay explores the life of a different kind of Puritan minister—a man who transformed banishment into a means for cultural mediation. Although Cotton had been forced out of Boston's elite ministerial circle, he still served as a liaison between Boston and Plymouth. Despite the scandal, he remained intimately connected with Boston ministers until his tragic death in 1699 in South Carolina.

Cotton accepted the call from the wilderness to preach on Martha's Vineyard beginning in 1664 and moved with his wife Joanna and their two young children. Hoping to preach in a native tongue, Cotton hired a young Indian to teach him the language of the Wampanoag who dominated the settlement on the island. According to his diary, he learned the language well enough and fast enough to preach comfortably in "their owne language." Cotton's "Indian" diary, which he kept from 1665 to 1678, documents his evangelism with the natives, which continued even after he left the island through his regular visits to the Vineyard to preach to the Indian church. Cotton embraced a flexible Christianity that recognized his parishioners as both Indian and Christian. Praying Indians fought to maintain their own culture, but they also sought the comfort and certainty that the church seemed to offer amid a world of disease, invasion, warfare, and death. Living alongside non-Christian natives sometimes complicated the praying Indians' sense of where they best belonged and of what God expected of them. As one native convert asked Cotton, "Must wee Love those that doe not Love Gods meetings?"[5] Due to the small numbers of white settlers, the missionaries on Martha's Vineyard were unable to demand complete cultural change from the Indians. The ratio of white to native was astounding and unusual in midcentury coastal Massachusetts. Even after the ravages of disease and warfare, there were more than 1,000 Wampanoag to the 180 English settlers on Martha's Vineyard in 1660, and most of the English population were densely established on the eastern tip of the island. Because of their numerical dominance, the natives on the island never felt pressured to become completely acculturated. The Wampanoag were never required to look like Englishmen—they could leave their hair long, wear traditional dress, and maintain mourning practices—nor was attendance at Christian weekly church meetings mandatory. Cotton entered a missionary effort where the ministers had long since abandoned hopes of cultural dominance, and his evangelism flourished in the space between Wampanoag and English cultures.

Native parishioners brought doctrinal and social questions to Cotton, which he recorded in his diary. Some of their questions reflect a language problem and illustrate the difficulties of translating English metaphor into native languages. One Indian asked Cotton how it was possible to kiss the son of God. Other queries echoed the concerns that many Protestants shared, both English and Wampanoag, especially about complicated questions of predestination. Their questions occasionally cut close to the apparent contradictions in Protestant theology. The convert Obadiah asked Cotton about the distinction between grace and works: "May not a man by his good works deserve faith?"[6] Their questions reveal Cotton's commitment to teaching natives about their new faith as well as their own sophisticated theological understanding.

Just as in most communities in New England, Cotton led his native congregations in the rituals that invited believers to count their blessings or recount their sins. A day of thanksgiving allowed the Wampanoag to rejoice at "the recovery of John Wanna's child from great sickness, when all hopes of its life were past."[7] During the public thanksgiving for God's mercy in sparing their child, both Wanna and his wife admitted their sinfulness and recommitted themselves to "walke with God." With the help of New England's leading native missionary, John Eliot, Cotton also ordained two Wampanoag preachers, John Tackanash and John Hiacoombes, to help spread the Word among the flourishing Christian native congregations on the island. Despite his cultural distance from them, Cotton encouraged his native church members to employ all the traditional church ordinances in order to remain God's children.

When Cotton first arrived on the Vineyard, there was no settled clergyman. Thomas Mayhew Jr. had led the missionary efforts there from 1642 until his death in 1657, when his ship was lost en route to England. After Mayhew's death, his father, Governor Thomas Mayhew, worked among the Indians, although he never formally trained as a minister. The elder Mayhew also served as the governor of Martha's Vineyard and held titles to vast lands on the Vineyard, the nearby island of Nantucket, and the Elizabeth Islands. Mayhew's dual role as landlord and minister confused the Vineyard Indians. Paskannahommen recognized the impropriety of such concentrated authority, and Cotton recorded his pointed question as to "whether it be a Righteous thing for Mr M[ayhew] to buy away soe much of the Indians lands?"[8]

Although Governor Mayhew had regularly appealed for missionary help after his son's death, Cotton was soon in a power struggle with Mayhew for the hearts and minds of the natives. Mayhew spread nasty rumors about Cotton, who noted: "Some of the Indians now told me that they thought Mr Mayhew was very much against my preaching bec[ause] he told some of them that last yeare I said the Indians stunk but now they were sweet."[9] Mayhew disliked Cotton's increasing influence with the natives; and, according to Cotton, Mayhew told them that he would not help them any more "unlesse [they] would promise to come noe more to my house for counsell."[10] The infighting hastened Cotton's departure from the Vineyard, but only after the authorities became involved. In September 1667 the Commissioners for the United Colonies called Cotton before them to explain his bickering with Mayhew. They worried that the fighting undermined their missionary work. The commissioners also knew that several mainland congregations were courting Cotton, and the Vineyard mission lacked money to pay ministerial salaries, so Cotton "was left to his libertie to dispose of himselfe as the Lord should Guid him."[11]

The Lord guided him to Plymouth. The congregation in Plymouth had struggled for more than twelve years without a permanent minister when they offered Cotton the job in September 1666. After some negotiation and hesitation, he accepted their call in November 1667, moving himself and his growing family to the coastal town in the Plymouth Colony (the "Old Colony"). Cotton's new home was in an agricultural town, quiet compared to his childhood home in Boston, the boisterous and transatlantic center of the neighboring colony of Massachusetts Bay. According to the church records, the congregation in Plymouth overlooked Cotton's sinful past and instead saw "a man of strong parts and good abilities to preach the Word."[12] News of Cotton's success with the struggling native church on the Vineyard had spread, including reports of baptizing dozens of Christian Indians and helping the Indian congregation to ordain native ministers. Cotton's evangelism attracted the desperate Plymouth congregation, and he was the first Harvard-educated minister to serve in the Plymouth Colony.

Cotton blossomed as a pastor in Plymouth. While his success at reawakening declining churches may have been the first attraction, his connections to a metropolitan world outside Plymouth proved useful as well. Throughout his thirty-year ministry in Plymouth, Cotton's congregation and fellow Plymouth Colony clergy used his connections to their advantage, and he relished his role as news correspondent and broker. Many other Harvard graduates followed his example and accepted invitations from Plymouth Colony churches, making Cotton's efforts to remain connected to former friends and colleagues even easier. His correspondence reveals both his powerful family connections—Mathers, Saltonstalls, Rossiters, and Cottons—and his extraordinary dedication to remaining informed about recent news and doctrine coming out of Boston. His work as a conduit between the remote villages in southeastern Massachusetts Bay and Plymouth colonies and the bustling centers in Boston and Cambridge enhanced both his ministerial work and personal prestige.

Immediately after his arrival in Plymouth, Cotton began preaching. After a customary trial period, the congregation voted to ordain him as pastor. Church members invited ministers from Barnstable, Marshfield, Weymouth, and Duxbury to join them for the ordination ceremony on June 30, 1669, and they all attended to support their new colleague. Cotton's evangelism began in earnest after his ordination. With only forty-seven full church members in 1667, the Plymouth church was desolate; one historian estimates that Plymouth's adult population was nearly three hundred. While everyone was expected to participate in the life of the church and attend regular services, only full church members could receive the Lord's Supper, have their children baptized, or vote. During initial home visits, Cotton met with each family in town "to enquire as to the state of soules." After speaking with all the members of the household, Cotton offered "counsells, admonitions, exhortations & incouragements." The effect was remarkable. As Cotton noted in the church records, his visitations seemed to "stirre them up . . . others were awakened more seriously to attend upon the meanes of grace & to minde the concernments of their soules, & practice family-prayer more constantly."[13] In addition to pastoral visits and weekly church services, Cotton began monthly administrative church meetings, and he catechized girls and boys in doctrine. Just as he had done with the Wampanoag, Cotton led days of thanksgiving and fast days, and he administered the Lord's Supper to full church members several times a year, occasionally as often as ten times in a single year.

By 1670, Cotton seemed justified in calling for a day of thanksgiving specifically for "the settlement of Gods ordinances after soe long a vacancy, & the good success of the Gospel amongst them."[14] With Cotton's vigorous evangelism, church membership had doubled in just three years, and more than a hundred babies were baptized into the newly awakened Plymouth church. As was common practice in New England churches, all potential members stood before the congregation and offered a conversion testimony. Women (and after 1688, shy men) were permitted to give their testimony in private to the minister and elders, which Cotton would then read from the pulpit. He wanted to be sure that no parishioners were dissuaded from entering into full membership because they were "bashfull" or unable to project their voices throughout the whole church.

Along with his active ministry in Plymouth, Cotton continued his missionary work with the natives, both on the Vineyard and closer to home on the mainland and Cape Cod. As he did in many years, in 1669 he sailed to Nantucket and spent several days ministering to the praying Indians. Cotton noted that on August 8, "neere an 100 of them were gathered together, to whom I then preached, who were very thankful of it, and desired more."[15] Cotton preached more than twenty-five sermons per year to natives in Plymouth Colony and beyond, until a devastating war between natives and English settlers interrupted his work. By spring 1676, Cotton could not actively preach to natives at all.

King Philip's War pitted Metacomet (called King Philip) and his Narragansett, Wampanoag, and Nipmuk allies against land-hungry English colonists and their native allies (often from the same groups), beginning in the summer of 1675. Metacomet, a Wampanoag sachem, encouraged some natives to abandon their peaceful alliance with Plymouth and rebel against English settlers who were relentlessly encroaching on native land, and whose free-range livestock destroyed native crops. Fearing armed attack, the Plymouth government had disarmed the natives, forcibly when needed. The assassination in January 1675 of one Christian Indian, John Sassamon, by three Wampanoag allies of Philip provided the immediate cause of the eruption into war. The trial in June found Philip's men guilty of murder, and they were hanged in Plymouth on June 8, 1675. Cotton preached a sermon to the Christian natives and English settlers who had come to watch the hanging. The "praying Indians" found themselves in an impossible dilemma—having to choose between the cultures that many had fought to straddle.

Philip's devastating raids in 1675 against towns in Plymouth Colony, the Connecticut River Valley, the Merrimack River Valley, and Rhode Island were extremely successful. By February 1676 attacks on Massachusetts Bay towns such as Lancaster, Medfield, and Weymouth continued Philip's encircling of Boston, bringing him within ten miles of the city. One in ten colonists perished, and native tribes in New England never recovered from the devastating casualties, making it the deadliest war in American history. Terrified colonists did not always distinguish between peaceful "praying Indians" and Philip's allies, and settlers indiscriminately attacked Christian Indian settlements throughout the war.

As the fighting raged in Plymouth Colony, Cotton appealed to his colleagues for news of worsening native attacks. Since his arrival in Plymouth, Cotton had cultivated relationships with his neighboring ministers, just as he maintained regular correspondence with leading clergy in Boston and Cambridge. His links in both directions—into the backcountry and out to the coast—empowered him to gather and distribute information as few others could. One of Cotton's hinterland colleagues was Noah Newman, the settled minister in the town of Rehoboth in Plymouth Colony. When war broke out, Cotton naturally turned to Newman for information.

Rehoboth was the central rendezvous for almost seven hundred

Massachusetts Bay and Plymouth Colony soldiers (and their native allies) who had gathered to fight against Philip's forces. Newman's location gave him access to late-breaking news from the officers and the soldiers who filled his town and church. He actively sought out information by interviewing participants, reading personal letters that addressees generously shared with him, questioning military postal riders, and ministering to the soldiers. Newman's letter to Cotton of March 14, 1676, about Philip's attack on Medfield, suggests how vicious the fighting was and how adept Newman had become in his role as news correspondent. Describing the early morning attack on Medfield based on information gained from a visit to the devastated town, Newman relied on the testimony of his colleague in Medfield, the Reverend John Wilson, who had survived the attack. Although Wilson was still unsure of the exact numbers who had died, he described some of the gruesome deaths, which Newman repeated in his letter to Cotton: "Samuel Smiths wife being big wth child & another child in her arms was crossing over an open field to a Garison house & was over taken by the enemy & kild, & her child left alive, found standing by its dead mother where they thought it had stood near an hour." Using vivid imagery, Newman shared with Cotton the "cry of terrifyed persons, very dreadfull" and the yells of Philip's men, "shouting so as the earth seemed to tremble."[16] In a follow-up letter to Cotton on March 27, Newman carefully listed the English casualties by town. His clear intention was for Cotton to help him spread the tragic news to people in nearby Scituate, Marshfield, Duxbury, Sandwich, Barnstable, Yarmouth, and Eastham, whose family members had perished in Rehoboth.

Some of Boston's leading ministers wrote to Cotton looking for trustworthy information about the native wars, and they relied on his newsletters. Cotton's information spread along a ministerial letter-exchange network that recognized the importance of rapid information diffusion, especially during crises. His letter exchange during King Philip's war traveled far beyond the small agricultural and frontier towns in Plymouth Colony. Joshua Moody, a minister settled in Portsmouth, New Hampshire, wrote to Cotton on April 1, 1676, thanking him for "ye Intelligence" about the Medfield attack, which Moody had received from colleagues in Boston: "I have read it & showed it unto many who have p[er]used it wth great Sympathy. . . . If anything of like hath occurr among you for ye future . . . your handing it to us w^d be a matter of great Satisfaction y^t we might know things pticularly & truly. Reports are so many & various y^t we know n^t what to believe."[17] Moody certainly shared the information as well, broadening Newman's (and Cotton's) audience with each retelling.

The war tested the faith of many English settlers who worried that their own sinfulness had provoked God's wrath and caused such a dreadful judgment. Hoping that fervent prayers to God might halt Philip's progress, Cotton turned to the traditional ordinances. To help his congregation confront their sins, Cotton called for days of humiliation on July 21, 1675, and January 5, February 2, April 19, and May 30, 1676. Following orders from the General Courts of both Plymouth and Massachusetts Bay, Cotton's church also joined all other churches in holding a day of humiliation on June 29, 1676. Cotton furthered the work of reformation by appointing additional days for the community to examine its sinfulness. The list of sins that he read before the congregation on July 18 included missing church meetings, losing their love of the Bible, abandoning the godly life, "polluting" the Sabbaths, and "frequenting such places & companyes not becoming christians." Considering their own vileness, Cotton argued, the rebuking hand of God as evidenced in Philip's wrath was only just. Cotton mourned that people died during the war, but he preached to his congregation that they deserved it: "Wee have provoked the Lord God . . . [and] by our sins have had a deep hand in procuring these calamities."[18] Like many New England ministers of his time, Cotton looked to the community's sinfulness to explain the war.

Once again, Cotton's pastoral work had astounding effects. In summer 1676 he marveled at "how ready God was to heare the cry of his poore people . . . for immediately . . . God turned his hand against our Heathen-enemies & subdued them wonderfully." As Cotton noted in the church records, just one month after the colony-wide day of humiliation, Philip was killed on August 12, and "his head was brought into Plymouth in great triumph . . . so that in the day of our praises our eyes saw the salvation of God."[19] The rituals to which Cotton's congregations turned in distress bent God's ear to their sorrow. No one would have suggested that the godly had persuaded God to do anything—they knew that humans were powerless to effect change with an omnipotent Father. Rather, God had heard the cries of the afflicted, and His mercy showered down on them. Apparently, the victors paraded Philip's head through the streets of Plymouth to remind all believers of the awesome power of God's love for them.

During the native wars of 1675–76, Cotton's ministry focused on the calamity befalling God's plantations in New England. During more peaceful times, Cotton was blessed with an effective ministry, and he devoted his pastoral work to ordinary concerns. The congregation in Plymouth grew with both the regular admission of new church members and the baptism of newborn children. Along with his elders and deacons, Cotton attended the ordinations of neighboring ministers throughout southeastern Plymouth and Massachusetts Bay Colonies, and reported back to his congregation about the ceremonies. Preaching weekly sermons and services, leading days of humiliation and days of thanksgiving, administering the Lord's Supper, and holding regular church meetings to decide disciplinary action and policy kept Cotton's ministry full.

Local (and sometimes even distant) clergy sought Cotton's help on many questions, and he and his colleagues debated theological and social concerns in their letters to one another. Scituate's Nicholas Baker shared news about the abuse that he suffered at the hands of Quaker "heretics," "coming in to oʳ publick meeting while we are worshiping . . . calling us false profits & a company of Hypocrits."[20] James Keith, the minister in Bridgewater, inquired about "the scandal & miscarriage of Robert Lathrop by excess of drinking," while Lathrop was visiting Plymouth.[21] Rehoboth's minister, Samuel Angier, admitted that his own "inexperiencedness" encouraged him to ask Cotton for more specific information about ordaining deacons and administering the Lord's Supper to "informe my young brain."[22] When Shubael Dummer's congregation suffered through a native attack that left York, Maine, in ashes, Cotton's congregation raised money to aid the survivors.

Family concerns also occupied Cotton's time in Plymouth, and his family connected him to his community in many different ways. Of the eleven children that Joanna bore, seven lived into adulthood. Most families in early New England expected some of their young children to die, but parents mourned their loss no less. Cotton wrote sadly to his stepbrother in Boston, the prominent minister Increase Mather, to tell him "of Gods holy hand in bereaving us of our deare little one." Four-year-old Josiah Cotton had died a week earlier in January 1677, joining four-year-old Sarah who had died in 1669, only to be followed by an unnamed stillborn son in 1674, and Samuel, another son who died in 1682. Of John and Joanna's remaining children, all but two had links to the ministry: their eldest son, John, became the settled minister in Yarmouth; Elizabeth married James Alling, the minister in Salisbury (and after he died, she married his successor, Caleb Cushing); Rowland served as the pastor in Sandwich; Josiah preached in Yarmouth; and Theophilus ministered to Hampton Falls, New Hampshire.

Like most fathers, Cotton worried about the health, safety, and education of his children. When sons John and Rowland seemed ready for higher education, Cotton sought the advice and help of Increase Mather. While Cotton felt confident that he could begin their education, he knew that Mather could instruct his sons as they matured. Increase sent his own son, Cotton Mather, to tutor the young boys and prepare them for college.[23] Ultimately, all of

Cotton's sons graduated from Harvard in preparation for the ministry. Apparently, John Jr. fell into sinful ways while attending Harvard, and Cotton hastily wrote to Increase to look into it. Both Cotton and his wife worried that John had lost his way: "I would entreat earnestly of you, that you would write . . . to my afflicted wife, to quiet her heart . . . that one so deare to her may be saved from sin. . . . Our soules are troubled for him. Wee heartily wish his hastening out of the schoole, that he might be under your roofe & eye."[24] (The letter does not disclose young John's specific sins, but many Harvard undergraduates left college with hefty bills for broken glass and furniture following rowdy gatherings.) Real affection filled Cotton's letters to his children, which he usually signed, "your loving Father." Not surprisingly, he rejoiced when his children returned home safely after a journey, succeeded in school, served their congregations well, fell in love, or blessed him with grandchildren.

Despite the sexual scandals early in their marriage, John and Joanna clearly loved each other deeply. As John wrote in 1694 describing Joanna's commitment to him, "Love carrys through many difficulties easily & makes heavy burdens Light."[25] Almost always referred to as "my Dearest," Joanna enriched Cotton's life beyond his considerable powers of description. When she traveled to Cambridge in 1688, Cotton asked his son Rowland, who was at Harvard at the time, to write to him when Joanna arrived safely. Rowland must have forgotten his father's instructions, because he received a scolding: "I thought you could not have been so unkind, knowing how much I longed to hear of your mother's welfare . . . but children know not the heart of a father or husband: my bowells yearn."[26]

In addition to helping him raise their children and often accompanying him on his pastoral work, Joanna was a paid midwife and healer. Her father, Bray Rossiter, was a physician in Connecticut, and he may have sparked her interest in medicine, which she enhanced throughout her life by studying medical books sent by relatives and friends in England. During Cotton's ministry on Martha's Vineyard, Joanna earned £10 a year for "Phisicke and Surgery" among the natives. Cotton's letters regularly refer to his wife's practice. Smallpox constantly threatened New England, and settlers remained wary of infected persons. During one outbreak in 1677, Cotton wrote to Increase Mather (this outbreak began in Boston) to ask Mather's advice on how best to treat it. But Cotton wrote on behalf of "wee" and "us"—clearly, Joanna wanted the information as well. Family letters illustrate her extensive healing abilities. Joanna often told her sons to purge their bodies in the spring, she sent her children vials of medicine for everything from congested chests to sore gums, and she always advised medicine over bloodletting, a practice increasingly popular among European-trained male physicians. Joanna also traveled throughout Plymouth Colony gathering pharmacological plants. Her prescription for infected breasts after childbirth is a good example of her medical philosophy: Joanna sent herbal medicines and warnings that her daughter must not nurse while medicated; therefore she instructed that someone must "draw her breasts" to alleviate the pain.[27]

While it seems that family illnesses alone were frequent enough to keep her busy, Joanna regularly attended to the sick in Plymouth and the surrounding area. If Cotton's casual record is any indication, her medical practice was steady. Consider this one workweek in 1698: "yesterday Rob Bartlett fetcht her to his very sick family . . . he had a lovely boy borne on Wednesday both its feet bending inwards, likely to be a cripple, she bound up, lay there all night, came home early, & ever since hurried, by Jos Churche for his son John, Will Harlow & Ben Warren for their wives, & Will Ring for his child . . . thus is she tired."[28] Joanna's medical work bound the Cotton family to the congregation and community in Plymouth just as his ministry did; like him, her work moved outward from the frontier to friends in other colonies, and even to English contacts, who sent her "tokens"—the word she used to describe the precious medical texts from London bookstalls.

Living in Plymouth meant that Cotton and other frontier preachers looked to Boston and to each other for current news, recently published tracts and broadsides, intellectual stimulation, and doctrinal information. Much of Cotton's correspondence during his thirty years in Plymouth focuses on needing, receiving, sharing, and requesting information. Many of these clergymen began their careers together as part of a vital intellectual community at Harvard. Being scattered in remote pulpits challenged their efforts to remain part of the intellectual life that they once had shared. Letters helped to bridge the distance between them. Although many hinterland ministers maintained regular correspondence with friends and classmates, few could rival Cotton's intercolonial and transatlantic letter-exchange network. Cotton's family, clerical, and governmental connections privileged his letters, since few others in Plymouth Colony had ties to so many leading men in Massachusetts Bay and beyond.

By the end of 1696, Cotton's spirits were soaring. The last of his four clergyman sons was ordained in November, his missionary work continued successfully, his salary arrived regularly, and he enjoyed frequent travel to Boston, which enabled him to share Boston's excitement and news with his loyal correspondents. His mood seemed to sparkle in the letters that he wrote in late 1696:

"On Friday morn I came from Boston, some horses had made a good track for me, at Milton Eben Allyn . . . rode with me . . . and that evening . . . wee came comfortably to Barker's [tavern] & the next morning home, my passage was as good as ever." Cotton had journeyed to Boston to attend the funeral of a Harvard classmate, and he enjoyed his stay in the intellectual center of New England. He attended the Boston ministers' meeting on Monday, where he listened to the colony's most prolific speakers, including his step-brother Increase, his nephew Cotton, and their colleague, Samuel Willard. Then Cotton reached a career high: the Boston clergy invited him to give the Wednesday sermon in Old South Church. His evangelism infected Old South's congregation, as six people swore their saving testimony and became church members "while I was in the pulpit." Prestigious Boston clergy were "very civille," and "courteous" in "entertainments," to Cotton.[29] If there were any remaining doubts about his gifts as a minister, they surely vanished from the heights of Old South's pulpit—until sexual scandal erupted in Cotton's congregation in June 1697.

On June 18, 1697, thirty-five Plymouth brethren met to "consider the sad & scandalous reports that hath bin raised & spread abroad concerning some miscarriages in the Pastor towards Rebekah Morton." Cotton was fifty-seven years old. The church meeting heard "her charges & the Pastors particular vindications of himselfe from all those scandals & his confession of one," and unanimously voted to ask Cotton to "carry on the Lords worke among them as formerly."[30] Evidently, the Plymouth congregation accepted Cotton's explanation and wanted him to continue serving as their pastor. Did Cotton's one confession refer to the earlier sexual misconduct in Wethersfield, or to just one instance of adulterous "miscarriages" with Rebekah Morton? (No written record remains to answer that question.) Not surprisingly, Joanna was devastated. Cotton wrote to Rowland in Sandwich, begging him to come to Plymouth to visit his mother: "Your mother hath bin . . . worse than ever she was since I knew her, soe much that I much question . . . your tarrying long before you see her, I wish she be alive when you come." [31] Joanna clearly had had enough.

While Cotton proclaimed his innocence, the same Boston clergy who had praised him in December called for his dismissal (or worse) in June. By October 1697 the council dispatched by the General Court ejected Cotton from his pulpit, but he was never excommunicated. Surprisingly, the ministers in Boston went against the wishes of the Plymouth congregation. This intervention may reflect Boston ministerial efforts to establish more centralized control in the last decades of the seventeenth century. Cotton's nephew, Cotton Mather, recorded the sobering news in his diary: "Under extreme Anguish of mind, from the terrible and amazing Circumstances, of my poor Uncle at Plymouth (condemned the last week, to Silence, by the just sentence of a Council)." He later referred to Cotton's life stripped of his pulpit as "the deplorable Condition of my fallen Uncle."[32] Other Boston observers were much less charitable. Samuel Sewall, a wealthy merchant who had trained for the ministry and later served as the chief justice of Massachusetts's highest court, dismissed Cotton completely: "Thus Christs words are fulfilled, Unsavoury Salt is cast to the Dunghill. A most awfull Instance!"[33]

Church relations in Plymouth had soured well before this latest adulterous charge, and some historians suggest that Cotton's attempt to prevent some church members from leaving to form a new church, his interfering with the laity's selection of elders, and other problems created an anti-Cotton faction that used his prior sexual misconduct to whip up another scandal. Most of the members of this splinter congregation had already ceased attending services when the church members voted on Cotton's future ministry, so their discontent is not reflected in the Plymouth congregation's unanimous support for him. Was Cotton guilty again? While the earlier adultery charges did not help, there is no reason to doubt the council's wisdom, Mather's and Sewall's judgment, or to think that any married woman would destroy her life just to spite an overarching minister.

After the Boston council removed Cotton from his pulpit, he journeyed to Yarmouth and Sandwich, spending time with each of his sons who lived nearby, and finally returning to Plymouth to settle his affairs and his future—all the time awaiting an invitation from another congregation. Joanna moved in with Rowland's family in Sandwich, which, according to John, only fueled rumors about their marriage: "Mercy Dunham . . . hath vindicated you & me from some considerable aspersions grounded upon your living so long at Sandwich."[34] Cotton knew that his remaining in Plymouth almost two years after the scandal occurred enraged the ministers in Boston, but he had nowhere else to go. Desperate for a call from some congregation, Cotton preached to several struggling native churches and hoped that rumors about a job in Barnstable or Malden were true. By July 1698 his letters to Joanna and Rowland were despondent, begging for prayers, help, and forgiveness: "I have a 1000 thoughts but think I shall do nothing at all but lye down under my burden til I die; Lord pitty, help, direct; think, think, think, pray, pray, pray."[35]

Salvation came in a familiar guise. As Cotton tells it, just when he was most desolate, God saved him: "Gods wayes are past finding out; when I came home I found Mr Robert Fenwick at my house where he waited divers houres for me with his call [from] the inhabitants of Charlestowne." Fenwick also gave Cotton letters of support from some of Boston's ministers encouraging him to go. Heartened by the new missionary prospect in South Carolina, Cotton immediately asked the Plymouth church for permission to leave its fellowship (a common practice when someone moved), and began packing. Believing that Joanna would join him, he told her about another minister, who would be journeying with them, whose wife "Mrs Lord . . . is ready to leap [out] of her skin for joy" that another woman will venture into such a dangerous frontier.[36] Chosen to be the hub of the new proprietary colony of Carolina, Charleston was founded in 1670 at the convergence of two rivers—an ideal location for trade, but also an ideal habitat for disease-bearing mosquitoes. As late as 1708 the entire population of the Carolina Colony was only eight thousand, and more than four thousand were slaves. Dysentery, malaria, and yellow fever gave Carolina the highest mortality rate in the mainland colonies. Recognizing how dangerous Charleston would be, Cotton asked a poignant question in the summer before his departure: "I sit down astonished, & am musing whether it be a beginning of mercy & deliverance, or a lightning before death."[37]

Joanna chose not to go to Charleston. Given her legal status as Cotton's wife—upon marriage, a woman moved from her father's control to her husband's—her choice was incredible. Women simply did not remain away from their husbands. Following Joanna's unusual decision, Cotton's letters refer to her as "my deare mourning dove."[38] Days before sailing on November 15, 1698, he wrote a farewell letter to Rowland, asking him to watch over Joanna and his brothers, to preserve Cotton's books, manuscripts, and letters, and to pray for him. He also wrote to his many correspondents asking them to write "tenderly compassionate letters" to Joanna to comfort her in his absence. Her nephew, John, wrote to reassure her that Cotton was doing God's will and redeeming himself for his sinfulness: "My Uncles going to Carolina may prove to [be] ye Saving of many soules alive, & ye best work y^t he ever did in his life . . . now he is restored wth reputation to his service in Gods house."[39] If Cotton could minister well to the struggling inhabitants of Charleston, maybe he could prove his worth once again to the Boston ministers and return to New England.

John and Joanna wrote letters for their mutual reassurance during his stay in South Carolina. Joanna constantly heard rumors that John had died, and his timely letters eased her worry. Stories of Charleston's Catholics, pirates, disease, and slaves did little to encourage her to move there, but the sight of his handwriting comforted her, and he shared news of his considerable progress with the "New England Meeting Church" in Charleston. Her letters struggled to keep John current with family and local news, and

Joanna busily delivered five new grandchildren (including a set of twins) in the spring of 1699. Husband and wife switched roles, with Joanna quietly assuming the job of news correspondent to her now remotely settled husband. Despite trying to keep active, she admitted to John in July 1699, "I am quite weary of Living."[40]

Cotton died of yellow fever in September 1699. Theophilus Cotton, the youngest, learned of his father's death on the street in Hampton Falls, New Hampshire: "I met with Mr Thomas Smith who told me he was sorry for my loss, what loss saith I? Why, saith he, havent you heard yet, who said I, why said he your father is dead. O never was I struck into such amazement in my life, he told me also that there was an [150] dead in [16] days & all the ministers of the town are dead with a plague. . . . Father died 3rd day. . . . I have heard no more about it yet. I am going to Deacon Bridgeham's he hath letters from thence. I must end."[41] While deeply saddened, Joanna and her children could agree with Cotton Mather's final assessment of his uncle's death: "I have Reason to give great thanks unto Heaven, in that the Lord accepted that poor Man, to dy in the Service of the Church, After the Death which there had been upon all hopes of any such matter, by his Abdication from his work at Plymouth."[42] Cotton's humiliating "Death" in Plymouth—his ejection from the pulpit and the end of his ministry—had been far worse than his death in Charleston. Despite dying in body, he had redeemed himself before God, and his work helped him atone for his sins. By dying with his faithful in Charleston, Cotton fulfilled the ministerial promise that so many had predicted for him, and God's blessings surely flowed to him through the souls of the converted.

Along with God's blessings, forgiveness shone down on John Cotton. Traditional interpretations of "Puritan" society leave little room for a sinner such as Cotton, except on the scaffold or in the stocks. His story highlights a flexible Puritanism. His sins did not prevent his community from loving him; and, despite his failings, they embraced him. From the elite clerical meetings in Boston to the wilds of Martha's Vineyard, Cotton traveled with the godly, who accepted him and even looked to him as pastor and informant. His journey, as retold here, echoes the cycle of redemption that all church members endured. Moments of redemption and salvation followed moments of sinfulness and despair in a never-ending circle. Sin, repentance, and readmission structured every believer's life, and Cotton's was no different. Once he was forced out of the church's protection into the wilderness, on the Vineyard or in Charleston, he truly saw his own sinfulness and sought God's mercy. Both times, his contemporaries believed that God heard Cotton's cries, and saved him.

Notes

1. Report of a Committee on Charges against John Cotton while Preaching in Wethersfield, March 20, 1661/2, Andrews-Eliot Papers, Massachusetts Historical Society, Boston (hereafter cited as MHS.)

2. Ibid.

3. John Davenport to John Cotton (1640–1699), March 23, 1662/3, MHS, *Collections*, 4th ser., 8 (1868): 547–49 (hereafter cited as *Colls*, MHS.)

4. "The Records of the First Church in Boston, 1630–1868," ed. Richard D. Pierce, Publications of the Colonial Society of Massachusetts, *Collections* 34 (1961): 60–61.

5. John Cotton Jr., "Diary of Preaching to the Indians on Martha's Vineyard, 1665–1678," MHS.

6. Ibid.

7. Ibid.

8. Ibid.

9. Ibid.

10. Ibid.

11. Quoted in "John Cotton," *Biographical Sketches of Graduates of Harvard University*, ed. John Langdon Sibley (Cambridge, MA, 1873), 1:497.

12. "Plymouth Church Records, 1620–1859," Colonial Society of Massachusetts, *Publications* 22 (1920): 111.

13. Ibid., 144.

14. Ibid., 146.

15. Cotton, "Diary," August 8, 1669.

16. Noah Newman to John Cotton, March 14, 1676, Curwen Family Papers, American Antiquarian Society, Worcester, Massachusetts (hereafter cited as AAS.)

17. Ibid., April 1, 1676, Curwen Family Papers, AAS.

18. "Plymouth Church Records," 149–51.

19. Ibid., 152–53.

20. Nicholas Baker to John Cotton, 1677, Curwen Family Papers, AAS.

21. James Keith to John Cotton, January 15, 1679, Cotton Family Papers, MHS. Original owned by the Boston Public Library, Boston.

22. Samuel Angier to John Cotton, October 27, 1679, Cotton Family Papers, MHS. Original owned by the Boston Public Library, Boston.

23. John Cotton to Increase Mather, October 20, 1677, *Colls*, MHS, 239–40.

24. Ibid., November 24, 1676, *Colls*, MHS, 229–30.

25. John Cotton to Rowland Cotton, November 21, 1694, Miscellaneous Bound, MHS.

26. Ibid., August 13, 1688, Thomas Prince Collection, MHS.

27. Ibid., September 13, 1694, Miscellaneous Bound, MHS.

28. Ibid., March 6, 1698, Miscellaneous Bound, MHS.

29. Ibid., December 1696, Miscellaneous Bound, MHS.

30. Church meeting records, as rewritten in ibid., June 1697, Miscellaneous Bound, MHS.

31. John Cotton to Rowland Cotton, June 1697, Miscellaneous Bound, MHS.

32. *The Diary of Cotton Mather, 1681–1708*, ed. Worthington Chauncey Ford, *Colls*, MHS, 7th ser., 8:236–37.

33. *The Diary of Samuel Sewall, 1674–1729*, ed. M. Halsey Thomas (New York, 1973), 1:378.

34. John Cotton to Joanna Cotton, July 10, 1698, Miscellaneous Bound, MHS.

35. John Cotton to Rowland Cotton, July 2?, 1698, Miscellaneous Bound, MHS.

36. Ibid., July 16, 1698, Miscellaneous Bound, MHS.

37. John Cotton to Thomas Prince, July 19, 1698, Miscellaneous Bound, MHS.

38. John Cotton to Rowland Cotton, November 3, 1698, Miscellaneous Bound, MHS.

39. John Cotton (1658–1710) to Joanna Cotton, November 15, 1698, Miscellaneous Bound, MHS.

40. Joanna Cotton to John Cotton, July 13, 1699, Miscellaneous Bound, MHS.

41. Theophilus Cotton to John Cotton (1661–1706), October 26, 1699, Miscellaneous Bound, MHS.

42. *Diary of Cotton Mather, Colls*, MHS, October 23, 1699, 1:319–20.

Suggested Readings

Cotton's "Indian Diary" has never been published, but the Massachusetts Historical Society holds the manuscript. The Society also holds most of Cotton's letters. John Cotton Jr. has never received a full-length biography, but Mark Peterson studied his Plymouth ministry in "Plymouth Church and the Evolution of Puritan Religious Culture," *New England Quarterly* 66 (1993): 570–93. David D. Hall's *Worlds of Wonder, Days of Judgment: Popular Religious Belief in Early New England* (New York, 1989) and Charles E. Hambrick-Stowe's *The Practice of Piety: Puritan Devotional Disciplines in Seventeenth-Century New England* (Chapel Hill, NC, 1982) offer the best descriptions of seventeenth-century religious culture. King Philip's War is the focus of Jill Lepore's *The Name of War: King Philip's War and the Origins of American Identity* (New York, 1998). For some more information about Plymouth Colony, see Darrett Rutman, *Husbandmen of Plymouth: Farms & Villages in the Old Colony, 1620–1692* (Boston, 1967); George Langdon, *Plymouth Colony: A History of New Plymouth* (New Haven, 1966); and John Demos, *A Little Commonwealth: Family Life in Plymouth Colony* (New York, 1970). The acceptable and unacceptable sexuality of early New Englanders is the subject of Roger Thompson's *Sex in Middlesex: Popular Mores in a Massachusetts County, 1649–1699* (Amherst, MA, 1986). Laurel Ulrich has re-created the rich life of one New England midwife and healer in *A Midwife's Tale* (New York, 1990). Both Neal Salisbury's *Manitou and Providence: Indians, Europeans, and the Making of New England, 1500–1643* (New York, 1982) and editors Henry W. Bowden and James Ronda's *John Eliot's Indian Dialogues: A Study in Cultural Interaction* (Westport, CT, 1980) discuss Native American missions and praying Indians. Ronda focuses specifically on Martha's Vineyard in "Generations of Faith: The Christian Indians of Martha's Vineyard," *William and Mary Quarterly*, 3d ser., 38 (1981): 369–94.

8

Isabel Montour
Cultural Broker on the Frontiers
of New York and Pennsylvania

Jon Parmenter

Madame Isabel Montour's extensive multicultural network of kin as well as her knowledge of languages, customs, and protocols made her a valued guide through the complexities of colonial frontier life. She was a rather different cultural intermediary from either Squanto or Pocahontas. Of mixed blood herself, Madame Montour (c. 1685–1753) lived in a variety of places where she was respected, not marginalized, for her links with various competing cultures: although born in New France, she translated for a British governor of New York during Queen Anne's War, and although the daughter of an Abenaki, she became a matron of a well-regarded Iroquois clan. Did her time of visibility in Pennsylvania coincide with the Proprietor's interest in orderly Iroquois overlordship along a frontier of fertile land peopled by numerous Native American groups? What does her obvious importance to the British and French colonials suggest about their views of female savants and Native American matrons? Perhaps her place and time lived with less rigid racial definitions than would be common soon thereafter.

Jon Parmenter completed his doctoral research at the University of Michigan. He has published "Pontiac's War: Forging New Links in the Anglo-Iroquois Covenant Chain, 1758–1766," *Ethnohistory* 44 (1997): 617–54.

On the evening of June 28, 1744, Witham Marshe, secretary to the Maryland Commissioners for the Indian conference then under way in Lancaster, Pennsylvania, took advantage of a break in the negotiations to visit "the celebrated Mrs. Montour." Intrigued by this elderly woman's reputation, Marshe conversed at length with her (in French) about her storied career on the early American frontier. Perhaps amused by the curiosity of the young gentleman, Madame Montour provided him with an account of her life, which, despite several flights of fancy, remains the best source of information for reconstructing her personal history. Madame Montour told Marshe:

> that she was born in Canada, whereof her father (who was a French gentleman) had been Governor; under whose administration the then Five Nations of Indians had made war against the French, and the Hurons in that government (whom we term French Indians, from espousing their part against the English, and living in Canada), and that in the war, she was taken by some of the Five Nations' warriors, being then about ten years of age; and by them was carried away into their country where she was habited and brought up in the same manner as their children: That when she grew up to years of maturity she was married to a famous war captain of those nations who was held in great esteem for the glory he procured in the wars carried on against the Catawbas, a great nation of Indians to the south-west of Virginia, by whom she had several children; but about fifteen years ago, he was killed in battle with them; since which she has not been married: That she had little or no remembrance of the place of her birth, nor indeed of her parents, it being nearly fifty years since she was ravished from them by the Indians.[1]

A key member of a remarkable family in the history of colonial North America, Madame Montour achieved considerable renown in her own lifetime, yet historians still lack a clear sense of her significance as a cultural broker between Indian and colonial communities in early eighteenth-century New York and Pennsylvania. The scattered and contradictory nature of the documentary sources on her career, along with the considerable romantic tradition that has accrued around her life story, complicate the biographer's task. Nevertheless, a closer look into Madame Montour's life reveals a complex, multifaceted individual who moved easily between native and settler communities, facilitating informed communication between different cultures. Her evident linguistic fluency, her far-ranging family and trading connections, and her ability to convey different understandings of events to different people kept Madame Montour in demand as a person "in the know" for much of her adult life. Most often identified as an "interpretess" who served at Iroquois conferences, Madame Montour, although she interpreted on several occasions, held other roles in her diplomatic career at once more important and less visible than that of an interpreter. Madame Montour's experience in the public and private spheres of early American Indian diplomacy was not always easy or secure, however, and her ability to penetrate the ambiguities of cross-cultural interactions won her both praise and condemnation from her contemporaries.

Existing sources do not permit a definite account of Madame

Montour's early years, but the weight of evidence indicates that she was most likely born about 1685 at the Indian village near the French mission of St. François-du-Lac (near modern Sorel, Québec), the daughter of one Louis Montour and a Sokoki (Western Abenaki) Indian woman with the Christian name of Madeleine. Louis Montour, himself the son of a Frenchman and an Algonquian Indian woman, had moved to a seigneury near St. François in 1676 (at the age of seventeen) and occasionally worked as a *coureur de bois*, trading furs with the Indians in the North American interior. Louis's knowledge of Indian languages, along with the attacks of the Iroquois Indians on Canadian mission villages after the outbreak of King William's War (1689–1697), combined to lead him away from the life of a farmer and toward that of an itinerant fur trader and interpreter.

Consisting of the Mohawk, Oneida, Onondaga, Cayuga, Seneca (and after 1722, the Tuscarora) peoples, the Iroquois (also referred to as the Five or Six Nations) resided in the colony of New York and took advantage of the war between the English and French colonies in North America to attack their Indian enemies living in Canada. Mixed parties of Iroquois warriors struck St. François in November 1689 and in September 1690. In early August 1693, probably in retaliation for a French and allied Indian attack on three of their villages in February of that year, a party of Mohawks raided the village again, returning to Albany, New York, with several prisoners. It is possible, given the details in Madame Montour's autobiographical account, that the Iroquois took her captive during one of these incursions as part of their traditional mourning-war, through which they replaced dead relatives with adopted prisoners from other nations. Shortly after this last Mohawk raid, Louis Montour relocated his family to the fortified Canadian village of Trois-Rivières and enlisted in the militia. On June 13, 1694, while scouting with two other soldiers near Fort Lamotte on Lake Champlain, Montour received a gunshot wound in the abdomen in a brief skirmish with some Mohawks. This incident apparently ended his interest in both military service and life in the colony of Canada. His family dispersed, and he relocated to the northern Great Lakes region (*pays d'en haut*), living at Michilimackinac (modern Mackinac City, Michigan) with his sisters Isabelle and Madeleine and their families. Ironically, these events also marked the beginning of an enduring relationship between the Montour family and the Iroquois.

Reduced for a time to clandestine, small-scale fur trading in the *pays d'en haut*, Louis Montour emerged as a key intermediary in the Iroquois-sanctioned efforts to divert the furs taken by the Great Lakes Algonquians from their traditional French customers in Canada to the Dutch traders at Albany. Following the conclusion of

King William's War, the Iroquois made separate peace treaties with the French and English in 1701, and after 1704 the Iroquois began to permit the western Indian groups allied with New France to trade at Albany. Attracted by high-quality trade goods and better prices for their furs than they could obtain in the glutted markets of French Canada, the western Indians had made some direct overtures to trade at Albany, but prior to 1707 the bulk of this trade went through smugglers between the French fort of Detroit (established in 1701) and the Iroquois, who accepted gifts from the western Algonquians in exchange for safe passage through the Five Nations' homeland. Louis Montour soon involved himself in this profitable enterprise, appearing at Albany with "severall farr Indians to trade" in June 1707. He received a payment of £5 in New York currency for his services, and left promising to "go among the farr Nations again and bring down more Indians."[2] Montour returned to Albany with twelve Miami and Huron Indians from the *pays d'en haut* in July 1708, much to the delight of New York Governor Edward Hyde, Lord Cornbury, who spoke highly of Montour's abilities and credited him with fulfilling his long-standing plan to open trade with the western Algonquians at Albany. Additionally, Montour's efforts prompted the Iroquois to make plans for a peace treaty with at least four different western nations early in 1709. He had won significant favor for himself among the Albany trading community, a development that would later contribute to the success of his daughter, Madame Montour.

Louis Montour's activities among the Indian allies of New France living in the *pays d'en haut* did not go unnoticed by Canada's Governor Philippe de Rigaud, Marquis de Vaudreuil. Although officially at war after 1702 (Queen Anne's War, 1702–1713), France and England enjoyed relative quiet in North America prior to 1709, owing principally to the Iroquois adhering to their 1701 professions of neutrality, and their refusal to ally exclusively with one or the other imperial contestant. Montour's attempts to foster closer ties between the Iroquois and the western Algonquians threatened to upset this delicate diplomatic balance, however, and Vaudreuil took steps to neutralize the problem. In late April 1709, Louis-Thomas Chabert de Joncaire, Vaudreuil's agent among the Seneca, encountered Louis Montour in Cayuga territory (near Sodus Bay, New York) with a vanguard of ten delegates from western Indian nations en route to trade and discuss peace with the Iroquois at Albany. After Montour rejected Joncaire's request that he return to the *pays d'en haut,* an unidentified Frenchman in Joncaire's party drew a hatchet from under his coat and "cut the sd. Montour into his head and killed him."[3] The outraged Algonquians accompanying Montour carried Joncaire to the Cayuga village and nearly killed him, but the intervention of one of Montour's brothers-in-law prevented further bloodshed. Whether Vaudreuil intended to execute Montour is not clear, but in a 1709 letter he railed against the offspring of marriages between Frenchmen and "savages," singling out Montour by name as a prime example of how these renegade mixed-bloods combined the worst traits of both societies.[4] Twelve years after the killing, Vaudreuil still refused to apologize for his action, claiming that Montour "would have been hanged had it been possible to take him alive and bring him to [Canada]."[5]

The violent death of Louis Montour permitted the public emergence of a woman intimately associated with him into the Albany diplomatic network. Variously identified in the sources as his widow or his sister, she appeared at Albany on May 17, 1709, with a party of Mississauga Indians under the headman Kaqucka, who stated that he had come on Louis Montour's invitation "to open the Path from our Country to this place, and if we are well treated here we shall always keep the path clean and open, and forget the old path to Canada wch we have hitherto used."[6] The female Montour accompanying Kaqucka turned over to the Albany Commissioners of Indian Affairs (composed largely of Dutch residents of Albany active in the Indian trade) one of Louis Montour's wampum belts, but she apparently received no special recognition at that time.

It remains open to question whether this woman was Louis Montour's sister, Isabelle Couc, or his daughter, known only as Madame Montour. More important, however, it seems clear that Isabelle Couc and Madame Montour were very likely not, despite the prevailing belief among many of her subsequent historians, one and the same person. Born in 1667, Isabelle Couc lived at Michilimackinac and Detroit after the 1693 dispersal of the Couc family. She never referred to herself by the Montour name, and a 1730 description by Pennsylvania authorities of Madame Montour's young son (Andrew Montour) suggests that Couc, born sixty-three years earlier, could not have been Madame Montour.

Parties of western Algonquians, "who said they were come by Montour's perswasion,"[7] continued to appear in Albany well into June 1709, complaining of their "great Loss by Montour's death."[8] New York authorities shared their concern, since Montour's demise came at a critical juncture in the North American theater of Queen Anne's War. Nevertheless, the Albany Commissioners of Indian Affairs took the opportunity to exploit his death in their own negotiations with the Indians. They sent belts of wampum to the *pays d'en haut*, claiming French responsibility for Montour's murder; and on July 14, 1709, when New York Lieutenant Governor Richard Ingoldsby met with delegates from all the Iroquois nations (except for the Seneca), to request their military assistance in a planned expedition against Canada, he made certain to remind them of French treachery, especially "their treacherous murthering of Montour one of your Brethren, before your faces, in your own country this Summer, an evident mark of their Insolence and how they intend to use you."[9]

Montour's murder helped Anglophile Iroquois headmen to persuade their warriors to accede to Ingoldsby's overtures, and they joined the ill-fated 1709 land expedition under the command of Colonel Peter Schuyler, a prominent Albany citizen, and Colonel Francis Nicholson, the former governor of Virginia. Unknown to the colonial military organizers, the English navy rerouted the fleet intended to reconnoiter with the land forces for the invasion of Canada, and Nicholson found himself bogged down with logistical problems south of Lake Champlain in October 1709, when news of the naval decision canceling the expedition finally reached him.

New York's new governor, Robert Hunter, arrived in June 1710, eager to continue his predecessors' policy of undermining Canada's commerce by fostering ties with the Great Lakes Indians through the Iroquois. By August 1710, however, the pro-French faction among the Iroquois, apparently unimpressed by the highly publicized visit of three Mohawk emissaries to England earlier that year, employed its renewed strength after the humiliating English military failure of 1709 and allowed the French to construct a small blockhouse in Onondaga country. This visit, organized by Schuyler and Nicholson, aimed to demonstrate the grandeur of England to the Iroquois and to facilitate a formal alliance between the Mohawk delegates and Queen Anne. When plans for another military expedition against Canada surfaced in June 1711, Hunter arranged to have Madame Montour assist him in what promised to be challenging negotiations with the Iroquois.

Although nothing is known about her life after being taken captive and adopted by the Iroquois, Madame Montour's linguistic accomplishments and her network of kin in the *pays d'en haut* represented valuable commodities in the world of Anglo-Iroquois diplomacy. Madame Montour was fluent in French, English, Oneida, Mohawk, Delaware, and quite possibly spoke Huron and Miami. Large families and multiple marriages among her kinfolk meant that Madame Montour had relatives scattered throughout Canada and the Great Lakes region. These included: cousins (descendants of her aunts Isabelle and Madeleine Couc) living at Montréal and Michilimackinac; cousins (descendants of her aunt Marguerite Couc) residing at Detroit; her brothers Joseph and Jean Montour, who alternated between Detroit and the Miami Indian country; a sister known as "femme Saint-Cerny," who was married to a Miami man and living among the Miami; her brother Jean-Baptiste

Montour, who married an unidentified Indian woman and lived at Lachine, Québec; her own son Andrew, who married twice (once to a Delaware woman and then to an Oneida); her daughter Margaret (known as "French Margaret"), who married a Mohawk named Katarionecha, and by him had two daughters, Catherine and Esther Montour; and a mysterious individual known as Lewis Montour, who lived at Detroit and whom contemporary observers identified as Andrew Montour's brother, but given the different means of reckoning kinship ties among Native American societies, he was more likely Madame Montour's nephew. The matrilineal orientation of the Iroquois kinship system may explain why Madame Montour's children bore her surname. No surviving source gives a definite statement of her Christian name, but she emerged from the shadows after the death of her father Louis and assumed a prominent position in New York's Indian affairs during Governor Robert Hunter's administration. Married to an Oneida war leader named Carondawana (who eventually took the name "Robert Hunter" himself), Madame Montour became one of the governor's most trusted advisers, as New York's surveyor, future lieutenant governor, and recognized "Indian expert" Cadwallader Colden attested:

> He [Hunter] had so great a diffidence of all the people at Albany that at the public meetings with the Indians he had allwise a French woman standing by him who had married one of our Indians to inform him whether the interpreters had done their part truely between him and the Indians, notwithstanding that Col. Schuyler was present at the same time. This woman, commonly called Madame Montour had a good education in Canada before she went among the Indians and was very usefull to Mr. Hunter on many occasions for which reason she had a pension and was sometimes admitted to his table in her Indian dress.[10]

Although Madame Montour served as an interpreter in formal conference proceedings on several occasions, Colden's description of her association with Hunter, combined with other documentary evidence and current understanding of Iroquoian diplomatic procedures, suggests that her most significant work was done "offstage," as an intercultural consultant of sorts who carried messages, supplied essential intelligence, and helped to compose, translate, and edit the texts of speeches before others delivered them in public at Iroquois conferences. Women in Iroquois society had real political power, but they wielded it in ways that few eighteenth-century white observers understood. The Iroquois structured their society on the bases of matrilocal residency and matrilineal descent. Communal longhouses were organized around extended families of female relatives, and senior women, known as clan matrons, selected and deposed the hereditary male chiefs allotted to their lineage. Military activities were often determined by whether or not the women provided supplies for the warriors, and women also had the power to decide whether captives taken in mourning-war raids would be adopted or ritually tortured and executed.

Iroquois women, however, did not usually interpret publicly the messages they had woven into wampum belts, and they did not make speeches, although they could nominate a speaker to voice their concerns. While these women had a significant degree of access to the public sphere of political life, it is important not to overstate the nature and extent of their authority. Given the concept of gender reciprocity in Iroquois society, the majority of female influence came not as a result of public expressions of their command over others, but through their fulfillment of reciprocal social obligations. While men spoke at council meetings, held office, and traveled far beyond the limits of their home villages on diplomatic missions, women gained prestige through their complementary role of managing the affairs of household and village. The influence of women at public councils occurred almost entirely "behind the scenes."[11] Madame Montour, as an adopted Iroquois and a cultural broker who mediated the conflicting cultural perceptions, expectations, meanings, and values between Indians and colonists, held a unique position and contributed to the improvement in understanding of Iroquois culture, language, and political practices in New York's Indian diplomacy after about 1710.

Certainly the people involved in Iroquois negotiations needed the kind of help that Madame Montour could provide. The different linguistic groups present at early eighteenth-century Iroquois conferences at Albany required the utilization of at least three languages. Governors prepared their statements in English, and these would be translated into Dutch by the secretary of the Albany Commissioners of Indian Affairs. The interpreters then related the message to the Indians in an Iroquoian language, usually Mohawk, owing to the proximity and long-standing economic ties of that nation to Albany. The Indians' replies followed the same linguistic pathway in reverse. Obviously, this process involved a risk of misunderstanding at every step, hence Madame Montour's important role in checking the translations.

In addition to these duties, evidence suggests that Madame Montour also played a key part in the preliminary negotiations that accompanied all public councils. While the public proceedings at Iroquois conferences occasionally lasted for weeks, most of the important transactions and agreements were hammered out at private meetings of a few individuals that took place off the record. Here, Madame Montour's expertise in communicating not only language but also ideas, mannerisms, and protocol could go a long way toward making a conference successful.

Madame Montour made her public debut as an interpreter at Albany on August 24, 1711. She assisted in Francis Nicholson's presentation of a framed set of woodcuts commemorating the Iroquois emissaries' visit to England in 1710 "to be hung up in the Onnondage [sic] Castle the center of the 5 nations where they always meet," and four days later she helped correct a potentially serious mistake in Governor Hunter's speech. After delivering a large present of weapons, ammunition, clothing, and tobacco to the Iroquois in recognition of their agreement to send more than six hundred warriors to accompany another expedition against Canada, Hunter proclaimed that he had "oversett the kettle of war." With Madame Montour interpreting, Onondaga speaker Teganissorens responded: "That the kitle may not be oversett nor turn'd upside down, but remain boyling which is our custom, meaning that the war may continue, but if God pleases to bless, that we reduce and wholly subdue Canada, then it is in your power to oversett the kitle of War and turn it upside down, which is as much to say that the Expedicon is over and then what is boiled in it meaning the Prisoners are at the disposal of the Lieut. Generall [Nicholson] as he shall see cause."[12]

Had Hunter's slip of the tongue gone uncorrected, he might have inadvertently called off the expedition before it began. As it turned out, another naval mishap ruined the 1711 Anglo-Iroquois expedition against Canada even before the land-based forces left Albany. Disgusted by the second English military disaster in three years, the Iroquois declared themselves "so ashamed that we must cover our faces," and French rumors of an English plot to exterminate the Iroquois began to circulate widely among the Five Nations.[13] By June 1712 alarming new reports of the French arming Iroquois war parties to assist their distant Tuscarora allies in the latter's war on the settlers of North Carolina forced the Albany Commissioners of Indian Affairs to take action. They recommended that "some men of Credit" be sent among the Iroquois to "indeceive them of the ill impressions they have received from the French," and to discourage them from any involvement in the Tuscarora War.[14] One day after learning of the Albany Commissioners' recommendation, the New York Assembly accepted Hunter's request that Madame Montour, Carondawana, and Peter Schuyler proceed to the Iroquois Grand Council at Onondaga (modern Syracuse, New York) to communicate this message to the Iroquois and provided £100 for the mission, one-half as a present to the Iroquois and one-half for expenses.

Hunter hoped that the efforts of this diplomatic legation would be sufficient to dissuade the Iroquois from allying formally with the

Tuscarora, since he did not wish to see Indians from New York attacking settlers in another English colony. On July 19, 1712, Schuyler presented his journal of the trip to the Albany Commissioners, and although no specific information on the activities of Madame Montour during the journey survives, the mission succeeded. Only a few Seneca warriors traveled south to assist the Tuscarora, and the Carolinians, with the assistance of the Yamassee Indians, eventually succeeded in dispersing them. Instead of joining in the war, the Iroquois made offers to mediate peace between the Tuscarora and the North Carolina settlers, and invited the defeated Tuscarora to move north and live on lands provided largely by the Oneida. Pleased with the work of Madame Montour and Carondawana, Hunter advised the Albany Commissioners in August 1712 of his desire "that in all propositions and messages to or from ye Indians Mrs. Montour and her husband be present."[15]

Despite this endorsement, Madame Montour disappears from the written record for seven years after her return from Onondaga. The 1713 Treaty of Utrecht concluded Queen Anne's War and led New York's political leadership to turn its attention away from Indian affairs to other matters. Governor Hunter seldom met with the Iroquois after 1713, and not at all after 1717, which limited his need for Madame Montour's services. As an Oneida wife and possibly a mother by this time, however, Madame Montour kept busy. Also, given her family contacts in the *pays d'en haut*, she spent some time traveling during this period.

A visit from one of Madame Montour's female relatives returned her to the attention of the Albany Commissioners in 1719. After Governor Vaudreuil sent Madame Montour's sister (who lived among the Miami Indians) to New York to try to persuade her to leave the English colony and relocate permanently to the *pays d'en haut*, the Albany officials immediately corrected the arrears in Madame Montour's salary. They also raised her pay to equal that of a soldier in one of the four independent companies of the British army serving in New York, which in 1701 had amounted to eight pence per day.

Madame Montour evidently stayed in New York for at least two years beyond 1719. In September 1721 the New York Assembly discussed a proposal for an officer and twenty men to be stationed in a blockhouse erected at Saratoga, with "Mrs. Montour interpreter at Saratoga to be paid." New York officials planned to employ this outpost "for stopping the trade to Canada."[16] Yet by June 1722 the Albany Commissioners determined that the illicit trade with Canada "was largely carried on from Sereghtoga [sic]," and "that the Officer posted there with a detachment of the Independent Company was expected to be concerned in the same."[17] Madame

Montour had relatives involved in the illegal fur trade between New York and Canada, in which Catholic Iroquois living in mission villages near Montréal carried furs obtained by French *coureurs de bois* and traded them in Albany for higher-quality and lower-priced goods, especially stroud blankets (made of coarse woolen cloth), than they could obtain in Canada. The Iroquois couriers then exchanged these goods in Canada with the French, for the latter to use in their trade with the Indians of the *pays d'en haut*.

It remains unclear whether Madame Montour ever assumed her post at Saratoga. Given the evidence available, it seems unlikely, since her experience to this date emphasized forging economic ties between Albany and the Great Lakes Algonquians. This economic policy was favored by New York governors such as Robert Hunter and his successor William Burnet, because it weakened French influence in the Great Lakes region. The clandestine trade between New York and Canada involved few risks for the Dutch traders at Albany, but it enabled the French to maintain their network of alliances with the western Algonquians by providing a supply of merchandise which the Indians demanded but which the Canadian merchants could not readily obtain from France.

How long Madame Montour resided in New York after 1721 remains a mystery. The 1720s witnessed widespread population movements among the Iroquois. After voluntarily ceding part of their own territory to the Tuscarora refugees, many Oneida families (including Madame Montour, Carondawana, and, very likely by this time, her children Margaret and Andrew) moved to multiethnic Indian communities in Pennsylvania's Susquehanna River Valley to live with Delaware, Conestoga, and Shawnee peoples affiliated with the Iroquois. By establishing closer ties with Pennsylvania, the Iroquois migrants sought a diplomatic counterweight to Canada and New York, both of which placed fortifications (Niagara and Oswego) in Iroquois territory shortly after 1725. Not surprisingly, Madame Montour had contacts in Pennsylvania, including a relative married into the Bisaillon trading family who, along with the Le Torts and Chartiers, conducted business with Pennsylvania Secretary James Logan. By 1727, Madame Montour made her family home at Ostonwakin (near modern Sunbury) on the west branch of the Susquehanna.

On July 3, 1727, Madame Montour appeared as an interpreter in Philadelphia with a delegation of Iroquois offering to sell land in the Susquehanna Valley to Pennsylvania in exchange for a pledge from the colony that no further settlement would occur beyond Paxton, in Lancaster County. Confused by this unsolicited offer, Governor Patrick Gordon declined, but council etiquette demanded that the Indians receive some remuneration for delivering the message, and he presented Madame Montour and Carondawana with three stroud blankets, a shirt, and a matchcoat, or mantle, for their trouble. Secretary Logan quickly realized the potential of this visit, and over the next decade he worked to extend the Six Nations' authority over their Indian allies in Pennsylvania as a means of expediting the colony's purchases of Indian land.

Shortly after her arrival in Pennsylvania, Madame Montour built a solid reputation for her knowledge of Indian affairs. As in her career in New York, she cultivated close personal ties with Pennsylvania authorities early on, but her role became increasingly that of a freelance consultant for persons willing to visit her hometown. In autumn 1727, when trader James Le Tort wanted to arrange a trading expedition to the Miami country, he consulted with Madame Montour, "who having lived amongst & having a Sister married to one of that Nation, he believed might be a proper person to advise him."[18] Initially excited about the prospect of Le Tort's venture, she even agreed to accompany him, but winter set in before Le Tort could depart. In the spring of 1728, when Le Tort called on Madame Montour again, she advised him against making the trip, citing hostile feelings toward white colonists among the Delaware stemming from the 1727 hanging of a Delaware named Wequela in New Jersey. Madame Montour reported that the Delaware complained to the Iroquois, who in turn sent a message to the Miami, "desiring to know if they would lift up their axes and join with them against the Christians, to which they agreed."[19] Thus discouraged from visiting the Miami, Le Tort questioned Delaware leader Manawkyhickon about the Iroquois-Miami message, and the Indian confirmed Madame Montour's report. The Pennsylvania Council, once apprised of Madame Montour's intelligence, ordered an inquiry into the affair and provided matchcoats for Le Tort to give to his informants. James Logan also sent word to Madame Montour "that I desire her on the faith of a Christian and the profession of fidelity to this Government w[hi]ch she made to me to be industrious in procuring all the certain intelligence she can, of all affairs transacted amongst the Indians that relate to the Peace of this Province and transmitt an acc[oun]t of them to me."[20]

Soon after this situation calmed down, Philadelphia politicians in 1728 made contact with Shickellamy, an Oneida headman sent by the Iroquois Grand Council to the west branch of the Susquehanna. Operating from the village of Shamokin (near Ostonwakin), Shickellamy looked after affairs for the faction in Iroquois leadership most interested in a new alliance with Pennsylvania, as an alternative to their relationships with New York and Canada. Shickellamy brought social and political prestige rather than cultural or linguistic expertise to his new role, and he often required translators and other advisers to help him communicate. Madame Montour's network of contacts helped Shickellamy to establish himself in Pennsylvania, and he owed his early influence in part to his status as a representative of the Iroquois Confederacy and in part to his association with Carondawana and Madame Montour. In October 1728, Carondawana accompanied Shickellamy to a conference in Philadelphia, where Delaware headman Allumapees (whose daughter later married Andrew Montour) informed Governor Gordon that "the Five Nations have often told them that they [the Delaware] were as women only, and desired them to plant Corn and mind their own business, for that they would take care of what related to peace."[21] In effect, Allumapees announced his acquiescence to the primary "go-between" position that Shickellamy had assumed in Pennsylvania on behalf of the Iroquois-allied refugee Indian groups residing in the colony.

Tragedy struck the families of both Shickellamy and Madame Montour in the spring of 1729, when Carondawana and one of Shickellamy's sons fell victim to a surprise retaliatory attack by the Catawba Indians while returning home through Virginia from a military campaign against these traditional enemies. On June 16, 1729, the Pennsylvania Council sent black stroud blankets to the Oneida in sympathy for Carondawana's death. Governor Gordon expressed his personal sorrow in letters to Shickellamy and Madame Montour in August 1729; and on May 29, 1730, Pennsylvania authorities forwarded "a suit of mourning clothes" for Madame Montour, along with a coat and handkerchief for her "little son."[22] Providing her son Sattelihu (Andrew Montour) with the linguistic and brokerage skills for a diplomatic career became the central focus of her life following the death of her husband.

Madame Montour remained an active part of official Oneida brokerage circles in Pennsylvania for only a short period after 1729. Carondawana's brother Sagogaliax represented the Oneida with Shickellamy at an August 1732 conference in Philadelphia, but Shickellamy by this time had already started to edge away from Madame Montour's family contacts. In 1733 he publicly discredited a report provided by fellow Shamokin resident Katarionecha, who had warned him "that the Friendship of the White People was from the Mouth only, and not from the Heart."[23] After about 1730, Shickellamy relied increasingly on the interpreting and brokerage skills of Conrad Weiser, a German immigrant living in Pennsylvania who had strong ties to the Mohawk. Madame Montour soon found herself on the margins of Pennsylvania's "official" Indian diplomacy.

Yet Madame Montour's reputation still commanded attention from the Pennsylvania Council. When a large party of Oneidas under headman Saristagoa arrived in Philadelphia on September 25, 1734, reportedly to confer with Proprietor John Penn on the subject of their "great loss" of warriors in 1729, the authorities called on her expertise. Uneasy and confused that these Oneida "had come hither without any Authority from the Six Nations, [and] had nothing of Importance to deliver," the Council discussed the need to discourage potentially costly future visits of this kind, and planned to set a precedent by giving these "private persons" a present equivalent in value to the single bundle of deerskins that the Oneida had presented. Consulted for her opinion, Madame Montour scrutinized the visitors and confirmed that these Oneida were "not persons of any great Note amongst the Six nations, yet they set out for this place at the Desire of some Chiefs of those Nations, who when just preparing to visit this Government & to follow those Indians hither, were stopped by the unexpected arrival of sundry Persons from Albany, charged with matters of consequence to be imparted to them, that hereupon orders were dispatched to countermand all the other Indians from proceeding, but that those Oneidas were far advanced on their Journey before those orders reached them."24

Madame Montour provided a believable story, and helped persuade the Pennsylvania Council to issue to the Oneida some £20 worth of "such Goods as they stand most in need of."25 Her all-too-accurate assessment of the Oneida party, however, alarmed both Iroquois and Pennsylvania authorities, who were anxious to promote the image of Iroquois control over the colony's native population. The absence of important Iroquois leaders from Pennsylvania's Indian conferences threatened to reveal the central premise underlying Secretary Logan's Indian policy: that Iroquois participation in Pennsylvania-Indian diplomacy in the 1730s represented the work of only a narrow faction of headmen in Six Nations home territory who lacked the prestigious official endorsement of the Iroquois Grand Council that they claimed to possess.

Shickellamy and Seneca headman Hetaquantagechty hastened to Philadelphia less than three weeks later and, through Weiser's interpretation, offered an explanation for the absence of the prominent leaders that actually corroborated Madame Montour's story. Nevertheless, Hetaquantagechty made a point of denouncing her in the presence of Proprietor John Penn, stating that

> he was sorely troubled to hear that some base representations had been made of those Indians that came hither to the Treaty, as if they were persons who had no Authority for their coming, and were not of any Credit amongst their own people and that this Government had been imposed upon and put to a needless charge on their account; that he believes this report has been in great measure owing to a certain woman whose old age only protects her from being punished for such Falsehoods, that in the meantime

they must resent it and hope to get rid of her. On this article he delivered some strings of wampum.

Unwilling to offend the Iroquois, Penn urged that Hetaquantagechty "disregard such Idle reports, for they can make no Impressions on us."[26] This speech effectively ended Madame Montour's public career. She never again appeared at a conference in any recognized capacity.

Supporting herself and Andrew by trade and by acting as a personal clearinghouse of intelligence on the western Indians, Madame Montour retreated to Ostonwakin after 1734. If she bore any hard feelings toward Weiser and Shickellamy, they did not prevent her frequent informal contacts with both men. When Weiser appeared at her home in March 1737, en route to speak with the Iroquois at Onondaga, he remarked that she "showed great compassion"; and despite "having very little to spare at this time, or perhaps dared not let it be seen on the account of so many hungry Indians about," Madame Montour secretly gave Weiser and his companions "as much as we could eat, which had not happened to us before for ten days."[27] By maintaining good relations with Weiser, continuing to live in proximity to the diplomatic hub of Shamokin, and imparting to her son the linguistic skills and the accumulated wisdom of her experience as an intermediary, Madame Montour established the groundwork for Andrew's future diplomatic career.

Andrew Montour began working formally as an interpreter in September 1742, when he served with Conrad Weiser as a guide for the visit of Moravian missionaries to Ostonwakin under the auspices of Count Nicholas Ludwig von Zinzendorf. Deeply affected by the appearance of these people, Madame Montour reportedly wept during Zinzendorf's sermon (delivered in French), and tried to persuade him to baptize two children, possibly her granddaughters Catherine and Esther. Unimpressed with Madame Montour's grasp of Christianity, which he attributed to "falsehoods" spread by French Jesuit missionaries, Zinzendorf refused her request. Nevertheless, Madame Montour apparently forged close ties with Moravian missionary Anna Nitschmann, and she reportedly told Nitschmann "among other things that she was weary of Indian life."[28] Weary or not, Madame Montour continued to live as an Oneida woman. She left Ostonwakin in 1743 and took up residence on a small island in the Susquehanna River near Shamokin, and her relocation brought Andrew into a prominent interpreting role in Shickellamy's diplomatic orbit.

After 1744, Andrew Montour built a reputation for himself as a skilled and trusted interpreter, and he often worked with Conrad Weiser. Andrew also took on the care of his mother, especially after she lost her eyesight and apparently withdrew from even informal contact with public life. Madame Montour lived with her son until January 1753, when Pennsylvania Indian trader John Harris reported her death.

An assessment of Madame Montour should take into account both the empowerment and tragedy in her life so as not to over-romanticize her career as a cultural broker, yet still recognize her accomplishments while living on a difficult, and sometimes chaotic, early American frontier. As an adopted Oneida woman, her life story definitely reflects the "sustained and enduring contact with new cultural ways" that faced most Indian women after the arrival of Europeans in America.[29] Although she left no written documents of her own to retrace her path, she lived and moved between several cultures. Her legacy derives from her mobility, her adaptability, and her family. Independent, trustworthy, and unafraid to tell the truth, Madame Montour bounced back from several devastating events in her life and labored to keep herself and her kin prominent in the minds of people on both sides of the early American frontier. Frequently identified as "white," or "French," the vagueness of Madame Montour's ethnic identity permitted her the freedom of emphasizing or withholding aspects of her background to her own advantage as the social situation demanded. Despite the difficulties of starting life as a captive of the Iroquois, apart from her mixed-blood family in Canada, Madame Montour's far-flung network of kin played a key role in her rise to influence by providing her with much of the intelligence about Indian country that generally eluded colonial officials. She must also have derived some satisfaction from living to see her son Andrew eclipse Shickellamy's role in Indian affairs in Pennsylvania after 1747, when that colony began direct negotiations with the Indians living in the Ohio Valley rather than continuing to work through Iroquoian diplomatic channels. Madame Montour's children, grandchildren, and other relatives lived for many years as cultural brokers and traders, taking different sides during the American Revolution. The Montour name still persists among the Iroquois people today.

Yet Madame Montour also paid a price for her role as a cultural broker on the colonial frontiers of New York and Pennsylvania. In retrospect, she received surprisingly little in the way of reward from the white colonial or Indian societies whom she served as an inter-cultural consultant. Her mixed racial heritage may have set her apart at an early date and left her little choice but to begin dealing with outsiders. The respect and influence accorded her by colonial authorities did not necessarily translate into acceptance among the Indians. As a widow, without her husband Carondawana as an ally, even the migrant Oneida community in Pennsylvania began to marginalize her family. Madame Montour spent many of her days on the move between different regions and assignments, alone or with only a small part of her extended family. Madame Montour's career as a cultural broker demonstrates that such a role was not always pleasant, or rewarding, or even sought after by native and white societies on the colonial American frontier.

Notes

1. "Witham Marshe's Journal of the Treaty Held with the Six Nations by the Commissioners of Maryland, and other Provinces, at Lancaster in Pennsylvania, June, 1744," Massachusetts Historical Society, *Collections*, 1st ser., 7 (1800): 189.

2. C. H. McIlwain, ed., *An Abridgment of the Indian Affairs Contained in Four Folio Volumes Transacted in the Colony of New York, from the Year 1673 to the Year 1751, by Peter Wraxall* (Cambridge, MA, 1915), 50 (hereafter cited as *WA*).

3. *WA*, 64–65. Cf. M. de Vaudreuil to M. de Pontchartrain, November 14, 1709, in E. B. O'Callaghan and Berthold Fernow, eds., *Documents Relative to the Colonial History of the State of New York*, 15 vols. (Albany, 1853–1887), 9 (1855): 830 (hereafter cited as *NYCD*).

4. "Letter from MM. Vaudreuil and Raudot, Quebec 14 November 1709," in Clarence M. Burton, comp., "Cadillac Papers," Michigan Pioneer and Historical Society, *Collections* 34 (1905): 453–54.

5. M. de Vaudreuil to Governor William Burnet, August 24, 1721, *NYCD* 9:902.

6. *WA*, 66.

7. "Cadwallader Colden's *History of the Five Indian Nations, Continuation, 1707–1720*," New-York Historical Society (hereafter cited as NYHS), *Collections* 68 (1935): 372.

8. *WA*, 67.

9. Minutes of the Albany Commissioners of Indian Affairs, July 14, 1709, in Lawrence H. Leder, ed., *The Livingston Indian Records* (Gettysburg, PA, 1956), 207.

10. Cadwallader Colden to his son, September 25, 1759, in "The Colden Letters on Smith's *History of New York*, 1759–1760," NYHS, *Collections* 1 (1868): 200.

11. Natalie Zemon Davis, "Iroquois Women, European Women," in *Women, 'Race,' and Writing in the Early Modern Period*, ed. Margo Hendricks and Patricia Parker (New York, 1994), 252–53.

12. "Conference between Governor Hunter and the Indians, August 17–28, 1711," *NYCD* 5:270, 273.

13. *WA*, 92–93.

14. "Council at Fort Anne, June 13, 1712," in *Journal of the Legislative Council of the Colony of New York, 1691–1775*, 2 vols. (Albany, 1861), 1:337.

15. Hunter to Albany Commissioners of Indian Affairs, August 13, 1712, in Francis Jennings et al., eds., *Iroquois Indians: A Documentary History of the Diplomacy of the Six Nations and Their League* (50 reels microfilm; Woodbridge, CT, 1985), reel 7.

16. September 11, 1721, Minutes, in Berthold Fernow and A. J. F. Van Laer, eds., "Calendar of New York Council Minutes," New York State

158   *The Human Tradition in Colonial America*

Library *Bulletin* 58 (1903): 281. Cf. *NYCD* 5:641–42.

17. *WA*, 141.

18. Samuel Hazard, ed., *Minutes of the Provincial Council of Pennsylvania*, 16 vols. (Harrisburg, 1838–1853), 3 (1840): 312 (hereafter cited as *MPCP*).

19. Charles A. Hanna, *The Wilderness Trail, or the Ventures and Adventures of the Pennsylvania Traders on the Allegheny Path*, 2 vols. (1911; reprinted., Lewisburg, PA, 1995), 1:94–95.

20. James Logan, "Instructions to J. Le Tort and John Scull, April 18, 1728," in Samuel Hazard, ed., *Pennsylvania Archives*, 9 ser., 138 vols. (Philadelphia and Harrisburg, 1852–1949), ser. 1, 1 (1852): 211.

21. *MPCP* 3:353–54.

22. Quoted in Katharine Bennet, "Madame Montour," Northumberland County Historical Society, *Proceedings and Addresses* 13 (1943): 37.

23. *MPCP* 3:537–38.

24. Ibid., 617–18.

25. Ibid., 618.

26. Ibid., 625, 628.

27. "Narrative of a Journey, made in the Year 1737, by Conrad Weiser, Indian Agent and Provincial Interpreter, from Tulpehocken in the Province of Pennsylvania to Onondago, the headquarters of the allied Six Nations in the Province of New York," trans. Hiester H. Muhlenberg, Historical Society of Pennsylvania, *Collections* 1 (1853): 8.

28. William C. Reichel, ed., *Memorials of the Moravian Church* (Philadelphia, 1870), 1:95–98.

29. Clara Sue Kidwell, "Indian Women as Cultural Mediators," *Ethnohistory* 39 (1992): 98.

Suggested Readings

The only full-length biographical treatment of Madame Montour (written in French) is by Simone Vincens, *Madame Montour et son temps* (Montreal, 1979), but the best scholarship to date on Madame Montour appears in several works by Nancy Hagedorn, including her " 'Faithful, Knowing, and Prudent': Andrew Montour as Interpreter and Cultural Broker, 1740–1772," in *Between Indian and White Worlds: The Cultural Broker*, ed. Margaret C. Szasz (Norman, OK, 1994), 44–60; idem, "Brokers of Understanding: Interpreters as Agents of Cultural Exchange in Colonial New York," *New York History* 76 (1995): 379–405; and idem, " 'A Friend to Go between Them': Interpreters among the Iroquois, 1664–1775" (Ph.D. dissertation, College of William and Mary, Williamsburg, VA, 1995). In addition to the literature cited in the notes, the following works also proved helpful in reconstructing Madame Montour's history: "The Montours," in *Notes and Queries, Historical and Genealogical, Chiefly Relating to Interior Pennsylvania*, ed. William H. Egle, 3d ser., 3 vols. (1895; reprint ed., Baltimore, 1970), 1:118–27; Charles A. Hanna, *The Wilderness Trail, or the Ventures and Adventures of the Pennsylvania Traders on the*

Allegheny Path, 2 vols. (1911; reprint ed., Lewisburg, PA, 1995), 1:198–202; Howard Lewin, "A Frontier Diplomat: Andrew Montour," *Pennsylvania History* 33 (1966): 155; Paul A. W. Wallace, "Montour, Madame," in *Notable American Women: A Biographical Dictionary*, ed. Edward T. James, 3 vols. (Cambridge, MA, 1971), 2:568–69; William A. Hunter, "Couc, Elizabeth," in *Dictionary of Canadian Biography*, ed. George W. Brown et al., 14 vols. to date (Toronto and Laval, 1966–), 3:147–48; and James H. Merrell, "The Cast of His Countenance: Reading Andrew Montour," in *Through a Glass Darkly: Reflections on Personal Identity in Early America*, ed. Ronald Hoffman et al. (Chapel Hill, NC, 1997), 13–39.

Important work on Iroquois women's history appears in William Guy Spittal, *Iroquois Women: An Anthology* (Ohsweken, Ontario, 1990); and Susan C. Prezzano, "Warfare, Women, and Households: The Development of Iroquois Culture," in *Women in Prehistory: North America and Mesoamerica*, ed. C. Claasen and R. A. Joyce (Philadelphia, 1996), 88–99. Scholarly literature on cultural brokers includes James A. Clifton, "Alternative Identities and Cultural Frontiers," in *Being and Becoming Indian: Biographical Studies of North American Frontiers*, ed. James A. Clifton (Chicago, 1989), 1–37; Frances Karttunen, *Between Worlds: Interpreters, Guides, and Survivors* (New Brunswick, NJ, 1994); Alan Taylor, "Captain Hendrick Aupaumut: The Dilemmas of an Intercultural Broker," *Ethnohistory* 43 (1996): 431–52; and James H. Merrell, "Shickellamy, 'A Person of Consequence,' " in *Northeastern Indian Lives, 1632–1816*, ed. Robert S. Grumet (Amherst, MA, 1996), 227–57. Finally, the best introduction to the early American *métis* may be found in Jacqueline Peterson, "Many Roads to Red River: Métis Genesis in the Great Lakes Region, 1680–1815," in *The New Peoples: Being and Becoming Métis in North America*, ed. Jacqueline Peterson and Jennifer S. H. Brown (Winnipeg, Manitoba, 1985), 37–71; and Harriet Gorham, "Families of Mixed Descent in the Western Great Lakes Region," in *Native People, Native Lands: Canadian Indians, Inuit, and Métis*, ed. Bruce A. Cox (Ottawa, 1987), 37–55.

9

Caspar Wistar
*German-American Entrepreneur and Cultural Broker**

Rosalind J. Beiler

The life of Caspar Wistar (1696–1752), like that of Daniel Clocker, is a success story that seems stereotypical. Changing conditions in his native Palatinate encouraged him to leave home, and his savings allowed him to pay his own passage and thereby avoid indentured servitude in Pennsylvania. By his own account, he arrived in Philadelphia without any money and with a fellow immigrant as his only friend. Through good fortune or careful planning, Wistar quickly gained access to cash and credit. Within seven years of his arrival, he was an established button maker, a Quaker convert, a naturalized British subject, a property holder, and a merchant. Two years later he married into a prominent pioneering German Quaker family, and Caspar's political and business associations thereafter seem prudent, yet profitable. His role as adviser, employer, master, and landlord to a large number of new German immigrants may well have been mutually beneficial, although he was certainly in a position to exploit these people. As a new migrant of good family, Caspar was able to attract other German migrants and to broker legal business between arrivals and their homeland. Caspar's own prosperity was impressive; his ability to establish his seven children as substantial property holders was remarkable.

Rosalind J. Beiler's most recent monograph is entitled Becoming American: The Transatlantic World of Caspar Wistar, 1650–1752. She teaches early American history at the University of Central Florida.

O n September 16, 1717, Caspar Wistar, a twenty-one-year-old German-speaking immigrant, stepped onto the dock in

*The research for this essay has been supported by the Fulbright Commission, The Philadelphia Center for Early American Studies, The Pennsylvania Historical and Museum Commission, Harrisburg, and The Henry Francis du Pont Library at Winterthur, Wilmington, Delaware.

Philadelphia. According to his own account, he had spent all but nine pence of his life savings on the voyage, and had borrowed three *pistolines* from Abraham Riehm, his only friend on the ship. When his shipmates went in search of something to eat and drink, the young man was forced to wander the streets because he could not afford the taverns' prices. Like his contemporary, Benjamin Franklin, Wistar purchased a loaf of bread and then set out to explore the city. He soon met a cider maker, who offered to pay him in apples in return for his help. His poverty and his first American meal of apples and bread made a lasting impression on the young immigrant.

Wistar may have been nearly penniless when he first arrived in Pennsylvania, but by the time he died in 1752, he was a prominent, wealthy leader among the German-speaking community in this British colony. The story of his position among fellow immigrants is intricately woven together with his meteoric rise from rags to riches. Wistar does not fit the traditional definition of a cultural broker; he never acted as an official interpreter or a treaty negotiator between European and Amerindian peoples, nor did he consciously set out to become a leader among his fellow immigrants. Instead, Wistar sought economic security and the social status that had eluded his family in Europe. A combination of the particular circumstances in Pennsylvania and his creative use of those conditions propelled him into his mediating role.

What were the strategies that Wistar used to secure his position in British America? How did his pursuit of wealth contribute to his rise as a leader? Wistar's role as a cultural broker evolved as he struggled for survival in the new and very different environment of eighteenth-century Pennsylvania. First, he set out to develop professional connections through religious institutions and family networks. Second, he shrewdly used his reputation, creativity, and credit to provide services to the Pennsylvania Proprietors. Finally, Wistar tapped into a common cultural identity to help other immigrants like himself begin their lives in America. By pursuing profits and simultaneously offering aid to immigrants, Wistar helped to bridge the gap between Anglo-American and German-speaking cultural groups in colonial Pennsylvania. In the process, he gained the economic stability that he had set out to achieve.

The young man's story begins, however, on the other side of the Atlantic in Waldhilsbach, a small village southeast of Heidelberg. Wistar was born and baptized there in 1696 as Hans Caspar Wüster.[1] The firstborn son of a forester or hunter, he and his family belonged to the growing government bureaucracy of the Elector of the Palatinate, a small principality in what is today Germany. That membership influenced almost every aspect of the Wüsters' daily lives: it determined their occupations and economic status, it affected their relationships with their neighbors, and it influenced their decisions about religious affiliation.

As foresters and hunters, Wistar's grandfather and father were responsible for protecting the state's natural resources and for helping to gain revenue from them. They also aided the Elector in his elaborately staged hunts designed to impress the aristocracy and heads of other states. At a time when burgeoning government bureaucracies symbolized the wealth and power of the state, official positions promised appealing social status and economic security.

Performing the tasks of a forester, however, required a fine balancing act. By the early eighteenth century, land and resources were shrinking as the Palatinate recovered from a century of wars and as the population once again began to expand. While the government sought to increase its revenues from the forests, villagers struggled to hold on to land and usage rights that they had claimed for centuries. Foresters were caught in the middle of this tug-of-war. If, in the line of duty, a forester denied his neighbors access to firewood or meadows too severely, villagers could make his life miserable—as Wistar's father discovered. His neighbors filed a lengthy suit against him when they believed he had abused his power as a forester, and they made it difficult for him to purchase village property. On the other hand, if he did not properly protect the state's resources from his neighbors, a forester could easily be replaced by someone whose patronage connections in the Elector's court were stronger. Wistar grew up in this world, where negotiating between various interests was interwoven with every aspect of his daily life and where opportunity was increasingly limited.

According to his own account, Wistar received little formal education as a child. Instead, he worked for his father, hunting and fowling, until he was a teenager. When he was seventeen, he went to the Elector's hunting lodge at Bruchhausen, where he served the chief huntsman, Georg Michael Förster, as an apprentice. The prestige associated with his position in the Elector's entourage is evident in the substantial salary he supposedly received: 69 *Gulden,* 20 *Kreuzer* (£7.5 sterling), a clothing allowance, and a per diem allowance while performing government duties. In comparison, his father received an annual salary of 64 *Gulden* (£7 sterling), 16 *Malter* of wheat, and free firewood for his tasks as a forester. (A Pennsylvania laborer's family of four needed £32 sterling to cover the costs of food, clothing, heat, and shelter for one year in 1762.) While Wistar was at Bruchhausen, however, a series of changes occurred in the government that created difficulties for foresters and hunters. The new Elector, who came to power in 1716, ordered a series of reforms and salary freezes in the forestry administration. For the next three years, foresters and hunters received little of their pay as their superiors worked to trim costs and positions from the bureaucracy.

In the midst of these freezes and at a time when prospects for newly trained hunters looked particularly grim, "the Lord of all Lords inspired" Wistar to travel to Pennsylvania.[2] Family traditions maintain that his father offered to give Wistar his forester's position, which the young man would have inherited as the oldest son, if he remained at home. But his own account notes that his heart was so taken with the "new land" that he refused to stay, despite the emotional trauma of leaving home against his parents' wishes. Instead, he said a tearful good-bye to family and friends, collected the money he had managed to save, and boarded a ship for Philadelphia.

When Wistar arrived in the city in 1717, the conditions he found in Philadelphia forced him to the bottom of colonial society. In contrast to the Palatinate, Pennsylvania had no forestry administration; William Penn and his descendants did not command a corps of hunters. The difference between the two worlds meant that Wistar could not do the job for which he had trained in Europe. Consequently, he was reduced to hauling ashes for a soap maker named John Bearde, a job well below the social status of a Palatine hunter and forester. To complicate matters, Wistar could not communicate well in English. As a result, he suffered from misunderstandings with his master's wife and feared that he was not working hard enough.

Although his station as a wage laborer made a lasting impression on the immigrant, Wistar did not remain in his humble position for long. Within a year and a half, he began an apprenticeship as a brass button maker, an occupation he continued to pursue throughout his life. Long after he became a wealthy merchant and land speculator, the immigrant still identified himself as a brass button maker. For Wistar, promotion from a wage laborer to an artisan was the first step in securing his place in his new home.

While he was working to obtain some job security, Wistar also set out to raise his social status. An apprenticeship as a button maker was one step above hauling ashes, but it carried little of the prestige that he associated with being a government official in the Palatinate. The young man had watched his father's status among his neighbors vacillate as changes at court shifted his patronage connections. He assumed that in America, as in Europe, his place in society depended on establishing relationships with the right people.

One of the ways that Wistar improved his position was by seeking out Quaker patrons. Shortly after his arrival, he realized the importance of Quaker merchants in Penn's colony. Wealthy Friends controlled much of Philadelphia's economy and dominated provincial politics. Like his grandfather and father, who sought patrons in the Elector's governmental bureaucracy to elevate their social position, Wistar understood the importance of finding Quaker sponsors.

Perhaps the most obvious group of Quaker patrons whom Wistar sought were the German-speaking Friends at Germantown who had preceded him to the colony. Common language and culture created an instant bond between him and the settlers there. A group of Quaker families from Krefeld, a town in the Rhine River Valley not far from the Palatinate, had settled Germantown in 1683. In the following twenty-five years, additional families from villages close to Wistar's home joined the earliest settlers of the town. When the young man arrived in 1717, many of his shipmates had family and friends who had already settled in Germantown. Although he claimed to have only one friend in the colony, the people at Germantown understood the world that Wistar had left behind, and he knew their leaders were well connected to Pennsylvania's government.

The immigrant's first step toward acquiring Quaker patrons was to change his religious affiliation. Wistar was the son of a Lutheran father and a Reformed mother. He and a sister were baptized in the Reformed Church, while their seven siblings were baptized according to Lutheran rituals. Furthermore, a brother and two sisters converted to the Catholic Church upon becoming adults. The ecumenical nature of Wistar's family resulted from the peculiar circumstances of the Palatinate during the period. Traditionally, the ruling Elector determined the official church. Consequently, Lutheran and Catholic subjects were baptized, married, and buried in the Reformed Church throughout the second half of the seventeenth century, while continuing to think of themselves as Lutheran or Catholic. Between 1680 and 1705, however, frequent changes in power led the government to recognize publicly the legitimacy of all three churches. Thereafter, Wüster family members chose the religious affiliation most likely to promote their positions as officials or within their communities.

Changes in public affiliation, however, did not diminish the importance of their religious beliefs. Family members shared personal assumptions about their spiritual lives that remained distinct from their stated affiliation with a particular church. The spiritual language that Wistar used in his American letters to his widowed mother and siblings in Europe indicates a common set of beliefs even though they all belonged to different churches. For the Wüsters, therefore, joining the church of one's patrons was not a sign of insincerity or a lack of religious conviction. It was simply the continuation of a long-standing division in the Palatinate between public religious affiliation and private belief.

Like his father and siblings in Europe, Wistar realized the importance of religious connections for establishing his reputation in Pennsylvania. As early as 1721, the immigrant indicated his Quaker sympathies by signing a declaration of allegiance to the King of England rather than swearing an oath. The declaration was a legal tool designed to permit Quakers, who had scruples against taking oaths, to promise loyalty to Great Britain. By 1726, Wistar had become a member of the Philadelphia Monthly Meeting of Friends and thereby gained entrance into the dominant network of merchants and political leaders in the province.

At the same time he was seeking Quaker patrons, Wistar joined the ranks of American property holders. In 1721 he purchased a prime city lot on High Street in Philadelphia. Precisely how he raised £210 "American Money" (£153 sterling) in less than four years to acquire the property remains a mystery. Wistar entered Philadelphia during a period when opportunities for artisans to invest in real estate were greater than in Boston or New York. While it seems unlikely that he saved the entire amount from his apprenticeship wages, he may have supplemented his savings with an informal loan from a Germantown or Philadelphia Quaker.

Wistar soon took further measures to secure his property. According to British law, the children of non-British immigrants could not inherit land unless their parents had become naturalized citizens. While provincial governments tried to guarantee such rights for their settlers, Parliament and the courts in the mother country did not always approve their attempts. News of the legal difficulties that Pennsylvania Germans faced in leaving legacies of land spread back to Europe. Several months after Wistar arrived, Pennsylvania's Commissioners of Property warned some of his shipmates that the government could not guarantee their rights to pass on land to their heirs. The newcomers replied that they were already aware of the colony's laws and responded favorably to the recommendation that they become naturalized British subjects.

Wistar, like his fellow immigrants, clearly understood the potential danger of losing his investment. While most of his shipmates did not become citizens until later, he submitted a petition to the legislature requesting naturalization in 1724. Within several months, the assembly passed an act that gave Wistar, fellow German John Cratho, and French immigrant Nicholas Gateau the right to "have and enjoy all lands and tenements . . . by way of purchase or gift of any person or persons whatsoever . . . as if they had been born natural subjects of this province."[3]

Wistar's naturalization act went beyond property concerns, however. It included an additional clause granting the petitioners the privilege of participating in international trade. The act stated that they were "free and fully able and capable to trade, traffic, load, freight and transport all and all manner of goods, wares and merchandises not by law prohibited to be imported or exported, as if they had been of the natural liege people and subjects of the King of Great Britain born in this province."[4] Wistar's bill was the third private naturalization act to be passed in the colony, and none of the previous ones had included trading privileges.

The success of Wistar's petition indicates that he had established his reputation among the "better sort" of Pennsylvanians. At the same time that his bill was under consideration, the assembly debated another naturalization petition from a group of nearly four hundred German-speaking settlers. Isaac Norris, a member of the Provincial Council, noted that the petitioners were "mostly unknown to the Assembly or the better sort of the Inhabitants."[5] The legislators echoed Norris's sentiment when they determined that local officials should inquire into the petitioners' "Characters, Belief and Behavior" before issuing certificates qualifying them for naturalization.[6] Interestingly enough, the assembly required no character references for Wistar; two days after its debate, it approved his bill. The fact that he was acquainted with at least one influential Quaker legislator, Anthony Morris, undoubtedly worked in his favor. Just three years earlier, Wistar had signed the will of his father, Anthony Morris Sr., as a witness.

Wistar's naturalization also signaled the beginning of his diverse American career. By 1724 he very likely had completed his apprenticeship as a button maker and set up his own business. Wistar had been in the colony long enough to be familiar with the career trajectories of Philadelphia's "better sort." Like many of them, he intended to add mercantile activities to his artisan profession. In 1725 he joined eight partners in establishing the Abbington Iron Furnace in New Castle County (in present-day Delaware). At least one of the partners, Thomas Rutter, was a Germantown resident of Quaker background. Many of the other investors were Philadelphia merchants; several served in the legislature. At the same time, Wistar began to import hardware and other merchandise from continental Europe. By 1726 the thirty-year-old immigrant was listed in the *Weekly Mercury* as one of the "principal" merchants of Philadelphia.

Having established himself as a merchant and investor, Wistar turned his efforts toward beginning a family. Early in 1726 he had applied to the Philadelphia Monthly Meeting for permission to marry, as was customary for Quakers in good standing. One of the men appointed to verify his status as an upstanding Friend was

Evan Owen, Wistar's partner in the Abbington Iron Furnace. In May his request was approved, and he married Catharine Jansen, the American-born daughter of Dirk and Margaret Milan Jansen. Catharine's parents were well-established Germantown Quakers who had lived in the colony for more than twenty-five years. By the time of Wistar's marriage, Dirk Jansen owned a considerable amount of land and was a justice of the peace for Philadelphia County.

In marrying Catharine Jansen, Wistar chose a wife from a background similar to his own family's class of officials in the Palatinate. A justice of the peace was the closest position in Pennsylvania's local government structure to Waldhilsbach's village magistrate. Just as his father had attempted to secure his position in the village by marrying the daughter of the magistrate and Reformed elder, so Wistar chose the daughter of a Quaker justice of the peace as his wife. An alliance with the Jansen family anchored his position in Pennsylvania society and signaled his acceptance among the German Quaker community.

By 1726, Wistar had succeeded in creating a place for himself in the British colonies. He had trained in a new occupation, built patronage relationships within religious and family networks, and entered the career path of prominent Philadelphia merchants. Wistar's success resulted from his creative adaptation of his European experience to his Pennsylvania context. Conditions in the colony, however, allowed him to move well beyond the world he had known as a child.

Having established his presence and reputation among Philadelphia and Germantown Quakers, Wistar turned his energies toward ensuring economic security for his children. The couple's first son, Richard, was born in 1727; and over the next thirteen years, there were six more children. To obtain the land and wealth necessary to ensure the future of his growing family, Wistar courted the favor of Pennsylvania's Proprietary family and their agents. Two specific sets of circumstances—the chaotic state of Pennsylvania's Proprietary affairs and the simultaneous influx of German-speaking immigrants—aided Wistar's entrepreneurial pursuits. He astutely recognized the governing family's needs and shrewdly set out to furnish a solution that would enhance his position and his income.

Wistar had entered the colony at a time when Pennsylvania's political affairs were in a state of confusion. One year after his arrival, Proprietor William Penn had died in England. In his will, Penn left most of his American holdings to his three sons: John, Thomas, and Richard. When Penn's children by his first wife contested the will, a lengthy legal battle for control of the colony ensued. While the suit wound its way through the British court system, the trustees assigned to oversee Penn's affairs in America hesitated to sell land to anyone. Since it was not clear who held the Proprietary rights to the colony, the appropriate authority for offering clear land titles also remained in doubt.

Penn's estate was finally settled in 1727, in the same year that Richard Wistar was born and Wistar's brother John arrived in the colony. By that time, the elder Wistar recognized the value of investing in Pennsylvania land. New settlers were arriving in large numbers, and anyone who owned property could make a nice profit. Since Penn's sons inherited a substantial mortgage with the colony, they were interested in generating as much revenue as possible from land sales. Consequently, anyone with access to capital could profit from buying land.

Wistar bought his first large tract in 1728 when the Commissioners of Property agreed to sell him two thousand acres in the colony's backcountry in return for £153 sterling in bills of exchange and £128 in Pennsylvania money. Not only was Wistar willing to pay the going rate of 50 percent on his bills of exchange, but he also paid cash for additional land. Having befriended James Steel, the Penns' land agent, Wistar persuaded the Proprietors to sell him twenty-five hundred additional acres the following year. Between 1729 and Thomas Penn's arrival in the colony in 1732, the immigrant was one of Pennsylvania's few sources of income for its debt-ridden Proprietors.

In addition to supplying revenue, Wistar also was willing to invest his capital in risky real estate ventures. Two tracts of land in his original 1728 purchase were in a territory that the Penns had not yet bought from the Delaware Indians. More than one-third of the immigrant's second major land transaction, which Steel had negotiated on his behalf, was in tribal territory. Although the Commissioners of Property discouraged the Penns from selling land before buying it from the Indians, the Proprietors were more concerned with raising money than with the legality of their land titles.

Wistar not only purchased land without clear title, but he also participated in some of the Penns' more controversial strategies to raise revenue. The immigrant was among the "eight close Proprietary associates" who received land in a private lottery after the Penns' public lottery scheme of 1735 failed. The Proprietors had hoped to net £15,000 by selling tickets for unsettled land. When they discovered that the plan was illegal because the colony had a law against lotteries, they held a secret drawing instead in which Wistar received over five thousand acres.

Once again, he purchased property that the Penns had no right to sell; efforts to clear the title to some of the lottery land resulted in the famous Walking Purchase of 1737, a legally questionable transaction. To justify the purchase, William Penn's sons produced an old document that Penn had negotiated with the Delaware Indians in 1686. According to the document, the boundaries of the purchase were to be measured by the distance a man could walk in a day and a half. Penn's sons claimed that although their father had paid the price for the land, the walk had never occurred. After careful planning, walkers marked off a region that was much larger than the Indians had intended and that included the land sold two years earlier through the private lottery. By investing in the lottery land, Wistar proved willing to take part in risky transactions while providing a solid source of revenue for the Proprietors.

A second set of circumstances that aided Wistar in his land speculation and in courting the favor of the Proprietors was the influx of immigrants into the colony. In the decade following Wistar's arrival, several shiploads of settlers had docked at Philadelphia's port and numerous German-speaking colonists from New York had migrated to Pennsylvania at the invitation of Governor William Keith. Issues of immigration quickly became intertwined with land-settlement policies and political maneuvering in the colony.

James Logan, one of the Trustees listed in Penn's will and the family's Pennsylvania agent, noted constantly the problems created by immigrants while the legal battle over Penn's legacy raged in England. He reported to Penn's widow in 1726 that the family's interests were suffering: "Your lands to the Northw[ar]d are overrun by a number of those unruly Palatines . . . invited hither in 1722 by Sr. William [Keith] . . . and the southern parts are in the same manner possessed by as disorderly persons who have lately floc'd in . . . from Ireland."[7] Because the Trustees could not grant clear titles to new settlers, immigrants simply squatted on land that appeared uninhabited and claimed they would pay for it when Penn's estate was settled. By 1726, Logan believed that nearly one hundred thousand acres were "possessed by persons, who resolutely sitt down and improve, without any manner of Right or Pretense to it."[8] While he may have been exaggerating the amount of land claimed by the squatters, new colonists were posing a very real problem for officials trying to settle the colony in an orderly fashion.

Nor did immigration problems subside. In 1727, Logan reported that instead of the three ships of German-speaking settlers that were expected, a total of six with more than twelve hundred foreigners had arrived. In addition, eight or nine ships had landed at New Castle from the north of Ireland. The Palatine and Irish newcomers all predicted large numbers of fellow countrymen planning to make the journey the following year. "Both these sorts sitt frequently down on any spott of vacant Land they can find without asking questions," Logan reported.[9] He believed that few of those who were settling the land had the means to purchase it. Consequently, Logan proposed that the Penns grant the land to others who could pay cash and extend credit to the new settlers. The only other option was for the Penns to rent to the squatters. Rents, however, had proven impossible to collect in the Lower Counties (Delaware), where a boundary dispute with Lord Baltimore of Maryland threatened the settlers' titles. Logan believed that the new squatters would use a similar rationale for refusing to pay rents until the family's legal affairs were clarified.

Isaac Norris, another Trustee, was pessimistic about how to obtain money from the German "free Booters or those voluntary or unlicensed settlers on your lands." Norris believed that the "large number, the insolence of some, & the povertie of most" would make the situation difficult to handle. He suggested that it would "require some person or Persons of great care & discretion to be the active agents in agreeing with those settlers."[10]

Although he was not officially appointed as such an agent, Wistar proved to be precisely the kind of person whom Norris was looking for. Wistar had established his reputation as a Philadelphia Quaker merchant and investor who was a partner with several political figures in the Abbington Iron Furnace. He was a solid source of credit and cash at a time when specie and bills of exchange were difficult to find in the colony. Wistar was also a German-speaking immigrant who could communicate with the new arrivals. Through his land purchases, Wistar allowed the Proprietors and their agents to settle German immigrants in a more orderly fashion.

At the most basic level, Wistar helped to sort out the trustworthy Germans from the "lower sorts." He gave advice on the reputations of his fellow countrymen who wanted to purchase land. The Commissioners of Property, for example, noted next to Thomas Hean's request for a warrant that Wistar had verified his honest character and promised that Hean would pay for his land. Throughout the next decade, Wistar and his father-in-law vouched for the credibility of German immigrants and submitted payments to the commissioners on their behalf.

As a land speculator, Wistar also provided a solution to the problems of German-speaking squatters. Between 1729 and his death in 1752, he received patents for more than twenty thousand acres of unimproved land in Philadelphia, Bucks, and Lancaster Counties. Most of that land he resold to German immigrants and their descendants; indeed, most of the purchasers of Wistar's land recorded in Philadelphia County deeds prior to 1777 had German names. Similarly, a majority of the people who bought his land in Berks,

Bucks, Lancaster, Montgomery, and Northampton Counties were of German descent. In many cases, Wistar's purchasers—the squatters about whom Logan and Norris had complained—were already living on the property he had sold them. By acquiring large tracts and reselling them to German immigrants, Wistar furnished the Proprietors with the means for clearing up titles in the colony's backcountry.

Thus Wistar, in pursuing financial security, surveyed the opportunities around him. He recognized that the Proprietors' agents controlled land, the primary form of wealth in Pennsylvania. By building on his reputation, his access to capital, and his cultural background, Wistar made his services indispensable to the Penns. In purchasing backcountry land, he provided them with much needed revenue and a solution to the problems of settling new immigrants.

The Penns were not the only ones to benefit from Wistar's land speculation, however. The newcomers needed someone to help them get a start in the New World in the same way that the Germantown Quakers had helped Wistar. By giving them advice, selling them land, lending them money, and purchasing the contracts of indentured servants, he aided German-speaking immigrants in adjusting to their new life. Wistar's attempts to help his fellow immigrants had begun even before their departure from Europe. In 1732, after conditions aboard the ships arriving in Philadelphia began to deteriorate, he wrote a letter to potential settlers in Europe that was published throughout the Rhine Valley. In it, Wistar described a ship in which a large number of the passengers had died as a result of the deplorable conditions on board. The survivors were "nearly all sick, weak, and worst of all, poor and without means, in consequence of which they are a heavy burden on the residents here, where money is very scarce."[11] Wistar recommended, therefore, that individuals make their decision to emigrate carefully, and he gave practical advice to those who determined to make the journey.

In addition to the conditions on the voyage, Wistar prepared potential settlers for what they might expect in Pennsylvania. He noted that the colony was "for some years past a very good country, and like all other new colonies, little inhabited." As a result, early immigrants such as he had been able to purchase large tracts for small amounts of money: "Because the wild land called for much labor . . . we were glad when ships arrived here bringing Germans, for these were at once redeemed, and by their labor earned so much that they too soon were able to purchase land." In the meantime, however, so many German, Irish, and English people had settled in Pennsylvania "that now he who wishes to obtain land must seek it far in the wilderness, and pay dear for it besides."[12]

While at first glance his letter seems to contradict the interests of a speculator who wanted purchasers for the forty-five hundred acres he had acquired, Wistar's advice actually worked to his advantage. Not only did the widespread circulation of his letter offer name recognition to potential immigrants, but it also portrayed him as a benefactor. Wistar became identified as someone who would help immigrants in need. Consequently, those who decided that they had the resources to travel to Pennsylvania often turned to him for help. At the same time, his letter forewarned settlers of the high prices that Wistar was charging for his properties. When families did not have sufficient cash to buy land, he provided them with mortgages.

Wistar also aided fellow Germans by extending them credit. As early as 1733 he was attempting to retrieve money from the family members of Heinrich Hiestand at Ibersheimer Hoff in the Palatinate. He had lent Hiestand, who lived in Pennsylvania, 130 *Gulden*, 2 *Kopfstück* (£14 sterling). It took Wistar nine years to retrieve the sum from Hiestand's creditors in the Palatinate, and the process involved numerous people and connections in America and the Rhine and Neckar Valleys. In addition to other debts he retrieved from Europe, Wistar's inventory listed bonds, mortgages, and book debts valued at £23,209 Pennsylvania currency due his estate at his death. The overwhelming majority of the names listed on the bonds were German.

As the immigrant population shifted in the 1740s from family groups with some resources to young single men with little money, Wistar found additional ways to offer aid. He purchased indentures for those who arrived without the means to pay for their passage. To fulfill their contracts, they worked as brass button makers, laborers at his new glass manufactory, or servants in his home or shop. In 1746, German immigrant John Peter Lambert, with the consent of his mother, indentured himself as an apprentice to Wistar for thirteen years. As part of this contract, Wistar promised to teach the young man to read and write English. In that same year, Wistar paid for the passage of Abraham Zimmerman, Melchior Zimmerman, and Ursula Dichter in exchange for indentures of five, six, and seven years, respectively. By the 1750s most of the sixty people who earned their living at Wistar's New Jersey glassworks were indentured servants. In the inventory of his estate taken in 1752, four "Servant Lads" with German names were listed along with Wistar's button-making tools, and three servant girls were listed with his shop goods. In offering contracts to immigrants, Wistar helped them learn a trade and become familiar with Anglo-American culture. Because he shared their heritage but also understood Pennsylvania's institutions, the entrepreneur acted as a cultural broker to the Germans migrating to the colony in the 1730s and 1740s.

While Wistar provided services to both the Proprietors and to other immigrants, his motives were not purely altruistic; he benefited tremendously from his position in the middle. His profits from land speculation were astounding. Of the 2,000 acres that he bought in 1729, Wistar sold 698 acres in parcels to Jacob Huddlestone, Henry Shate, Peter Andrews, and Jacob Stauffer. From the tracts sold, Wistar netted a profit of almost 200 percent. The remaining plantation, with 1,300 acres and all of the cattle belonging to it, he willed to his daughter Margaret. The profits from his 1729 purchase were typical of his speculation. In another series of transactions for land that he purchased in 1732, Wistar paid about £12 Pennsylvania currency for 100 acres and resold it at a rate of £50 for 100 acres.

Wistar's land speculation supplied him with extensive amounts of capital, but it also allowed him to furnish his children with impressive legacies. In his will, written less than one month before his death, he left his wife and children cash disbursements totaling £4,450, eleven city lots, and over five thousand acres of Pennsylvania land. Each of his children received at least one city lot in Philadelphia and land in the outlying counties. His only surviving sons, Richard and Caspar, and his oldest daughter, Margaret, each received a plantation with household goods and cattle. His three younger daughters, Catherine, Rebecca, and Sarah, inherited undeveloped land in Bucks and Philadelphia Counties. Although many of Philadelphia's leading Quakers sought to leave legacies of land to all of their children, Wistar's bequests were unusual in their size and value.

In addition to his wealth, Wistar's mediating role also gave him an international reputation as a leader among American Germans. The letter that he wrote in 1732, warning immigrants of deplorable ship conditions and giving them advice about Pennsylvania, was published throughout continental Europe. Moreover, he corresponded regularly with business associates in the Rhine and Neckar Valleys. These men purchased goods for Wistar and distributed and collected money and letters on his behalf.

Wistar's international reputation and business networks led to his involvement in retrieving numerous European legacies on behalf of friends and acquaintances in America. Georg Friedrich Hölzer, his business associate in the Palatinate, sought to obtain money in Europe that Wistar's siblings in America had inherited. Before long, other immigrants also were using his connections to retrieve legacies. By 1742, Hölzer was reporting his progress on five different inheritance cases that he was working on for Wistar.

Name recognition and a dependable transatlantic network helped to turn Wistar's house and shop into a communication center for Pennsylvania Germans. In 1737, Durst Thommen, a Swiss immigrant who settled with his family near Wistar's backcountry land, wrote to his European friends that they should send their letters addressed to him at Wistar's house in Philadelphia. Wistar, whose acquaintance he had made when he first arrived, would be sure to forward messages or letters. Wistar and his brother John, who was also a Philadelphia shopkeeper and shared the same business connections, provided an informal postal service for the immigrant community.

Wistar's success in using his transatlantic networks for communication and financial transactions, in turn, increased his reputation among American Germans. In one case, John Theobald Endt, a merchant in Germantown, recommended to a European friend that he send his American niece's legacy to Pennsylvania to invest because the interest rate was so much higher than in Krefeld. Endt suggested that his friend appoint three trustees for the money, among whom were Wistar's brother John and his cousin, David Deschler. Previously, Endt had suggested Wistar as one of the trustees, but he had died in the meantime. Wistar's reputation for handling money responsibly and for helping other Germans begin their new lives in America allowed him to become a patron to the Pennsylvania settlers and their European families.

His position of prominence among the immigrant community became well known among Anglo-American colonists as well. In 1738, John Bartram, a naturalist with whom Wistar had become friends, mentioned him in a letter to William Byrd II, a wealthy planter in Virginia. Byrd was advertising for people to settle his land at Roanoke. Bartram reported that he had presented Byrd's scheme in a favorable manner to Wistar, "to whome many of ye Palatines resorts both for advice & assistance."[13] In his reply, Byrd offered Wistar or any of his countrymen as much of his Roanoke land as they wanted to buy.

By the late 1730s, Wistar's position as a leader among German immigrants was well established, and his wealth and social status made him less dependent on the Proprietors. Between 1738 and 1742 a series of events occurred that led the Penns and their supporters, who had once relied on Wistar's help for settling their colony, to recognize the influence he had gained. Throughout the 1730s, the period during which Wistar purchased most of his land, the relationship between the Proprietors and the assembly was relatively cooperative. Thomas Penn's presence in the colony and his land purchases from the Indians partially resolved the tensions of the previous decade. In addition, an ongoing boundary dispute between Lord Baltimore of Maryland and the Penns created an outside threat that encouraged compromise within the province's government. In order to strengthen his claim to the disputed territory, Thomas Penn allowed immigrants to settle on the land without paying the full purchase price.

Toward the end of the decade, however, the political climate began to change. In 1738, Lord Baltimore and Penn reached a compromise on the border dispute between Maryland and Pennsylvania. Penn immediately set out to reform his land policies. He issued a mandate requiring settlers who had not paid for their land in full to remit their remaining balances within a short period or face legal proceedings. At the same time, Penn replaced several well-known, trusted Proprietary officials with outsiders less sympathetic to the colonists' interests. Finally, in early 1739, news reached Pennsylvania that King George's War had broken out.

For the next several years, tensions between the Quaker-dominated assembly and the Proprietors' supporters, led by prominent Anglicans, increased. Preparing the colony for defense was central to the conflicts. The Quaker assemblymen, who had religious scruples against going to war, refused to allocate money to support a militia. To raise the necessary funds, Proprietary officials tried to unseat the Quaker majority in the assembly. As a result, the elections of the early 1740s became hotly contested, tumultuous affairs.

It was during the election for assembly representatives in 1742 that the extent of Wistar's influence among the German population became apparent. In past elections, most Pennsylvania German voters had supported Quaker legislators, for many of the early immigrants belonged to religious groups that shared the Quakers' pacifist positions. However, the majority of the more recent arrivals belonged to the Reformed and Lutheran churches and had no scruples against going to war. This was the constituency whose vote the Proprietary faction worked hard to win.

When mobs of Germans from the backcountry arrived in Philadelphia for the 1742 election, however, they sided with the Quakers. According to Richard Peters, an Anglican and a staunch supporter of the Penns, Wistar, his brother John, and Christopher Sauer had ruined the tenuous coalition of support that the Proprietary party had constructed among the Germans. Whenever backcountry settlers had come to Philadelphia, the Wistars had told them the real purpose for raising a militia was to eject colonists who had not paid for their land. As proof, the Wistars cited the Proprietors' arrest of settlers who refused to pay back rents and fines in the Lower Counties (Delaware), where the assembly had passed a militia act. The Wistars implied a connection between the two events. Peters noted that "these storys were greedily swallowed by those ignorant People & being improved by Sower [Christopher Sauer], who took care to see his Countrymen as they returned thro'

Germantown, they were fix'd beyond a possibility of stirring them."14

Wistar, who had used his capital and credit to help the Proprietors solve the immigrant problem in the previous decade, became a patron who now protected the interests of his own constituency. He and his brother had convinced their fellow countrymen that the prospect of Proprietary supporters gaining a majority in the assembly was a greater threat to the immigrants' property than the impending war. By doing so, Wistar demonstrated his ability to turn his role as a broker into a position of political power.

Nor did Wistar's influence over the Pennsylvania Germans diminish. In 1750, Governor James Hamilton wrote a letter to Thomas Penn in which he used Wistar as an example of the dangers in conferring the rights of Englishmen on German immigrants "before they know how to use them." Hamilton noted that Wistar, "whom I remember wheeling ashes about this Town," was now worth £60,000, an estate that placed him among the wealthiest men in the colony. The governor believed that German-speaking immigrants such as Wistar would soon have "the wealth & power of the province in their hands," and that they would "either make a bad use of it themselves, or devolve it on some Demagogue, who may thereby be able to give the Government perpetual uneasiness." Hamilton acknowledged "the benefits that accrue to this province from the Industry of these people," but viewed them as a threat to the provincial government. The immigrants, he argued, did not understand Pennsylvania's laws or language, and "yet they are become the most busy at all Elections, which they govern at pleasure."15

Hamilton's paranoia captures beautifully the results of Wistar's activities as a cultural broker. By 1750 he had used his mediating role between the Proprietors and the other German-speaking immigrants to amass a fortune. The wealth and power that he had accumulated in the process now posed a threat to Proprietary supporters trying to secure their own political control. Hamilton feared that Wistar, his brother, and the small group of businessmen who had arrived early in the flow of German-speaking settlers might gain control over the growing crowds of immigrants. If they did so, neither the Proprietary supporters nor the Quakers would be able to manipulate their support, and Pennsylvania's politics would dissolve into chaos.

Wistar did not, however, become the "demagogue" feared by Hamilton. Within two years, the successful immigrant died, leaving his widow and sons to carry on his various business enterprises. His six surviving children married Anglo-American Quakers and became fully integrated into Philadelphia's elite society. If the legacies he left to his children are any indication, Wistar success-fully achieved economic security for his family.

In part, timing and good fortune influenced Wistar's accomplishments; he arrived in Philadelphia at a period when the city's economy and social structure were particularly fluid. Wistar's success was also shaped by the way that he maneuvered within the colony's relationships of power. He began by learning a profession and establishing a religious identification to help him solicit patronage and build new family networks. Like his father, who constantly negotiated between conflicting interests, Wistar then took a position in the middle, between Pennsylvania's Proprietors and the newly arriving immigrants. As a land speculator, he offered solutions and his services to the Penns. The success of those services, however, depended on a steady stream of German-speaking settlers. At the same time, his role as a cultural broker would have failed without the resources of his business enterprises. Wistar's climb from hauling ashes to his position as a wealthy merchant was determined by his ability to combine entrepreneurial pursuits with mediating Anglo-American culture for his fellow immigrants. That combination, in turn, allowed him to become a powerful patron within Philadelphia's German community.

Notes

1. "Wistar" was the English phonetic spelling of his name, which he began to use in legal documents after 1721. German-language documents in America and Europe continued to use the original spelling, "Wüster."

2. "Ein Kortzer Bericht von Caspar Wistar," Morris Family Papers, Historical Society of Pennsylvania, Philadelphia (hereafter cited as HSP).

3. James T. Mitchell and Henry Flanders, eds., *The Statutes at Large of Pennsylvania from 1682–1801* (Harrisburg, 1895), 3:424–26.

4. Ibid.

5. Isaac Norris Sr. to S. Clements, April 30, 1725, Norris Papers, Isaac Norris Sr. Letterbook, 1716–1730, 422, HSP.

6. Gertrude MacKinney and Charles F. Hoban, eds., *Pennsylvania Archives*, 8th ser., 8 vols., *Votes and Proceedings of the House of Representatives of the Province of Pennsylvania, 1682–1776* (Harrisburg, 1931–1935), 2:1569.

7. James Logan to Hannah Penn, February 9, 1726, Penn Papers, Official Correspondence, HSP, 1:181, 313 (hereafter cited as PPOC).

8. James Logan to Hannah Penn, March 11, 1726, PPOC, 1:185.

9. James Logan to the Penns, November 25, 1727, Logan Papers, James Logan Letterbook, 4:153–54, 160, HSP.

10. Isaac Norris to John Penn, April 30, 1729, Isaac Norris Letterbook, 1716–1730, 522–25, HSP.

11. "Caspar Wistar's Letter of December 4, 1732," in Henry S. Dotterer, ed., *The Perkiomen Region, Past and Present*, 3 vols. (Philadelphia, 1899–1900) 2, no. 8:120. Another translation of this letter is in *Pennsylvania German Society Proceedings and Addresses* 8 (1897): 141–44.

A partial copy of the original is in Morris Family Papers, HSP.

12. Ibid., Morris Family Papers, HSP.

13. Edmund Berkeley and Dorothy Smith Berkeley, eds., The Correspondence of John Bartram, 1734–1777 (Gainesville, FL, 1992), 98–99.

14. Richard Peters Letterbook, 1741–43, 28, Peters Papers, HSP.

15. Governor James Hamilton to Thomas Penn, September 24, 1750, PPOC, 5:55.

Suggested Readings

The sources for information on Wistar's life are extensive on both sides of the Atlantic but of varying nature. The history of his family in the Palatinate is drawn from court records and government administrative documents in Abteilung #77 (*Pfalz Generalia*) in the Badisches Generallandesarchiv in Karlsruhe, Germany. The family's genealogy and references to its members' religious affiliation are based on church records at the Evangelisches Oberkirchenrat, Karlsruhe. A draft of Wistar's autobiography and a series of letters between him and a business correspondent in the Palatinate form the core of primary sources about his life in Pennsylvania. These documents are in the Morris Family Papers and the Wistar/Wister Family Papers at the Historical Society of Pennsylvania, Philadelphia. Information from wills, land records, Quaker Meeting minutes, and letters in the Logan, Peters, Norris, and Penn Papers, all available at the Pennsylvania State Archives, Harrisburg, or the Historical Society, supplemented the data drawn from private manuscripts. For general reading on German immigrants or Pennsylvania during this period, see Aaron S. Fogleman, *Hopeful Journeys: German Immigration, Settlement, and Political Culture in Colonial America, 1717–1775* (Philadelphia, 1996); Gary Nash, *Urban Crucible: Social Change, Political Consciousness, and the Origins of the American Revolution* (Cambridge, MA, 1978); Sally Schwartz, *"A Mixed Multitude": The Struggle for Toleration in Colonial Pennsylvania* (New York, 1987); and Alan Tully, *William Penn's Legacy: Politics and Social Structure in Provincial Pennsylvania, 1726–1755* (Baltimore, 1977).

10

Lewis Morris Jr.
British American Officeholder

Michael Watson

Lewis Morris Jr. (1698–1762) was fortunate without being famous. As the eldest son of one of colonial New York's wealthiest orphans and most talented politicians, Lewis had every career opportunity. He eventually gained what proved to be the very influential and profitable office of vice-admiralty court judge and displayed how an imperial office could be used for colonial benefit. He was not unusual in this achievement; prominent colonials such as Wait Winthrop of Massachusetts, Edward Shippen of Pennsylvania, Daniel Dulany of Maryland, and John Randolph of Virginia were all vice-admiralty court judges. In each colony the vice-admiralty court decided most maritime cases, including those concerning privateering, sailors' wage disputes, and violations of the imperial trade laws. New York became the capital for colonial privateers, in large part because Morris "bent" the law in their favor. New York prospered, Morris prospered, and the imperial war effort was supported by private ships of war. British imperial law was often applied, negotiated, and appropriated through colonial-born attorneys-general and judges of superior, county, and vice-admiralty courts. How does Morris's career, and those of dozens of others like him, question traditional views about imperial officeholders in colonial America? And did the leadership style of governors of New York vary during Morris's career?

Lewis Morris fathered a large family, as had his father, and it is noteworthy that three of his sons became prominent in Revolutionary America. How valuable were marriage alliances in consolidating this dynasty? Was there any social or political stigma attached to the profitable office that Morris held?

Michael Watson, at the University of Western Ontario, London, has completed a book-length study of colonial American vice-admiralty courts, and his published work includes "Captures and Condemnations: Judge Lewis Morris, the New York Vice-Admiralty Court and Colonial Privateering, 1739–1762," *New York History* 78 (1997): 117–46.

Lewis Morris was born into fortunate circumstances, the eldest son of a wealthy and prominent New York family. Although overshadowed by his father for most of his life, and by his sons in later times, Morris's life shows how British Americans could appropriate imperial government for themselves. Lewis Morris's tale reveals much about the lives and circumstances of British America's native-born elite. Understanding this group's interests and concerns is essential if we are to understand how the process of political accommodation and development worked within the British Empire.

Lewis Morris came into the world in 1698. He was born on his father's estate of Morrisania (now an area of the Bronx) into a family that, in the short period of thirty years, had established itself as one of the wealthiest and most significant in the region. Morris's grandfather had come to New York in 1670 from Barbados. He married a local woman and had a son, Lewis Morris Sr., in 1671, but both he and his wife died a year later, leaving their infant son orphaned. Until his death in 1691, an uncle oversaw Lewis Morris Sr.'s upbringing and education. Then, the twenty-year-old inherited the family's extensive property holdings, which included the 2,000-acre estate in what was then part of Westchester County, later known as Morrisania, 1,500 acres on Long Island, 6,200 acres in New Jersey, and a house in New York City.

His inheritance made Lewis Morris Sr. one of the largest land-holders in the area. Seeking to placate a potentially useful ally, New Jersey's governor bestowed public offices upon the young man commensurate with Morris Sr.'s obvious economic and social prominence, appointing him a provincial sessions judge and naming him to that colony's council in 1692. Once in the public sphere, Morris Sr. realized that he had found his niche. He was a gifted and exceptional politician. Later that year he extended his influence when he married the daughter of New York's attorney-general.

The marriage of the younger Morris's parents may have been convenient at the beginning, but the match proved to be a happy and fruitful one. Lewis Morris Jr. was the couple's first son, after two daughters. In adulthood, Morris was surrounded by ten siblings, eight sisters and two brothers, all of whose doings he carefully kept abreast of and whose marriages provided the family with an extensive network of useful connections, both in England and British North America. By all accounts, Morris and his siblings grew up in a lively household. Morris's youngest brother told Benjamin Franklin that Morris Sr. had taught his brood to be argumentative and assertive, encouraging them, as youngsters, "to dispute with one another for his Diversion while setting at the Table after Dinner."[1] All of the children were taught to read and write, and the sons were sent away to the best colonial schools for further education. Lewis Morris Sr. took special care to educate his eldest son for public affairs. Lewis Morris Jr. graduated from Yale College and trained as a lawyer in New York City.

When he married in 1723, the younger Morris followed his father's lead and allied himself with a prominent family. His wife was Katerina Staats, the daughter of a politically well-connected Dutch family. Morris proved to be nearly as prolific as his father. Before Katerina died in 1731, the couple had three sons and two daughters. Then, fifteen years after his first wife's death, Morris married again, this time to Sarah Gouverneur, the daughter of another prominent New Yorker. With his new wife, Morris had three more daughters and another son. He carefully educated all of his children, although the two eldest sons, Lewis and Staats, never completed their degrees at Yale.

His father dominated the first half of Lewis Morris's life. Morris Sr. was a gifted politician, and Morris Jr. dutifully acted as his father's lieutenant. There was little doubt that Morris would follow his father into public life. Not only had his education and upbringing prepared him for it, but his father's political activities, which had broadened in the years since Morris's birth, had a direct impact upon the family fortunes. During the eighteenth century, substantial colonial citizens such as the Morrises paid close attention to public affairs, vigilant for any threat to their position and alert for any opportunity to profit. The easiest way to protect their interests was to ensure that they controlled the local positions of power. The appearance of native-born political elites was one of the most significant indications of the increasing social maturity of the British American colonies. These individuals, who had the time, resources, and education necessary for public service, controlled and articulated local political debate and eventually came to monopolize colonial positions of authority. Although the political dynamic of each British American colony differed from its fellows, each witnessed the rise of its own native-born political elite. Lewis Morris Jr. was born into this world and this role.

The appointment of an acquaintance, Robert Hunter, as New York's governor in 1710 gave Morris Sr. the opportunity to expand his political activities in New York and New Jersey. He gained election to the assembly and became the governor's chief political collaborator. Grateful for his support, Hunter rewarded Morris Sr. by appointing him New York's chief justice in 1715 and favoring Morris Sr.'s supporters whenever possible. Morris Sr.'s political influence continued to grow during the governorship of Hunter's successor, William Burnet, who showed his regard for the chief justice by adding his son, the twenty-three-year-old Lewis Morris, to the colonial council in 1721.

Morris's designation as one of New York's twelve councillors was a propitious start to the youngster's public career. His father had been a New Jersey councillor for two decades, and Morris's appointment gave the family a seat on the most important political bodies in both New Jersey and New York. Save for the position of governor, a council seat was the highest and most prestigious British American colonial political office. Most colonial councils, which acted both as the governor's major advisory body and the legislature's upper house, were appointive bodies that drew their membership from a colony's most influential, affluent, and important families. Along with the considerable prestige that attached to the position, councillors enjoyed easy access to the governor and an enhanced ability to influence the course of public debate within the colony. More material advantages, for New York's councillors, included protection from lawsuits, a closer proximity to patronage networks, and a hand in the distribution of unassigned tracts of land. Morris's appointment to the council at such an early age virtually ensured that his public career would be both substantial and rewarding.

The death of Burnet and the arrival of a new governor, John Montgomerie, in 1728, presaged a darkening of the Morris family's political fortunes. The intimate association that the Morrises had enjoyed with New York's executive for the past two decades and the manifest patronage rewards that the family and their supporters had accrued had given the group a well-deserved reputation of privilege, which made them a focus for popular resentment. Ironically, just as popular feelings began to turn against the Morrises and their allies, the group found itself unable to come to an understanding with Governor Montgomerie, which plunged them into opposition for the first time. Montgomerie had different objectives from his predecessors; the insolvent governor's overriding goal was to accumulate a fortune during his tenure. He sought allies who would help him achieve this aim, something the Morrisites were unlikely to do.

The stimulus for the Morrises' break with Montgomerie came in 1729, when the governor refused to condemn an assembly proposal to regulate the salaries of the colony's royal officers. This measure would have reduced Morris Sr.'s salary as chief justice from £300 to £250 per year, but it was the assembly's usurpation of power that most angered the Morrises. For two decades the Morrises and their associates had accumulated New York's most promising political offices. The assembly's action threatened their ascendancy. At the next meeting of the council, in June 1729, Lewis Morris Jr. rose and delivered an ill-tempered, and ultimately ill-timed, censure to the governor for consenting to a diminution of the executive's privileges without consulting his councillors. Morris asserted that the assembly's action would "render the members of the councill Insignificant and as so Many cyphers." It would also incline the assembly members "to persist in their claims of such things, as are inconsistent with their Dependence upon a British Government."[2]

Unwilling to tolerate such impudence, and glad of the pretext to enlarge his support by dissociating himself from the Morrises, Montgomerie suspended Lewis Morris Jr. from the council. His denunciation of Montgomerie had been the act of a political novice. He had come to maturity comfortable in the knowledge that his family and friends enjoyed easy access to the sources of public power and preferment in New York and New Jersey. These years had made young Morris complacent, and his public career to date had been too easy and too sheltered. Now his gesture of support for his father had not brought either of them any political benefit, but instead had deprived the family of a useful forum. The Morrises and their supporters hoped that Morris Jr.'s stated support for the royal government would incline colonial officials in London to look mildly upon his case and revoke his suspension, a wish that proved illusory.

For his part, Morris Jr. learned a valuable lesson. As he sardonically informed the Board of Trade, governors did not come to New York "to take the air" but "either to repair a shattered fortune, or acquire an Estate," and only those colonials who would help them achieve either of these goals could expect to prosper.[3] Losing his council seat as well as the privileges and opportunities that came with it was a serious setback for young Morris's public career. If he wanted to remain in public life, he would have to stand for the assembly, the elected body of representatives.

Even Montgomerie's death in 1731 could not halt the decline in the Morrises' political fortunes. Where once incoming colonial governors had found the family's support essential to governance, new executives now had alternate avenues through which to accomplish their objectives. The most telling blow to the Morrises' fortunes came in August 1733, when a new governor, William Cosby, angry at Morris Sr.'s temerity in ruling against him on an important point of law, suspended Morris Sr. from the chief justice's office. This action galvanized those opposition politicians who had begun to gather around the Morrises.

This group, loosely composed of naturally conservative landowners like the Morrises, found themselves allied by their personal dislike for Cosby and their desire to regain some measure of political power for themselves. While they tended to their own interests, the competitive nature of British American politics meant that political elites had to appeal to a wider constituency to retain power. To accomplish their ends, the Morrisites organized themselves as an opposition party. They reached out to New York's electorate through their endorsement of a broad series of reform policies designed to regulate the colony's administration, promote judicial reform, and encourage more equitable government. To advance their cause, they established a party newspaper, the *New-York Weekly Journal*, which lampooned and ridiculed the governor and his supporters, thus stirring up popular indignation over Cosby's policies. Morris Jr. and Sr. also won assembly seats for themselves in a series of by-elections in 1733, giving leadership to that body's discontented members. The Morrisites' platform soon became a rallying cry for New Yorkers hit hard by the colony's economic stagnation.

Building upon their recent successes, in late 1734 the Morrisites resolved to attack Cosby on another front. The party leaders decided to take their complaints about Cosby directly to London in hopes of having him recalled. To this end Morris Sr., accompanied by his youngest son, Robert, optimistically set out from New York in November 1734. His sojourn in London lasted eighteen months. Although Morris Sr. had been in London three decades earlier upon official business, few of his acquaintances from that time still wielded political power or influence, nor did the Morrisites, who were mostly landowners and not merchants, have an extensive circle of English business contacts to introduce them to London's official circles. So Morris Sr. mobilized his family connections and set about the laborious work of building a network of informal contacts who would assist him. This task made Morris Sr.'s time in England longer, more frustrating, and ultimately more expensive than the Morrisites had anticipated. In London's official circles, Morris Sr. wrote, "An universall avarice and corruption Predominates."[4] Each petition and every complaint that Morris Sr. circulated against Cosby was costly. In letters to his fellows, Morris Sr. wearily recounted his visits to various government officials and the heavy monetary burden involved in suborning a governor.

Accomplishing the recall of a colonial governor was a frustrating task in eighteenth-century Britain. Government officials, concerned with matters closer to home, rarely considered complaints of alleged colonial misgovernment on their own merit, but evaluated each charge in terms of its possible domestic impact upon the ministry that had appointed the governor. Despite the odds against him, and the obvious self-interest in his charges against Cosby, Morris Sr. proved adept at presenting a case against the governor. He acquired a network of useful patrons, the most important of whom included First Lord of the Admiralty Sir Charles Wager. Eventually, word got to Morris Sr. that if he would abandon his attack on Cosby, whose patrons were anxious to avoid the embarrassment of having their protégé's supposed misdeeds further bruited about, it might be arranged that he become New Jersey's next governor. Rightly wary of the value of such a promise, Morris Sr. did not accept this offer immediately. However, by the time of his departure in 1736, Sir Charles had the appointment in hand, although it took nearly two years to confirm.

Morris Sr. arrived back in New York in the autumn of 1736 to find that his party had achieved a number of successes in his absence. The failure of previous efforts to silence the Morrisites' *Weekly Journal* had caused a frustrated Cosby to have its editor, John Peter Zenger, arrested and charged with libel in August 1735. To ensure a guilty verdict in the case, Chief Justice James De Lancey disbarred those Morrisite lawyers who might have defended Zenger, but the party's leaders outmaneuvered the chief justice when they imported lawyer Andrew Hamilton from Philadelphia to plead on Zenger's behalf. Hamilton's rousing speech to the jury, designed to convince its members that truth could be an effective defense against libel, resulted in Zenger's acquittal as well as a resounding defeat for Cosby and his supporters. A year later Governor Cosby died; and although his successor, George Clarke, was scarcely more well disposed toward the Morrises than the late governor had been, the party's fortunes were clearly on the mend.

Morris Jr. had written a number of the lampoons and sardonic verses that appeared in the *Weekly Journal* and so incensed Cosby. During his father's absence in England, Morris had gained political stature and self-assurance, as George Clarke ruefully admitted: "Tho Morris himself be in England yet his son fills the place in the faction."[5] Although not a brilliant politician in the manner of his father, Morris proved to be a sound political manager. The brash young councillor of the 1720s had been tempered by his years in opposition. In 1737 he managed his most significant political achievement to date. In the assembly elections that year, the Morrisites won control of the house, and its members elected Morris Jr. as its speaker. He was emerging from his father's shadow.

In 1738 colonial officials finally confirmed Morris Sr.'s appointment as governor of New Jersey. Upon accepting the post, Morris Sr. resigned from New York's assembly and abandoned his political activities in that colony, leaving his son and remaining colleagues to their own devices. Until his father's death in 1746, Morris Jr. maintained a close contact with Morris Sr. Although Morris Sr. had bequeathed Morrisania to his eldest son when he retired to New Jersey, the old patriarch continued to bother the younger man about the estate's management, offering him detailed advice about how to deal with the slave laborers or increase crop yields. The two men also exchanged frequent letters about family matters, and Morris sent his youngest son, Richard, to New Jersey where his grandfather supervised the youngster's education. But as the political focus of Morris father and son diverged, their relationship altered. Morris Jr. continued to share his political thoughts, insights, and problems with his father, but the quandaries that Morris Jr. faced as a party leader in New York had little to do with the challenges that confronted Morris Sr. as the governor of New Jersey. As Morris Sr. commented to his son, Robert, whom he had appointed New Jersey's chief justice, "Lewis means well but is not enough Acquainted wth our affaires" to provide useful advice or assistance.[6] Lewis Morris and his father did not pursue any mutual political projects from Morris Sr.'s departure until his death in 1746.

The last political favor that Morris Sr. did his son was to use his influence with Sir Charles Wager to secure a commission from the Admiralty appointing Morris vice-admiralty judge of New York, New Jersey, and Connecticut in January 1739. The colonial vice-admiralty courts had jurisdiction over the British Empire's maritime commerce. These courts, which operated in the major colonial ports, settled wage or contract disputes between masters and mariners or shipowners and suppliers, decided salvage cases involving wrecks and damaged cargo, and assessed responsibility for collisions or other accidents at sea. They also adjudged infractions of the Navigation Acts, those infamous mercantilist parliamentary statutes designed to restrict British trade to British carriers. This was the position that history would associate with Lewis Morris Jr. For the first forty years of his life, Morris had been a noteworthy player in one of the most contentious and controversial political eras in colonial New York's history, but throughout that period his father had consistently overshadowed him. Now Morris had his own stage to perform upon, and he proved himself a worthy actor.

The Morrisites had been striving to gain the vice-admiralty judgeship for Lewis Morris since at least 1734. Morris Sr., who had acted as New York's deputy vice-admiralty judge from 1715 to 1721, grasped the consequence of the office. The vice-admiralty judgeship was a prestigious appointment; according to British precedence circulars, the vice-admiralty judge ranked below a colony's councillors, but above members of its assembly. Most important to Morris, the judge's commission originated with the Admiralty and could not be revoked by the governor, except on the grounds of proven judicial misconduct. Colonial vice-admiralty courts sat without juries, thus making the judge the sole arbiter of any disputes brought before him. So his commission gave Morris sole judicial control over an important segment of New York's economy and made him responsible for deciding cases that concerned the very basis of the British maritime trading empire. The only appeal from his rulings was to the High Court of Admiralty in London.

In the past, and despite its status, the vice-admiralty judgeship in New York had not been a remunerative office. Morris's predecessor had heard fewer than two cases per year. This changed during the mid-eighteenth-century war years, when the vice-admiralty court became one of New York's busiest public institutions. From 1739 to 1748, and again from 1756 to 1763, Great Britain was at war with other European powers. Fortunately for Morris, the colonial vice-admiralty courts' responsibilities expanded during times of war to include prize cases involving enemy merchant ships captured by privately financed warships known as privateers. Governments of the time, reluctant to make the capital investment that a large navy would require, incited privately financed warships to capture enemy vessels and cargo.

Colonial privateers depended upon the vice-admiralty courts from beginning to end. With the approval and consent of the governor, the vice-admiralty judge commissioned local privateers. This commission, without which no privateer could sail, contained instructions and a code of behavior and provided for a bond of £3,000 or (£1,500, depending on the size of the ship), which would be forfeited if the captain violated the conditions of the commission. Once the captain set out on his cruise, should he contravene any of the manifold parliamentary rules and regulations that governed a privateer's actions, it was the vice-admiralty judge who punished the transgressor. Finally, after the privateer returned to port, the vice-admiralty judge inquired into the circumstances of any prizes captured to ensure that they were legitimate targets of war and officially condemned the captured ships, after which the privateer's crew, officers, and investors shared the proceeds.

Until this last stage had been reached, the privateer's investors realized no profits from their outlay, so it was essential that the vice-admiralty judge not complicate the final condemnation. Morris proved to be a good friend to colonial privateers, and rightly so, according to local lights. Privateering was big business in mid-eighteenth-century New York. Before setting out, vessels had to be manned, outfitted, and provisioned, which kept local shipyards, suppliers, lawyers, and taverns busy. Following the cruise, condemned prize ships and their cargoes were sold at public auction, which circulated prize money throughout the colony and gave local citizens the opportunity to purchase bargains. Morris's reputation for interpreting difficult questions of law in the privateers' favor and for not inquiring too closely into the circumstances of questionable captures reassured investors. In response, New York's merchants and entrepreneurs equipped a large number of privateers from 1739 to 1748 and from 1756 to 1762.

The large number of prize cases he judged gave Morris the

opportunity to make some money from his office. The vice-admiralty officers received a parliamentary-stipulated payment of £15 sterling for sitting in judgment on prize ships over one hundred tons, and £10 sterling for smaller prizes, the largest proportion of which accrued to the judge. There is no evidence that Morris took greater fees than allowed, but colonial vice-admiralty judges made money in other ways. Morris charged a fee for issuing and renewing privateer commissions; and he advanced funds, at appropriate rates of interest, to privateer litigants who lacked ready funds to prosecute their cases, an action that nowadays would be considered a conflict of interest. He also employed his son Richard as his deputy, once that young man had completed his legal studies. His father's patronage ensured that Richard Morris, when not acting as deputy vice-admiralty judge, had a thriving practice representing privateer captains before the vice-admiralty court.

Morris grasped quickly how privateering could benefit New York economically and worked diligently to make the colony an attractive destination for prize-laden privateers. He persuaded his fellow assembly members to pass an act whereby sugar captured from enemy merchant ships could enter the colony as if it were British produce. British law permitted prize goods such as sugar to be imported from the colonies as if they were colonial produce, but the same prize goods still remained subject to colonial tariffs. Rhode Island, for example, had an impost on foreign sugar that applied to all prize sugar condemned in its vice-admiralty court. A similar duty on foreign sugar existed in New York, but when the first prize cargo of sugar reached his jurisdiction, Morris ruled that prize sugar brought into his court became English upon condemnation and hence was not subject to New York's duties on foreign sugar. Morris followed up his ruling by taking the lead in having the assembly pass a "Prize Goods Exemption Act," reminding his fellow members how it was to "the Greatest Advantage to the Inhabitants of this Colony that Prize-Goods be brought into this Port."[7] Despite opposition from the colony's customs officers, the assembly followed Morris's lead and promulgated an act that abolished the duties on all prize goods condemned in New York. Morris's promise to the assembly rang true when privateers soon arrived at the port with six more French sugar prizes, worth in total £23,600 sterling.

Securing the passage of legislation permitting the free export of prize sugar was a significant achievement on behalf of the colony's privateer investors. New York's governor gave Morris full credit for his achievement, explaining to colonial officials that "the Merchants of the City has [sic] been extremely alert in fitting out Privateers, at a very great expence, and have brought in several prizes, consisting chiefly of sugars, which, from the nature of the Duty claimed, wou'd anticipate most of their gains."[8] Having the assembly pass such an exemption was a legitimate and justified assistance to privateers, but Morris was often less scrupulous in his encouragement. Since the beginning of hostilities with Spain in 1739, Morris had given errant privateer captains a great deal of latitude in regard to their behavior. When Governor George Clarke insisted that the vice-admiralty court prosecute Captain John Lush in 1741 for attacking a neutral ship and threatening to sink the naval vessel that had arrested him, Morris, who had very profitably condemned two of Lush's prizes, set the captain's bail at £40, instead of the £20,000 that Clarke had suggested, and granted the defense so many continuations that the governor abandoned the suit.

Tacitly endorsing the actions of privateer captains who abused their commissions so flagrantly was not a wise decision. Morris's increasingly arrogant actions as vice-admiralty judge made him vulnerable to replacement. Because Morris's judicial commission originated with the Admiralty, he could not be replaced unless evidence of misconduct was presented in London. New York's new governor, Admiral George Clinton, was a regular naval officer who regarded privateers as semilegal opportunistic pirates who deprived the navy of much-needed men and resources. Like Governor Clarke, he tried to compel Morris to punish errant privateer captains whose excesses needlessly complicated wartime diplomacy. Clinton needed only persuasive evidence of judicial misconduct on Morris's part to secure his dismissal. The governor got his opportunity in 1746.

Earlier that year, Morris had rejected Clinton's command that he punish two New York captains, Arthur Helm and Michael Beezley, for violating the conditions of their privateering commissions. Although the governor presented convincing information that the two men had captured noncombatant ships that they had plundered before releasing, Morris dismissed the suit against the two captains. When a frustrated Clinton angrily canceled Helm's and Beezley's commissions, Morris drew upon his father's connections in New Jersey to secure new ones for the two captains from that colony. Set loose upon the high seas again, Beezley promptly committed another outrage, bilking two Dutch merchant ships of 18,000 pieces of eight, an action that caused the governor of Dutch Surinam to vow vengeance against any New York merchants unwary enough to enter his colony.

Clinton conveyed his complaints about Morris to the Admiralty, insisting that Morris's judicial warrant be terminated. In this instance, Morris had miscalculated the governor's resolve and over-estimated the effectiveness of his own resources. At the age of forty-seven, Morris had become one of New York's most notable public figures, but his standing still rested, to an uncomfortable degree, upon his father's connections. After Morris Sr.'s death in 1746, the fundamental weaknesses of Morris Jr.'s position became apparent. Sir Charles Wager had died in 1742, depriving Morris of his most effective Admiralty advocate. Moreover, Admiral Clinton had strong patrons within the Admiralty, and his recommendation that Morris be replaced received prompt attention. The Admiralty, which had already suspended a number of colonial vice-admiralty judges for various offenses during the war, canceled Morris's warrant in September 1747 and issued a commission to James Alexander as New York's new vice-admiralty judge. News of Morris's ouster was slow to reach New York, and by the time Clinton learned of the Admiralty's action, Morris had made his political peace with the governor.

Morris's timely accommodation with Clinton saved his judgeship. Alexander, a longtime political associate, refused to displace Morris; and the governor, who had since entered into a close friendship with Morris's brother Robert, and confident that he had successfully demonstrated his authority, did not pursue the matter. But Morris's new association with Clinton caused opposition politicians in the colony to target him. Chief Justice James De Lancey's party, eager to demonstrate their power, made a special effort to defeat Morris during the assembly elections of 1750. In a close election, characterized by fraud, intimidation, and other electoral irregularities, Peter De Lancey, the chief justice's brother, defeated Morris in Westchester by fewer than ten votes. This election, which saw a sweep by De Lancey's party, whose supporters dominated the new assembly, finished the Morrisites as an effective political force within New York.

Defeat in the 1750 election marked the end of Morris's legislative career. He never again stood for election to the assembly, nor, despite his periodic inquiries, did he ever regain his council seat. Despite his enforced retirement from the legislature, Morris's control of the vice-admiralty court continued to give him an important and influential public voice in New York. His actions on behalf of the colony's privateer investors from 1739 to 1748 had established Morris as a firm friend to the privateering interests. He enhanced this reputation during the Seven Years' War (1756–1763). More so than other North American colonial vice-admiralty judges, Morris treated privateering as a business that measured its success by the number of prize ships captured. If he erred, it was on behalf of the privateers' interests rather than in the interest of justice or any strict interpretation of the statutes governing prize trials.

From 1739 to 1748, privateers carried ninety-one prizes into New York, a level of activity that easily outdistanced rival North American ports in South Carolina and Rhode Island. New York witnessed even more prize business during the Seven Years' War, especially after Morris had digested the implications of the British Parliament's Rule of 1756. This legislation declared that neutral ships carrying an enemy cargo were legal prizes. Once newspaper reports appeared in 1757 that West Indian vice-admiralty judges had used this legislation to condemn a number of the Dutch traders who crowded the Caribbean, Morris began to vent his spleen against the Dutch carriers who had been profiting from the war by carrying contraband to enemy ports. From November 1757, when he condemned the first Dutch prize, to the end of the war, Dutch neutral prizes made up 21 percent of the captures libeled in Morris's court.

More than one colonial vice-admiralty judge had released a Dutch ship suspected of carrying cargo to or from an enemy port because no absolute proof of the offense could be found, only to have evidence of the wrongdoing surface later. Morris made no such mistakes. He carefully studied Dutch trading patterns and flattered himself on his ability to unravel the varied skeins of deception that he detected in the ships' papers. His propensity for condemning nearly every Dutch ship libeled in his court, regardless of the circumstances of their capture, inevitably led the owners of the seized ships to appeal his judgments to London. A typical example is that of the *Elizabeth*, a Dutch carrier with an innocuous cargo of bricks, coal, and boards, captured by a New York privateer off the coast of Hispaniola.

During the trial, the Dutch captain contended that he had been driven off course and that his destination had been the Dutch island of Curaçao. Morris derided this defense, calling it a "stale pretence . . . because it is the general answer all the Captains give, when they are taken going into the french ports." He found it suspicious that the captain did not use a £1,000 letter of credit known to be in his possession to acquit his ship: "The cap't is conscious to himself that the ship and cargo is french property . . . had the ship and cargo been bona fide Dutch property and destined to Curaco [*sic*] as he pretended, surely no man in his senses would have declined a Defence that could fully prove the property. . . . As being french property I adjudge & condemn her & her lading as Lawfull prize."[9] The *Elizabeth*'s owners appealed Morris's decision to the prize commissioners in London. This tribunal, which found the captain's tale to be more to its liking, reversed Morris's sentence and restored the *Elizabeth* to its owners.

Morris's bitterly expressed antipathy to the Dutch nation, which he castigated as "public factors for the enemy," or worse, is unsettling. His judgments in cases involving Dutch prizes prove him to be a very arrogant and haughty man, in the mold of his father. They make startling reading for the intemperate abuse that he heaped upon the Dutch. No other British American judge put on record in their judgments, as Morris frequently did, declarations that the Dutch were a traitor nation whose citizens could not be trusted. Morris's strong feelings were not apparent before the Seven Years' War. Many of New York's prominent families had Dutch antecedents, including his first wife's family, so an overt prejudice against the Dutch would have handicapped Morris in colonial politics and his personal life. His feelings seem to have been actuated by the exigencies of war and strong patriotic impulses. Morris's public-spirited declarations against what he considered Dutch perfidy and his official duties as a vice-admiralty judge coincided nicely for him.

During his twenty-four years as New York's vice-admiralty judge, Morris personally condemned more than 260 prize ships, worth over £2 million, captured by colonial privateers. In this capacity, he acted as an intermediary between Britain's imperial needs and colonial economic ambitions during the mid-eighteenth-century European wars for empire.

Lewis Morris Jr. died in 1762. His health declined toward the end of his life, which made traveling difficult, but he simply shifted the vice-admiralty court's proceedings to Morrisania, forcing court officers, lawyers, libelants, and defendants to undertake the journey to his home. There is no record that any of the participants found this arrangement at all peculiar, or that any complained publicly about the inconvenience, which showed how identified Lewis Morris Jr. had become with the court. (Probably none would have dared antagonize the old judge.) In deference, New York's governor immediately commissioned his son, Richard Morris, as the colony's new vice-admiralty judge.

The political world that Lewis Morris Jr. had navigated during his life disappeared within fifteen years of his death, when New York, along with twelve other British American colonies, moved to sever its connection with Great Britain. The shattering impact of the American Revolution has eclipsed the public accomplishments of men such as Morris, while it has magnified those of his sons. While Morris's sons showed little interest in New York's political life before his death, all four became prominent public figures afterward. The second son, Major-General Staats Morris, a career officer in the British army, served in India and sat in Parliament during the Revolutionary period. The other three—Lewis, Richard, and Gouverneur—made their mark in New York during those years. Lewis, Morris's first son, signed the Declaration of Independence; Richard moved from the colonial vice-admiralty judgeship to become the chief justice of New York; and Gouverneur helped write the final draft of the U.S. Constitution and served as American minister to

France for many years.

Lewis Morris Jr. is representative of those colonial-born politicians who came to dominate public life in eighteenth-century British America, during a time of frenetic colonial economic and demographic growth but ostensible imperial neglect. His family connections and his profession, the public offices he occupied and the politics he espoused, all marked Morris as a typical member of New York's political elite. A study of his public career is valuable for what it indicates about colonial America's native-born elite: how they engaged in public debate, the political strategies that they employed, and the fluid nature of transatlantic political life. The development of this class within the British Empire was a critical trend historically, especially because an overwhelming majority of the generation of political leaders who rose to power in Revolutionary and post-Revolutionary America came from these elite colonial families.

Notes

1. Leonard W. Labaree et al., eds., *The Autobiography of Benjamin Franklin* (New Haven, CT, 1964), 212.

2. "Representations of Lewis Morris Junr.," New York Council Minutes, June 13, 26, 1729, Public Record Office, Richmond, England, Colonial Office Papers, 5/1055, fols. 66–69, 71–78.

3. Lewis Morris Jr. to Board of Trade, July 19, 1729, in E. B. Callaghan, ed., *Documents Relative to the Colonial History of the State of New York*, 15 vols. (Albany, NY, 1853–1887), 5:887.

4. Lewis Morris Sr. to James Alexander, August 25, 1735, in Eugene R. Sheridan, ed., *The Papers of Lewis Morris, 1731–1737*, 3 vols. (Newark, NJ, 1993), 2:191.

5. George Clarke to Horace Walpole, March 16, 1736, in Callaghan, ed., *Documents Relative to . . . New York*, 6:48.

6. Lewis Morris Sr. to Robert Morris, July 26, 1743, in Sheridan, ed., *Papers of Lewis Morris*, 3:265.

7. Votes and Proceedings of the New York Assembly, July–September 1744, Colonial Office Papers, 5/1214, fols. 44–73.

8. George Clinton to Board of Trade, October 9, 1744, in Callaghan, ed., *Documents Relative to . . . New York*, 6:262.

9. Devereaux v. *Elizabeth* (1758), New York Vice-Admiralty Court Records, Office of Clerk, U.S. District Court, New York, NY, vol. 3, fols. 27, 28, 34, 39, 47–49, 52, 53.

Suggested Readings

Although there is no biography of Lewis Morris Jr., the fortunes of the Morris family in colonial and post-Revolutionary New York are well chronicled. S. S. Smith, *Lewis Morris, Anglo-American Statesman, ca. 1613–1691* (Atlantic Highlands, NJ, 1983), and Eugene R. Sheridan, *Lewis Morris, 1671—1746: A Study in Early*

American Politics (Syracuse, NY, 1981), are biographies of Morris's great-uncle and father, respectively. In addition, biographical sketches of three of Morris's sons, Lewis (1726–1798), Richard (1730–1810), and Gouverneur (1752–1816); two of his grandsons, Lewis Richard (1760–1825) and Richard Valentine (1768–1815); a nephew, Robert (1745–1815); his brother Robert Hunter (1700–1764); plus his father and great-uncle, appear in Dumas Malone, ed., *Dictionary of American Biography*, vol. 7 (New York, 1934). Stanley N. Katz, *Newcastle's New York: Anglo-American Politics, 1732–1753* (Cambridge, MA, 1968); Patricia Bonomi, *A Factious People: Politics and Society in Colonial New York* (New York, 1971); and Alan Tully, *Forming American Politics: Ideals, Interests, and Institutions in Colonial New York and Pennsylvania* (Baltimore, 1994), provide interesting and complementary overviews of colonial New York's often confusing political scene. James G. Lydon, *Pirates, Privateers, and Profits* (Saddle River, NJ, 1970), discusses privateering in eighteenth-century New York, while Lewis Morris's career as a vice-admiralty judge is explored in Michael Watson, "Appropriating Empire: The British North American Vice-Admiralty Judges, 1697–1775" (Ph.D. dissertation, University of Western Ontario, London, 1997). The articles in Bruce C. Daniels, ed., *Power and Status: Officeholding in Colonial America* (Middleton, CT, 1986), discuss British North American elites and officeholders in a larger context.

11

Pierre Pouchot
A French Soldier Views America

Brian L. Dunnigan

As an ambitious European military officer, Pierre Pouchot (1712–1769) saw North America, and himself, rather differently than our other witnesses. Born and raised in a French merchant family, he was anxious to advance himself through a military career. How did his early soldiering, especially in Italy and Corsica, prepare Pouchot for irregular or partisan warfare in North America? While his talent for engineering advanced his career, it may also have limited it in an army that did not regard engineering as noble. Pouchot was not only observant of topography, as was any good military engineer, but he was also curious about Native Americans. Is it coincidental that both Sagard and Pouchot recorded what they saw of Native Americans with genuine curiosity and acceptance, or did both these Frenchmen have professional reasons to do so?

How was a French soldier's view of the Seven Years' War likely to differ from that of a British or American colonial soldier? Regular troops of Britain and France were promoted in analogous ways, so that the career of most regular military officers was limited by birth, patronage, and marriage connections. Was access to higher political and judicial office, in Europe or America, similarly limited? Pouchot thought that tensions between French and Canadian troops and leaders were a major military problem, although he bridged these communities himself. What does his comfortable life in New York as a British prisoner of war suggest about the conventions shared by European regular troops? Would native and white Americans hold similar views? Does the fall of Niagara indicate the competition and confusion between distinct military cultures concerning prisoners?

Brian L. Dunnigan has edited a translation of Pouchot's *Mémoires* (1994) and published a study of the siege of Pouchot's Fort Niagara. He is curator of maps at the William L. Clements Library at the University of Michigan.

On the cold, gray morning of March 8, 1761, the British cartel transport *James* swung at anchor off Havre de Grâce, France. The ship had just made a stormy, nine-week crossing from New York, battered by the wintry North Atlantic and driven to temporary shelter in Portsmouth before at last raising the French coast. Crowded aboard *James* and her consort *Boscawen* were 504 French prisoners of war: officers and men of the army and colonial forces. New France had succumbed in September to overwhelming British military power, and the soldiers now preparing to disembark were the last remnants of the colony's defenders being repatriated to Europe.

Among the enlisted men and the dozen officers patiently waiting to go ashore was one Pierre Pouchot, captain in the Régiment de Béarn, Knight of the Royal and Military Order of St. Louis and former commandant of the fortresses of Niagara and Fort Lévis. As Pouchot contemplated his future, he could hardly have avoided reflecting on his experiences of the past six years. The captain had last seen France in April 1755, when he and more than five hundred officers and men of the Second Battalion of the Béarn Regiment sailed from nearby Brest. Béarn and five other regular army battalions were bound for North America to bolster the meager defenses of New France against Britain and her American colonists. Since that earlier crossing of the Atlantic, Pouchot had marched or sailed across most of New France and the enemy province of New York. He had designed buildings and fortifications, survived the most desperate battle of the French and Indian War, defended two fortresses, and besieged a third. He had twice been a prisoner of war and acquitted himself with honor before and during his captivity. And, in the midst of nearly constant campaigning, Captain Pouchot had also mapped a large part of North America while carefully observing and recording the culture and habits of the Canadian colonists and many of the Indian nations of the northeastern part of the continent. By 1761 his journals and maps brimmed with the raw material for a chronicle of the 1754 to 1760 period of the North American war. Pouchot's coming years would be filled with personal and professional disappointments, but those frustrations would motivate him to shape his collected material into three volumes of *Mémoires*.[1] This, Pierre Pouchot's most lasting achievement, would prove to be the only history of the French and Indian War from the French perspective published during the eighteenth century.

Pierre Pouchot was a remarkable man in any sense of the term. His abilities as an engineer, cartographer, military leader, and envoy to the Indian allies and enemies of New France set him apart from his fellow officers of the *troupes de terre*, the French regular army, who served with him in America. Military and civil officials alike recognized Pouchot's talents and consistently called upon him to accept responsibilities far beyond the normal duties of a company commander, including specialized assignments and independent commands that, in the British service, would have been entrusted to an officer with the rank of colonel or even general. And yet Pouchot never rose above the rank of captain, in large part because he was, by class, a *roturier,* or commoner, in an officer corps whose upper echelons were drawn almost exclusively from the ancient nobility of France. Two generations later, during the wars of Revolutionary France or the empire of Napoleon, Pouchot might have risen to grand heights of command. Instead, he served at a time when his efforts to obtain the preferment of superior rank foundered on the increasing unwillingness of traditional officers to promote capable *roturiers* to senior positions.

The Seven Years' War placed many European soldiers in unfamiliar, unique situations and exposed them to other cultures. Pouchot embraced the North American world that he and his fellow officers encountered between 1755 and 1760 with interest and a surprisingly open mind. He possessed an energetic and ambitious attitude, a scientific inclination frequently expressed in engineering and cartography, and the personal discipline and experience needed to gather and use information effectively. These were the tools of a capable soldier and a keen, objective observer. Pouchot was also particularly fortunate in that the independent commands accorded him because of his varied skills provided opportunities to encounter the full range of cultural and social groups involved in the North American war. At one time or another, he served with or commanded French, Canadian, and German troops. He successfully worked with the colonial French population and the *marine,* or navy, officials responsible for the colony. He rapidly gained esteem among the native peoples, knowing them both as firm allies and formidable enemies. Pouchot had the opportunity to learn about the culture of the Iroquois nations as well as the Algonquian peoples of the Great Lakes region, and he was able to master their rhetoric and military strategy in order to motivate diverse and independent groups to work together against the British foe. Pouchot was also one of the few French or Canadian officers who came to know his enemies personally during two periods as a prisoner of war in New York. These circumstances, set amid the chaos of a war that would end French control of half a continent, placed Pierre Pouchot in a position to record the events of his time with accuracy and style.

Pouchot, a native of Grenoble, was born on April 8, 1712. His father was a merchant with several children, although Pouchot's *Mémoires* mentions only a brother. The senior Pouchot died before 1733; and when his widow soon remarried, the children by her first husband embarked upon extended litigation (still ongoing in 1781) with their mother and stepsiblings over the family fortune. This unhappy situation influenced Pierre's decision to follow a military career. He had demonstrated an early interest in engineering, and in 1733, at the age of twenty-one, he entered the army as a volunteer seeking a commission as an officer. The eighteenth-century editor of Pouchot's *Mémoires* claims that he joined in the capacity of engineer, but the fact that his entire service was with the infantry and that there is no indication he seriously sought an appointment to the Royal Corps of Engineers suggests that he began his service in the Béarn Regiment and remained with it for most of his career.

During Pouchot's stint as a volunteer, he learned the military craft on the job as, in effect, an officer-trainee. He continued to study engineering from texts by such masters as Sébastion Le Prestre de Vauban and Menno van Coehoorn. This apprenticeship came to an end on May 1, 1734, when Pouchot obtained a commission as lieutenant *en second*, junior officer of a company of infantry, in the Régiment de Béarn. It is possible that Pouchot family funds played some part in this event, for, although junior commissions were not purchased outright as in the contemporary British army, it was relatively common for money to be directed to the colonel of the regiment and the Ministry of War to facilitate approval of a candidacy.

Pierre Pouchot's embarkation on a military life came at a favorable time for a young man of ambition, for France was at war. The conflict known as the War of the Polish Succession (1733–1738) sent Pouchot's regiment against the Austrians along the River Po in northern Italy. Although his *Mémoires* only briefly touch on these events, Pouchot very soon gained the practical engineering and reconnaissance experience that would influence the rest of his career and enhance his ability to observe and record. Lieutenant Pouchot's talent for engineering was recognized by his superiors, and he was posted away from his regimental duties to assist Pierre-Joseph de Bourcet, an engineer with fresh ideas in the use of field fortifications who was beginning to establish a reputation as an expert in Alpine campaigning.

This early exposure to irregular forms of warfare would pay dividends during later European and American service. In 1739, Pouchot got his first taste of overseas service when the Béarn Regiment was shipped to Corsica, where French troops had been introduced at the request of the island's Genoese overlords who had been unsuccessfully attempting to pacify its fractious and hardy population. Pouchot was introduced to partisan warfare in difficult terrain, where he spent the greater part of his time fortifying positions and establishing roads to improve communications between French garrisons. By November 1739 the Corsicans had laid down their arms. Less than three years later, in May 1742, Pouchot was appointed lieutenant of the colonel's company, the senior and most prestigious unit of the regiment. His career was now advancing at a respectable pace, especially during a nominal peacetime.

Renewed warfare was just the tonic to accelerate the preferment of a young officer, for it was the surest way for personal merit and achievements to advance a career in the army of Louis XV. Although France would not formally declare war until 1744, an army of French "volunteers" joined the Bavarians in an invasion of Austrian Bohemia in 1741. Two years later, Pouchot experienced a full-scale battle against the British at Dettingen in Germany. In September 1743 he advanced to the rank of assistant major of his regiment, which placed him in a position to aid the chief administrative officer and learn the involved financial system of the French army.

The War of the Austrian Succession (1741–1748) would carry Pouchot across large areas of Germany, Flanders, Italy, and Austria. It would also provide opportunities for engineering and independent service. In April 1744 the Béarn Regiment and Pouchot participated in a formal siege of Freiburg, Germany. The 1745 campaign found Pouchot involved in another siege at Tournai in Flanders, where he had the mundane but important task of fortifying the attackers' camp. Between these sieges, Pouchot was again off on his own in an undertaking that could only have been assigned to him because of influence and a regard for his engineering talents. At some point during 1744, he was ordered to reconnoiter the road through the Tyrol that provided Austria's chief land link with Italy. Pouchot claimed that he had been given this duty by the Court itself, and that he prepared a map and a memorandum on the road between Innsbruck and Verona through the Brenner Pass. This would have taken him deep into Austrian territory. This further experience in rugged country honed his skills as an observer and cartographer. It is likely that his former superior, the engineer Bourcet, influenced the choice of Pouchot for this assignment. By this time, Bourcet was serving on the Italian front, the area most affected by Austria's ability to move troops through the Alps.

Although details of Pouchot's Tyrolean adventure are sparse, this dangerous reconnaissance behind enemy lines and the more pedestrian services at Freiburg and Tournai brought him to the most significant watershed of his military career. In August 1745, twelve years after entering the army as a volunteer, Pouchot was advanced to the rank of captain. About the same time, he was rewarded for his 1744–45 services with the coveted *croix de St. Louis*, which made him a *chevalier*, or knight, of the premier military order of France. The promotion came without command of a company, but Pouchot could only have viewed the decoration as a sign that he had at least a chance for further advancement. The title of *chevalier* implied an elevation to the nobility; and, in 1750, Louis XV issued an edict that officers who received the *croix de St. Louis* were to be so honored.

Pouchot thus entered the final years of the War of the Austrian Succession with greatly increased prestige and clearly demonstrated abilities as a dependable officer and competent engineer. During the Flanders campaign of 1746 he served primarily as an infantry officer. He would thus have participated in the French victory at Rocoux on October 11. His final wartime service in 1747 took him again to the Maritime Alps and a far less satisfactory action at the Colle dell'Assieta near Turin where, on July 19, a French army was bloodily repulsed. This ended Pouchot's active fighting in Europe, and the Treaty of Aix-la-Chapelle terminated the war in 1748. His next few years would be spent at peaceful garrison duties in France.

Although the fighting was over for a time, Captain Pouchot was planning assaults of another kind. His commission as captain was a promising step, but without command of a company his status was little higher than that of a senior lieutenant. There remained that last bit of gulf between the status of the junior *officiers subalternes* and the *officiers supérieurs* who commanded companies and regiments. From the latter position, Pouchot could hope to continue his advancement to command a battalion or even a regiment, and from there the rank of general was not unthinkable.

The first step came in 1749. Facilitated, perhaps, by the fact that the Béarn Regiment had been doubled in size in 1746, Pouchot obtained his company in the Second Battalion. The nature of the vacancy that opened for him is unknown, but it is likely that, in the aftermath of the 1748 peace, captains retired or moved on from the newly raised junior battalion of a solid but not particularly prestigious regiment. Command of a company also brought the captain certain personal financial responsibilities for its maintenance, and perhaps the lingering family litigation initially delayed Pouchot's ability to muster the resources needed to exploit the opportunity provided by meritorious services in 1744–45.

Successful preferment required a continuous effort, and Pouchot was not content to remain a captain. His next step was to obtain a lieutenant colonelcy, probably in the role of "battalion commander" of a junior battalion in an infantry regiment. Between 1749 and his departure for New France in April 1755, Pouchot had at least one interview in Paris with Antoine-René de Voyer d'Argenson, Marquis de Paulmy, then serving as general secretary to the minister of war, his own uncle. Paulmy gave the impression that he would look favorably on the captain's efforts to improve his lot while serving King Louis. This must have been reassuring, for by that time Pouchot had passed the age of forty and was becoming apprehensive, he wrote a few years later, that "my time is passing."[2] For a moment, the captain seemed to have gained access to the precincts of power, especially since Paulmy succeeded to his uncle's post in February 1757, but he lasted only a year, and with his departure vanished the nearest thing that Pouchot had to a patron in high places.

Peacetime garrison duty did not provide fertile ground for martial ambition, but opportunity was soon to present itself again. The treaty signed at Aix-la-Chapelle in 1748 was, then and now, considered little more than a truce in an increasingly earnest worldwide conflict between the powers of Europe. The results of unfinished business were particularly apparent in North America, where British and French interests increasingly overlapped. America had already seen three inconclusive and rather desultory offshoots of European wars since the 1690s. Old disputes over the boundary between Acadia and New France remained unresolved in 1748. The volatility of that situation was matched in the west by increasing rivalry over trade in the Ohio River region, known to the French as *la belle-rivière*. Tensions had been growing since the signing of the Aix-la-Chapelle treaty, and the subsequent commercial and military expeditions of both sides resulted in renewed confrontation in the spring of 1754.

When the first round of shooting was over, the French had the upper hand in the Ohio, but by autumn Britain had resolved to dispatch regular troops from Ireland to reassert the claims of George II to the backcountry of Pennsylvania and Virginia. News of this escalation brought a corresponding reaction from France, whose colonial garrisons had heretofore comprised only companies of infantry maintained by the *marine* and led chiefly by colonial-born officers. For the first time in nearly a century, battalions of the metropolitan army, the *troupes de terre*, would be committed to New France. These units were considered to have the experience and discipline needed to conduct a war against British regulars.

Early in April 1755, six infantry battalions marched to the naval port of Brest to take ship for New France. Two were bound for the maritime stronghold of Louisbourg on Cape Breton Island. The others, including the Béarn Second Battalion, would be transported to Québec, there to take whatever action might be necessary to defend the colony. There was a general enthusiasm among the troops for the American adventure. Pouchot's opinion is not apparent in his *Mémoires*, other than discontent at seeing *troupes de terre* units placed under overall *marine* command (the governor-general of New France was a *marine* officer, and the naval administration assumed responsibility for the army troops, even down to providing uniforms of their own pattern). This was worse, Pouchot opined, "than if they had passed into the service of an absolutely foreign prince."[3] The innate tensions between the two branches of service and their leadership would ultimately have a negative effect on the prosecution of the war in America. Despite Pouchot's comments, he proved able to bridge this gap between the two military services committed to the defense of New France.

The small army of which Pouchot and the Béarn Regiment were a part was provided with its own staff and supporting troops, including engineers. Pouchot himself set off for America as an infantry officer, but fate once again intervened to place a premium on his talents. The troops were carried to New France in a number of 74-gun ships-of-the-line armed *en flûte*—that is, most of their guns had been removed to convert them to transports. These vessels were escorted by fully armed warships in the hope that the flotilla would rapidly move its human cargo to Canada. But the British Royal Navy had been alerted to the move and given orders to prevent its arrival. Most of the French ships got through, but two, *Alcide* and *Lys*, were captured, even though France and Britain were still officially at peace. Although the loss was not devastating, it revealed that an egregious error had been made at Brest, where all three of the expedition's engineers had been assigned to one vessel, the *Alcide*.

The Béarn Regiment arrived safely at Québec in June. There, Pouchot and his superiors realized that he was the most experienced military engineer in the colony: his extensive service in Italy, Corsica, and Flanders had made him the officer best qualified to design or attack fortifications. Once he proved his expertise as an engineer to his superiors, particularly to Governor-General Pierre de Rigaud, Marquis de Vaudreuil, Pouchot saw little of his company of infantry during the next six years of campaigning. He would, instead, find himself serving consistently as an engineer or being given independent assignments.

The troops arrived at an opportune time, for New France was being pressed at four points. The Béarn Regiment was sent to cover the Lake Ontario frontier, posted at Cataraqui, or Fort Frontenac, at the head of the St. Lawrence River. There Pouchot resumed familiar duties, designing an entrenched camp to protect the troops. Although the westernmost British attack under General Edward Braddock was routed early in July, Governor Vaudreuil remained deeply concerned about the security of communications between distant French territories: Canada and the Great Lakes, the Ohio River Valley, and Louisiana. This required holding the portage around Niagara Falls, and its defense was, in the summer of 1755, dependent upon Fort Niagara, a stone house surrounded by a rotten stockade. Prudence required that it be made defensible against the heavy artillery that any British expedition would bring against it.

In October, Pouchot was sent to Fort Niagara, accompanied by the Guienne Regiment. He enthusiastically set about transforming the thirty-year-old post into a formidable, European-style fortress in the best traditions of the French master, Vauban. Pouchot would spend most of the next two years perfecting his fortress (see map), and in so doing he drew the favorable attention of Governor Vaudreuil, who would remain an enthusiastic patron for the balance of the war. The new defenses of Fort Niagara established Pouchot's reputation in the colony to such a degree that even a very junior

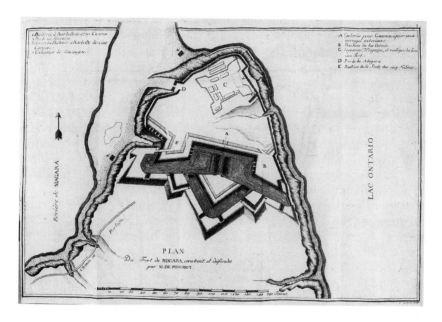

A plan of Fort Niagara reflecting the situation during the winter of 1755–56, soon after Pouchot's arrival. The map was engraved and published with Pouchot's *Mémoires* in 1781. The key in the upper left-hand corner indicates the positions of: 1. a battery of five cannon, 2. the relief gate, 3. a second battery of five cannon, and 4. Indian cabins or huts. The key in the upper right-hand corner indicates the positions of: A. the galleries to communicate with the outer defenses, B. the Lake Ontario bastion, C. quarters, storehouses, and traces of the old fort, D. Niagara Gate, and E. the bastion of the Gate of the Five Nations. The Chemin du Portage (Portage Road) in the lower left-hand corner leads to a point above Niagara Falls where boats could safely be put in the water. *Courtesy of William L. Clements Library*

marine cadet could answer to British interrogators that the captain was "esteemed a very good engineer."[4]

Niagara introduced Pouchot to other facets of North American life. Although he applied himself chiefly to designing and constructing buildings and fortifications during the winter and spring of 1756, he was also exposed for the first time to large numbers of Indians. Fort Niagara was a major trading and supply post for the western nations of the Iroquois as well as for the Mississauga from the north shore of Lake Ontario. These people, as well as French officers and traders, brought to Fort Niagara intelligence of military movements, posts, and topography that could be applied to the making of maps. Niagara was commanded by a *marine* officer, however, and for the first year Pouchot had little responsibility for French-Indian relations or for making maps other than some fine plans of the new fortifications.

The summer of 1756 found the defenses of Niagara in an acceptable state, though far from perfected. A new *troupes de terre* general, Louis-Joseph de Montcalm, had arrived in New France that spring, and he was intent on a bold offensive stroke to forestall an attack by the numerically superior British. He decided to attack the forts at Oswego on the southwest corner of Lake Ontario, and for that he recalled Pouchot and the *troupes de terre* detachments at Fort Niagara. Pouchot was once again expecting to resume his role as an infantry officer, for Montcalm had arrived in the colony with additional troops and engineers to replace those lost aboard the *Alcide*.

Pouchot rejoined Montcalm's army only to find that fate had intervened once more. Soon after the French army landed near Oswego, Montcalm's new chief engineer had undertaken an evening reconnaissance. Shedding his heavy blue coat in the warm weather, he set off on this hazardous duty clad in his red waistcoat. The French-allied Indian who saw him in the dusk naturally assumed him to be an Englishman and fired a fatal shot. When the engineer's assistant admitted virtually complete inexperience in the conduct of a formal siege, Montcalm called for Pouchot, since he had already received favorable reports of his work at Niagara. For the next few days the captain would direct the successful French siege of the British forts at Oswego. The surrender of this major British garrison secured the Lake Ontario frontier for the next two years.

The capture of Oswego, and the high regard in which his superiors held his skill and energy in refortifying Niagara, brought Pouchot several honors that he could only have assumed would lead to advancement. The list of recommendations forwarded to France in the autumn of 1756 included a request that Pouchot be promoted to lieutenant colonel. Coming from Governor Vaudreuil, and seconded by General Montcalm, this recommendation must have seemed the culmination of a long-sought ambition, especially with the Marquis de Paulmy and his uncle still in the Ministry of War. A second honor conferred on Pouchot was command of Fort Niagara, a ticklish appointment for the governor, who had previously maintained that only *marine* officers should command the frontier posts of New France. Vaudreuil's naming of Pouchot drew the ire of *marine* officers who believed that the opportunity for profitable personal trade, one of the perks of the command, was wasted on an officer of the *troupes de terre*. The governor's regard must have been substantial for, in addition to weathering such political criticism, he had to be confident that Pouchot could handle the crucial matter of Indian relations at the post.

As it turned out, the Niagara appointment proved to be the most substantial of Pouchot's personal honors granted in the aftermath of Oswego. When the list of *grâces*, or favors, reached the colony in 1757, there was no promotion for Pouchot, only a small pension. He would be granted three more pensions in the next three years as rewards for devoted service, but senior rank and command of a battalion eluded him. The war in Europe, finally declared in 1756, had brought a backlash by noble officers against the promotion of *roturiers* to senior positions in the army. When Paulmy was replaced as minister of war by Marshal Louis-Charles Auguste Fouquet, Comte de Belle-Isle, in the winter of 1758, Pouchot's last hope vanished. Belle-Isle was foremost among those advocating that senior positions be given only to members of the nobility. He agreed with the king "that the regiments which are most used in the war be commanded only by those of quality."[5] Despite the status conferred by the *croix de St. Louis*, Pouchot was not of the true nobility and had become one of many victims of a conservative shift in the French army.

As yet unaware of the futility of his ambitions, Pouchot assumed command of Fort Niagara in October 1756. There he applied himself in several ways, first completing the fortifications and erecting adequate buildings for a substantial garrison. This work was finished by the fall of 1757 to general acclaim. Fort Niagara had been transformed from a virtual ruin into the strongest position in New France west of Québec. Any attack on Niagara would necessitate logistics and the transportation of heavy artillery bound to delay, if not stop, the British.

With his engineering duties accomplished, Pouchot devoted increasing attention to one of the chief reasons for his post: maintaining the allegiance of the Indians. Fort Niagara was a supply base, trading post, and diplomatic station critical in recruiting and retaining Indian allies for New France. It was even more important because of its location on the western margin of the Six Nations of the Iroquois. The Seneca, the most populous of the Six Nations and the most inclined to favor the French, particularly gravitated to Niagara. Their support was needed, and Fort Niagara was no place for a man unable to deal effectively with diverse groups of Indians.

Captain Pouchot's success as envoy to the Iroquois and other nations was nothing less than astounding. Admittedly, he undertook the responsibility at a propitious time, for the capture of Oswego had elevated French prestige and seriously weakened the British position. No sooner had Pouchot returned to Niagara, in October 1756, than numerous Loups or Delawares from Pennsylvania arrived to confer with him. Groups of Iroquois followed during the winter, and by the summer of 1757 some Seneca chiefs had even declared outright in favor of the French. The Iroquois soon gave Pouchot a name—"Sategariouaen," or "the center of good dealings"— a sign of genuine regard, very likely for his honesty and straight-forwardness. More Indians than usual were seen at Fort Niagara during 1757, in part because of the enhanced French position but also because a host of western Indians was passing through on the way to Montréal to join that summer's campaign on Lake George. They came too because of Pouchot, and the summer of 1757 was the high-water mark of French relations with the Iroquois. General Montcalm was convinced that Pouchot was "wonderfully liked by the Indians," while Governor Vaudreuil praised his "talent for dealing with the Indians and enticing them for the good of the service."[6]

Pouchot, though clearly motivated by his sense of duty, seems to have possessed a deep interest in the people whom he served as the representative of Governor Vaudreuil and King Louis XV. He could not entirely bridge the cultural gulf between Europeans and Amerindians, but at least he opened his mind to the other culture. Pouchot avidly collected first- and second-hand information about the way his allies lived, and a substantial part of his *Mémoires* is devoted to his account of the "manners and customs" of the people whom he encountered, chiefly at Niagara. Virtually every aspect of their culture was of interest to him, from clothing to family life. He set about collecting information in an organized and, for his time and background, surprisingly objective manner, and he presented his data in a way that can be read today with a great deal of benefit.

Pouchot collected other data as well, for he retained an interest in cartography and a goal of gathering enough information about the western theater of the war to produce a map that could adequately define the frontiers of the English and French domin-ions. There is clear evidence that he was busily assembling carto-graphic intelligence as early as the winter of 1757, and this activity was probably only a continuation of efforts begun soon after he arrived in New France. Ultimately, much of this information would also find a place in his book where it provides geographical and topographical context for the historical events described in it.

Captain Pouchot's duties at Fort Niagara kept him from the main theater of fighting during 1757. French arms reached their zenith that summer with the capture of Fort William Henry and the forestalling of a British attack on Louisbourg. The period also coincided with the completion of the fortifications at Niagara, and with that the end of the governor's best reason for having a *troupes de terre* officer in command there. In October, Governor Vaudreuil gave in to pressure from within the colony and appointed a *marine* captain to replace Pouchot.

Although this appointment freed a versatile officer for frontline service, it proved a fatal blow to French-Iroquois relations. Pouchot's replacement was not well regarded by the Indians and soon threw away Pouchot's diplomatic accomplishments. It was a bad time to change the equation in the Iroquois country, for British agents, led by Sir William Johnson, were unrelenting in attempts to pull the Six Nations into their camp. The Iroquois who had most enthusiastically supported the French took the replacement of Pouchot as an affront. A warrior who swam out to Pouchot's ship, as it was about to leave Niagara, expressed their disappointment most eloquently. When told that the captain was leaving under orders from Governor Vaudreuil, the warrior declared that "our father no longer loves us then, since he is taking from us a chief whom we all love."[7] Iroquois support for the French eroded from the time of Pouchot's departure, and by the autumn of 1758 they would be ready to support British moves against Niagara and the St. Lawrence.

With Pouchot's departure from Niagara, the whole tone of the narrative in his *Mémoires* changes. It becomes much more detailed for the campaigns of 1758, 1759, and 1760, largely because the captain faced British attacks in all three years. The winter of 1758 provided an interlude, however, during which he worked with Governor Vaudreuil and General François Lévis, second-in-command to Montcalm, to complete a large map of the French and English frontiers. The governor had become increasingly critical of Montcalm, and their strategies for the defense of the colony were rapidly diverging. Vaudreuil's interest in cartography was due in part to his own ambitious plans for an invasion of New York during 1758. He kept these strategic ideas from Montcalm, whom he outranked, until the very beginning of the campaign.

Despite clear signs of a gathering British threat on the Lake Champlain frontier, Vaudreuil suddenly shifted portions of Montcalm's army away for his invasion scheme. Pouchot was assigned to a mixed detachment of *troupes de terre*, colonial, and Indian forces that was to descend the Mohawk River from Lake

Ontario. Before Vaudreuil's ambitious plan could be carried out, it became clear that every available man was needed to face a British thrust against Ticonderoga. Pouchot and his men were ordered back to the army; they arrived only hours before the assault began. Captain Pouchot fought in the front lines of the battle of July 8, when British General James Abercromby's army was repulsed at Ticonderoga with horrific losses. This was the last significant French victory, however. By the end of the year British successes elsewhere—at Louisbourg on the Atlantic, Fort Duquesne on the Ohio, and Fort Frontenac on Lake Ontario—made it clear that the days of successful offensive action by French forces were over.

The French commanders spent the winter of 1758–59 planning how best to preserve the colony, but the disagreements between Vaudreuil and Montcalm became ever more pronounced. The governor wanted to retake *la belle-rivière* and hold the west, while the more conservative general wished to concentrate his forces for the defense of the settled part of the colony and the cities of Québec and Montréal. Eventually, a compromise was reached, by which some western forces would be maintained and supported from the fortress at Niagara. Pouchot was everyone's choice for the command. Not only had he designed the fortifications, but he also had a proven record of success with the Iroquois and other Indian nations. Perhaps it was not too late to keep them from wholeheartedly supporting the British. Montcalm expressed it best: Pouchot was "assuredly . . . better qualified to defend that place than any Colonial Captain."[8]

Before assuming his post, Pouchot was involved in discussions of strategy because of his knowledge of Niagara and the Indians of the region. Up to this point, he had successfully negotiated the widening chasm between the governor and general, remaining trusted by both men. But, during the winter of 1758–59, it became necessary to support one strategy or another. Pouchot at some point must have expressed too much support for Vaudreuil and the defense of Niagara and the Ohio River, because the attitude of Pouchot's own general rapidly changed. He became sarcastic about Pouchot's abilities and the regard in which he was held by the governor. Later, Montcalm would disparage the "Canadian arguments" of Pouchot who, it must have seemed to him, had deserted his own *troupes de terre* and thrown in with the *marine* faction. Pouchot therefore left Montréal with a cooler relationship with Montcalm. With a few reinforcements, sweeping powers that placed him in command of French forces from Detroit to the head of the St. Lawrence, and a mandate to recover the situation at Niagara, Pouchot set out up the St. Lawrence on March 17, 1759.

He came very close to success. Between March and July,

Captain Pouchot reestablished French naval power on Lake Ontario, repaired the neglected fortifications at Niagara, and organized a substantial French-Indian army to evict the British from their new fort at Pittsburgh on *la belle-rivière*. Success, however, was dependent upon early notice of any British advance on Niagara, and here Pouchot failed, primarily because he relied on Iroquois promises to warn him. Perhaps he believed too much in his own "Canadian arguments" and overestimated his regard among the Iroquois. They had, in fact, decided to support the British, and one thousand warriors eventually joined the attack on Fort Niagara.

Pouchot had some six hundred men to defend Fort Niagara when thirty-five hundred British and Iroquois landed nearby on July 6. The defenders were stubborn, however, and they were led by a man who had carefully studied the manuals of fortification and had helped besiege at least three fortresses. The garrison held out for nineteen days, longer than almost any other North American fortress had to that time. When a French relief force was destroyed within sight of the walls on July 24, however, Pouchot believed further resistance to be futile. He capitulated the next day.

By this time, Captain Pouchot had become intimately familiar with his Canadian and Amerindian allies. During the next five months he would come to know his British enemies as well, something that few French officers had the opportunity to do. Taken to New York as a prisoner of war, Pouchot became something of a celebrity in the colonial capital, dining with Sir William Johnson and other British officers as well as meeting General Jeffrey Amherst and many important New Yorkers. He finally got to see the Mohawk and Hudson Rivers, and the experience was duly recorded among his topographical observations. When he was exchanged and returned to Montréal on Christmas Eve 1759, Pouchot had much to relate about British strength, which had not been concealed from him during his captivity.

Pouchot's news was bad, and he returned to New France to find Montcalm dead—mortally wounded in September in the defense of Québec—and Lévis in command. At least the new general was capable, and he was on good terms with Vaudreuil, but the loss of Niagara, Ticonderoga, Crown Point, and Québec in 1759 left little hope for the declining number of French and Canadian defenders. Lévis attempted a bold stroke at Québec in April 1760, but the city walls and the Royal Navy turned an initial success into a futile gesture. By summer, the French were being forced toward Montréal by British armies approaching from three directions.

Pouchot's demonstrated dual talents for fortification and Indian relations were again summoned for the final campaign of 1760. His assignment was to defend Fort Lévis, an island post in the upper

St. Lawrence that blocked the route to Montréal from Lake Ontario. Pouchot approached the task with his customary vigor, working tirelessly to maintain Indian alliances and forestall British influence. He gathered intelligence and passed it promptly to Lévis while preparing his garrison for the inevitable assault. It came in August, and this time Pouchot had only three hundred men to face General Amherst's ten thousand. The fate of Fort Lévis was a foregone conclusion, but Pouchot held out through six days of violent bombardment and again earned the admiration of his enemy, many of whom he had met during 1759. On August 25, 1760, Pouchot surrendered his shattered fort and became a prisoner of war for the second time. He and his men were conveyed once more to New York, while Amherst's army swept down the St. Lawrence. Two weeks later, cornered at Montréal by three British armies, Lévis and Vaudreuil surrendered their remaining troops and all of New France.

The capitulation ended the fighting in Canada and the participation of the *troupes de terre* in New France. Those soldiers and officers who remained were immediately sent off to France, not to serve again until the war had been concluded. Pouchot and his little garrison were treated otherwise since their surrender was tendered under terms predating the Montréal agreement. They were, once exchanged, still eligible for further service. While British officials awaited instructions on how to treat the more than six hundred French prisoners from Fort Lévis and earlier engagements being held in and around New York, Pouchot spent the autumn of 1760 in a comfortable captivity. He lived in the home of the British commissary of prisoners and came to know the cosmopolitan seaport as someone akin to an honored guest. Finally, on January 1, 1761, Pouchot boarded the *James* and set out on the voyage that would return him to the shores of France.

Captain Pierre Pouchot returned to his native land with little to show for his dedicated efforts over the past six years and with a most uncertain future ahead of him. The cause for which he had fought, the preservation of New France, had been unsuccessful despite the sacrifices of the soldiers of the *troupes de terre* and *marine*. The captain was a paroled prisoner of war and could not serve again until formally exchanged. Most disappointing personally, his highly recommended service in New France had brought him only some small pensions and not the hoped-for advancement. By the winter of 1761 he was largely convinced that he was unlikely to "cross the barrier that separates subordinate functions from upper ranks."[9]

Despite these disappointments, Pouchot was not yet prepared to give up his quest for preferment. His first stop after landing was Paris, where he sought out the Marquis de Vaudreuil. The former governor promptly wrote Pouchot an enthusiastic letter of recommendation, but by the end of 1761 Vaudreuil and other colonial officials had been charged with rank corruption in their administration of New France. This *affaire du Canada*, as it was called, soon touched Pouchot himself. He was in Grenoble, early in 1762, when he heard of the arrests of Vaudreuil and many others. Pouchot also learned that inquiries about his own whereabouts were being made in Béziers, Grenoble, and Metz. Certain that he was to be charged as well, he went immediately to Paris to clear his name. Although he was no doubt relieved to learn that only his testimony was needed, he knew that his Canadian patronage was now worthless. Then, in November 1762, came a final blow when his Béarn Regiment was disbanded in a reorganization of the army. Pouchot could do little else than retire on his pensions.

It was apparently at this low point of his military career that Pouchot returned to Grenoble and began forging his North American notes and data into a book. He had several purposes in mind. One clearly was to record the honorable service of his regiment and other *troupes de terre* units in what had proved to be one more lost cause in a disastrous war for France. In the course of doing so, he ensured that his own achievements were recorded and emphasized as far as was prudent. Another purpose, no doubt spurred by his brush with the *affaire du Canada*, was to distance himself from and expose the unethical and illegal dealings of colonial financial personnel, particularly Intendant Militaire François Bigot and his minions. His personal agenda was wrapped in a rich account of the war from 1754 to 1760 that fills two of the three volumes of his narrative. This history was particularly detailed for the campaigns in which Pouchot had participated. His third volume comprises two invaluable sections: topographical observations on the main routes for traversing the theater of the war in Canada, New York, and the Ohio Valley; and a long and well-organized discussion of the manners and customs of the Indians of North America.

Sadly, Pouchot was unable to complete his book himself, and it shows many signs of haste in its composition. What is fortunate is that he assembled as much as he did before returning to the army. Perhaps Pouchot continued to hope that distinguished field service would obtain for him the elusive preferment he sought. Perhaps his pensions were inadequate. Or perhaps he simply missed the martial life that had occupied him for nearly thirty years. His eighteenth-century editor maintained that he "could imagine no other way of avenging himself on the ingratitude of his country than further service."[10] At any rate, when trouble erupted once more in Corsica during 1768, Pouchot seized the opportunity to go there as an engineer. To gain such employment, the fifty-six-year-old captain might have turned to the only area of influence left to him—officers familiar with his sterling service during the War of the Austrian Succession. One of these, Lieutenant General Noel Jourda, Comte de Vaux, was given command in Corsica in the winter of 1769, and Pouchot served on his staff. In the three months before his departure for Corsica, Pouchot finished arranging his material and hastily composed what he could of his book.

It was well that he did so, for Corsica would be his last campaign. On May 3, 1769, Vaux began a three-pronged offensive to crush the Corsican rebels led by Pasquale Paoli. As his columns marched south from the northern end of the rugged island, Pouchot was ordered to reconnoiter a strategic road, a task familiar enough to him from his service of thirty years before. The reconnaissance was important enough for the engineer to be escorted by the grenadiers of the Royal-Italien Regiment. Despite this precaution, Pouchot's party was ambushed on May 8 by the rebel inhabitants of the village of Vignale. The grenadiers panicked and fled. Pouchot, veteran of sieges, battles, and Indian warfare in North America and Europe, was abandoned to be killed by the Corsicans. He lies in an unknown grave.

The manuscript, which Pouchot had entitled *Mémoires sur la dernière guerre de l'Amérique septentrionale . . . ,* had been left behind in Grenoble, where it passed into the hands of his brother. It languished for a decade before he took it to be published in Yverdon, Switzerland, a logical and prudent place considering the author's blunt comments about a number of influential French officials. The three slim volumes came off the presses in 1781, at a time of renewed interest in France and Europe about North America because of the American Revolution and the support being provided the rebels by the French army and navy. Echoes and lessons of the former war, as well as the insatiable curiosity of Europeans about the native peoples of America, gave the book a currency that it probably would not have had if Pouchot himself had published it in the aftermath of the Seven Years' War.

Pierre Pouchot, soldier, engineer, cartographer, diplomat, and observer of other cultures, never achieved his narrower personal goals of advancement to senior rank in the army of Louis XV. But through his talented and energetic services in America, he influenced the course of the war more than any other battalion officer of the *troupes de terre.* Even more important, he documented the struggle from the French perspective and left us a vivid picture of a war that had far-reaching implications for all the peoples of North America.

Notes

1. Published as Pierre Pouchot, *Mémoires sur la dernière guerre de l'Amérique septentrionale entre la France et l'Angleterre. Suivis d'Observations, dont plusieurs sont relatives au théâtre actuel de la guerre, & de noveaux détails sur les moeurs & les usages des Sauvages, avec des cartes topographiques,* 3 vols. (Yverdon, Switzerland, 1781). The most recent English translation is by Michael Cardy, *Memoirs on the Late War in North America between France and England,* ed. Brian Leigh Dunnigan (Youngstown, NY, 1994). Citations here are from the 1994 translation. The descriptive extended title of the 1781 edition translates as: *Memoirs on the Late War in North America between France and England. Followed by observations of which several are pertinent to the current theater of the war, and fresh details on the customs and habits of the Indians, together with topographical maps.*

2. Captain Pierre Pouchot to Marquis de Paulmy, November 3, 1757, in E. B. O'Callaghan, ed., *Documents Relative to the Colonial History of the State of New York,* 15 vols. (Albany, NY, 1849–1851), 10:668 (cited hereafter as *DRCHSNY*).

3. Pouchot, *Memoirs,* 73.

4. Examination of Michel La Chauvignerie *fils,* October 26, 1757, in Sylvester K. Stevens and Donald H. Kent, eds., *Wilderness Chronicles of Northwestern Pennsylvania* (Harrisburg, PA, 1941), 117.

5. Belle-Isle to Cadillac, March 18, 1758, quoted in Lee Kennett, *The French Armies in the Seven Years' War: A Study in Military Organization and Administration* (Durham, NC, 1967), 59.

6. Montcalm to Argenson, April 24, 1757, *DRCHSNY,* 10:548; Testimonial of Vaudreuil, May 6, 1761, in Pouchot, *Memoirs,* 51.

7. Pouchot, *Memoirs,* 126.

8. Montcalm to Belle-Isle, October 27, 1758, *DRCHSNY,* 10:860.

9. Pouchot, *Memoirs,* 49.

10. Ibid.

Suggested Readings

The most concentrated body of information about the life and military career of Pierre Pouchot is his own *Mémoires.* The original edition of 1781 was published under the title *Mémoires sur la dernière guerre de l'Amérique septentrionale entre la France et l'Angleterre. Suivis d'Observations, dont plusieurs sont relatives au théâtre actuel de la guerre, & de noveaux détails sur les moeurs & les usages des Sauvages, avec des cartes topographiques,* 3 vols. (Yverdon, Switzerland, 1781). This edition has been translated by Michael Cardy and edited and extensively annotated by Brian Leigh Dunnigan as *Memoirs on the Late War in North America between France and England* (Youngstown, NY, 1994). The 1994 translation includes an extensive bibliography of many of the most important sources for the study of the French and Indian War, particularly those that touch on Pouchot's service and campaigns. A brief analysis of the form and purpose of his writing may be found in Michael

Cardy, "The Memoirs of Pierre Pouchot: A Soldier's View of a Doomed Campaign," *War, Literature and the Arts* 4 (Spring 1992): 1–23.

For an understanding of the workings of the French army and officer corps of the era of Louis XV, consult Lee Kennett, *The French Armies in the Seven Years' War: A Study in Military Organization and Administration* (Durham, NC, 1967). The functioning of the military administration of New France is discussed in René Chartrand, *Canadian Military Heritage*, vol. 1, *1000–1754* (Montreal, 1993), and in the opening chapter of *Canadian Military Heritage*, vol. 2, *1755–1871* (Montreal, 1995). The same author's *The French Soldier in Colonial America* (Ottawa, 1984) offers an overview of the history of French colonial military practices.

Pouchot's construction and defense of Fort Niagara is presented in Brian Leigh Dunnigan, *Siege, 1759: The Campaign against Niagara*, rev. ed. (Youngstown, NY, 1996). For a general work on France's American colonial experience, see W. J. Eccles, *France in America* (Toronto, 1972). Surveys of the French and Indian War, as the North American manifestation of the Seven Years' War is commonly known in the United States, are numerous. Among them is Guy Frégault, *Canada: The War of the Conquest*, trans. Margaret M. Cameron (Toronto, 1969); George F. G. Stanley, *New France: The Last Phase, 1744–1760* (Toronto, 1968); and vols. 4 through 7 of Lawrence Henry Gipson's monumental *The British Empire before the American Revolution*, 15 vols. (Caldwell, ID, and New York, 1936–1970).

12

George Whitefield
Transatlantic Revivalist

Nancy L. Rhoden

George Whitefield (1714–1770) was an innkeeper's son who became the leading religious figure of the British Atlantic world and an indefatigable touring celebrity. He denounced the theater that he so enjoyed but employed theatrical techniques for what he saw as a higher purpose. How do Whitefield's evident ambitions in life compare with those of our other guests? He used newspapers to advertise his gatherings and sold his sermons and journals to prolong his influence on those who were moved by his impressive sermons. This stirring speaker seemed able to draw together denominations, races, classes, and regions of a disparate empire, yet he split many parishes irreparably. Eventually, antiauthoritarian elements in his message would be adopted in Revolutionary American rhetoric. How would the itinerant Whitefield compare, as a religious leader, with Anne Hutchinson, John Cotton Jr., or Samson Occom? In the lives assembled here, it seems a telling coincidence that the only known personal contacts between guests were those of Whitefield with both Occom and Olaudah Equiano.

Nancy L. Rhoden's *Revolutionary Anglicanism* (1999), like her other publications, concentrates on early American religious history. She teaches early American and English history at the University of Southern Indiana, Evansville.

George Whitefield, the "Great Itinerant," was a masterful minister of revivalism and the most widely recognized personality in North America in 1740. An ordained minister of the Church of England, Whitefield preached an unorthodox, revivalist message in his travels throughout the British Empire, including several trips to the colonies in America, where he delivered sermons from Georgia to Maine. Whitefield and his followers exchanged detailed information about the spread of revivalism, and in so doing forged ties of cooperation and friendship within the empire. In bitter fights with antievangelicals, Whitefield and his contemporaries also debated the very meaning and character of religion. His life and work demonstrate the role of revivalism in both anglicizing and americanizing the mainland English colonies of America.

Born on December 16, 1714, George Whitefield (pronounced Whit-field) was the son of a successful innkeeper of Gloucester, England. His father died when George was two years old, but the family, consisting of the widow Elizabeth and her seven children, managed to remain one of the largest taxpayers of St. Mary de Crypt's Parish throughout Whitefield's childhood. In his autobiographical writings, however, Whitefield contributed to his own myth by portraying more humble beginnings. Whitefield spent much of his early life at the family inn, observing people of many different walks of life. He was educated at a local grammar school and later attended Pembroke College at Oxford University as a "servitor," one of a select number of non-elite students who had their lecture fees paid in exchange for services they provided to gentleman students and scholars. As Whitefield reflected in his autobiographical work, *A Short Account of God's Dealings with the Reverend Mr. George Whitefield* (1740), his mother had long supported his ambitions. "[Mother] has often told me how she endured fourteen weeks' sickness after she brought me into the world; but was used to say, even when I was an infant, that she expected more comfort from me than any other of her children."[1] Immodestly, Whitefield noted, too, that in his background he shared a certain affinity with Jesus Christ: both had been born at an inn.

At Oxford, Whitefield was not particularly taken with scholarly studies, but he enjoyed the theater, a passion that he would later denounce. Here he also met Charles and John Wesley, who had started an Oxford "Holy Club," a society that promoted spiritual improvement. Their rigorous and methodical practices, including fasting until they could hardly walk, caused scoffers to label them "Method-ists." Whitefield frequently neglected his studies in his search for piety, and it was under the Methodist influence that he had a personal conversion experience. Like the Wesleys, Whitefield did not aim to create a new denomination, Methodism. Rather, his goals more closely resembled seventeenth-century Puritan attempts to purify the Church of England from within. In the early eighteenth century, a number of Anglican officials had pointed to the need for spiritual reform, although Methodism was certainly not their preferred solution. Nor would most of Whitefield's innovative techniques meet with the approbation of the Church of England.

Whitefield's long career would be characterized by conflict and controversy, but this was barely evident when he was first ordained into the ministry in June 1736. In fact, young Whitefield had attracted the attention of some powerful Anglican figures who believed that he held great promise as an evangelist, even if they were less certain about Methodism. As his friend John Wesley remembered (or as Wesley paraphrased it from Whitefield's published account of the tale), at the age of twenty-one Whitefield feared that he was not worthy of Holy Orders, but the bishop of Gloucester told him, "Tho' I had purposed to ordain none under three and twenty, yet I will ordain *you* whenever you come."[2] Whitefield had also remembered and retold this story in an effort to demonstrate his precocious nature and his early favor among Anglican elites.

When Whitefield graduated from Oxford in 1736, the Wesleys' example and advice encouraged him to become a foreign missionary. This career decision began his lifelong itinerancy; unlike most ministers and missionaries who had a fixed parish granted them by church officials, Whitefield preferred a traveling ministry, which opponents charged was unethical competition. From 1738 until his death in 1770, George Whitefield made seven trips to America and fourteen to Scotland, in addition to his frequent travels in England and Wales. Before sailing to Georgia in February 1738, young Whitefield put his ministerial skills to the test in London. As a member of the Church of England, he preached while wearing the required surplice and holding the Book of Common Prayer, as he did throughout his career, but even from the beginning, his body did not remain fixed. Using dramatic gestures and an inclination to tears, he soon learned that he had a great capacity for inspiring his audience with sermons that spoke more to the passions than the intellect. Whitefield was a complete success, both in terms of the numbers who flocked to his services and in the unprecedented donations he received. By the age of twenty-five, he was well on his way to developing a unique professional style.

Georgia, the destination of his first overseas journey, was a remote and largely unsettled part of the English Atlantic in the late 1730s. It provided a challenge for the "boy preacher" who usually delivered his sermons in urban centers, such as London, but within a few months Whitefield managed to find his calling and a justification for his controversial itinerancy. Adopting Charles Wesley's idea, Whitefield founded in Savannah an orphanage, which he called Bethesda, and financed the expensive project through preaching and fund-raising. After returning to London in 1739 and being ordained a priest of the Church of England, Whitefield secured a post in Georgia that consisted of the orphanage and surrounding parish. With this official charge, he could then explain his itinerant preaching throughout the empire as an effort to raise money for the orphanage. If denied the pulpit, he could use the same reason, his legitimate charity, to preach outdoors.

After ordination, Whitefield remained for a time in England and experimented with open-air preaching and an extemporaneous style. The two techniques reinforced each other nicely, since he could move about freely without a pulpit or notes. Although both would become his personal trademarks, neither was completely new. Earlier, when he had forgotten his notes, John Wesley had accidentally discovered the power of extemporaneous prayers. Whitefield noticed that this seemingly spontaneous style could energize interested listeners, even when the message had been memorized, as an actor would a script. He borrowed the technique of outdoor preaching from a Welsh minister by the name of Howell Harris, who employed field preaching in his rural itinerancy. Whitefield adopted this style in the urban setting whenever crowds grew too large or wherever he was denied the pulpit. Both problems arose frequently. Many English ministers forbade Whitefield access to their pulpits because they disapproved both of his itinerancy and his criticism of nonevangelical ministers. Whitefield labeled such behavior "persecution," but ultimately the publicity attracted both the interested and the curious until congregations swelled beyond the capacity of most churches. From his first experiment in Kingswood, a coal-mining community close to Bristol, Whitefield argued that the size of the crowd justified his novel methods.

In the wake of such English success, Whitefield made his second journey to America from October 1739 to January 1741. In 1738 he had visited only Georgia; but his second trip was a triumphant tour that stretched from Pennsylvania, New Jersey, and New York, then back to the southern colonies for the winter, to the middle colonies again in the spring of 1740, back to Georgia, and finally to New England in the autumn of 1740. An indefatigable lecturer, Whitefield traveled constantly and often preached several times per day. While on tour, he probably spent forty to fifty hours per week delivering his message, either in a pulpit or out of doors. When he visited New England, beginning in September 1740, Whitefield traveled 800 miles and preached 130 sermons in just over 70 days. This daunting pace succeeded in transforming personal charisma into an international reputation.

Campaigning on behalf of the Bethesda orphanage in Georgia, Whitefield touched off a "great" or "general awakening," which has subsequently been termed the "First Great Awakening." This interdenominational religious revival drew upon American elements, in particular the experiences of a number of congregations that had already felt the effects of local revivalism. Jonathan Edwards, a Congregationalist minister in Northampton, Massachusetts, Theodorus Frelinghuysen, a Dutch Reformed minister in New

Jersey, and Gilbert Tennent, a Presbyterian minister also of the middle colonies, had all witnessed a revival in their own parishes in the 1720s and 1730s, and they welcomed Whitefield's efforts as a way of renewing that religious fervor. Whitefield came to personify the movement, and the spread of revivalism matched closely his own travels up and down the Atlantic seaboard. Sometimes his preaching built upon the work of others, on other occasions he began work for colleagues to finish, but in either event he considered his labor part of an international effort to encourage God's presence in specific communities.

In England, Scotland, and America, Whitefield popularized the message of revivalism. Through extensive letter-writing networks, he and his numerous correspondents traced the development of revivalism as well as its spread through America and Europe. By 1739, Whitefield had become convinced that God was beginning a great work, and that Providence had placed him in a special position to forge transatlantic ties that would produce a general revival throughout the British world. Such confidence won him not only supporters but also a growing number of critics, who claimed that he was an arrogant "spiritual pick-pocket" who invaded parishes and illegally competed for parishioners. His "enthusiasm" and theatrical style especially concerned Anglicans, who feared the social consequences of an aroused mob and disapproved of his theatrical impersonations of Christ and God. Depending on who was consulted, Whitefield's character might be described as saintly or satanic.

As colonial audiences soon learned, Whitefield possessed a powerful and compelling voice, which could both intrigue and frighten his listeners. He could incite both an ecstatic appreciation of Heaven and a tormented fear of damnation. Such a balance was important for Whitefield, and yet he frequently preferred to emphasize loving aspects of God's character. By using theatrical techniques, Whitefield also demonstrated the importance of passion, or an emotional approach, to religious expression. Skillfully he used dramatic pauses, subtle inflections, perfect enunciation, and a plain style. The oratorical skills of eighteenth-century evangelists were innovative, since in that era only well-educated elite men tended to be public speakers, and such gentlemen typically directed their message to the educated. Although an Oxford graduate and an ordained minister, Whitefield cultivated an image of himself as a man of humble origins. This image, he believed, would increase his appeal to American audiences as well as to the common man and woman in Britain. By avoiding most complicated theological issues, except when his audience was especially knowledgeable in such matters, Whitefield could transcend denominational differences and appeal to a wider spectrum of religious opinion. He knew how to address plain people in plain language; usually he appealed to their imaginations. Plain language, however, should not be confused with a matter-of-fact approach. Emotionalism could be both straight-forward and compelling. Reportedly, Whitefield was able to bring tears to the eyes of his listeners with his pronunciation of the word "Mesopotamia," and frequent passages in his journal describe his audience (and himself) in tears.

Benjamin Franklin, who attended an outdoor Whitefield sermon in Philadelphia, found the young minister a most compelling orator and "in all his Conduct, a perfectly *honest Man*." As Franklin wrote in his *Autobiography*,

> [Whitefield's] Eloquence had a wonderful Power over the Hearts and Purses of his Hearers, of which I myself was an Instance. I did not disapprove of the Design [the building of an orphanage], but as Georgia was then destitute of Materials & Workmen, and it was propos'd to send them from Philadelphia at a great Expense, I thought it would have been better to have built the House here & Brought the Children to it. This I advis'd, but he was resolute in his first Project, and rejected my Counsel, and I thereupon refus'd to contribute. I happened soon after to attend one of his Sermons, in the Course of which I perceived he intended to finish with a Collection, & I silently resolved he should get nothing from me. I had in my Pocket a Handful of Copper Money, three or four silver Dollars, and five Pistoles in Gold. As he proceeded I began to soften, and concluded to give the Coppers. Another Stroke of his Oratory made me asham'd of that, and determin'd me to give the Silver; & he finish'd so admirably, that I empty'd my Pocket wholly into the Collector's Dish, Gold and all.[3]

Given his initial reluctance and his international reputation as a man of science and Enlightenment rationalism, Franklin's change of heart suggests that Whitefield's performance must have been truly amazing. Although elite men (and even deists such as Franklin) could be seen in the crowd, Whitefield found great popularity among the common people and especially among women. Indeed, his critics scoffed that his followers consisted of large numbers of women who came either because of his emotional (and therefore irrational) style or because they were attracted to him. After hearing a Whitefield sermon, a German woman from the middle colonies proclaimed to her minister that she had never been so powerfully affected by a sermon, even though she could not understand a word of English.

Nathan Cole, a Connecticut farmer and carpenter, had been working in the fields when a messenger alerted him that Whitefield was to preach at neighboring Middletown that morning. Cole recorded in his spiritual narrative that he dropped his tools, ran for his wife and his horse, and raced to the old meetinghouse, following a cloud of dust made by "a steady Stream of horses and their riders, scarcely a horse more than his length behind another." There he found three or four thousand people and noted that "the land and banks over the river looked black with people and horses all along the 12 miles I saw no man at work in his field, but all seemed to be gone." Cole also described the authority with which Whitefield spoke: "When I saw Mr Whitefield come upon the Scaffold he Lookt almost angelical; a young, Slim, slender, youth before some thousands of people with a bold undaunted Countenance, and hearing how God was with him every where as he came along it Solemnized my mind; and put me into a trembling fear before he began to preach; for he looked as if he was Cloathed with authority from the Great God. . . . And my hearing him preach, gave me a heart wound; By Gods blessing: my old Foundation was broken up, and I saw that my righteousness would not save me."[4]

At first glance, American, English, or Scottish audiences must have wondered if someone who appeared so young could be worthy of their attention. Not only was Whitefield a mere twenty-five years old when he began his 1739 tour, but his fair complexion and boyish looks emphasized his youth. At least the first several rows in the crowd would also have noticed his crossed eyes, a feature quite visible in most of his portraits. The intensity of his stare added to the mesmerizing quality of his sermons.

Nathan Cole's account also suggests how Whitefield's other listeners might have interpreted his message. Despite innovative evangelical techniques, his theology was fundamentally traditional. Above all else, Whitefield insisted on the importance of the New Birth, or a "born again" conversion experience, which was thought to be a sign of assurance from God that one was among the saved and so would go to Heaven. A committed Calvinist, Whitefield accepted the doctrine of predestination and argued that personal salvation was less a human accomplishment than a result of God's saving grace. Later, his relationship with the Wesleys became strained because of their increasing emphasis on human free will and the performance of good deeds. Whitefield's preaching attempted to reverse this "Arminianism" within the Church of England in the eighteenth century, but his traditional Calvinist opinions also had meaning and relevance to New England dissenters who had long lamented the waning religious values in their communities. Whitefield's solution was to return to those central ideas of the Puritan founding fathers. As Cole noted, he, too, had been influenced by freewill arguments, but in the course of Whitefield's sermon, Cole became convinced that his good deeds would not save him; instead he accepted the doctrine of election, that God "had decreed from Eternity who should be saved and who not."5 Looking back on that day in 1740, Cole remarked that his "old Foundation was broken up" by the Whitefield message, although it would still be some months before Cole felt any assurance. Whitefield believed that the conversion experience need not take months of preparation, but rather could be compressed by the techniques of revivalism into a single meeting, much as his own conversion had occurred in one night. That was the fundamental power of revivalism: to compress a lifelong search for assurance of salvation into a single moment.

Favorable reports of Whitefield's second journey to America, including those recorded by Benjamin Franklin and Nathan Cole, also estimated the success of his preaching by the crowds he drew. Cole found a few thousand along the river bank, but urban figures were more impressive. Franklin paced off the distance from Whitefield to the edge of his audience and estimated that thirty thousand people could have heard him. Although Whitefield's own figures, recorded in his journal, may well have inflated some estimates, his critics as well as his friends noted impressive crowds that regularly numbered several thousand or more. Even though a single American meeting could not surpass the record throng of eighty thousand people who listened to his Hyde Park sermon in London, American audiences sometimes exceeded the population of the town in which he preached. Boston's population of seventeen thousand produced crowds that rivaled many of his regular London audiences. At Old South Church on the second Sabbath in October, so many people attended that Whitefield had to climb in through one of the windows. His farewell sermon at Boston drew an estimated twenty to thirty thousand listeners. The crowd consisted of rich and poor, friend and foe; it included magistrates, Harvard students, residents of an almshouse, and slaves. It was such an important public event that everyone wanted to attend. Most ministers could harness the emotional power of a farewell sermon only a few times in their career, but Whitefield's constant itinerancy allowed him to use the technique regularly and to great effect. Newspaper accounts of farewell sermons frequently noted that Whitefield's imminent departure not only drew a great crowd but also left his distraught audience in tears.

On another occasion in Boston, at Mr. Checkley's meetinghouse, the audience had filled the building beyond capacity before Whitefield's arrival. A noise in the gallery started the rumor that it was collapsing due to the excessive weight. A panic ensued. Some worshipers jumped from the gallery into the pews or out the windows, while the crowd below pressed toward the door. When it was all over, five persons had died and others were injured. Despite the tragedy, or perhaps because of it, Whitefield did not cancel the sermon. Instead, the group reassembled outside where he preached in a driving rainstorm. Wet and no doubt frightened, his audience stayed for the lesson. As Whitefield put it, "God was pleased to give me presence of mind; so that I gave notice I would immediately preach upon the common. . . . I endeavoured, as God enabled me, to improve what had befallen us."[6] Such a tragedy demonstrated the unexpected nature of death and, consequently, the necessity for immediate spiritual improvement.

Not only was Whitefield met by great crowds in America, but also during the 1739–1741 tour the dissenting ministers of Boston and the leaders of Harvard and Yale warmly welcomed this Anglican minister with the unorthodox message. Many acknowledged the massive number of worshipers to be a sign that God approved of Whitefield's ministry and methods, but colonial clergymen of the Church of England often considered such crowds as evidence of a spreading general delusion. The opposition of those whom Whitefield labeled "Arminian" helped to fuel popular interest. In particular, Whitefield emphasized that ministers who had not personally experienced "New Birth" were unfit for duty. Consequently, he attacked not only current Anglican priests and some ministers of other denominations but also Anglican ecclesiastical icons such as the very respected John Tillotson, a seventeenth-century archbishop of Canterbury. Whitefield claimed that since Tillotson had not been born again, he knew no more of God's saving grace than "Mohamet." Similarly, Whitefield denounced the widely distributed Anglican educational tract, *The Whole Duty of Man*, which he believed had consigned thousands of readers to Hell. A most public conflict involved Alexander Garden, Anglican commissary, or bishop's representative abroad, for the Carolinas and Bahamas, whom Whitefield characterized as "an unconverted man, [and] an enemy to God."[7] Garden summoned Whitefield to an ecclesiastical court to answer charges of preaching without using the Book of Common Prayer, but it was unclear whether he had any such authority over Whitefield. Garden appealed to London but failed to obtain a decision. For dissenting friends of Whitefield, Garden's actions only confirmed their long-standing beliefs about the oppressive nature of the Anglican hierarchy. American dissenters found in Whitefield a refreshing inside critic of the Church of England; most Anglicans found a turncoat priest.

His attraction for many different classes, races, and religious communities owed a great deal to an early ecumenical approach and an ability to adapt his teachings to particular regions. Whitefield's message transcended particular denominations and so could be termed ecumenical. Nonetheless, opposition within Anglicanism proves that his ecumenical worldview had its limits; it was decidedly Calvinist and so could not include any Arminian opinion. But within Calvinism, Whitefield seemed as comfortable with Presbyterians, Baptists, Congregationalists, or awakened Anglicans.

He also considered his messages valuable to Native Americans and to African-American slaves. Evangelical ministers of this era encouraged the rebirth of interest in Indian missions. From his first visit to Georgia, Whitefield had accepted and endorsed slavery, unlike the Wesleys whose earlier denunciation of the institution had given Methodism a bad name throughout the southern colonies. Whitefield had early recognized that planters would be uninterested in his message if he did not accept their social values, including slavery. In fact, he himself was a slave owner, since his orphanage depended upon slave labor, but he did firmly believe that planters had an obligation to teach the Gospel to their slaves. In Philadelphia, perhaps a thousand slaves heard Whitefield during his first tour; in the middle colonies as well as New England, debates ensued concerning the souls of black folk.

To appeal successfully to different regions, classes, races, and denominations, Whitefield appropriated techniques from the developing commercial world of the eighteenth century. A growing imperial consumer society offered a litany of mass-marketing techniques, which could be adapted to evangelism, and consequently newspapers and printing presses became allies of revivalism. Whitefield understood the power of self-promotion; instead of writing an introspective private diary, he composed and published several of his journals. Deliberately written for a mass audience, these journals created a public image of a tireless and heroic revivalist who witnessed the spreading of God's influence wherever he went. Newspaper accounts of Whitefield's sermons, often written by Whitefield himself or (early in his career) by his traveling companion and publicist, William Seward, promoted attendance and donations at the next town on the tour. Newspaper announcements of a Whitefield sermon were careful to include details about the spread of revivalism at his last stop and so heightened interest. Contemporaries noted with amazement how much money he was able to collect for his orphanage, as well as the spiritual effects of his preaching. By the time Whitefield arrived at Jonathan Edwards's congregation in Northampton, Massachusetts, local residents expected that a momentous revival would occur. Predictably, Whitefield did not disappoint them; he reported moving his audience, including the Reverend Mr. Edwards, to a flood of tears.

By learning the art of advertisement and self-promotion, Whitefield shaped his own popular image, and his preaching techniques further enhanced this public persona. His extemporaneous prayers and open-air preaching transformed the sermon into a popular event that assaulted traditional rules of assembly. Prayers that did not follow a set liturgy seemed to address the common man and woman and minimize the intellectual distance between clergy and people. As the crowd gathered around Whitefield, men and women, whites and blacks, rich and poor—all found themselves rubbing elbows. Contemporaries must have been struck by the egalitarian implications of such an assembly, especially since Anglican churches of this era had assigned seats that reflected the social rank of everyone in the community. Pews at the front of the church were reserved for and often commissioned by the parish's elite families, while poorer families sat farther back. Servants, slaves, and other members of the "lesser orders" typically stood at the back or might sit above in the gallery.

Whitefield left the colonies in January 1741 to return to Britain, where he continued to preach, ostensibly to raise money for his orphanage. His reception in England was not particularly warm, since his criticism of *The Whole Duty of Man* and of Archbishop Tillotson had not endeared him to his fellow Anglican priests. Although dissenters from the Church of England had welcomed Whitefield warmly in America, ministers of English dissenting churches did not officially cooperate with him. Since English dissenting ministers were licensed to particular churches, they lacked the freedom to preach in open fields, a tactic that probably would only have unleashed the ire of Anglican officials. In fact, some dissenters may have feared that their audience was being lured away by Methodism, or perhaps they were suspicious of Whitefield's enthusiasm. Furthermore, Whitefield appeared content to continue his affiliation with the Church of England. He could still draw large English crowds despite the reactions of the ministers, but throughout his career he made his greatest impression outside England in America, especially in New England and the middle colonies, and in Scotland.

During one visit to Wales, Whitefield met a widow, Elizabeth James, whom he married in November 1741. His journals and correspondence do not provide many clues about this relationship. After all, the journals were not intended as an introspective diary but rather as a forum to convey a certain public image; moreover, while on tour, Whitefield wrote to his wife infrequently. The courtship and proposal had been concluded within four days, and Whitefield seemed quite pleased that he had no intense, romantic feelings for Mrs. James. Romantic love may have been on the rise among courting couples in certain English families by the late eighteenth century, but Whitefield, in his time, denounced such notions. He reserved his passion for the ministry, and so married a woman whom he described as ten years his senior, not particularly attractive, but a good Methodist. He also knew that Mrs. James did not have deep feelings for him. She was in love with Whitefield's friend and fellow revivalist, Howell Harris, who had similar feelings for her but who sanctioned her union with Whitefield. Harris, too, must have agreed with Whitefield that romantic passion should be avoided in the interest of evangelism. Two years after their marriage, the couple had one child, John, who died at age four months. Elizabeth Whitefield also had four miscarriages, which left the couple childless. They were frequently separated while Whitefield toured; his wife remained in London from the mid-1740s until her death two decades later.

Whitefield's marriage had occurred between two important trips to Scotland, his visits of 1741 and 1742, during which he assisted in touching off another general awakening, known as the Cambuslang Revival, which began outside Glasgow and peaked in the summer of 1742. The Cambuslang Revival was less a spontaneous occurrence than a carefully planned and orchestrated event. The parish minister there, the Reverend William McCulloch, had been corresponding with Whitefield as well as with Jonathan Edwards until he saw the telltale signs of revival— "severe bodily agonies, outcryings and faintings" —which spread in less than two months to most parishes within twelve miles.[8] In fact, Scottish revivalists had been reading Edwards's publications as well as Whitefield's journals and sermons. They had followed news of Whitefield, much of it unfavorable, from the English newspapers, but there was also an admiring weekly Methodist journal started in England in the summer of 1740, then renamed *The Weekly History*, and sanctioned by Whitefield the following year. For some time, a transatlantic evangelical letter-writing network had operated with Whitefield at the center. Letters, newspapers, and magazines spread the news of approaching revivalism and generated considerable popular interest. Noting the revivals in England and America, Scottish evangelicals expected that Whitefield's visit there would similarly spread God's message. Again, he did not disappoint them. As in America, he utilized an interdenominational approach and resisted invitations, or demands, of both Presbyterians and Secessionists to join their churches. So anxious were these Scots to duplicate Whitefield's pattern of revivalism that they also invited revivalist preacher Gilbert Tennent of Pennsylvania to visit the same parishes, just as he had done in New England, but he declined. The Reverend Mr. McCulloch had studied Whitefield's methods and began to use them in his preaching, and many parishioners, especially those who had seen Whitefield in Glasgow, noted the improvement.

The revival then spread to western Scotland, and Whitefield, returning to the area, participated directly in the revival in Edinburgh and the western towns. In the middle of July, Cambuslang held a Communion service, at which twenty thousand attended and seventeen hundred received Communion. Although typically ministers celebrated the Eucharist only a few times per year, another Communion service was called for the next month. Whitefield himself was amazed at the gathering of thirty thousand people, three thousand of whom were communicants. Cambuslang proved that Whitefield's brand of revivalism was not only effective, but that it was also transferable. The sharing of his methods generated a community of evangelicals that included Americans, Englishmen, and Scots; opponents of revivalism also found transatlantic allies and so compared their particular criticisms and complaints. Opposition to Scottish revivals, however, was relatively mild. Unlike America, Scotland did not witness the rise of radical itinerant preachers whose actions encouraged condemnation from both opponents and supporters of revivalism. In addition, revivalists' efforts to work within the established Scottish Church, which favored Calvinism, minimized internal denominational differences.

Opposition to Methodists was turning violent in England. Mob violence had resulted in the death of Whitefield's advance man and traveling companion, William Seward, in 1740. For a time, Whitefield himself managed to avoid injury and luckily escaped unharmed from an attempted stabbing. While preaching in Plymouth, England, in June 1744, however, he admitted to his quarters a naval officer pretending to be an interested layperson, who beat Whitefield very badly with a cane. Whitefield's powerful screams prevented permanent injury, but he still needed some weeks to recover before he could sail to America for another tour.

When Whitefield returned to America in 1744, he found not only large crowds but also considerably more opposition. A few dissenting ministers in New England may have had reservations about his brand of "enthusiasm" when he visited in 1740, but, if so, they held their tongues. When Whitefield arrived at York, Maine, in October 1744, after an eleven-week journey, he must have noticed that times had changed and, with them, people's reactions to revivalism. By then the preaching of some of Whitefield's followers, especially Gilbert Tennent and James Davenport, had threatened to bring the whole notion of revivalism into disrepute. Their itinerant and emotional methods, adopted from but also exaggerating his example, affected the community's reaction to Whitefield. Davenport, most of all, had taken emotionalism to its extremes by preaching twenty-four hours straight, dancing in the candlelight, and wrestling the devil to the ground as well as by encouraging his followers to destroy their material possessions, including their clothes and nonevangelical books. Judged insane by civil authorities in Connecticut and Massachusetts, Davenport acknowledged his errors, publicly recanted, and published his *Confession and Retractions* in 1744. Antirevivalists wondered, however, if all revivalists were victims of delusion.

As a result of Whitefield's earlier tour and his imitative followers, itinerancy as a method drew intense criticism. Opponents denounced outdoor preaching in particular, warning that it unleashed the enthusiasm of the uneducated and impressionable crowd. To counter the presumption that such large groups were naturally riotous, evangelicals introduced evidence of their good behavior. John Wesley noted that Whitefield's hearers, though numbering in the thousands, were "as quiet as they could have been in a church."[9] Puritan New England, like the Church of England, did not have a permanent itinerant ministry; both organizations firmly believed in settled clergy, officially attached to a specific parish. In 1700 the Puritan minister, Increase Mather, had attacked the notion of an itinerant ministry by warning: "To say that a *Wandering Levite* who has no Flock is a Pastor, is as good sense as to say, that he that has no Children is a Father."[10] As many contemporaries reasoned, itinerancy invaded the rights of parish clergy, since itinerant ministers always competed with the assigned parish clergy not only for the parishioners' attention but also for their limited financial resources. Since Whitefield was particularly skilled at fund-raising, local charities must have been affected when generous parishioners gave freely to the Bethesda orphanage.

Fundamentally, Whitefield and his imitators posed a serious challenge to the established churches. While he was not directly hostile to authority, his condemnation of "unregenerate" ministers encouraged a certain strain of anticlericalism. He did not directly denounce hierarchy, but his public disputes with officials in his own church, including Alexander Garden and adherents of the legacy of Archbishop Tillotson, could easily be interpreted as attacks on a hierarchical system. Regardless of his intentions, Whitefield's followers understood a more radical social message from his actions. Although Whitefield urged his listeners to cooperate with their local churches, schisms developed instead. The speed of evangelical conversions and the indifference of revivalists to denominational boundaries inevitably caused disputes. Many ministers, noting how appealing revivalism seemed to be, opened their church doors and hoped that the techniques would improve the religious zeal of their flocks. In other situations, parishioners were divided among themselves about the merits of revivalism; sometimes the minister and parishioners held opposing opinions. Where the congregation favored an emphasis on New Birth and the minister opposed it, he could be accused of working against God's will. Ministers who had not personally experienced conversion were chastised as unregenerate. Divisions became bitter and new churches proliferated. Congregationalists divided into New Lights (prorevival) and Old Lights (antirevival), while Presbyterians split into New Sides and Old Sides.

In 1740, Whitefield had directly questioned the effectiveness of ministers who had not yet had their conversion experience, but in the next few years Davenport and Tennent made this issue even more controversial. Davenport (in an act reminiscent of Anne Hutchinson in the seventeenth century) claimed to know for a fact that many New England ministers were not among the saved. Reportedly, he told one audience that it might be better to consume rat poison than to listen to the sermon of an unconverted minister. Tennent's scathing publication, *The Danger of an Unconverted Ministry* (1740), fanned the flames by asking, "[Is] a Leper, or one that has Plague-sores upon him, fit to be a good Physician? Is an ignorant Rustick, that has never been at Sea in his Life, fit to be a Pilot, to keep Vessels from being dashed to Pieces upon Rocks and Sand-banks? *'Is'nt* [sic] *an unconverted Minister like a Man who would learn others to swim, before he has learn'd it himself, and so is drowned in the Act, and dies like a Fool?'* "[11] In the face of such criticism, New England ministers assumed a defensive posture. Previously, only Anglican ministers such as Timothy Cutler had warned against such enthusiasm. Now dissenting clergy, such as the Congregationalist Charles Chauncy of the First Church of Boston, picked up the gauntlet. In his *Seasonable Thoughts on the State of Religion* (1743), Chauncy blamed George Whitefield for instigating all the evils associated with itinerant preaching. In another publication, Chauncy accused Whitefield and his colleagues of "enthusiasm," by which he meant religious delusion, or "a bad temperament of the blood and spirits; 'tis properly a disease, a sort of madness" that disregarded reason. For Chauncy, real religion did not originate with the emotions, but rather it had to be grounded upon a solid, intellectual foundation. As he wrote, " 'Tis, in it's [sic] nature, a sober, calm, reasonable thing."[12] In such debates, contemporaries discussed the very nature of religious expression, whether religion was a matter of the head or of the heart.

Opposition to Whitefield's later tours had also resulted, more directly, from his own commentaries about his New England experiences, which had been published in his journal since his last visit. Although he wrote that New England could very well surpass other parts of the world in its level of religious interest, Whitefield criticized both its educators and its ministers, who apparently had treated him quite civilly. He complained that Harvard instructors assigned bad books, by which he meant Tillotson and other nonevangelical authors, and he warned that "Discipline is at a low ebb."[13] Consequently, Whitefield argued, New England colleges were no longer sources of light, but bastions of darkness. In a published account of a New England sermon, Whitefield brashly criticized the region's ministers: "The Lord enabled me to open my mouth boldly against unconverted ministers; for, I am persuaded, the generality of preachers talk of an unknown and unfelt Christ. The reason why congregations have been so dead is, because they have had dead men preaching to them."[14] When revivalists such as Whitefield claimed that religion was dead, decayed, or darkened, usually they meant that it was uninfluenced by the conversion experience. Opponents, however, believed that they were being accused of a harsher indictment: complete religious disinterest. After all, Whitefield charged that most New England ministers did "not experientially know Christ."[15]

Predictably, New England ministers and the professors at Harvard and Yale considered these characterizations to be personal attacks, and they responded in kind. The Harvard faculty's testimony of December 1744 condemned Whitefield's brand of itinerancy: "We look upon his going about in an itinerant way, especially as he hath so much of an enthusiastical turn of mind, [as] utterly inconsistent with the peace and order, if not the very being, of these churches of Christ." Furthermore, they characterized him as "an uncharitable, censorious and slanderous man."[16] In their minds, Whitefield had committed, among other sins, a crime of arrogance by criticizing Archbishop John Tillotson and Commissary Alexander Garden and by presuming to tell Harvard professors what books their students should and should not read.

Despite this strong opposition from a mobilizing contingent of antirevivalists, Whitefield's tour of 1744 and his later tours enjoyed some limited success. He never managed to surpass the dramatic awakening of 1740 and 1741, but attendance at his meetings was still excellent. Perhaps people came to such meetings out of nostalgia; more likely, he appealed to a new audience in search of the same spiritual assurance. To calm his opponents and answer some of their charges, Whitefield publicly condemned the excesses of revivalism, including separatism. But perhaps the event that helped most to restore his reputation in America was his participation in the successful New England military campaign against the French fortress of Louisbourg. This fort, the so-called Gibraltar of the New World, was located on Cape Breton Island, Nova Scotia, where it guarded the entrance to the St. Lawrence River. Whitefield would not serve as a military chaplain, but, instead, his enlistment sermon in 1745 helped to assemble a large and committed expeditionary force. When Louisbourg fell, praise came not only to William Pepperrell, the colonial commander, but also to George Whitefield, the colonial inspiration. Although his critics would continue to follow him closely in England, his controversial years in America had ended.

Whitefield's legacy to American history is a broad one. While he had introduced religious concepts that would grow into nineteenth-century evangelicalism and be further refined in the Second Great Awakening, contemporaries in America and throughout the empire observed that his efforts had caused an upsurge in religious expression. In America, membership increased in those churches that favored revivalism, but even nonevangelical groups, such as the Church of England, gained members by offering refuge to those grown weary of evangelical emotionalism. Whitefield's efforts also contributed to a shift of religious sensibilities, which had latent political consequences. Revivalists emphasized the experience of the individual and, above all, the need for a personal and recognizable conversion experience. Salvation became more of an individual journey than a community process. The empowerment of the individual American in the religious sphere might be a precursor of the subsequent development of popular sovereignty in the political arena.

Whitefield also contributed to both the anglicization of the American colonies and their americanization. While the First Great Awakening may be considered the first protonational "American" event because it linked together large sections of the continent, Whitefield's transatlantic journeys and evangelical techniques also tied together an empire of British revivalists. The colonies did not find in revivalism a quality that distinguished them from England, but rather a point of commonality. American Revolutionaries, however, later could draw upon the antihierarchical, antiauthoritarian language of revivalists as well as their deliberate appeal to a mass audience.

In 1770, after three decades of transatlantic evangelism and on his seventh trip to America, George Whitefield died in Newburyport, Massachusetts. He had managed thirteen successful crossings of the Atlantic. John Wesley's account of his last days is true to the image that Whitefield had long cultivated: that of the tireless preacher. Wesley claimed to be relying on a report from a Boston gentleman when he related that Whitefield's health had been failing for some time, and yet he had continued to preach regularly and relentlessly. When Whitefield rose on the morning of September 30, 1770, he "went into his closet; and his companion observed he was unusually long in private. He left his closet, returned to his companion, threw himself on the bed, and lay about ten minutes. Then he fell upon his knees, and prayed most fervently to God, 'That if it was consistent with his will, he might that day finish his Master's work.' He then desired his man to call Mr Parsons, the clergyman at whose house he was: But in a minute, before Mr Parsons could reach him, [he] died without a sigh or groan."[17]

Wesley delivered this account as part of his November 18 eulogy in England. American newspapers carried other accounts of Whitefield's final hours and the public services that followed in every colony. The seventeen-year-old Boston slave and poet, Phillis Wheatley, even wrote a poem in his memory. Predictably, a tremendous crowd attended his funeral at the Presbyterian meetinghouse in Newburyport. The procession, over a mile long, ended at the meetinghouse, where the crowd crammed through the door and thousands of others mourned outside. Whitefield's coffin was buried in a renovated tomb under the pulpit.

Long after his death, Whitefield continued to have an impact on the American colonists as they prepared for revolution. Before a military expedition against Canada in 1775, a group of colonial officers and soldiers in Massachusetts dug up Whitefield's grave, pried open the coffin, and respectfully removed the clerical collar and wristbands from the skeleton. These patriot grave robbers hoped that Whitefield's relics would ensure them victory in their contest against Britain. Very likely they remembered his role in the successful Massachusetts campaign against Louisbourg three decades earlier. This particular military campaign did not succeed, but Whitefield's inclusion suggests that his public image had transcended the physical and the religious spheres. More than a former evangelist, he had become an American legend.

Notes

1. George Whitefield *A Short Account of God's Dealings with the Reverend Mr. George Whitefield, A.B. Late of Pembroke College, Oxford from His Infancy, to the Time of His Entering into Holy Orders* (1740), as reprinted in William Wale, ed., *Whitefield's Journals, to which is prefixed his "Short Account" and "Further Account"* (London, [1905]), 27.

2. John Wesley, *A Sermon on the Death of the Rev. Mr George Whitefield, Preached at the Chapel in Tottenham-Court-Road, And at the Tabernacle near Moorfields, on Sunday, November 18, 1770* (London, 1770), 6.

3. Benjamin Franklin, *Autobiography and Other Writings*, ed. Kenneth Silverman (New York, 1986), 116–21, esp. 118, 119.

4. Michael J. Crawford, ed., "The Spiritual Travels of Nathan Cole," *William and Mary Quarterly*, 3d ser., 33 (1976): 93.

5. Ibid., 94.

6. George Whitefield, [Seventh Journal], *A Continuation of the Reverend Mr. Whitefield's Journal from a few Days after his Return to*

Georgia to his Arrival at Falmouth, on the 11th of March 1741, as reprinted in Wale, ed., *Whitefield's Journals*, 462.

7. As quoted in Joseph Tracy, *The Great Awakening: A History of the Revival of Religion in the Time of Edwards and Whitefield* (Boston, 1842), 81.

8. Ibid., 268.

9. Wesley, *Sermon on the Death of the Rev. Mr George Whitefield*, 10.

10. Increase Mather, *The Order of the Gospel* (Boston, 1700), as quoted in C. C. Goen, *Revivalism and Separatism in New England, 1740–1800: Strict Congregationalists and Separate Baptists in the Great Awakening* (New Haven, CT, 1962), 9. Italics are Mather's.

11. Gilbert Tennent, "The Danger of an Unconverted Ministry" (Philadelphia, 1740), as excerpted in Richard L. Bushman, ed., *The Great Awakening: Documents on the Revival of Religion, 1740–1745* (Chapel Hill, NC, 1989), 91. Italics are Tennent's.

12. Charles Chauncy, *Enthusiasm Described and Caution'd Against* (Boston, 1742), as excerpted in Darrett B. Rutman, ed., *The Great Awakening: Event and Exegesis* (Huntington, NY, 1977), 55, 60.

13. Whitefield, [Seventh Journal], in Wale, ed., *Whitefield's Journals*, 463.

14. Ibid., 471.

15. Ibid., 485.

16. As quoted in Tracy, *Great Awakening*, 347–48.

17. Wesley, *Sermon on the Death of the Rev. Mr George Whitefield*, 14–15.

Suggested Readings

Two excellent studies of Whitefield are Frank Lambert, *"Pedlar in Divinity": George Whitefield and the Transatlantic Revivals* (Princeton, NJ, 1994); and Harry S. Stout, *The Divine Dramatist: George Whitefield and the Rise of Modern Evangelicalism* (Grand Rapids, MI, 1991). For related material on Whitefield and/or the First Great Awakening, see Patricia U. Bonomi, *Under the Cope of Heaven: Religion, Society, and Politics in Colonial America* (New York, 1986); Jon Butler, "Enthusiasm Described and Decried: The Great Awakening as Interpretative Fiction," *Journal of American History* 69 (1982): 305–25; Michael J. Crawford, *Seasons of Grace: Colonial New England's Revival Tradition in Its British Context* (New York, 1991); C. C. Goen, *Revivalism and Separatism in New England, 1740–1800: Strict Congregationalists and Separate Baptists in the Great Awakening* (New Haven, CT, 1962); William Howland Kenney, "George Whitefield, Dissenter Priest of the Great Awakening, 1739–1741," *William and Mary Quarterly*, 3d ser., 26 (1969): 75–93; Frank Lambert, "The Great Awakening as Artifact: George Whitefield and the Construction of Intercolonial Revival, 1739–1745," *Church History* 60 (1991): 223–46; Susan O'Brien, "A Transatlantic Community of Saints: The Great Awakening and the First Evangelical Network, 1735–1755," *American Historical Review* 91 (1986): 811–32; Harry S. Stout, "Religion, Communications, and the Ideological Origins of the American Revolution," *William and Mary Quarterly,* 3d ser., 34 (1977): 519–42; Timothy D. Hall, *Contested Boundaries: Itinerancy and the Reshaping of the Colonial American Religious World* (Durham, NC, 1994); and Joseph Tracy, *The Great Awakening: A History of the Revival of Religion in the Time of Edwards and Whitefield* (Boston, 1842).

The most useful documentary collections are Richard L. Bushman, ed., *The Great Awakening: Documents on the Revival of Religion, 1740–1745* (Chapel Hill, NC, 1989); Perry Miller and Alan Heimert, eds., *The Great Awakening: Documents Illustrating the Crisis and Its Consequences* (Indianapolis, 1967); and Darrett B. Rutman, ed., *The Great Awakening: Event and Exegesis* (Huntington, NY, 1977). For two contemporary accounts that mention Whitefield, see Michael J. Crawford, ed., "The Spiritual Travels of Nathan Cole," *William and Mary Quarterly,* 3d ser., 33 (1976): 89–126; and Benjamin Franklin, *Autobiography and Other Writings,* ed. Kenneth Silverman (New York, 1986), 116–21. The most important primary source collection of Whitefield's writings is John Gillies, ed., *The Works of the Reverend George Whitefield,* 6 vols. (London, 1771–72), but William Wale, ed., *Whitefield's Journals, to which is prefixed his "Short Account" and "Further Account"* (London, [1905]) is also useful.

13

Samson Occom
Mohegan Leader and Cultural Broker

Margaret Connell Szasz

Samson Occom (1723–1792), like Pocahontas more than a century earlier, was a well-born Algonquian convert to Christianity, an intermediary between Native Americans and Europeans, and a visitor celebrated in England. Occom's language facility must have been remarkable. Despite growing up Mohegan, far from the English settlements, he learned enough of that language to be converted by an itinerant minister before his formal education prepared him to become a famous preacher. He readily grasped the Latin, Greek, and Hebrew needed for the Puritan ministry. He acquired enough Mohawk and Oneida to recruit students for the Reverend Eleazar Wheelock and to preach in those languages as well. What other aspects of his life indicate an openness to other cultures and a capacity to use what he learned to protect his own people? Occom can profitably be compared with Squanto and Montour as a cultural broker.

Samson Occom knew our previous guest, George Whitefield, a famous fellow evangelical Calvinist minister; both were successful in crossing the Atlantic and preaching to raise funds for charitable institutions. In order for Christian missions to succeed in Native American communities, or to become more universal, it was necessary to separate Christianity from European culture. What does Occom's career, and Wheelock's refusal to regard him as an equal, tell us about that process? Would such a change be more difficult for Puritans, who required literacy for laypersons' practice of their religion, compared to work at Gabriel Sagard's mission? Occom could believe that he had contributed to such a transformation of Christianity when preaching in England or in New England to the Montauk and Mohegan or when establishing the multitribal and multilingual Christian settlement at Brothertown in Oneida territory.

Margaret Connell Szasz is the author of *Indian Education in the American Colonies, 1607–1783* (1988) and the editor of *Between Indian and White Worlds: The Cultural Broker* (1994). She teaches U.S., American Indian, and frontier history at the University of New Mexico.

> Since there is great miss
> Representation by Some concerning my Life
> and Education, I take this opportuniaty to
> give the World in few Words, the true account
> of my Education—I was Born a Heathen . . .[1]

In this fashion, Samson Occom introduced himself to the eighteenth-century New England worlds. Mohegan by birth and upbringing, missionary and schoolmaster by profession, Occom walked the cross-cultural borderline through most of his life. More than two centuries after his death, we can still reflect on his role, despite the vast temporal distance that separates his world from ours.

Although Occom's story remains distinctive, his experiences were not unique to eighteenth-century America. Throughout the nation's past, whenever cultures have grated against each other, intermediaries or cultural brokers have emerged. Although Occom's life was molded by cultural and historical circumstances, his role as cultural broker followed a pattern similar to that of the many intermediaries who have influenced America's past.

Like other brokers, Occom reached across the cultural divide through a singular path of understanding. Some cultural brokers communicated through interpreting, others through art or music, and still others through teaching. In Occom's case, he followed the path of Reformed Protestantism—namely, Congregationalism and Presbyterianism. During his initial encounters with the leaders of these denominations, he accepted the idea that their faith transcended the cultural barriers separating Natives and outsiders. Further encounters taught him that the universality promised in Christianity remained bounded by the cultures of those who heeded its message. It, too, was culturally specific. This painful lesson led Occom to alter the balance of his own brokerage. Although he continued along the path open to the spiritual intermediary, he directed his primary attention to the spiritual sustenance of his own people.

Unlike most eighteenth-century Natives, Occom left a written legacy. Because pre-contact indigenous people of North America relied on oral memory for recording their past, few Natives in colonial America became literate in English, and still fewer learned to write in this foreign tongue. By contrast, Occom mastered both skills; he kept a personal journal, carried on considerable correspondence, and published some of his works as well. As a literate Native, whose language repertoire also included Latin, Greek, and some Hebrew, Occom had access to several cultures beyond those of the Native peoples, including English, Dutch, and Scots.

Through his written legacy, he has provided us with an entrée into the multiple worlds of New England, New Jersey, Pennsylvania, and New York as well as England and Scotland.

The land that Occom cherished lay along the southern edge of the coastal Northeast woodlands. The Natives of this region had known the land to be their lifeblood for many generations before Samuel de Champlain, the French explorer, caught his first glimpse of its heavily populated shoreline, or Captain John Smith, once of Virginia, dubbed it "New England." Over time, Native communities had made this land their own.

Less harsh than the northern reaches of the region—Maine and the Maritimes—Occom's homeland, while sufficiently rigorous to deter anyone from south of the Potomac River, nonetheless proffered a relatively benign growing season. It yielded ample harvests of corn, beans, squash, sunflowers, and tobacco, plentiful fish and shellfish, and an abundance of game, birds, and waterfowl along with nuts, berries, and edible roots. By regulating the environment through controlled burning and other practices, the Native groups had generally found the land to be responsive to their needs.

Occom's neighbors, who lived along the river valleys and coast, spoke a form of Algonquian, a major language of indigenous North America. Whether they identified themselves as Mohegan or Pequot, Montauk or Shinnecock, Niantic or Narragansett, Tunxis or Nipmuck, these groups were both linguistically and culturally related. Following a seasonal cycle of planting, gathering, fishing, harvesting, and hunting, they moved in semisedentary small bands. They selected their own leaders, followed their spiritual customs, and taught their children to become knowledgeable and responsible community members.

Northwest of these Algonquians lay the villages of Iroquoian speakers. Located up the Susquehanna River and lying between the Great Lakes and the Hudson River, these villagers called themselves, collectively, the *Hodenosaunee* or People of the Longhouse. By the time of Occom's birth, the League of the Iroquois included the Cayuga, Seneca, Onondaga, Tuscarora, Oneida, and Mohawk. Sometime in the late fifteenth or early sixteenth century, these villagers had crafted an internal alliance to bring an end to the internecine warfare within Iroquoia. Consequently, the league had a decided advantage over their Algonquian- and Iroquoian-speaking neighbors, such as the Huron. Their aggregate numbers and their appetite for expansion led them to emerge as major players in the international colonial rivalry for control of the Great Lakes and St. Lawrence River region.

As a spiritual broker, Samson Occom negotiated with many of

these bands and tribes, both Algonquian and Iroquois. In his relations with Natives, especially of southern New England, he maintained a depth of understanding never duplicated in his contacts with the English and Dutch. Despite the Protestant connection that enabled him to move among these Natives and outsiders, he was invariably more at ease among his own people.

Occom's early years molded his perceptions of the world. Born along the Mohegan (Thames) River in Connecticut in 1723, he grew up in a well-respected Mohegan family. On his father's side, he traced his ancestry to Tomockham, a supporter of Uncas, the well-known seventeenth-century Mohegan sachem. On his mother's side, he was said to be descended from Uncas himself. As a youth, Occom absorbed the ancient survival patterns that had persisted into the early eighteenth century. His family "Chiefly Depended upon Hunting, Fishing & Fowling for their Living." "My parents," he recalled later, "lived a wandering life, as did all the Indians at Mohegan."[2] When Occom wrote this account for an English audience, he stressed "wandering" with the implication that their lives had no structure. Ethnographically, however, this word meant that they followed the semisedentary life characteristic of the subsistence pattern of the region.

During his childhood, Occom, like his friends, lived in a wigwam, a dwelling long familiar to northeastern Algonquians. Changes, however, had already differentiated his world from that of his parents and grandparents. By the early eighteenth century, the Algonquian communities in Connecticut and Rhode Island had become islands surrounded by English settlers. When Occom was still a child, the English were pressuring the Mohegans to relinquish the remaining remnants of their lands.

Pressures came in other areas as well. Occom's youth coincided with the Great Awakening, the widespread religious revival that swept across colonial America in the 1740s, touching both Native and African communities in its wake. New England ministers immersed in the enthusiasm of the revival often linked the goal of Native literacy with that of Native conversion. Like their well-known predecessor, John Eliot, the Congregational minister who engineered the "Praying Towns" of the mid-seventeenth century and helped to publish the first bilingual Bible in Massachusetts and English, these eighteenth-century Protestant clergymen saw schooling as a powerful tool for change among neighboring Indians.

Among the Natives of southern New England, however, the twin thrusts of Protestantism and literacy failed to achieve any momentum until the mid-eighteenth century, when Occom was already an adult. Occom maintained, therefore, that in the 1720s and 1730s the

Mohegans "had no Connection with the English, excepting to Trifle [trade] with them in their small Trifles." Although Mohegan families sometimes attended English preaching, their incentive was economic rather than spiritual: "They had Blankets given to them . . . and for these things they would attend."[3] Mohegan families responded with similar disinterest to schooling. An Englishman would go "about among the Indian wigwams, and whenever he would find the Indian Children, would make them read, but the Children used to take care to keep out of his way; and I believe he used to Catch me Some times and make me Say over my Letters, and I believe I Learnt Some of them. But this was Soon over too."[4]

In 1739–40 the reluctance of Mohegan families to connect with the English began to crumble under the insistent appeal of the itinerant preachers of the Great Awakening. As Occom wrote, "We heard a Strange Rumor among the English that there were Extraordinary ministers Preaching from Place to Place. . . . When some Ministers began to visit us and Preach the Word of God. . . . I was one that was Imprest with the things we had heard."[5]

Occom's conversion would change the direction of his life and, by extension, would alter the lives of those Natives, English, and Dutch whom he would encounter in the future. At this auspicious crossroad, Occom and his mother, Sarah Ockham, reached an understanding that emerged from their common conversion as well as their unique relationship. Occom's family included at least four children, but only Occom and his two younger siblings, Jonathan and Lucy (Tantaquidgeon), shared the same parents, Sarah and Joshua Ockham. The eldest sibling, Joshua, probably had a different mother. Samson, therefore, was not only the eldest child of Sarah and Joshua but also had the strongest potential for leadership. In 1742, when the Mohegan sachem, Benjamin Uncas, chose twelve councillors for the tribe, his choices included Joshua Ockham, Samson's father, and the nineteen-year-old Samson. Within a year, Samson's father died, an event that probably tightened the relationship between Samson and his mother. As a widow, Sarah would become even more dependent on her eldest son.

During this tumultuous interlude in Occom's life, his conversion convinced him that he must prepare himself to teach Christianity to Mohegan families. He saw the key to this goal as literacy: "If I could once Learn to Read I would Instruct the poor Children in Reading."[6] Thereupon he applied himself to the task, struggling to make some headway in the New Testament. Soon he saw the need for a tutor, and here, Sarah came to his aid. Occom had heard stories about an English Congregational minister by the name of Eleazar Wheelock, who lived in Lebanon, a short distance to the north, where he was said to tutor English pupils. When he learned that his mother planned to travel to Lebanon, Occom asked her "to ask Mr. Wheelock whether he would take me a little while to Instruct me in Reading."[7] Sarah Ockham was persuasive. Moreover, she struck a responsive chord in Wheelock, who had himself been deeply committed to the revival. With his interest piqued in the conversion of Natives, Wheelock sent his acceptance in the care of Occom's mother, who carried it to the eager young convert.

In 1743, the year that he began his studies with Wheelock, Occom made the journey north, "thinking I should be back again in a few days."[8] In 1749, six years later, he had achieved his goal and was preparing to "Instruct the poor Children" in a Native community he might not have considered earlier. In the interim, Occom had studied with Wheelock for four years, mastering English, Latin and Greek, some Hebrew, and also some English music, before moving on to further tutoring with nearby ministers, who proposed that he enroll at Yale. Further pressure on his strained eyes precluded this possibility, however, and forced him to search for a post where he could teach Native pupils.

During his six years of study, Occom had not neglected his people. To have done so would have been as uncharacteristic for a responsible tribal member in the eighteenth century as it would be today. Occom followed the pattern of the itinerant ministers, preaching to Native communities in the region, which ranged from his own Mohegans to the Pequots of Groton and the Montauks at the eastern end of Long Island. He also continued to counsel the Mohegan, advising them on a variety of matters, such as their ownership of land that was claimed by Connecticut. Occom's growing knowledge of the colonial English world increased his stature and usefulness, but it also would become a bone of contention within the splintered loyalties of the Mohegan tribe.

In 1749 one of his journeys took him across Long Island Sound to Montauk, where he planned to go fishing with friends. As was his custom when he visited Native villages, he paused to preach to community members. In this instance, his attentions proved so successful that the Montauks engaged his services as schoolmaster for their children and as preacher for the entire community. At the age of twenty-six, Occom had obtained his first job.

Occom would look back on his years at Montauk with some bitterness, but he never directed his regrets toward the Montauks or the neighboring Shinnecocks, who often sent their children to him for instruction. The poverty of these people removed them from the contentious issue of his salary, the source of his grievance. Moreover, after two years, Occom cemented his ties with the community by marrying a Montauk woman, Mary Fowler, and beginning a large family.

After his marriage, Occom gained financial support from the Boston Board of Commissioners for the New England Company, an English-based missionary society, but the funds—£15 per annum—did not stretch far enough to meet the needs of his growing family. Even his belated ordination in 1759 as a Presbyterian minister failed to nudge the board's initial salary offer, which remained frozen for twelve years. By contrast, the board paid a missionary who was English, and a bachelor besides, the sum of £100 for one year and for the same assignment, provided an additional £50 per year for an interpreter, plus £30 for an "introducer." In this instance, the Boston board in a single year reimbursed three Englishmen with the same sum that they paid Occom, the Indian missionary, for twelve years. Yet Occom's uniqueness enabled him to combine all three positions in one person: "In my Service . . . I was my own Interpreter I was both Schoolmaster and Minister to the Indians, yea I was their Ear, Eye, & Hand, as well as Mouth."[9]

Occom's relationship with the Boston board served as the first of many reminders that most of the English ministers and their missionary societies saw him as a means to achieve their own ends, rather than as a fellow minister with equal stature. The board's double standard also forced him to scramble in order to support his wife and children. When he was not in the schoolroom or preaching, he was raising pigs, catching fish, hunting for game, or tending his garden, which he planted in corn, potatoes, and beans. He also trained himself as an artisan. He "Bound old Books for Easthampton people, made wooden Spoons and Ladles, Stocked Guns, & worked on Cedar to make Pails, Piggins, and Churns, &c." When he ran into debt, the board, on one occasion, grudgingly provided extra funds; on another, they refused, accusing him of being "Extravagent."[10]

Although Long Island Sound separated Occom from the Mohegan during his mission at Montauk, he still advised his own people and also corresponded with Wheelock (who persisted in addressing him as "Dear child") and other English ministers. In Occom's absence, Wheelock had been mulling over the accomplishment of his first Indian pupil. As Wheelock considered the implication of Occom's achievements, he resolved to introduce a charity boarding school that would educate both Indian and English youth.

Wheelock's resolve led to a labored educational undertaking that would consume his energies over the next twenty-five years. The boarding school that sprang from a mixture of Occom's successes and Wheelock's political fund-raising acumen was dubbed Moor's Indian Charity School, in honor of a neighbor who had donated the land. In 1754, when Wheelock enrolled the first Native students, two boys from a Christianized Delaware group in New Jersey, he foresaw a community of young male Algonquian scholars who, like Occom, would arrive from their villages as pupils and return to them as schoolmasters or missionaries. Native missionaries, Wheelock reasoned to potential donors to the school, would be less expensive to maintain than their English counterparts. Occom could already attest to that benefit.

After the school was well under way, Wheelock altered its mission and diversified its student body. Occom was directly involved in these changes. On Wheelock's request, in 1761, Occom and David Fowler, his brother-in-law, a twenty-one-year-old student at Moor's School, traveled to Iroquoia, where they garnered the school's first Iroquois pupils, one of whom was Thayendanegea (Joseph Brant), who would become the best-known Iroquois warrior and British ally during the Revolutionary War. Through his several trips to Iroquoia, Occom furthered Wheelock's goal of tribal diversification. Occom also had family ties with at least one of the sixteen Indian girls whom Wheelock enrolled—his sister-in-law, Hannah Garrett Fowler.

By serving as liaison between Wheelock and the Iroquois, Occom also became a catalyst for Wheelock's determination to move Moor's School from Connecticut to a location within the Iroquois League. Even though the move was stalled, then blocked, Occom maintained close contact with Moor's School students whom Wheelock sent as schoolmasters to the Iroquois children. Twenty-two students—Algonquian, Iroquois, and English—tested their skills as schoolmasters or missionaries within the Iroquois villages during the decade before the Revolution. Two of those who made the long trek from Connecticut to the vicinity of the Mohawk River were David and Hannah Fowler, Mary Occom's brother and his wife.

Throughout the 1750s and 1760s, therefore, Occom's fortunes continued to be closely entwined with those of his former tutor. The relationship would intensify in the mid-1760s, when Wheelock's dreams of expansion into Iroquoia coincided with Occom's move to Mohegan. In this decade, when Occom was entering his forties, he would undertake two of the major endeavors of his life: He would return his family to his home community, where he would build a large, two-story frame house; and he would sail to Britain, where he would raise funds for Wheelock's final educational venture: the founding of Dartmouth College in Hanover, New Hampshire.

The shift to the English-style house was symbolic. For colonists and Natives alike, it implied that Occom had left his wigwam origins and crossed over the cultural divide into the arms of English material culture. Whether that was entirely true is difficult to ascertain. Some characteristics of English culture did intrigue Occom. On his first trip to the Iroquois League, he affronted the Oneida by ordering them to grow their hair long "as the English do," and advising them not to "wear the Indian ornaments, as wampum and the like: but put them off and burn them in the fire."[11] Incidents such as this suggest that in these early missionary years Occom, like the English, inflated the importance of conformity. But the Oneida exchange occurred when Occom was still in his thirties. As he grew older and confronted further episodes of English antagonism, his admiration for these outsiders moderated while his appreciation for his own culture grew deeper.

A breakthrough in Occom's attitude toward the English came when he traveled to Britain. The impetus for the trip had lain with Wheelock. When his plans to shift Moor's School from Connecticut to a location within the Iroquois League met forceful opposition from two sources—Sir William Johnson, ally of the Mohawk, British superintendent of Indian affairs for the Northern District, and a strong Anglican, as well as from among the Iroquois themselves—Wheelock chose a pragamatic alternative: a location to the east of the league.

Financial support loomed as the chief impediment to this plan. Although Wheelock intended to move Moor's School, he also envisioned a college to educate colonial youth. But Wheelock was no fool. His wide experience in fund-raising had taught him a harsh lesson: any appeal for financial assistance depended upon the prominence of Indian students. When Wheelock highlighted the role of Indians in the promotion of an educational institution, as he had at Moor's School, he generally attracted generous donors. If he focused on the role of English youth, he found a less sympathetic response. This formula dictated a singular goal for Dartmouth College. Its primary target would be Native youth, which would guarantee a sympathetic ear in England and Scotland. Moreover, British sympathy should translate more rapidly into pounds sterling if colonial ministers made a personal appeal by traveling across the water to solicit funds directly.

In this context, Wheelock's thoughts turned to Occom. With his formidable political insight, he realized that no one would epitomize the educational needs of Native youth more than an Indian minister. Grasping this idea, Wheelock began to lay plans for what would prove to be his most brilliant success as a fund-raiser. But the undeniable accomplishments of the British tour would not be achieved without a price, to be paid by both Wheelock and Occom. Moreover, Wheelock could not accept exclusive plaudits for this scheme. He contributed only the comprehensive plan and arrangements. Occom and his singularly drab counterpart and fellow fund-raiser, Nathaniel Whitaker, the English minister of Norwich, Connecticut, bore the burden of success. Only their skill in attracting donations would confirm Wheelock's gamble.

The tour would bequeath Occom an ambivalent legacy. Above all, it forced him to undergo intensive physical and psychological strain. Sailing from Boston on December 23, 1765, on what would be a grueling voyage, he could not know that he would not see his family again for almost two and one-half years. When the vessel landed in England, he faced another ordeal: the mid-eighteenth-century smallpox vaccination. Occom, like Abigail Adams, described this experience as difficult. For another well-known minister of this era, Jonathan Edwards, it had proved fatal.

With that ordeal behind him, for two years Occom endured the privileges and frustrations of being a public figure. The British found Occom a unique attraction: he appeared as both symbol and reality. His appeal lay in the fact that he was the first Native American minister to visit Britain; simultaneously, he came on a mission. Curiosity drove enormous crowds to hear the "Indian minister." Observers did not depict Occom as a sophisticated theologian. He reached his audiences through an evangelical style, which may have been derived in part from his observation of George Whitefield, and also through his frequent use of illusion and allusion. Although he was more comfortable preaching in Mohegan, the conviction of his message touched his British listeners. Delivering sermon after sermon, Occom crossed much of England before heading north beyond the crumbling stones of Hadrian's Wall and into Scotland.

For the Scots, Occom held a special appeal. Scottish Presbyterians knew well the work of this Presbyterian Mohegan and his English mentor, because their missionary society, the Society in Scotland for the Propagation of Christian Knowledge (SSPCK), had funded Wheelock's ventures. Lowland Scottish Presbyterians used a common cultural lens through which to view the conversion and schooling of "Red Indians" as well as the conversion and schooling of Highlanders and Islanders. Schoolmasters approved by the SSPCK traveled into the rugged Highlands and Isles of Scotland expecting to turn illiterate, Gaelic-speaking Roman Catholics into Presbyterians. In the same fashion, SSPCK funds were intended to turn illiterate, Native-speaking Algonquians and Iroquois into Presbyterians. The Scots, therefore, saw Occom as living proof of their commitment to education and conversion. In response to his visit, they donated £2,529, an astonishing sum considering Scotland's level of poverty and the fact that the nation was still recovering from the effects of the 1745 Stuart uprising led by Bonnie Prince Charlie. For the Scots, this was an outpouring of faith and a testimony to Occom's stature.

The Boston Board of Commissioners for the New England Company had also supported Wheelock and Occom, but Wheelock's failure to solicit its advice in planning the tour had led the group to oppose the trip, a position that poisoned Occom's relations with company members in Britain. As a result, on their arrival, Occom and Whitaker found their crucial supporter to be George Whitefield, the renowned evangelist who had attracted vast audiences on his tours of the American colonies during the Great Awakening. The entrée among nobility and royalty that Whitefield graciously provided Occom and Whitaker, mixed with the magnetic attraction of Occom's preaching, led to an electrifying experience for the transplanted Mohegan. One English minister wrote to Wheelock: "As far as I hear he pleases in every Town & city—So much Simplicity appears in the man: So honest, guiles [guileless] a Temper, with Seriousness in his public Service."[12]

For more than two years, Occom met with adulation from those who came to hear him and with respect, indeed deference, from his fellow ministers in Britain. One of the few discordant voices to shatter this harmony came from Wheelock, who persisted in viewing Occom as a pupil, an inferior, and subject to stereotypical Indian weaknesses. Although Wheelock's chiding of Occom may have reflected his own insecurities at the time—the Native students whom he tutored at Moor's School were not living up to the expectations he held for them—it nonetheless contrasted harshly with the recognition that Occom was garnering from ministers in England. Although Wheelock had urged Occom to make the journey, Wheelock feared that once he had arrived in Britain, his popularity would inflate his ego. He wrote: "I hope God has made you more humble than you have commonly been."[13]

Given Wheelock's increasingly skeptical attitude toward his Indian pupils, perhaps the most revealing legacy of the British tour emerged in the division that it engendered between Occom and Wheelock. When Occom returned to America in the spring of 1768, Wheelock had changed little, still viewing his former pupil as he had before. Occom, however, had undergone a transformation, and therein lay the rub. Upon his arrival in Mohegan, Occom brought with him a sense of stature and self-worth—what Wheelock would have termed Indian "pride." The forthcoming division, however, moved beyond the issue of self-esteem. Although Occom felt personal satisfaction about the sum collected on the tour, which totaled £12,026, the fund-raising and all that it had entailed for him retained one overriding purpose: Occom had committed his energy because he believed in the cause of schooling for Natives. The £12,026 was a guarantee that Natives would be supported in their efforts to attend Wheelock's college.

Within two years after his return, Occom learned of Wheelock's duplicity. Dartmouth College, touted as a home for Indian youth, would be directed primarily toward serving English young men. As its carefully worded charter promised, the purpose of the college was "for the education and instruction of Youth of the Indian Tribes in this Land in reading, writing & all parts of Learning . . . and also of English youth and any others."[14] Although Indians might attend, Wheelock began to direct the primary funding toward "English youth." Believing his former mentor had deceived him, Occom was crushed. His efforts on the British tour had been for naught. When he shared his bitter reactions with others, one of the former English pupils from Moor's School wrote to Wheelock of Occom's dismay: "The Indian [school] was converted into an English School & . . . the English had crowded out the Indian youth."[15] So great was his disillusionment that Occom broke off relations with Wheelock and never visited Dartmouth College.

Occom was not mistaken in his assessment. Although Wheelock did transplant Moor's School to Hanover in 1769, it became a college preparatory school for English students, and few Indians attended. Moor's School closed in the mid-nineteenth century, but throughout that century, Dartmouth College maintained the facade of involvement with Native youth because of its "tetchy" relationship with the SSPCK. The archives of the Scottish Record Office in Edinburgh hold a bristling correspondence between the two entities, Dartmouth claiming selective interest in Natives and the SSPCK continually requesting proof. The SSPCK-Dartmouth correspondence, which continues into the early twentieth century, attests to this. The college did not begin a vigorous program to attract Native American students until 1969, when it established a goal of 3 percent Indian undergraduate enrollment, or 120 of 4,000 students. According to Jere Daniell of Dartmouth, even this number enrolled in a single academic year would have equaled the total number of Natives who attended the college between 1769 and 1969.

Occom, however, could not foresee the change of emphasis that lay so far in the future, and in the years following his return, his disillusionment persisted. Poverty also played a role in his depression. For two years after the British tour, he received no income from the Boston board due to a misunderstanding between Occom and Wheelock and the board. The Mohegan-Connecticut land dispute, a century-old disagreement that addressed Mohegan versus Connecticut ownership of a large tract, also disrupted his life. When the Mohegans splintered over this contentious issue, Occom sided with the losing faction, which had favored the Mohegan land claim.

Even though Occom continued to advise his people, he found his counseling interrupted by the ill health that both he and his wife Mary suffered during this time. This interval marked the low point in their lives.

In the early 1770s their hopes returned. One of the events that lifted Occom's spirits bore an uncanny resemblance to the movement that had initially catapulted him into the Protestant orbit more than three decades earlier. At the beginning of the decade, he led a local Native revival that spread through nearby Algonquian villages, including both the Mohegan community and that of the Tunxis, located in the vicinity of Farmington, just west of Hartford and the Connecticut River.

The energy that Occom brought to the revival reflected his renewed sense of self-worth, which emerged in part because of the publication of his own works. In 1772, when he preached a sermon preceding the execution of Moses Paul, a Mohegan who had committed a murder while drunk, a New Haven printer shrewdly gauged the potential popularity of the piece and published it. His gamble paid off. Because it was probably the first published sermon by a Native minister, it sold out quickly and was reprinted numerous times as a temperance tract. Occom's reputation was spreading. The second publication was a personal venture, which drew on his interest in music, especially hymns. His lengthy stay in Britain had coincided with a revitalization of hymn writing. As a result, he had returned with a large collection of hymnals and an increasing fascination with hymnody. Shortly thereafter, he published *A Choice Collection of Hymns and Spiritual Songs Intended for the Edification of Sincere Christians of All Denominations*, which included his favorite hymns, along with some that he had probably written himself. The *Choice Collection* was an important publication; it celebrated Occom's Christian faith along with his faith in himself as a Native minister who had led a remarkable tour on behalf of his people.

For the Christianized Algonquians of this region, music formed an integral part of their fellowship and worship. Consequently, they welcomed the hymnal. Among those who began to participate in these gatherings of fellowship and singing was a young Mohegan by the name of Joseph Johnson. In the early 1770s, like Occom, Johnson was recovering from a traumatic stage in his life.

When he was a mere lad of fifteen, Johnson had traveled north from Moor's School to the Iroquois villages. As a student at the school from the age of seven, Johnson was deemed sufficiently prepared to serve as an apprentice schoolmaster in the Oneida village of Kaunoaurohaure, where he was to assist David Fowler, who had moved to Oneida country with his wife Hannah. Soon the schoolmaster position fell into Johnson's lap when the Fowlers left after an acrimonious dispute with Samuel Kirkland, one of Wheelock's English students and a missionary to the Oneida. Although Johnson had followed David Fowler's example, holding evenings of music and singing with the pupils, he found the task overwhelming. After a trying season attempting to instruct young Iroquois, with the aid of another teenaged Algonquian from Moor's School, Johnson and the other youngster returned to Connecticut. The responsibility of teaching, combined with a meager diet due to widespread poverty among the Oneida and what appeared to these Algonquians as a completely foreign way of life, led the two young men to seek release through alcohol. Disgraced in the eyes of Wheelock, Johnson, again like Occom, found his self-esteem battered by the indefatigable director of Moor's School. Before he left Kaunoaurohaure, he wrote to Wheelock, concluding with these words: "So I remain your Ignorant Pupil & good for nothing Black Indian."[16]

Once he was back in Connecticut, Johnson's restlessness led him to embark on a lengthy sea voyage, which helped to restore his self-confidence. On his return to Mohegan, he moved into a comforting circle of relatives with whom he shared the revival experience led by Occom. Once more like Occom, who would become his spiritual mentor, Johnson was converted. Shortly thereafter, he received the approval of the Boston board to teach the Tunxis and other Algonquian youth near Farmington, and he was also licensed as a preacher of the Gospel to the Indians. In his second stint as schoolmaster, Johnson described himself: "I am, kind friend, an Indian of the Mohegan tribe. . . . I keep a School at Farmington amongst my Indian brethren. And it is to be hoped that I maintain a Good Character both among the English; and also among my brethren."[17]

Johnson's appearance on the scene at this time was no mere coincidence. His youthful energy and conviction would interact with Occom's stature and experience to create a volatile mixture. The two appeared almost to be alter egos. Their relationship was further strengthened by Johnson's marriage to Occom's daughter, Tabitha. Within a short time, Johnson would enliven an earlier proposal for Mohegans and adjacent Algonquian groups to move to lands among the Oneida. Occom had been weighing the merits of this move, initially suggested by Wheelock, for several years, but the disillusionment that plagued his spirit in the period immediately following his return from abroad had dampened any spark of interest. Moreover, since Wheelock's betrayal, he had become wary of any further proposals emanating from that source.

In the early 1770s, however, as his spirits quickened and he began to respond to the infectious enthusiasm of his son-in-law, Occom saw the proposed emigration in a new light. He had lived among the English since his childhood and, until recent years, had always managed to maintain a balanced relationship with them. The Mohegan-Connecticut land dispute and Dartmouth College's hypocrisy had tipped the balance. By the time of the Native revival, Occom's view of the English as arrogant, strong-willed, and covetous convinced him that he and his people must remove themselves as far as possible from these outsiders. The path opened to him through Reformed Protestantism, once seemingly available and cleared of obstacles, no longer beckoned to the other side. While Occom's faith in Protestant Christianity held strong, his faith in the English had severely diminished. Under these circumstances, he viewed Protestantism as a single dimension of English culture that he and his people would adopt for themselves while resisting other English ways that they found abhorrent. A move that would take them beyond the English presence in southern New England was clearly in order.

At Mohegan in the spring of 1773, Samson Occom, Joseph Johnson, and the Fowlers, along with other hopeful emigrants, held a long-anticipated meeting to make plans for the move. Representatives from several communities attended. Besides the leaders from Mohegan and the Tunxis at Farmington, the delegates traveled from the Narragansett community at Charlestown, Rhode Island, the Pequot at Stonington, the Pequot at Groton, and the Niantic, also of southern Connecticut. Between that spring and the fall of 1774, they negotiated with the Oneida and Sir William Johnson for a land base within Oneida country.

The Oneidas, though circumspect, were gracious. Addressed by the Algonquians as "elder Brothers," a traditional acknowledgement of Iroquois power and status, the Oneidas answered a speech delivered by Johnson during the January 1774 negotiations. "Brethren, since we have received you as Brothers, we shall not confine you or pen you up to Ten miles square. We have much Land at our disposal and you need not fear that you shall [not] have Land sufficient for you and your Children after you."[18]

In these final months before the Revolution, neither the Oneidas nor the Algonquians could anticipate further migrations that would affect them in the early nineteenth century. By the 1830s, most of the Oneida lands would be overrun by Americans, and many of the Oneidas and Algonquians would move to the vicinity of Green Bay and Lake Winnebago, Wisconsin, where their descendants live today. In 1774, however, both parties were hopeful, and their hopes appeared to have been borne out in March 1775 when the first group of Algonquian emigrants left their homelands, traveled north, and formed the new community among their "elder Brothers," the Oneida.

The spring of 1775, however, was an inauspicious time to begin an emigration, since the journey coincided with the encounters at Concord and Lexington, which ignited the spark for revolution. The War for Independence brought a lengthy hiatus in the establishment of the transplanted community. It also brought an end to Joseph Johnson's life. He died in 1776 in the service of General George Washington, who had asked the young Mohegan to carry a message from the Americans to the Six Nations, urging Iroquois neutrality. There are no details of how or where he died. Other Algonquians, along with Oneidas, would also lose their lives for the American cause, and the ancient League of the Iroquois would be torn asunder when individual Iroquois tribes split their loyalties between the British and the Americans.

Although the founders of the Algonquian community had been forced to delay their migration until the end of the war, in 1784, only one year after the Peace of Paris was signed, Occom and the Fowlers, along with other supporters, made the long-awaited trek to their northern lands. Throughout the journey they must have felt keenly the absence of Joseph Johnson. On November 7, 1785, they organized formally, naming their town Eeyamquiltoowsuconnuck, or Brothertown. Gradually, others joined them, but the exodus was not universal, and eventually some of those who had emigrated returned to their old homelands, thus splitting these tribes. Today, the descendants of those who returned live on ancestral sites, including the best known of the southern New England Algonquian, the Mashantucket Pequots.

For Samson and Mary Occom, the decision to move loomed as a wrenching choice. Occom had reached his early sixties; Mary was probably younger but must have been in her fifties. For Mary, who had left her Montauk home across Long Island Sound for Mohegan, moving meant a second major upheaval in her married life. The Brothertown migration also meant leaving the two-story house in which the family had lived for twenty-five years. Consequently, Mary Occom did not travel north with the first group. Although she had once been willing to transplant their children to Mohegan, in 1784 she was not ready to travel a greater distance.

For several years after he helped to form Brothertown, therefore, Occom found himself once again separated from his wife, who faced with him the experience of a "commuter marriage." Throughout his life, Occom had filled his journal entries with cryptic notes alluding to his various migratory locations and sleeping conditions. On one occasion, he noted, "I had but poor rest all Night, they [the Oneidas] have too many Vermin for me."[19] Often traveling as an itinerant preacher, whether during his student years, at Montauk, between Montauk and Mohegan, in Britain, or between Brothertown and Mohegan, he had spent much of his life away from home. On his travels he had preached to Algonquians and Iroquois, to the English and then Americans in southern New England, to Dutch families en route to Iroquoia, and before rapt audiences in England and Scotland. The relationship between Samson and Mary Occom, therefore, resembled that of their contemporaries, John and Abigail Adams, who were separated for over half of the first fourteen years of their marriage. Although the Adamses' position in American history is well established, the Occoms' position among northeastern Natives is less well known. Yet the Occoms' contribution to Native groups and to the network of English, Dutch, and American communities reached by Samson's spiritual brokerage should also be viewed as an integral part of America's past. They, too, speak for the eighteenth-century worlds of the colonies and the young Republic.

By 1789, Mary Occom had chosen to leave Mohegan and travel north to Brothertown. In that same year, the Brothertown Indians won an important victory in their ongoing land dispute with the Oneidas, who had questioned the Algonquians' right to the lands from the moment the migrants arrived. Largely due to Occom's perseverance and his careful recordkeeping, plus the persuasive powers of New York Governor George Clinton, the Brothertown Indians retained their lands, which comprised approximately 24,000 acres.

Occom's leadership and experience in land negotiations, along with his spiritual guidance, had made him an invaluable member of the newly established community. Upon his death in 1792, Samuel Kirkland, the missionary to the Oneida, wrote in his journal: "The Indians were so alarmed at the sudden death of Mr. Occom that they began to collect at Tuscarora from the various settlements very early in the morning. . . . We moved about a mile to a bower [arbor] near the center of the town . . . there being no house sufficiently large to contain one half of the Indians who were assembled on the occasion." Kirkland preached "from Math. 24.44 in both the Indian and the English languages: that all might understand me on that solemn occasion."[20]

Given the course of Occom's life as a cultural intermediary, the circumstances of his memorial service were fitting. Like the wide range of people who would mourn his passing, those who were drawn to the service were both Iroquois and Algonquian, but the man who spoke to them was an Englishman/American who, coincidentally, had also broken off his relationship with his mentor,

Eleazar Wheelock. The location of the service was also fitting, as it testified to Occom's withdrawal from outsiders and his return to his own people. Despite the earlier attraction of cultural brokerage through the path of the spiritual intermediary, Occom had reshaped Reform Protestantism for his brethren and brought that message to his own community in a Native environment. In the final years of his life, Samson Occom had come home.

Notes

1. File 765628.1, Dartmouth College Archives, Hanover, New Hampshire (hereafter cited as DCA).
2. September 17, 1768, Transcript of Samson Occom's Journal [Diary], 1:82, DCA.
3. Ibid., 82–83.
4. Ibid.
5. Ibid., 83.
6. Ibid., 84.
7. Ibid.
8. Ibid.
9. Ibid., 91
10. Ibid., 90–91.
11. Samuel Hopkins to Wheelock, September 30, 1761, file 761530, DCA.
12. Peter Jilliard to Wheelock, March 2, 1767, quoted in Leon Burr Richardson, *An Indian Preacher in England* (Hanover, NH, 1933), 227.
13. Wheelock to Occom, April 9, 1766, file 766259, DCA.
14. The Dartmouth College charter can be found in Jere R. Daniell II, "Eleazar Wheelock and the Dartmouth College Charter," *Historical New Hampshire* 24 (Winter 1969): 3–44.
15. David McClure to Wheelock, May 21, 1770, file 770321, DCA.
16. Joseph Johnson to Wheelock, April 20, 1768, file 768270, DCA.
17. Joseph Johnson to "All Enquiring Friends," ca. February 1772, file 772900.2, DCA.
18. "The [Oneidas'] Third Answer, given on Monday January 29th 1774 at Kaunoaurohaure," file 774122, DCA.
19. Occom's Journal, 2:242.
20. W. Pilkington, ed., *The Journals of Samuel Kirkland* (Clinton, NY, 1980), 223.

Suggested Readings

For further studies of Occom, see the works by his two biographers, W. DeLoss Love, *Samson Occom and the Christian Indians of New England* (Boston, 1899; reprint ed., Syracuse, NY, 1998); and Harold Blodgett, *Samson Occom* (Hanover, NH, 1935). Shorter accounts of Occom occur in Margaret Connell Szasz, *Indian Education in the American Colonies, 1607–1783* (Albuquerque, NM, 1988); idem, "Samson Occom: Mohegan as Spiritual Intermediary," in *Between Indian and White Worlds: The Cultural Broker*, ed.

Margaret Connell Szasz (Norman, OK, 1994), 61–78; and John A. Strong, "Samson Occom," in *Encyclopedia of North American Indians*, ed. Frederick E. Hoxie (Boston, 1996), 434–36. For the British tour, see Leon Burr Richardson, *An Indian Preacher in England* (Hanover, NH, 1933).

14

Susannah Johnson
Captive

Ian K. Steele

Susannah Johnson's narrative reveals much about her Abenaki and Canadian captors, and even more about herself. Susannah (1730–1810) reckoned her mother's life as successful because she had had twelve children, and she proudly counted the descendants of her own children. Although she never managed entirely to reassemble her family after their capture, Susannah recounts her extraordinary efforts to do so. In her later years, she was anxious to commemorate her adventures, note her personal faith and endurance, and see her account published and revised.

Captivity had radically changed life for Pocahontas and Equiano, seized in their youth "and never returned." How much did the age or gender of the Johnson family members when taken determine the impact of the experience? Susannah's adoption into an Abenaki family was common for young women and children captives of any race. Both adoption and ransom practices ameliorated Native American warfare, although British American colonists were invariably surprised by their treatment. The captivity of Susannah and her husband was unlike that of Pierre Pouchot; Indian, colonial, and imperial military conventions were mixed in the complex struggle called the French and Indian War.

Susannah seemed remarkably able to adjust to Abenaki and then to Canadian ways, and to attract and remember the kindness of others wherever she went. While war tore apart her life and her family, it also provided memorable high points. She empathized with people across cultural divides, and her account challenges preconceived notions about the Abenaki, Canadian, and English peoples, indicating that the capacity for kindness is not the monopoly of any culture. Does her story question our stereotype of a New England Puritan woman?

Ian K. Steele teaches British Atlantic and American colonial history at the University of Western Ontario, London. His books include *Betrayals: Fort William Henry and the "Massacre"* (1993) and *Warpaths: Invasions of North America* (1994).

257

Born in 1730 into the Massachusetts frontier family of Moses and Susannah (Hastings) Willard, Susannah proudly traced her father's family back to a Major Willard who was active in King Philip's War (1675–76). Her autobiographical *Narrative of the Captivity of Mrs. Johnson* includes a few approving mentions of her mother (1710–1797) as having a full and long life, with 12 children, 92 grandchildren, 123 great-grandchildren, and 4 great-great-grandchildren, still working on a quilt of her own design at her death at age eighty-eight. Susannah's father was from Lancaster, in Worcester County, Massachusetts, but migrated northwestward at least twice to develop a farm that could support his growing family. By 1742, Moses Willard and his family had followed relatives to the northern edge of European settlement along the Connecticut River, farming in what would become Charlestown, New Hampshire. Susannah did not accompany her parents; from age eight until her marriage, she served in the household of a Colonel White of Leominster, Massachusetts, whom she remembered with gratitude. Although she dictated rather than wrote what we know of her life, Susannah probably learned to read and write. She valued family very highly, naming her first daughter Susannah (as had at least four generations before her) and struggling to keep her brood together in the face of disruptive events.

Susannah's detailed recollection of a visit to her parents in 1744 reveals her strong preference for a cleared landscape settled with European farming families. Meeting only "a few solitary inhabitants, who appeared the representatives of wretchedness," she recalled traveling cautiously "through the gloomy forest." She also encountered her first party of friendly Amerindians, who were dancing, shouting, and drinking rum that white frontiersmen had apparently shared while celebrating the opening of their first sawmill. She remarked that Amerindians and settlers then lived in "such a mixture on the frontiers," and found it threatening that they were "without established laws to govern them."[1]

Susannah presumed Amerindian hostility during Anglo-French wars, but saw no connection between that anger and the encroachment of European settlement. Although the governments of Massachusetts and New Hampshire both claimed the site, it was the settlers themselves who built Number 4, an elaborate stockaded fort that included accommodations for their families. Susannah recounted the entire catalog of Amerindian attack and colonial defense of this fort throughout King George's War (1744–1748).

In 1747, at seventeen, Susannah married James Johnson, a twenty-seven-year-old Irishman who had been kidnapped at age ten and sold into servitude in Boston. James had been indentured to one of Susannah's uncles for ten years, not an uncommon term for one so young. An "enterprising spirit," James bought out the last year of his service and became a farmer and trader. Within a year of marrying Susannah, he became a militia lieutenant. Peace supposedly reached the New Hampshire frontier in May 1749, and James, Susannah, and their baby Sylvanus promptly moved to war-battered Number 4, now renamed Charlestown, where Susannah's parents, brothers, and sisters lived. Within days of her arrival, Susannah was huddled in the fort, which was under attack by Abenaki who had not yet made peace. She recalled her "anxiety and grief" that her husband, father, and brothers were not in the comparative safety of the stockade during what proved to be the final blow of what she called "the Cape Breton War." One neighbor was killed and another captured, but her relatives all survived; the settlers lived in the fort for most of the next three years.

By late 1752, James and Susannah felt confident enough to move, with their children Sylvanus, Susannah, and newborn Polly, to their farm a third of a mile from the fort. In the next year, James traded blankets "and other necessaries" with neighboring Amerindians for furs; Susannah recalled that most of those natives given credit made punctual payments. In the summer of 1754, with James away for three months buying supplies, she managed both the farm and her family amid frightening rumors of renewed war. In August, in the last days of another pregnancy, Susannah was relieved and happy when her husband returned with a large stock of trade goods. Neighbors and relatives gathered nightly to drink fresh supplies of liquor, eat ripe watermelons from Susannah's garden, and talk of precautions to be taken before the war that was expected the following spring.

Susannah's world exploded just before sunrise a few days later. On August 30, Peter Labarree arrived at the house at dawn to join other hired men intent on doing a long day's work for James. As the door was opened, a number of Abenaki, who had been hiding in the woods, attacked. Susannah recalled screaming and urging the outnumbered men to surrender rather than fight; they were soon all prisoners. Then, "I was led to the door, fainting and trembling; . . . to complete the shocking scene, my three children were driven naked to the place where I stood. On viewing myself I found that I too was naked."[2] The eleven attackers were in too much of a hurry to ransack the house thoroughly, but one had found three of Susannah's dresses and handed them to her. All five Johnsons as well as Labarree, Susannah's sister Miriam Willard, and her kinsman Ebenezer Farnsworth were forcibly hurried away. The sound of the fort's alarm guns made the captors even more anxious to quicken the pace of the very pregnant Susannah and her three terrified youngsters. She later learned that the garrison intended to give chase, but her father had convinced his militia captain that the raiders, if pursued, would kill their slowest captives. The eight were forced through thorny thickets, and Susannah lost a shoe and was winded within a mile and a half. When she sat down, a warrior pulled out his scalping knife, but only used it to cut the waistband of her dress before pushing her onward. The group hurried on for another three miles before the Abenaki felt confident enough to stop and eat. As she sat looking at her bleeding legs and feet, the Abenaki offered Susannah bread, raisins, and apples taken from her own house, and James, who had earlier been untied in order to hurry along his children, helped catch a stray horse. The eleven Abenaki warriors, none of whom spoke English, resumed herding Susannah, now on horseback, the three captive men, Miriam (age fourteen), Sylvanus (six), Susannah (four), and Polly (two), none of whom spoke Abenaki or French.

On the rainy second day of their captivity, Susannah's labor pains prompted the group to stop and build a shelter. Her husband and sister were allowed to help with the birth of Susannah's third daughter. The Abenaki, along with the other prisoners and the crying children, remained at a distance throughout the birthing. Her Abenaki captor, whom she regarded as clever and "by no means void of compassion," was pleased, announcing "two monies for me."[3] He helped clothe the infant, whom Susannah rather whimsically named Captive, and the group spent the rest of the day preparing another shelter for the mother and baby, and building a litter for the next day's journey. The litter for transporting Susannah and her baby was useful as long as the male captives could carry it, but they were exhausted after only two miles. The Abenaki considered leaving Susannah behind; she accepted the nearly-as-terrifying alternative of riding a horse one day after childbirth.

Their food proved insufficient and, on the fifth day, the Abenaki killed the horse and spent the evening "drying and smoking" some of the meat. Susannah had not walked more than half a mile on the sixth day before she fainted. In a third contentious discussion among the warriors, Susannah's "master" again defended the life of his bothersome captive. Saved again, Susannah stumbled on, amazed that the Abenaki were so much more humane than their reputation. They built shelters for her to sleep in, stopped to dry her clothes after a river crossing, and shared scarce food generously, be it horse, duck, woodchuck, squirrel, or hawk. The provident Abenaki, having killed a bear on their way south to raid Charlestown, had suspended a cache of bear fat sausage, flour, and tobacco from a high tree limb. This food saved the finicky English from the horse meat.

The only irritants that Susannah recalled came from the

youngest of the Abenaki, who "delighted himself by tormenting my sister, pulling her hair, treading on her gown, and numerous other boyish pranks."4 Susannah could not walk; James was now carrying her in an improvised pack saddle. Near the middle of the ninth day the procession finally reached East Bay on Lake Champlain, ending the tortuous 100-mile walk of the poorly shod captives. Susannah did not present her story as a conscious religious allegory, as numerous other captives had done; yet at this point she noted, "The same Providence who had brought us so far, and inclined our savage masters to mercy, continued my protector." Thus, "few will deem it less than a miracle, that we were still among the living."5

After a night in canoes, the Abenaki held a victory dance near the fringe of the Canadian settlement at Fort St. Frédéric, presumably for the benefit of the commandant. Each prisoner was given a song to sing and was forced to dance around the fire. Susannah did not know whether this was a religious ceremony or simply a diversion, but found it painful and offensive. Then they were all taken into the fort, where the commandant treated them to brandy, a good dinner, and a change of clothing. After four days of French civility, they were returned to their Abenaki captors, "to our great grief and mortification." Susannah recalled subsequent kindnesses from the commander at Chambly, where she slept in a bed for the first time since her captivity, drank brandy again, and "lived in high style."6 At another village, the parish priest was hospitable but, like the other Canadians, was also unwilling to interfere in an accepted traffic that saw the prisoners off once again with their Abenaki masters.

As the Abenaki approached their home village of St. François, another halt was made. The captives were again made to dance and sing, and this time they all had their faces painted with stripes of vermilion and bear grease for the triumphal arrival. As the canoes landed, there was tremendous yelling, and the village emptied to form a gauntlet to the water's edge. Susannah expected a severe beating, but the prisoners were given only a ceremonial pat on the shoulder by each villager as their masters led them to their wigwams. At a council the next day, Susannah's master traded her and Captive for Sylvanus, who was to be taught to be a hunter. Susannah and Captive were formally adopted by a principal chief, Magouaouidombaouit, also known as Joseph-Louis Gill. The son of two New England captives, Magouaouidombaouit had been born in St. François and had married the daughter of the chief sachem, Nanamaghemet. This white chief of the Abenaki lived as the most prosperous farmer and trader in the settlement.

Of the now nine captives, Susannah, her baby, and her young son, Sylvanus, were the only ones adopted by the Abenaki. Sylvanus was destined to become a hunter, a considerable investment in a six year old unless he was also being adopted to replace a lost son. Peter Labarree was apparently tested as a hunter by his captor and found unsatisfactory. He and the others, including Susannah's husband and their two other daughters, were taken away and sold in Montréal. The adoption process might be expected not to favor adult males, but it also bypassed three girls aged fourteen, four, and two. The choice of Susannah may have been compassionate, or even involved some clever calculation of a mother's ransom, but it seemed to her simply a matter of chance.

Susannah lived in a village of some thirty wigwams inhabited by people who were devout and deferential to their aged Jesuit missionary. There were, however, recognized boundaries between the powers of the missionary and those of the grand sachem, differences that Susannah compared to those between legislative and executive power in New England government. She had some difficulty in adjusting to life in a large wigwam with two or three Abenaki couples. It was awkward to kneel and eat with a spoon from a large, communal wooden bowl placed on the floor or to sleep on a board covered with a blanket. This Puritan mother found the Abenaki rather indolent "and not remarkable for neatness," but thought "they were extremely modest, and apparently averse to airs of courtship."[7] Susannah milked cows twice per day but overall considered herself idle. Much of her time was spent visiting among her new relatives, and she became particularly fond of her young adoptive brother Sabatis, who was about the age of her own son, away hunting. Susannah was a novice at canoe making and hence agreed with her adoptive sister's occasional complaints that she was a "no good squaw." Her general appraisal of the community within which she lived for two months was very favorable, for none of her family suffered wanton cruelty, and she was confident that no "civilized conquerors" would have been so considerate or would have adopted her as a sister.

Susannah's two-year-old daughter Polly was bought by the mayor of Montréal, whose wife seemed determined to raise her as her own. Four-year-old Susannah was sold to three elderly and prosperous sisters, who doted on her. Her own sister, Miriam Willard, was bought by Governor Ange Duquesne de Menneville, Marquis Duquesne, whose personal concern for the Johnsons made it clear that he was no more buying a worker than were the purchasers of the two little girls. James Johnson was probably sold to the Canadian authorities, like an indentured servant once again, but was soon treated as a captured militia officer. Ebenezer and Peter were sold to prosperous Montréal gentlemen. After being with the Abenaki for two months, Susannah and Captive were brought to

Montréal, where the governor paid a surprising 700 livres for them, a price comparable to that paid for adult slaves.

James managed to borrow 300 livres to pay his own ransom and was given two months' parole to return to New Hampshire and gather cash to repay the governor for the ransom for Susannah and their children. Only a day after being reunited with her husband, Susannah watched him leave for Albany with two Amerindian guides who were to remain there until he returned. From Albany, James went to Boston and applied to Governor William Shirley and the General Court of Massachusetts for redemption money. The General Court gave him a mere £10 (about 150 livres) toward his expenses; Massachusetts authorities usually refused to redeem captives, claiming that it would just encourage the taking of more of them. His own New Hampshire government granted James £150 sterling to redeem his group as well as eight other colonials who had been captured on the Merrimack River that summer. Johnson set out for Albany overland, but he had gone no farther than Worcester before being stopped on orders of Governor Shirley. Because Massachusetts was preparing expeditions against Acadia and Fort St. Frédéric, Johnson was forbidden to proceed for fear that the Canadian government could extract strategic information from this frantic husband and father.

The best days of Susannah's captivity had been those spent in Governor Duquesne's house that winter. Although she needed an interpreter in Montréal, as in St. François, Susannah recalled dining frequently with prominent families and receiving numerous "general tokens of generosity which flow from a humane people."[8] She found special kindness in the home of a merchant, Louis Charly Saint-Ange, where another Englishwoman, captured in Maine and purchased as a servant, was being treated like another daughter of the family. Susannah and Miriam enjoyed the company of the young Saint-Ange ladies. Susannah also met Captains Robert Stobo and Jacob Van Braam of the Virginia militia, who were hostages for unfulfilled terms of Washington's surrender at Fort Necessity the previous summer. As hostages taken in peacetime by a formal government force, these men were given considerable freedom, including the license to trade. They were affluent enough to give Susannah a substantial gift of cash.

Susannah adapted quite well to her new environment. After a tearful and direct appeal, she recovered her daughter from the mayor's wife. Susannah had been particularly upset that Polly was living with a poor nurse rather than in the mayor's household, but she later understood "that it was fashionable among the higher class people in Canada, to have their own children nursed out till they were about three or four years old."[9] Polly, accompanied by a considerable wardrobe, was finally returned to her mother, without repayment of any of the ransom. Susannah's adaptability also showed when Captive became seriously ill. Not only did Susannah yield to exhortations to have her infant daughter baptized a Roman Catholic, but the governor stood as godfather, and the child was given the baptismal name of Louise, after Madame Duquesne. Susannah was less anxious about her eldest daughter, living "with the three old maids, who treated her tenderly," confident "that every attention was paid to her education and welfare by her three mothers."[10]

Once the guides returned from Albany without James Johnson, life quickly became much harder for Susannah, her two youngest daughters, and her sister. Governor Duquesne's military code of honor could not tolerate this unexplained breach of protocol. The sisters were immediately banished from his household and from polite Canadian society. After their funds were exhausted, they survived by working as seamstresses.

It was a very different Montréal to which James Johnson finally returned at the end of June 1755. Canadian-born Governor Pierre de Rigaud, Marquis de Vaudreuil, had just arrived, and was taking New France into the war that had evidently begun on the Ohio the previous year. Even before General Edward Braddock's captured papers revealed that Captain Stobo had smuggled a plan of Fort Duquesne to his superiors, Vaudreuil was furious that the hostage Virginians had been given the freedom of Montréal and neighboring Indian villages. Not only was James Johnson considered a prisoner who had violated parole, but he was also carrying bills of exchange that represented credit available from prominent Canadians who were thereby implicated in an illegal trade between empires. In effect, these documents from Albany merchants instructed their Canadian customers to pay the money owed them to Johnson. The named Canadians denied any connection with Albany and refused to pay. The Johnsons were left penniless. War not only made breach of parole a more serious offense but also turned Lieutenant Johnson into a potential source of damaging military intelligence about the defenses of New France. He would also be useful in subsequent exchanges of prisoners of war. James was promptly jailed in Montréal, while Susannah commiserated with former acquaintances who began arriving as newly taken prisoners of war. Members of her own party, taken as slave captives of the Abenaki and redeemed by Canadians expecting repayment in cash or labor, were now also seen as legitimate prisoners of war. Even though Miriam, Farnsworth, and Labarree had all managed to pay their entire ransom, they were not allowed to go home.

A few weeks later, Susannah, James, and their two youngest

daughters were sent to Québec, where they were initially incarcerated in the criminal prison. All four survived smallpox and six months of close confinement in filthy surroundings. Infant Captive was allowed to live with a nurse after an appeal to Intendant François Bigot, the senior administrator who eventually intervened to relocate the other Johnson prisoners. The Johnsons then moved to a civilian prison where they were given beds, fuel, and candles and were advanced James's pay as a lieutenant. Confinement here was a major improvement over the cell that they had occupied in the criminal prison, but more restrictive than the free range given many other prisoners of war. Although grateful for the change, Susannah remained the industrious New Englander, again complaining of enforced indolence. She and James had a small garden within the prison yard and could now get their clothes washed. Susannah was even allowed a weekly outing to buy provisions.

On one of her days of freedom, Susannah visited two recently captured girls who had been bought by Governor Vaudreuil and sent to the Ursuline convent in Québec for their education. In addition to meeting the two girls and being impressed with how well they were being treated, Susannah had a conversation with the assistant superior, Sister Esther-Marie-Joseph de l'Enfant-Jésus, formerly Esther Wheelwright. She asked to be remembered to her brother in Boston, whom she had not seen in the fifty-two years since she had been taken captive in an Abenaki raid on the Maine frontier. This visit indicates the comfort and support shared by the captives and former captives who had settled in New France.

In August 1756 the entire garrison of captured Fort Oswego, numbering more than eighteen hundred people, arrived in Canada as prisoners of war. These prisoners increased the population of New France by more than 3 percent and outnumbered all of the New Englanders brought to Canada as captives over the previous eighty years. Feeding so many people strained the food supplies of the colony, eventually making the release and exchange of prisoners more likely. For the Johnsons, the most appreciated among these captives was Peter Schuyler, the wealthy and generous colonel of the New Jersey Blues, who lent and spent his fortune in aid of his fellow captives. Schuyler gave the Johnsons a cash gift soon after his arrival and continued to help them throughout the rest of their captivity.

Susannah found the winter of 1756–57 particularly difficult. She gave birth to a son who died within a few hours, and she learned that her father had been killed and her brother Moses, named after his father, had been wounded in yet another Abenaki raid on Charlestown. Although hospitalized again briefly, Susannah recovered her health and spirits when Governor Vaudreuil granted a petition to allow her sister Miriam to join them. Miriam had spent the previous two years with a prominent family in Montréal, comparatively well treated and working as a seamstress. By this time, Captive had become a "very pert and talkative" three-year-old who was "accustomed, at Québec, to go to market, or anywhere among the shops, just as she pleased," where she was often given biscuits or gingerbread treats. Captive spoke only French, but, by this time, Susannah had learned enough of the language at least to understand her daughter. Although the flood of military prisoners also lowered the diplomatic value of the Johnsons, it was May 1757 before they were given even as much freedom as Schuyler and his fellow officers already enjoyed within the town of Québec.

A month later, the Johnsons were among those promised an indirect route home via England. Just before sailing, Vaudreuil ordered James to stay but gave permission for Susannah, Miriam, Polly, and Captive to go. Susannah agonized about leaving her beloved husband in Québec, her eldest daughter in Montréal, and her son among the Abenaki. A coffeehouse conference "of all the prisoners in the city," chaired by Colonel Schuyler, "voted, by a large majority, that I should go—I, with hesitation, gave my consent." Susannah found that the decision to leave without her husband "shook my boasted firmness"; and, as the ship left Québec, "I gazed, as long as sight would permit, at the place where I had left my dearest friend."[11]

Like many English captives and commentators, Susannah considered the treatment of captives in Canada unfair and hypocritical. She retained, and published, these views long after the United States of America became independent and France had become its valued ally. From the beginning of the eighteenth century, France had set Europe's standards for humane treatment of prisoners of war, yet civilian captives were enslaved in peacetime by Amerindian captors, often sold to Canadians, and then required to redeem themselves in cash. The Johnson case indicates that Governor Vaudreuil did not distinguish clearly among captives (the Johnsons), hostages taken in peacetime (Captains Stobo and Van Braam), and prisoners of war. The coming of war had prompted Vaudreuil to consider James Johnson a captured military officer, and then a criminal who broke parole rather than a captive who had paid his ransom. Susannah somewhat condescendingly "pardoned" her Abenaki captors but still felt that she and her family had been victims of capricious French and Canadian authority.

Susannah had never been to sea, but she recorded no fear of sailing; instead, the relatively quick one-month crossing from Québec to Plymouth, England, was marked by fine weather, cheerful sailors, and commodious accommodations. "It will be thought singular, that a defenceless woman should suffer so many changes, without meeting some insults and many incivilities." Susannah, Miriam, Polly, and Captive were celebrated by the "charitable ladies" of Plymouth, and they stayed in the home of Captain John T. Mason, holder of a major New Hampshire land patent. Although she was in Plymouth and Portsmouth for only a few weeks, Susannah received a substantial sum of money donated by sympathetic people in Plymouth and London. By mid-October, the four female venturers sailed with a fleet of British troopships bound for New York. After a stopover in Cork, Ireland, "We had a passage of seven weeks, remarkably pleasant, to New York." Susannah remembered "the supreme felicity to find myself on shore in my native country, after an absence of three years, three months, and eleven days."[12]

At New York, then a town of fewer than 18,000 people, Susannah met her neighbor Peter Labarree, who had just arrived after escaping overland from Canada. Colonel Schuyler was there, too, on parole to assemble funds in support of captives in Canada. Schuyler reported having "redeemed" Susannah's son Sylvanus from the Abenaki, and passed on the news that James had finally been released and was returning via Halifax. On his arrival in Boston, James was initially imprisoned because he had no receipts for the expenditure of the redemption money. Released, and granted $100 by the governor of Massachusetts, James made his way to Charlestown without knowing that Susannah was already home. They were joyously reunited there on New Year's Day of 1758, but their restored happiness was not enduring. After accepting a captain's commission in a newly raised Massachusetts regiment, James was killed at the battle of Ticonderoga on July 8.

Susannah found her years of widowhood "particularly afflictive," although she was as grateful now as she had been earlier to God, friends, and kind strangers.[13] To settle James's estate as a trader, she undertook twenty journeys to Boston, Portsmouth, and Springfield. To dispose of his stock of goods, she and her brother Moses ran a store in Charlestown for three years. Neither travel nor storekeeping appealed to her.

Returning to New England was hard at first for Susannah's children. Sylvanus, now fifteen, arrived through redemption and a prisoner exchange in October 1758, sick and remembering little of his family or of the English language. He could speak to his mother only in broken French, for she could not understand his fluent Abenaki. Susannah says little about him, except that he lived for a few years with her relative, Colonel Aaron Willard. Sylvanus had become an Abenaki, resented his redemption, and "always maintained that the Indians were a far more moral race than the whites."

He was known as an "honest, upright man" and lived on in Charlestown and its vicinity to the age of ninety.[14] Susannah's eldest daughter did not arrive home from Montréal until after the conquest of Canada in 1760. In her six years there she had become a well-educated twelve-year-old, speaking only French, thus making Susannah's family "a mixture of nations." In her mother's telling, young Susannah had not been disadvantaged by a captivity in which she had been loved by three Canadian spinsters who still wrote letters after her return; she would marry well and be "the mother of fifteen children, among which were five at two births."[15] Polly and Captive apparently adjusted easily to life back on the New Hampshire frontier, and both eventually married men of sufficient standing to become militia colonels. Captive, who arrived in New England at age three, lost her French and Catholic beginnings readily, although she would later live with her husband in Canada for a time before returning to be of special help to her aged mother.

Susannah recounted a more troubling meeting with another relative. In October 1759, Major Robert Rogers's rangers returned from a raid in which they burned the entire village of St. François. They had brought back Sabatis, Susannah's adoptive Abenaki brother, as one of their few prisoners: "He was transported to see me, and declared that he was still my brother, and I must be his sister. Poor fellow! The fortune of war had left him without a single relation, but with his country's enemies, he could find one who too sensibly felt his miseries: I felt the purest pleasure in administering to his comfort."[16] The rangers, who also brought Susannah a bundle of James's carefully preserved papers "found in pillaging St. Francis," soon took Sabatis away to Crown Point. Susannah, who apparently never heard of him again, reflected that "I shall ever remember this young Indian with affection; he had a high sense of honor and good behaviour, he was affable, good natured and polite."[17]

Susannah ended her four years of widowhood in 1762 by marrying an early settler of Charlestown, John Hastings. She had seven more children, five of whom died in infancy, as had three of her seven children by her first husband. In an obvious comparison with her mother, Susannah calculated her total of thirty-eight grandchildren and twenty-eight great-grandchildren. She was also proud to have lived most of the rest of her life "on the same spot where the Indians took us from in 1754, but the face of nature has so changed that old savage fears are all banished."[18]

As an aunt and grandmother, Susannah relished telling of her youthful adventures, which she came to see as an instructive tale of suffering and redemption. At age sixty-six, she dictated her recollections to John C. Chamberlain, with some help from her fellow prisoner Peter Labarree and from James's salvaged notes as well as her own. Susannah's memoir was first printed in 1796 as *A Narrative of the Captivity of Mrs. Johnson, containing An Account of her Sufferings during Four Years with the Indians and French* in Walpole, New Hampshire. In each of the next three summers, Susannah and her daughter Captive tried to locate the exact spot where she had been born: "The keenest anguish of soul, the providential deliverance, and the almost miraculous preservation, has ever rendered the recollection of that spot dear to me."[19] On their third attempt in 1799, accompanied by Peter Labarree, the site was finally identified, and a "birthstone" was placed there: "On the 31st of August 1754 Capt. James Johnson had a Daughter born on this spot of Ground, being Captivated with his whole Family by the Indians." To help others find the place she cherished, half a mile from a road that then linked Weathersfield and Reading, Susannah had another stone set by the roadside: "This is near the spot that the Indians Encampd the Night after they took Mr. Johnson & family Mr. Laberee & Farnsworth August 30th 1754 And Mrs. Johnson was Deliverd of her Child Half a mile up this Brook." Beneath these lines was inscribed a verse that gave God credit for Abenaki kindness:

When trouble's near the Lord is kind
He hears the captive's cry
He can subdue the savage mind,
And learn it sympathy.[20]

Susannah's *Narrative* proved very popular, going through at least five printings before her revised edition appeared in 1807. This much enlarged edition included the account above and various additional documents, including a 1799 testimonial to her veracity signed by eighteen people, including her son, her brother, and Labarree. Her account was already in danger of being regarded as fictional. Susannah concluded by recounting being thrown from a horse in 1801, at age seventy-one, eating a good meal at Captive's birthsite on her last visit there in 1808, and breaking an ankle when a wagon overturned on her the following year. She was disturbed that she and her second husband had imprudently given their estate to a son-in-law; Susannah found living under his control "almost as painful to be borne, as my savage captivity."[21] After the intervention of Captive and other relatives, the Hastingses apparently regained some freedom.

Before she died in Captive's arms in November 1810, Susannah had asked the Reverend Abner Kneeland, who had shown an interest in preparing a new edition of her memoir, to preach her funeral sermon and append it to a third edition of her *Narrative*. Susannah's choice of the radical Mr. Kneeland is intriguing. By 1810 he was minister of both the Congregational and Universalist communities of nearby Langdon, New Hampshire, openly preaching that all humans would ultimately be saved by a merciful God. His sermon for Susannah's funeral interpreted her life as a display of human fortitude and faith as well as God's grace. Kneeland did not inflate the real but limited signs of piety in earlier versions of Susannah's story and joined others in vouching for the truth of her seemingly fantastic adventures.

Notes

1. Susannah Johnson, *A Narrative of the Captivity of Mrs. Johnson*, 3d. ed. (1814; reprint ed., Springfield, MA, 1907), 8–9.
2. Ibid., 27–28.
3. Ibid., 31, 36.
4. Ibid., 47.
5. Ibid., 52, 54.
6. Ibid., 59, 61.
7. Ibid., 71.
8. Ibid., 85.
9. Ibid., 75. This situation was not mentioned in the first edition.
10. Ibid., 91, 133.
11. Ibid., 105–11.
12. Ibid., 119–23.
13. Ibid., 136.
14. Emma Coleman, *New England Captives Carried to Canada*, 2 vols. (Portland, ME, 1925), 2:311–12.
15. Johnson, *A Narrative,* 138.
16. Ibid., 132.
17. Ibid., 133.
18. Ibid., 138.
19. Ibid., 36n.
20. Ibid., 38.
21. Ibid., 142.

Suggested Readings

The fullest edition of Susannah's *A Narrative of the Captivity of Mrs. Johnson* is the third, printed in Windsor, Vermont, in 1814 and reprinted in Springfield, Massachusetts, in 1907. The second edition has been reprinted in Colin G. Calloway, *North Country Captives: Selected Narratives of Indian Captivity from Vermont and New Hampshire* (Hanover, NH, 1992), 45–87. Parts of her story are verified by Nathaniel Bouton, ed., *Documents and Records Relating to the Province of New Hampshire from the Earliest Period of Its Settlement*, 7 vols. (Concord, NH, 1867–1872), vol. 6; *Scout Journals. 1757. Narrative of James Johnson, a Captive during the French and Indian Wars* (Manchester, NH, 1902); and Johnson's petition of February 24, 1758, in Loudoun Papers, LO 5655, Huntington Library, San Marino, California.

Susannah's story has interested Henry H. Saunderson in his *History of Charlestown, New Hampshire* (Claremont, NH, 1876); Emma Coleman, *New England Captives Carried to Canada*, 2 vols. (Portland, ME, 1925), 2:302–13; and Ian K. Steele, *Betrayals: Fort William Henry and the "Massacre"* (New York, 1993), esp. 10–18. Of related interest are James Axtell, "The White Indians of Colonial America," *William and Mary Quarterly*, 3d ser., 32 (1975): 55–88; Alden T. Vaughan and Daniel K. Richter, "Crossing the Cultural Divide: Indians and New Englanders, 1605–1763," American Antiquarian Society *Proceedings* 90 (1980): 23–99; Barbara E. Austen, " 'Captured . . . Never Came Back': Social Networks among New England Female Captives in Canada, 1689–1763," in *New England/New France, 1600–1850*, ed. Peter Benes (Boston, 1992), 28–38; June Namias, *White Captives: Gender and Ethnicity on the American Frontier* (Chapel Hill, NC, 1992); and John Demos, *The Unredeemed Captive: A Family Story from Early America* (New York, 1994).

15

Bryan Sheehan
Servant, Soldier, Fisherman

Margaret Kellow

Bryan Sheehan (1732–1772) apparently valued his Catholic faith highly enough to emigrate rather than convert to escape oppression and poverty. His quest took him to Newfoundland, Massachusetts, and Maine without obvious success, although his marriage may have indicated that he had some prospects. Time, place, and personality may all have helped make his indentured servitude less satisfactory than Daniel Clocker's. While the French and Indian War (1754–1763) was Pierre Pouchot's professional opportunity, it disrupted Sheehan's life, as it did Susannah and James Johnson's. Bryan joined the British army, rather than a privateering vessel that a sailor might be expected to prefer, and gambled his life to fight his fellow Catholics, French and Spanish. He won in two senses: he served in the victorious armies taking Louisbourg, Montréal, Martinique, and Havana; and he survived despite the risk of fatal diseases, especially high in the West Indian campaigns.

In spite of six years with the same winning regiment, an impoverished Bryan returned home to face more disappointment. He had been presumed dead and his wife had remarried. This situation was not at all uncommon, especially for those who were unable or unwilling to write and were rumored to have been in horrendous battles. What would such errors, and their correction, do to the inheritance of property, the payment of debts, and the disruption of families? Although he was his wife's "husband of choice" in this awkward circumstance, Bryan never quite recovered. He was disgraced and dead at forty, a stark reminder that the New World did not automatically bring success.

Margaret Kellow has published a study of colonial indentured servants, and her biography of Lydia Maria Child is forthcoming. She teaches U.S. and women's history at the University of Western Ontario, London.

Other people told Bryan Sheehan's story, people who judged him and found him wanting. A printer in Salem, Massachusetts, hoped to capitalize on Sheehan's notoriety by publishing a sensational account of his offenses. Like the printer, a local minister thought there was capital to be made from Sheehan's history. He saw Sheehan's life as an object lesson: from a bad beginning, the Irishman had come to a worse end, and a determined deviant had received his just reward. In the minister's hands, the story became a cautionary tale that might save some other wayward souls. While the printer and the minister articulated the community's sense of outrage, Sheehan's view of things must have been very different. The lesson he took from his life was one of anger, frustration, and failure. No matter how hard he tried, he was never able to bend events to his will. Whatever youthful ambition he might once have had, his luck was always bad. Eventually, he just stopped trying. To someone who had never managed to grasp even the first rung of the ladder of success, the values upheld by the printer and the minister, and indeed by the respectable citizens of Salem and Marblehead, Massachusetts, made little or no sense.

Sheehan was born into a large family in Ireland in 1732, to a Catholic father and a Protestant mother. As in so many Irish Catholic families, the Penal Laws, designed by successive British Parliaments in the early eighteenth century to coerce the Catholic Irish into Protestantism and loyalty, dominated Sheehan's early life and fostered in him a deep sense of grievance and resentment. His parents' generation had seen these laws come into force, and his own generation would experience the full weight of their impact. His parents' marriage was not considered legal; consequently, his mother forfeited any property she might have had. Being raised as a Catholic, as the boys in the Sheehan family were, denied Bryan access to an education. Moreover, Catholics could not make a legal will, so even if Sheehan's father had owned any property, the best that Bryan could hope for was a minuscule inheritance, as Catholic estates had to be divided among all the children. More important, if any one of his brothers decided to convert to Protestantism, he alone would inherit everything. Judging by his reading later in life, Sheehan did receive some education; he was certainly literate. But with no land and no credentials, and a resolve to adhere to his faith, he had few prospects. Rural Ireland in Sheehan's youth was beset by rising rents and falling commodity prices and punctuated by periodic bad harvests. In this environment, and like many landless youths, he had drifted about in search of work, eventually to a seaport on the southern coast of Ireland. In 1752, having exhausted other possibilities, Sheehan decided to emigrate. There were few material goods in his meager baggage, but at twenty years old, he appears to have left Ireland with a chip on his shoulder and little respect for the powers that be.

Along with hundreds of other Irish youths in the 1750s, Sheehan signed on for the Newfoundland fishery. Over the preceding century, cod fishing had become an international industry and cod a staple in the diet of people on both sides of the Atlantic. Fishermen, not only from England but also from France, Spain, and Portugal as well as the American colonies, competed in the fisheries off Newfoundland, Nova Scotia, and New England. Initially, men worked inshore from small boats. Over the course of the eighteenth century, however, larger vessels began to fish out on the banks. The English fishery on Newfoundland was a "dry" one; that is, once caught, the cod were cleaned and dried ashore on open wooden platforms called flakes. When thoroughly dried, the cod were packed and shipped to waiting markets all around the Atlantic and into the Mediterranean.

Sheehan had probably never been to sea previously; indeed, part of the great value of the cod fishery to the British government was that it took untried men like Sheehan and turned them into sailors. The summer fishery was very labor intensive, but little permanent settlement had taken root, so it depended on a large migrant labor force. Most of the Irish were shoreside workers, employed in drying or "curing" the fish. Ship captains from the West Country in England scooped up dozens of young men like Sheehan in Waterford, Youghal, or Cork early each spring and set out for Newfoundland. The captains were either fishermen themselves or merchants who sold the labor of their passengers as servants to the "planters," as the permanent settlers on Newfoundland were known. From Sheehan's point of view, if the catch was good, he could learn a trade, accumulate some money, and be back in Ireland by the fall.

Eager to get an early start on the season, the fishing captains headed out into the North Atlantic in late March. Leaving the soft Irish spring behind and sharing the vessel with livestock and other provisions, Sheehan and his fellow servants battled westward against the prevailing winds for about a month. Arriving in late April or early May, they found spring in Newfoundland to be very different from the one they had left behind. Sheehan's heart must have sunk at his first sight of the cold barren shore, still ringed by the last vestiges of ice. Scattered tiny settlements, separated by deep bays and rocky peninsulas, were filled primarily by young men like him, summer servants between the ages of eighteen and twenty-five. In these encampments, there were scant comforts and next to no women to be found. Whatever life Sheehan had known in Ireland, little in Newfoundland resembled it. In the meager summer, warm days might be followed by days of cold and fog. There were work and wages, to be sure, but the barren land and fitful weather meant that few crops could be cultivated. Planters, and especially servants, relied heavily on imported food and comforts. Although the Penal Laws did not apply in Newfoundland, the planters and their families, most of whom were English Protestants, took few pains to hide their disdain for the Catholic Irish servants.

Fishing camps were known as rambunctious places. Shore workers lived in an essentially male community. They had no hope of attracting the attention of the few planters' daughters in the neighborhood. In the long summer twilights, Sheehan and his companions sang and drank and gambled and planned what they would do when they returned to Ireland. But as September approached, hopes for a better standard of living when they returned home gave way to anxiety over whether or not they could pay their passage home. Much depended on how good the catch had been, but even when it was good, merchant captains with their holds full of cod had no reason to concern themselves with the fate of the summer servants. Some deliberately cheated their employees of their wages. Those servants who could not pay were abandoned on the shore. Indeed, this happened so frequently that the planters began to complain of it. With no money and no food, these servants soon were destitute, for they could not hope to survive on their own through a Newfoundland winter. Whether he gambled away his wages or his master cheated him, Bryan Sheehan was among those stranded when the fishing fleets returned to Britain in the fall of 1752.

Fortunately, there was another option—indeed, one that occurred so often that, by Sheehan's time, it had become a well-established pattern. Most of the provisions for Newfoundland came from the British colonies in New England. In the fall, ships from Massachusetts and New Hampshire carried many of these stranded servants back to the North American mainland. In this manner, Bryan Sheehan arrived in Massachusetts late in 1752.

In some respects, Boston must have seemed like paradise after the monotony and desolation of Newfoundland. Though far smaller than Cork or Waterford, Boston, with its taverns, coffeehouses, stores, and newspapers, throbbed with life compared to the forlorn little settlements that he had just left. Here surely was a place where he could make his way in the world. Sheehan quickly found work in Charlestown, just outside Boston, as a carter, but if he was to get ahead, he knew he would have to learn a trade or skill. Luck seemed finally to be with him, and he bound himself as a servant for a year to Benjamin Hollowell, an ambitious shipbuilder. Despite appearances, Sheehan had come to Boston at a troubled time. In the wake of King George's War, high taxation had thrown the town into an economic decline. Nor was it a center of tolerance: Congregationalists were not just disdainful of Irish Catholics, they were openly hostile. Boston's working men annually celebrated Pope's Day (November 5) with anti-Catholic rioting with the anxious approbation of the town fathers. In addition, a serious smallpox epidemic earlier in 1752 had exacerbated tensions. Perhaps the mortality occasioned by the epidemic explains Hollowell's willingness to employ the young Irishman.

Sheehan's indenture, as was usually the case, provided for him to live in the home of his master, and life in the Hollowell household was a far cry from what Sheehan had known among the summer servants in Newfoundland. Master Hollowell, on his way to becoming Collector of Customs and a wealthy and prominent Tory, insisted on certain standards. Sheehan was forced to attend family prayer meetings daily. Not content with that, Hollowell's thirst for respectability drove him to compel Sheehan and his other servants to attend Sunday worship with the family in Boston's Old South meetinghouse. It was not enough that Sheehan must endure the colorless forms of Congregational worship, which seemed to him to consist of little more than a droning harangue from the minister, but after the service, Hollowell regularly quizzed Sheehan on the substance of the sermon. The master's concern for the religious conformity of his servant was almost certainly matched by stern oversight of other aspects of Sheehan's life. Thus not only his work but also Sheehan's recreation and socializing regularly came under Hollowell's scrutiny, and, as master, this was his right. As Hollowell vigorously pursued the approbation of his peers by his conduct of the household, Sheehan's resentment began to fester. For his part, Sheehan made no secret of his antipathy toward Hollowell's religious practices and the part he was required to play in them. Hollowell interpreted Sheehan's indifference and outright balkiness as evidence of stubborn, ignorant papistry. Given the tensions between the two, it is scarcely surprising that Sheehan left Hollowell's employ at the end of his term. Shortly afterward, following a night of drunken carousing, Sheehan found himself bound to another master, probably as a sailor. Whether in the service of this master or to escape him, Sheehan left Boston in the winter of 1753–54 and settled soon afterward in Casco Bay, near what is now Portland, Maine, becoming a fisherman once more.

As the inshore fishery gave way to larger, more commercial endeavors out on the banks, places such as Casco Bay became distanced from the international trade. Harassment by French-sympathizing Abenaki Indians made settlement in these Maine villages somewhat precarious. In 1754, Casco Bay was a stopping place on the coastal shipping route from Boston to Nova Scotia.

Sheehan hired himself out as a sailor and fisherman, trying doggedly to get some kind of economic toehold. If later reports are to be believed, he did little to endear himself to respectable folk in this small community. He drank heavily and was notoriously profane in his language. Thus it is surprising that within two years of his arrival at Casco Bay and still very much an outsider, he married a young woman from the village. Patterns that Sheehan had observed in Ireland might have led him to court a girl whose father owned property or a boat. As an extra hand, and claiming skills in seamanship and the fishery, he might well have been welcome in the young woman's home. On the other hand, later accusations of sexual impropriety raise the possibility that Sheehan may have seduced her and, indeed, both might have been the case. However, although there is no record of the woman's name, later events would show that Sheehan genuinely loved her.

The Casco Bay region was not much more hospitable than Newfoundland had been; the same rocky shores and icy winters made agriculture a doubtful proposition. Yet if the climate was only marginally more benign, Casco Bay was far less isolated. Through the summer and the fall of 1754, rumblings of a new war between England and France echoed through the region. In July, Captain John Winslow of the 40th Regiment of Foot set out from Bang's Island in Casco Bay with 800 men to find an alternate route overland to Québec via the Kennebec River. Winslow took with him carpenters and other laborers to build fortifications along the way. It is not likely that Bryan Sheehan was among them, but Winslow's expedition can only have made the possibility of war more real. Tensions in the area continued to rise, culminating the following year in the deportation of the Acadians from the eastern shore of the Bay of Fundy, not far to the northeast of Casco Bay. People in the settlement eagerly awaited newspapers and word of mouth, but the news when it came was not good. After hearing of the British defeats in the Ohio Valley, few could have been surprised when war was formally declared in 1756.

War, bringing with it the threat of privateers, disrupted the fishery and the coastal trade and thus disrupted Sheehan's livelihood. It brought with it an opportunity of sorts, however, especially for a young man inclined to be footloose. Recruiters passed through the region seeking men willing to enlist. At the behest of Governor William Shirley, Massachusetts began to raise companies of soldiers for Provincial regiments. Enlistment into the Provincials often drew strongly on local and kinship ties; thus, as an Irish outsider, these regiments had little appeal for Sheehan. Moreover, as recruiters whipped up support for the conflict in local communities, they often did so with fiercely anti-Catholic rhetoric, a poor inducement for

Sheehan to throw his lot in with his neighbors to fight Indians and the French far away across the mountains to the west. Yet his religious background made him suspect in the small community. Some proof of loyalty was necessary.

There was no question that enlistment brought bounties and the promise of further rewards at the war's end. The fishery could only offer him long years of hard labor and low profits. When Samuel Mackay, a recruiting officer for the 40th Regiment of Foot, passed through the Casco area in the spring of 1757, offering two hundred acres of land and steady wages in return for four years' service in the regular army, Sheehan had to consider the proposition seriously. There was his wife to think about, but the enlistment bonus would help her, and perhaps she could return to her parents' care. Fisherfolk were accustomed to long periods of separation. Sheehan and his wife may have reasoned that the prize at the end would make the years apart worthwhile. Sheehan's religion might have posed a problem, since Irish Catholics had previously been barred from the army, but in the early years of the war the need to raise troops outweighed this concern. A new act of Parliament would soon require recruits to attest that they were Protestants, but Sheehan either lied or the officials raised no difficulty on this score. Nor were his American-born neighbors likely to protest an enlistment that relieved the pressure on them and their sons. What role that Sheehan's apparent wanderlust might have played is difficult to assess, but the strongest inducement was the land. Two hundred acres seemed a fortune—the very fortune he had been seeking since he left Ireland. It was a gamble; he had to survive to obtain the prize. If he stayed in Casco Bay, the sea might kill him as effectively as any French soldier. Events had already shown that he was both a gambler and a survivor, so he took the King's shilling and reported for duty in Halifax in 1757.

Much newer and rawer than Boston, Halifax in 1757 was bursting with British troops when Sheehan arrived. Dozens of ships rode at anchor in Bedford Basin. The commander in chief in North America, John Campbell, Earl Loudoun, had just arrived from England, and plans were afoot for an assault on Louisbourg, the great stone fortress that guarded the entrance to the Gulf of St. Lawrence for the French. Sheehan's first few weeks were taken up with ceaseless drilling. Mastering his musket, learning to load and fire it accurately and quickly, absorbed much of his attention. With no experience of battle, he had difficulty in understanding the rationale behind endless commands to march, wheel, turn, halt, load, and fire. Still, the sense of impending adventure struck him as a vast improvement over the monotony of the fishery.

Loudoun planned the attack on Louisbourg for late August 1757, and troops had begun loading onto the transports early that month when news reached Halifax that the fortress was now protected by a French fleet. Loudoun rescinded his orders, and Sheehan's regiment was detailed to relieve troops in some of the captured French forts around the Bay of Fundy. Sheehan soon found himself at Fort Cumberland (formerly Fort Beauséjour) at the head of Chignecto Bay. Surrounded by broad tidal flats, the empty fields of the banished Acadians, and the Tantemar marshes, the setting seemed pleasant enough as the detachments rebuilt the fort's defenses in the crisp fall air. However, small parties of French soldiers constantly picked off squads of laboring British soldiers and then disappeared back into the forest. The need for constant watchfulness and the unceasing sense of threat escalated tensions even within the safety of the fort. When the regiment sailed back to Halifax in late October, their work on Fort Cumberland complete, Sheehan along with his fellow soldiers felt a deep sense of relief. He had yet to see a pitched battle, but it was already clear to him that his two hundred acres would come at considerable cost.

The winter in Halifax passed with more drilling, broken by hours on watch. Although his superiors were probably glad of the time to continue transforming their relatively new recruits into effective soldiers, Sheehan found the intensive regimentation oppressive. It was Master Hollowell's all over again, with a drill sergeant instead of a parson. Harsh military discipline did little to diminish Sheehan's antiauthoritarian streak. Conditions in the crowded town were poor, but Sheehan survived a smallpox epidemic that raged through Halifax that winter, while many other soldiers did not. Yet despite the sickness, the damp, and the cold, the food came fairly regularly, and in off-duty hours there was rum to be had in the alehouses of the town.

The spring of 1758 brought news that the assault on Louisbourg was certain to go ahead. As the fleet under Admiral Edward Boscawen and the army under General Jeffrey Amherst converged on Halifax, drilling and training took on added urgency. After the boredom of winter quarters, Sheehan was only too pleased when his regiment received orders to embark. On the bright, sunny morning of May 28, the fleet of 157 ships sailed out of Halifax with orders to rendezvous at Gabarus Bay, just west of Louisbourg. Amherst's plan was to surprise the French. Strict and detailed orders had been given to land the army in silence on the night of June 2; however, the weather soon began to deteriorate. Harsh, unpredictable winds dispersed the fleet. Although most vessels reached Gabarus Bay by the appointed date, they could do little when they got there. A huge, battering surf made landing impossible. Sheehan and hundreds of his companions sat packed in the transport ships as heavy seas and high winds tossed them about through June 3 and 4. Periodically, French shells hurtled toward them, falling short but adding to the din. Although Sheehan's days as a fisherman stood him in good stead, many of his peers were not so fortunate, and seasickness added to the misery of their cramped quarters. The waves abated somewhat on June 5, but thick fog swathed the fleet and a heavy swell continued to torment queasy stomachs and preclude any chance of landing. On June 6 the weather at first seemed to improve. After three days of bobbing about offshore, Sheehan and the rest of his company eagerly made ready to land, but the fog returned and with it the waves rose once more. Again the landing was put off; when the weather moderated slightly the following day, preparations were made to land at dawn on June 8.

All hope of surprise was gone, and the French, using their time wisely, had reinforced the cove where the British planned to land; still, Amherst and his subordinate, General James Wolfe, thought that it might be done. As they sat in the boats in the early light after nearly a week of being buffeted by wind, waves, and French shells, their men, Sheehan among them, were only too eager to get ashore. British ships opened fire to cover the landing, but as the first boats rowed in they came under French fire. More important, the waves were so enormous that the men could scarcely find a place to beach the small craft. In the midst of roaring seas and French shells, the first ones began jumping into the water and wading ashore. However, the huge waves overturned boats, breaking some to pieces. Empty boats were sucked back out to sea, crushing some of the men in the water. Conditions were so bad that Wolfe, at the head of one of the first parties, attempted to abort the landing, but some of his younger officers mistook his cautionary gestures for encouragement and with their men clambered over the rocks and up the low cliffs to the level ground above. At this, Wolfe took heart and soon followed.

Sheehan watched this drama from the transport boats. His company landed to the left of Wolfe's position in the cove and began the difficult and time-consuming work of landing men and supplies in order to fortify their position. The French soon began to fall back. In persistently dreadful weather, Sheehan's company was put to work erecting batteries and digging trenches for the siegeworks. All the while, firing continued from both sides. By July 13, still in foul weather conditions, the French attempted a sally out of the town, but a company of Sheehan's regiment soon drove them back. On the same day, he watched in awe as a British shell struck the powder magazine of *L'Entreprenant*. In the explosion that followed, two other French ships caught fire and sank; their men leapt overboard and were killed either by the explosions or by British gunfire. The bombardment continued night and day. Despite the weather, the

British advanced steadily, and by July 22 the citadel was in flames. On July 25 the last two French ships were destroyed, and the following day the French commander surrendered.

Sheehan's regiment watched as the French garrison was paraded out as prisoners in early August. After two months of tumult, he was not sorry to see things settle down into a quieter routine. Other regiments embarked, but Sheehan's was among those designated to occupy Louisbourg. Encamped just outside the fortifications, Sheehan and his companions helped build a block-house, repair the defenses, and dig wells in addition to preparing for winter. It was fortunate that they did, for the bad weather of the summer continued into the fall. By winter, bitter winds, plunging temperatures, and scarce fuel shortened tempers, and disputes began to arise over rates of pay. Money mattered, as there was a world of difference between Halifax merchants eager to do business with His Majesty's forces and the sullen townspeople of Louisbourg, who cheated and bilked their enemies at every turn. The soldiers took heart when the ice in the harbor broke up at last in the spring, especially as a huge army assembled for the assault on Québec. A portion of the 40th Regiment was ordered to join the attacking force, but when the fleet sailed on the first of June, Sheehan's company remained behind at Louisbourg for another winter, cheered by news of the British victory on the Plains of Abraham and saddened by the death of General Wolfe.

By the summer of 1760, Sheehan had been away from home for three years. When the remainder of the 40th received its orders to join the attack on Montréal, Sheehan and his peers must have hoped that the end of the war would not be long in coming. In mid-August, Sheehan's company was among those landed above Québec, just east of Trois-Rivières. Under Captain Mackay, Sheehan's company, just over one hundred men, marched through the villages of Champlain and Ste. Magdalene on the north shore, disarming the local population as they went. Following the surrender of Governor Pierre de Rigaud, Marquis de Vaudreuil, on September 7, Sheehan's company was sta-tioned first at Berthier, where the St. Lawrence broadens into Lake St. Pierre, and then in Montréal itself.

In the town of Montréal, Sheehan spent his third winter among the Canadians. One assumes that by now he had acquired a smattering of French. Similarly, the residents of Montréal, from encounters with English traders and captives, had learned at least a little English. Still, as they waited for the peace treaty, which would end the formal state of war and determine how the Canadians would subsequently live, the two sides regarded each other warily. Food was scarce in the town, and bread riots erupted as angry women struggled to feed their children. Some marriages took place between British soldiers and French Canadian women, but sexual assaults by soldiers on women of the town poisoned the atmosphere despite severe punishments. What Sheehan made of it all is difficult to say, but having survived this long he almost certainly must have looked forward to returning to his home and wife in Casco Bay.

That return was further away than he could have imagined. Sheehan had enlisted for four years or the duration of the war, probably hoping that the latter would be the shorter. The fighting might now be over in North America, but the British had ambitions elsewhere; and with the French apparently on the ropes, British Prime Minister William Pitt was determined to press the attack. As a consequence, a force under General Robert Monckton was ordered to proceed to the West Indies for an attack on the rich French sugar islands. In August 1761 the 40th Regiment received orders to assemble on Staten Island, New York, for transport to Barbados. Bryan Sheehan was not going home just yet.

After reaching Barbados in December 1761, the 40th set sail for its first target, Martinique. Despite strong French defenses, on January 16, 1762, Sheehan's regiment and numerous others waded ashore through the warm, blue Caribbean waters at a small inlet on the southern shore of Martinique. Conditions could hardly have been more different from the landing at Louisbourg two-and-one-half years earlier, but Sheehan found no time to enjoy them. In spite of difficult terrain, the British quickly captured the heights of the island with surprisingly few losses. Although the French offered vigorous resistance, on February 3 the garrison surrendered. Within days Grenada, St. Vincent, and St. Lucia followed suit. With so much of France's colonial empire now in British hands, how much longer, the men of the 40th Regiment wondered, before the French came to terms and a peace could be signed? The French and the British, however, were not the only European powers with Caribbean interests. No sooner had the sugar islands fallen to the British than news came from Europe that Spain had entered the war on the French side. As a consequence, Britain now turned its sights on Cuba, the largest Spanish possession in the Caribbean. The 40th Regiment of Foot, and Bryan Sheehan with it, was now detailed to be part of an assault on Havana.

As Sheehan's company waited on Martinique for the invasion force to assemble, sickness—yellow fever in particular—began to make serious inroads on the British forces. What was true of all warfare was especially valid in the Caribbean: sickness was far more deadly than gunfire. Newcomers were most at risk for yellow fever, and water barrels, crucial to sustain large encampments, were the chief hatchery for the mosquitoes that carried the virus.

Once the disease became established among the troops, it spread exponentially. None of this was understood by Sheehan and his contemporaries, but the generals did know that in planning a campaign in the Caribbean, it had better be a short one—one that could be brought to a successful conclusion before the inevitable epidemic began to take a significant toll on the army's fighting capacity.

The heart of Cuba was Havana, and the key to Havana was a large fortress known as the Moro, which guarded the entrance to the harbor. The British regarded the Moro as virtually impregnable. Captured Cuban sailors warned them that the Spaniards intended to hold the fortress at all costs. Accordingly, and as yellow fever continued to devastate their ranks, the British assembled a massive attack force. A total of 217 ships approached Cuba from the northeast, and landings began approximately six miles east of the Moro on June 7. The dimensions of the undertaking were considerable, especially because the British had no previous knowledge of the terrain. Above the rocky shore, the hills were densely forested. Guns and supplies would have to be dragged ashore over the rocks and up roads hastily built into the jungle to encampments and depots—all under Spanish fire.

The British determined to construct batteries on the landward side of the Moro. The grueling work began on June 13. The plans located the largest, named the Grand Battery, just 190 yards from the Moro. Under steady bombardment from the Spanish guns, Sheehan and his companions labored in the hot sun alongside African slaves to erect fascines, embankments of earth reinforced with bundled logs. Collecting the earth proved especially onerous. The area around the site of the batteries consisted mainly of bare rock. Soil had to be scraped up from the crevices and carried long distances. In addition, there was little food. Provisions rotted in the heat, and there was virtually no fresh water in the vicinity. Heat and thirst tormented the work parties, as yellow fever sapped their strength. Some men literally died of thirst, while others succumbed to yellow fever in a matter of hours. Still others, falling sick, lingered two or three weeks before the fever carried them off. Men died in such numbers that vultures hovered over their encampments, and graves could scarcely be dug fast enough to bury the dead.

On June 29 the Spaniards sallied forth from the fortress and were only beaten back after a desperate fight, one that cost many British lives. Worse disaster struck a few days later when the Grand Battery caught fire, rapidly destroying two-and-one-half weeks' work by six hundred men. By July 2, half of the British forces were too ill to work as a result of the combination of sickness and the brutal environment. Despite the appalling conditions and yet another fire at the Grand Battery, the British slowly advanced.

British ships shelled the fortress and the Spanish ships in the harbor constantly. Although more soldiers and sailors fell sick with each day, by July 16 only five or six Spanish guns still were firing. Sheehan's regiment now worked with the sappers to mine the foundations of the fortress. The Spaniards, increasingly desperate now, attempted once more to break out of the fortress, and once more were beaten back. On July 30 the British exploded their mines and breached the walls of the Moro. After an assault on the fortress itself, Havana surrendered two weeks later. Nearly three thousand British soldiers and sailors had died in the attack, and the survivors, among them Bryan Sheehan, had endured horrendous conditions.

Sheehan must have come through the experience relatively unscathed. He was not among a large complement of soldiers invalided home to North America as soon as the fighting ended. Bitter though he may have been at having been left in Cuba, it turned out to be his good fortune, as virtually all of those soldiers died en route. By September, out of an invasion force of more than eleven thousand, barely seven hundred were fit for duty. The men of Sheehan's regiment must have been a particularly hardy lot because they were among the forces detailed to garrison Havana, and there they stayed until the following summer. On June 30, 1763, in accordance with the terms of the Treaty of Paris, Cuba was handed back to Spain. The war had ended. On the same day, the 40th Regiment of Foot received orders to embark for England.

After more than six years of war, Sheehan and his companions must have despaired of ever seeing their homes again. Resentment simmered in the lower ranks of the 40th, ostensibly over stoppages in their wages for provisions, but since the regiment had initially been raised in Nova Scotia, a longing for home must have also fed the unrest. Whether superior officers recognized this discontent is hard to say, but though already under way for England, on July 18 the regiment was ordered to make for New York, where it arrived at the end of the month aboard the transport *Minerva*. From there, the regiment was ordered to Halifax, and it is likely that there, having enlisted for four years or the duration, Bryan Sheehan was finally mustered out of the 40th Regiment of Foot.

As Sheehan searched about for a ship to take him back to Casco Bay, he carried no fortune and apparently no land patent with him. Stoppages for provisions had consumed any wages that he might have been owed, so much so that his companions in the 40th registered a formal complaint from Halifax about the conduct of their officers in this matter. The officers also did a lively trade in the land patents of their subordinates, buying these up at a substantial discount from men eager for ready cash. After six and one-half years of war, Bryan

Sheehan had survived, but he does not appear to have accumulated anything more than experience. His gamble had not paid off.

Walking through the village on his return to Casco Bay, Sheehan, now thirty-one years old, could take comfort in the fact that he was still alive. If no farther ahead in the race, at least he could pick up the pieces of his prewar life and begin again. After his long absence, his former neighbors greeted him with amazement, but Sheehan sensed an unease on their part that puzzled him. The reason for it soon became clear. The war in North America had ended three years earlier to all intents and purposes. When he did not return at that point, his neighbors assumed that he had died. And so had his wife. She had married again, this time a Frenchman, and they had had a child.

Something broke inside of Sheehan at that point. Rage consumed him. He wanted nothing more than to kill the French scoundrel who had stolen his wife. At first he plotted to do just that, intending to stab his rival. Focusing his anger on the Frenchman deflected it from what he clearly felt was his wife's betrayal. Neighbors intervened and tried to reason with Sheehan. They attempted to negotiate some kind of resolution to the problem. The woman had apparently acted in good faith and she had a child. Gradually, Sheehan's anger cooled somewhat. He agreed that the woman must choose with whom she would live, and although she chose Sheehan, the relationship was not what it had been. The sight of the Frenchman's child never failed to remind Sheehan of his wife's inconstancy.

Over the next four years, Sheehan and his wife lived together unhappily. Deeply embittered now, he returned to the fishery and the sea and the meager subsistence that they offered. Together, he and his wife had three or four children, but only the Frenchman's child survived. Wherever Sheehan looked, the evidence of his disappointments lay all around him. The quality of his relationship with his wife deteriorated steadily. He drank heavily, taunted her with her past, and subjected her to both verbal and physical abuse.

Apart from his domestic unhappiness, Sheehan never settled back well into his community. He had not resided in Casco Bay prior to the war long enough to make a permanent place for himself in the region. His neighbors' war had been over for three years by the time that he returned. His experiences had been utterly different, even from those who had served with the Provincials. Merchants who had grown rich on war contracts looked down on his poverty and criticized him for his drinking and, increasingly, for his treatment of his wife. When the Stamp Act crisis erupted, Sheehan had no clear ties to either side of the conflict. His Irish background gave him little reason to love royal officials, nor was he inclined by nature to be deferential to authority; thus, he had no reason to identify with the Tory position. Yet to a man raised under the Penal Laws and clinging to the margins of subsistence, the essence of the colonists' grievance against Britain seemed hard to grasp. His war experience also tended to alienate him from the Patriot side. His background and term of service in the army bound him neither to a specific community network nor to a particular geographic locale. Moreover, as the American colonists began to construct their identity in opposition to royal authority, Sheehan's service with the British regulars put him increasingly on the wrong side of the political divide.

In about 1768, Sheehan found work in Marblehead, Massachusetts, an important center in the commercial fishery and the international trade to which it was linked. It is possible that work had dried up in Casco Bay and that Sheehan migrated to Marblehead in search of employment, but it is also possible that he had resolved his domestic problems by deserting his wife and her child. Rumors of serious crime began to attach themselves to his name about this time. In Marblehead, Sheehan hired himself out as a sailor, sometimes on fishing vessels, sometimes in the coastal trade, and sometimes on foreign voyages. His career in the fishery coincided with the completion of a massive transformation in the industry. Bank (offshore) fishing now dominated. Individual fishermen no longer worked inshore in their own small shallops but instead hired themselves out to masters of larger ketches and schooners, for "shares." Over the course of the eighteenth century, in the fishery as in mercantile shipping, the gap between owners and workers widened rapidly, and the consequences of this transformation were quite evident in Marblehead. Next only to Boston in population density in Massachusetts, Marblehead abounded with men looking for work. As he approached the age of forty, Bryan Sheehan was old for a sailor. Captains sought younger men. For Sheehan, the waits on the wharves and in the taverns between voyages grew longer.

Sheehan's fall into poverty and ultimately into crime accelerated. In addition, his determination to show his contempt for the respectable citizens of the Salem-Marblehead region marked him increasingly as a social outcast. Never seen in church, Sheehan could usually be found in the dramshops and alleyways of Marblehead's poorest quarter. As with many sailors, his language was foul and abusive. Notoriously quarrelsome, he drank heavily and brawled at the slightest provocation. Shunned by decent folk, he passed his time with known prostitutes and criminals. The respectable citizens of Marblehead and Salem took note of his behavior, heaving sighs of relief when he sailed out of port and rolling their eyes when he returned.

Merely to see Sheehan near a building was to suspect him of

planning a burglary. In the winter of 1770–71 he was accused of plotting to break into a store, simply because he and a companion were loitering nearby. In response, Sheehan threatened and then attacked his accuser, the "gentleman" who owned the store. For this crime, he was jailed in Salem and publicly whipped. The designation of his victim as a "gentleman" suggests that Sheehan's most serious offense was his stubborn refusal to conform to Salem and Marblehead's notions of deference and propriety. Early in 1771, while incarcerated in Salem, Sheehan received word that his wife had died. Observers noted that he grieved deeply for his loss, but this did little to rehabilitate him in the eyes of the townsfolk.

What happened next depends on whom one believes. In September 1771, Sheehan was arrested and charged with the rape of Abiel Hollowell, the wife of Benjamin Hollowell—not the shipbuilder to whom Sheehan had been indentured when he first arrived in Boston, but possibly his former master's son. Sheehan had apparently met Mrs. Hollowell at the home of another woman in early July. Sheehan began to importune her, even after he discovered that she was married. Whether Sheehan may have believed that she was connected to his former master is not clear. Witnesses testified later that Sheehan offered the woman drink and money, both of which she insisted that she had refused. He continued his pursuit of her over several weeks so insistently, Mrs. Hollowell stated, that she finally hid from him in the home of a friend. One night early in September, having discovered her whereabouts, Sheehan entered the house in which she had taken refuge and, according to Mrs. Hollowell, raped her in a particularly violent manner.

The case attracted enormous attention. Rape was a capital crime and no one had been executed in Salem since 1692, "the witch time," as one bystander put it.[1] In the Provincial Court House on the south side of the town square in Salem in November, witnesses came forward to support Mrs. Hollowell's charge and to testify to Sheehan's brutality. Sheehan admitted that he was guilty of adultery but claimed that Mrs. Hollowell had consented to have intercourse with him, and thus he was innocent of rape. The judges believed her. Sheehan was convicted and sentenced to hang in December.

Some people in the community clearly had doubts about Abiel Hollowell's story. Sheehan was repeatedly urged to admit to the rape, but he maintained his innocence. Observers noted that his stance had "induced many to entertain hard thoughts of the woman."[2] Among the morals that were drawn from the case by the minister who wrote about it was the following: "Let women consider their danger from whoremongers and adulterers: And let them be so far from trusting themselves in their power, as to shun and avoid them, as they would bears and tygers."[3] All of which suggests that some questions had been raised in the community about the firmness with which Mrs. Hollowell had rejected Sheehan's initial advances. Sheehan's execution was delayed at least twice, possibly in the hope that he would confess to the rape. As he waited, Sheehan asked that Mrs. Hollowell visit him. She agreed, but in their conversation and before witnesses, he still adhered to his version of the affair. Protesting his innocence even on the scaffold, he was hanged on January 16, 1772.

It is impossible to know at this remove who was telling the truth. Was Sheehan's stubborn insistence on his innocence the cry of a man condemned as much by his reputation as by the facts? Or was he compounding his physical attack on Mrs. Hollowell by destroying her reputation and thus passing out of this world with one last defiant gesture? What is certain is that the vindication of Abiel Hollowell and the condemnation of Bryan Sheehan continued after the latter's death. Eager to thrill their readers with details about the monster who had lived among them, Samuel and Ebenezer Hall, the Salem printers, included explicit details of Mrs. Hollowell's testimony in their broadside accompanied by a vivid sketch of Sheehan's depraved career. The Reverend James Diman, minister of the Second Church in Salem and related to several of Salem and Marblehead's most prominent citizens, made special arrangements so he could preach to Sheehan and the enormous crowd that had assembled on the day of the execution. He then published his sermon, to which he appended his version of Sheehan's life. Diman did all in his power to induce Sheehan to admit to the rape and thus exonerate Mrs. Hollowell. When he failed in that endeavor, Diman turned his attention to discrediting Sheehan. In outlining Sheehan's dissolute life, the minister strove to destroy any vestige of Sheehan's credibility. Linking him to other crimes and criminals, Diman also implied that it was foolish to expect truth from a Papist. In the final analysis, Bryan Sheehan may well have been guilty. But if he was innocent, if Abiel Hollowell had willingly consented as at least some of her contemporaries believed, this outsider, drifter, and troublemaker could marshal few resources to save himself. People with power and influence believed Abiel Hollowell. Bryan Sheehan had lost again.

Notes

1. Joseph Seccombe, Diary entry for January 16, 1772, reproduced in "Diary of Deacon Joseph Seccombe," *Essex Institute Historical Collections* (Salem, MA, 1899) 34: 27.

2. James Diman, *Mr. Diman's Sermon on the Day of The Execution of Bryan Sheehan* (Salem, MA, 1772), 23.

3. Ibid., 24.

Suggested Readings

Two accounts of Sheehan's life were printed at the time of his execution: *The Life of Bryan Sheehan* (Salem, MA, 1772); and *Mr. Diman's Sermon on the Day of The Execution of Bryan Sheehan* (Salem, MA, 1772). Parts of these accounts are verified by reports in the *Boston Post-Boy* of November 18 and 25, December 30, 1771, and January 20, 1772; and by the "Diary of Deacon Joseph Seccombe," which is reprinted in the *Essex Institute Historical Collections* 34:23–39; and by the "Almanac of Nathaniel Bowen," also reproduced in the *Essex Institute Historical Collections* 91:268–71. Captain R. H. Raymond Smythies, *History of the 40th Regiment of Foot* (Devonport, United Kingdom, 1894), tracks the experience of Sheehan's regiment through the Seven Years' War. See also Thomas Mante's *History of the Late War in North-America and the Islands of the West Indies* (1772; reprint ed., New York, 1970).

More recently, the accounts of Sheehan's life have been examined by Daniel Williams in "The Gratification of That Corrupt and Lawless Passion: Character Types and Themes in Early New England Rape Narratives," in *A Mixed Race: Ethnicity in Early America*, ed. Frank Shuffelton, 194–221 (New York, 1993). Of related interest is Daniel Vickers, *Farmers and Fishermen: Two Centuries of Work in Essex County, Massachusetts, 1630–1850* (Chapel Hill, NC, 1994).

16

Olaudah Equiano
An African in Slavery and Freedom

Robert J. Allison

Olaudah Equiano (1745–1797) is the quintessential captive in our gathering, and telling connections can be made between his experiences and those of our other captives. Although he spent little time in colonial America, his boyhood and kidnapping were well-remembered experiences common to thousands of Africans who ended their days in plantation slavery. Captives often cope with their trauma by identifying with their captors, which may help to explain something about Squanto and Pocahontas as well as Equiano. Yet his exceptional life came to include achieving personal freedom, publishing his autobiography, and generally defying all the usual bounds of slave life. Equiano's unusual slavery meant that he grew up among the English, became a sailor, made friends among the English, and married an Englishwoman, eventually becoming an activist prominent in the British abolition movement. How important was race to Equiano? He organized the Sons of Africa and fervently promoted the abolition of the slave trade, but he recounted that fellow Africans were the ones who initially captured and sold him. He assisted in slave trading and plantation management for a time after he bought his freedom, and he advocated interracial marriage. His *Interesting Narrative* was very consciously a part of the abolition movement; how would that purpose affect his version of his own story?

Robert J. Allison is the editor of Equiano's *The Interesting Narrative of the Life of Olaudah Equiano, or Gustavus Vassa, the African* (1995) and the author of *The Crescent Obscured: The United States and the Muslim World, 1776–1815* (1995). He teaches American history at Suffolk University in Boston.

Olaudah Equiano (pronounced o-lah-OO-day ek-wee-AH-no) was born in the Ibo village of Isseke (in present-day Nigeria) in 1745. At the age of eleven he was kidnapped by slave traders; he spent ten years as a slave in the West Indies, in America, and in the

British navy before buying his freedom in 1766. As a free man, Equiano traveled throughout the Western world, from the Arctic to Nicaragua and the West Indies, from Cádiz to Genoa, Philadelphia, and New York. Living in London in the 1780s, when the slave trade reached its peak, Equiano contributed to the international movement against it. With other Africans in London, he formed the Sons of Africa to promote the interests of Africans in England and its colonies. As part of this lobbying effort, Equiano wrote newspaper articles, petitioned Parliament and the Queen to end the slave trade, and in 1789 published his autobiography, *The Interesting Narrative of the Life of Olaudah Equiano, or Gustavus Vassa, the African*. One of the first abolitionist books by a former slave, Equiano's story is unique because he recorded virtually every part of the slave's experience: childhood in Africa, capture and sale to other Africans and to Europeans, the Middle Passage from Africa to the Americas; plantation labor in the West Indies and America; and the American slave trade from the Caribbean to the mainland. He also wrote about life after slavery, his twenty years as a freeman of color in England and America.

Equiano was the youngest son of seven children, six boys and one girl. His name connoted good luck: the word *ola* means ring, a sign for luck, and *ude* means a pleasant sound. His father was one of the village leaders, and his mother was active in the marketplace. He thought of his childhood as happy and prosperous, as the farming village produced plenty to feed the people. Equiano remembered the abundant corn, poultry, goats, tobacco, pineapples, yams, and cotton, and the women weaving and dyeing colorful calico cloth to wear and trade. The market drew buyers and sellers from distant areas, trading for the cloth and produce of Isseke. From the south, African traders brought European goods: guns, woolen cloth, and hats. These African traders also dealt in slaves.

Slavery in traditional African societies was a form of punishment for crimes such as adultery or robbery, or it could be a penalty for prisoners of war. Slaves were exiled from their own communities and forced to join another. While they were denied certain privileges in their new homes—in some cases, they were not allowed to eat with their masters—in other respects, slaves in African society did not live differently from free people. Equiano's father owned slaves, and some slaves even had slaves of their own, who could one day become free members of their new society. The European demand for slaves had changed the nature of this African trade. European slave merchants typically did not leave the coast of Africa but found willing African partners to kidnap slaves in the interior. The Aros, another Ibo clan living between Isseke and the coast, profited from the European demand. Equiano remembered that the Aro traders "carried great sacks with them" in which to confine unwilling captives.

Equiano recalled in his autobiography that when the adults were at work in the fields, a lookout was posted in the village to watch for slave catchers. He remembered once raising the alarm; but on another day, when "only I and my dear sister were left to mind the house, two men and a woman got over our walls, and in a moment seized us both, and, without giving us time to cry out, or make resistance, they stopped our mouths, and ran off with us into the nearest wood."[1] They were forced into the sacks and carried from the village. When they were some distance away, they were released from the sacks and marched off. Ultimately, they were separated. Equiano was sold in a distant village to an African goldsmith; after some months he was sold again, in another village, to serve as companion to a boy his own age.

Over several months as a slave in what is now southern Nigeria, Equiano wrote that he

> continued to travel, sometimes by land, sometimes by water, through different countries and various nations, till, at the end of six or seven months after I had been kidnapped, I arrived at the sea coast.... The first object which saluted my eyes when I arrived at the coast, was the sea, and a slave ship, which was then riding at anchor, and waiting for its cargo. These filled me with astonishment, which was soon converted to terror, when I was carried on board. I was immediately handled, and tossed up to see if I were sound, by some of the crew; and I was now persuaded that I had gotten into a world of bad spirits, and that they were going to kill me. Their complexions, too, differing so much from ours, their long hair, and the language they spoke (which was very different from any I had ever heard), united to confirm me in this belief. . . . When I looked round the ship too, and saw a large furnace of copper boiling, and a multitude of black people of every description chained together, every one of their countenances expressing dejection and sorrow, I no longer doubted of my fate.... [He fainted, but some of the traders revived him.] I asked them if we were not to be eaten by those white men with horrible looks, red faces, and long hair.[2]

The African merchants who had brought Equiano on board assured him that the white men would not eat him. The merchants collected their pay and left him. He never saw his home or family again.

Equiano and the other slaves loaded at this port were "soon put down under the decks, and there I received such a salutation in my nostrils as I had never experienced in my life: so that, with the loathesomeness of the stench, and crying together, I became so sick and low that I was not able to eat, nor had I the least desire to taste anything."[3] A slave ship usually carried up to four hundred captives, chained together in the hold for the two-month voyage across the Atlantic. With little ventilation, the crowded hold was hot, dark, and filthy. European traders spent months on the African coast visiting different ports to collect captives from as many different nations as possible so that the slaves would not be able to communicate with one another and rebel as a group. Despair among the captives was so great that many did rebel, or take the opportunity, when on deck for a brief gasp of fresh air, to throw themselves into the ocean to drown.

The Europeans saw Equiano's refusal to eat as rebellious, and he was beaten. Among the other captives he found some Ibos who gave him to understand that "we were to be carried to these white people's country to work for them. I then was a little revived, and thought, if it were not worse than working, my situation was not so desperate."[4] After all, he had worked at home and during his months of slavery in other African villages. He had questions: Did these white people live "in this hollow place (the ship)"? He did not see any European women: Were there only men in their country? And what made the ship go? No one could answer this question, since the slaves were packed below where they could not witness the art of navigation. Were the whites spirits who controlled the ship through magic? He began to fear them, he wrote later, because they "looked and acted, as I thought, in so savage a manner; for I had never seen among any people such instances of brutal cruelty; and this not only shown towards us blacks, but also to some of the whites themselves." One white sailor was "flogged so unmercifully with a large rope near the foremast, that he died in consequence of it; and they tossed him over the side as they would have done a brute."[5]

Equiano was one of fifty thousand Africans carried to the New World in the 1750s. The Portuguese had brought the first African slaves to Europe in 1441, and in the 1490s the practice had extended to the Americas. By 1756 it was well organized and brutally efficient. Of the estimated eleven million Africans brought to the Americas between 1518 and 1850, more than half came after 1750. Nearly half were taken to the sugar plantations of Brazil, about 40 percent to the Caribbean. The rest, or about 7 percent, were taken to mainland North America, principally to work on rice, tobacco, or (in the nineteenth century) cotton plantations, although slaves also worked on small farms, as urban servants, and as skilled craftsmen and sailors. The ship carrying Equiano landed first at Barbados, whose sugar plantations made it one of British America's wealthiest colonies. Equiano was astonished here to see two-story brick houses and men riding on horses. He had never seen a horse and thought that "these people were full of nothing but magical arts."[6]

More memorable than the horses, however, was the slave

market. The arrival of a ship from Africa was an important event in Barbados, and planters and their agents would assemble at the marketplace early, hoping to have the first choice of the new laborers. Equiano wrote that on the beat of a drum, "the buyers rush at once into the yard where the slaves are confined, and make choice of that parcel they like best. The noise and the clamor with which this is attended, and the eagerness visible in the countenances of the buyers, serve not a little to increase the apprehension of terrified Africans, who may well be supposed to consider them as the ministers of that destruction to which they think themselves devoted. In this manner, without scruple, are relations and friends separated, most of them never to see each other again."[7]

No one bought Equiano. He was young and small, apparently not suited to the hard labor of sugarcane cultivation. He was taken on board a sloop and sent to Virginia, where he stayed briefly on a tobacco plantation. Years later he remembered a few details of his weeks in Virginia. The cook, a black woman, wore an iron muzzle. A wall clock and a portrait both seemed to watch Equiano, who was put to work brushing flies away from the dozing planter. From this plantation, where he was called "Jacob," Equiano was bought by a British sea captain, Michael Pascal, who planned to bring the young slave to England as a gift for a friend. Equiano was taken on horseback to Pascal's ship, the *Industrious Bee*. Pascal renamed the boy after the sixteenth-century Swedish king and hero of a popular English play, "Gustavus Vasa, the Deliverer of His Country." Equiano at first resisted the new name, a resistance that "gained me many a cuff" before he submitted to being Gustavus Vassa.[8]

Also sailing on the *Industrious Bee* was Richard Baker, a Virginian just a year or two older than Equiano. Baker explained the ways of white people to the young African, becoming his companion and interpreter. Equiano had often noticed his master and Dick reading and "had great curiosity to talk to the books as I thought they did, and so to learn how all things had a beginning. For that purpose I have often taken up a book, and have talked to it, and then put my ears to it, when alone, in hopes it would answer me; and I have been very much concerned when I found it remained silent."[9] Although the books kept silent, Equiano soon learned how to read them, an unusual achievement for a slave. He spent the spring of 1757 on the Channel island of Guernsey, with the family of Captain Pascal's mate. The mate's wife, who was teaching her own daughter to read and write, gave Equiano the same lessons.

This interlude on Guernsey did not last. As Equiano had sailed from Virginia, England and France had gone to war. Captain Pascal was called into the King's service on the warship *Roebuck*, and Equiano would serve his master and the Empire in Canada, the

Atlantic, and the Mediterranean. The ability to read and to write down his experiences during these years of war marked a transition in Equiano's thinking. When he had first encountered Europeans on the coast of Africa, he had thought them spirits who moved their ships by magic. Now, just a few years later, he "was so far from being afraid of anything new" that he longed to get into battle, and his grief at losing his home and family faded in the excitement of war and the company of other boys on the ship. He began to box in shipboard matches arranged by the captain and other officers.[10]

After a long cruise north of England, which to his regret did not involve any battles, Equiano returned to London, ill with chilblains, a painful swelling of the feet and hands caused by prolonged exposure to cold. He remained in the hospital for months, visited by two cousins of Captain Pascal, the Guerin sisters. Dick Baker having died in the war, the Guerins became Equiano's newest European friends, and the three remained close for the rest of their lives. They began to tell him of the Christian faith, and the Bible stories of the ancient Hebrews reminded him of his own Ibo childhood. Equiano began his conversion to Christianity, a faith that would deepen throughout his life. He recovered from his illness and crossed the Atlantic to participate in the siege of Louisbourg, a French fortress at the mouth of the St. Lawrence River. He remembered years later seeing a British officer shot in the open mouth by a French musketball, holding in his hand an Indian's scalp. After the British victory, he returned to England in February 1759 to be baptized in the Anglican Church at St. Margaret's, in Westminster.

Equiano began to feel more at home in this new world. In 1760, then a swaggering fifteen-year-old veteran of the British navy, he had a furlough on the Isle of Wight. Just four years after his kidnapping, he relates, "I was one day in a field belonging to a gentleman who had a black boy about my own size; this boy having observed me from his master's house, was transported at the sight of one of his own countrymen, and ran to meet me with the utmost haste. I not knowing what he was about, turned a little out of his way at first, but to no purpose: he soon came close to me, and caught hold of me in his arms, as if I had been his brother, though we had never seen each other before."[11] Equiano did not immediately perceive a kinship with this black boy on the Isle of Wight. Now calling himself Gustavus, he said that he felt more English than African.

Nevertheless, his status was still ambiguous. He may have felt English, but not all English people would   treat him as an Englishman. The next years would bring many painful reminders of his status. Having served both his master and the Empire, Equiano, when the war ended, expected and was told by other sailors that he deserved freedom as well as a share in his ship's prize money.

Instead, Captain Pascal sold him. Equiano was forced onto a ship for the West Indies, where he was sold on the island of Montserrat. His new owner was a Philadelphia Quaker named Robert King, a slave trader even though Quakers had condemned slavery in 1727, and Philadelphia's Quakers would bar slaveholders from their meetings in 1774. Perhaps his involvement in the slave trade led to his move from Philadelphia to Montserrat, where he shipped sugar and slaves from the West Indies to Georgia and South Carolina and bargained there for rice and beef to feed the Caribbean workforce. King recognized Equiano's value as a skilled sailor able to read, write, and calculate. Pascal had even sent a character reference noting Equiano's honesty. He became part of the trade network holding together the British colonial system in America.

Equiano had been part of the community of sailors in the British navy; his growing Christian faith also made him part of a larger world. But in the West Indies he was cut off from these ties of community; he was constantly cheated in his business transactions, as the word of a black man counted for nothing in the courts of the British West Indies. He was always in danger of being kidnapped to work on the sugar plantations, of which he had heard incredible but true tales of horror: of free men kidnapped into slavery; of slaves branded, tortured, and beaten to death; and of owners and overseers raping women and young girls, then selling the children of their lust. Equiano recorded all of these stories as well as his own experiences to convince people in England of slavery's brutal nature. West Indian slavery was considered to be its most savage form.

Working for King made Equiano part of the slave system. One option to improve his lot was to become a merchant. He started with three pence and "trusted to the Lord to be with me." On a voyage to St. Eustatius, a Dutch island that served as a general trading post in the West Indies, Equiano used his three pence to buy a glass tumbler. On his return to Montserrat he sold the tumbler for six pence, which he used on his next trip to St. Eustatius to buy two more tumblers. Through several trips between the two islands, Equiano continued to double his capital, until after a month he had more than a dollar and "blessed the Lord that I was so rich."[12] Equiano continued this slow but steady accumulation of capital, combining his trust in divine Providence with his own business skill, investing not only in glasses but in gin, oranges, and chickens. After three years he had accumulated more than £40, enough to invest in his largest purchase. On July 10, 1766, he bought himself. Ten years after he had been kidnapped, Equiano became free.

For his first two years as a freeman, Equiano continued to work for King, trading slaves from the Caribbean into Georgia and South Carolina. On one trip the captain died, and Equiano, who had learned some sailing and navigation, steered the ship safely into port. But skilled as he was, Equiano was not given the job of captain. King hired an inexperienced white man to command the next trading voyage, and against Equiano's judgment the young captain sailed too close to the Bahama reefs. The ship foundered. The captain ordered Equiano to nail down the wooden planks over the hold so the cargo of slaves could not escape. The ship was in danger of sinking, and the white crew raided its rum supply and drank themselves into a stupor. Equiano disobeyed the order and released the slaves. With their help and that of one Dutch sailor, he repaired the ship's longboat and made for a nearby island. The captain warned them not to leave the ship, as he thought he saw cannibals walking on the beach. Equiano ignored his warning, and as he rowed nearer to shore, he watched the captain's cannibals one by one take to the air. They were flamingos.

Equiano now acted as captain, forcing the drunken sailors into the longboat to row them to safety. Although saved through his own efforts, Equiano attributed the miracle to God, and he vowed that if he survived to leave the West Indies, he would return to London and pursue his religious faith. He considered the shipwreck a warning; and when he published his *Interesting Narrative* twenty years later, he included an appropriate verse from the Book of Job about men who do not listen to the voice of God.[13]

Equiano did listen, and he took the shipwreck as a sign to leave the West Indies and the sinful world of American slavery. His work on the slave ships was a reminder of his own failings. Trips to Savannah were especially difficult. In Savannah, black people, either slave or free, were kept under tight control. Equiano himself was arrested there for having a light on after 9 P.M., when all blacks had to put their lights out. He was beaten almost to death by a drunken doctor and, another time, nearly kidnapped and sold as a slave. He was astonished then, in this place of brutal immorality, to pass a church packed with white and black Georgians. Full churches, he had noted, were rare in the West Indies. He was even more intrigued to learn that George Whitefield, the great evangelist, was preaching inside. Equiano pushed through the door to see him "sweating as ever I did on Montserrat beach," as he exhorted the Georgians to lead Christian lives.[14] Equiano did not know that Whitefield had long been a friend of Georgia, nor did he know that Whitefield and the colony's founder, James Oglethorpe, had envisioned it as a utopia. It became a utopia based on slavery, however, and by 1765 even Whitefield's Georgia orphanage was supported by slave labor.

Hoping to free himself from the sinfulness of the New World, Equiano returned to England and looked up his friends, the Guerin sisters. He told them of his adventures "at which they expressed great wonder, and freely acknowledged it did their cousin, Captain Pascal, no honor."15 A few days later, Equiano encountered Pascal in a Greenwich park: "When he saw me he appeared a good deal surprised, and asked me how I came back? I answered, 'In a ship.' To which he replied dryly, 'I suppose you did not walk back to London on the water.' As I saw, by his manner, that he did not seem to be sorry for his behavior to me, and that I had not much reason to expect any favor from him, I told him that he had used me very ill, after I had been such a faithful servant to him for so many years; on which, without saying any more, he turned about and went away."16

Equiano thought he was through with the sea. To support himself, he learned to dress hair. He studied mathematics, and for entertainment he learned to play the French horn. He went to work for Dr. Charles Irving, an inventor who was perfecting a machine to make seawater fresh—an important innovation for the British Empire, which relied on long ocean voyages to connect its far dominions. In 1773 he and Dr. Irving joined an expedition to the Arctic to try to find a northwest passage and also to test the machine. After being icebound, and nearly drowned, Equiano and the expedition returned safely to England. He left Dr. Irving and sailed on a merchant vessel to Smyrna, where he saw the Greeks "kept under by the Turks, as the Negroes are in the West Indies by the white people,"17 and to Genoa, whose grandeur was diminished in his eyes by the wretched life there of galley slaves.

Back in London, Equiano enjoyed a relatively good life, although wages on land were far below those he could earn at sea. In 1774 he prepared to ship out as a steward on a voyage to Turkey. The ship needed a cook, and Equiano recommended his friend John Annis, who immediately went on board to work as it lay at anchor awaiting its cargo. Annis had been a slave on the island of St. Kitts; his owner, a Scotsman named John Kirkpatrick, had brought him to England and now was trying to get him back to the West Indies. In 1772, England's Lord Chief Justice William Mansfield had ruled in a case involving a Massachusetts slave, James Somerset, that once a slave set foot in England, he could not be returned to slavery against his will. Thus, under English law, Annis was free. Kirkpatrick did not care much for the law. While Equiano hired a lawyer to protect his friend's rights, Kirkpatrick hired some men to kidnap Annis and take him back to the West Indies. Equiano received a letter describing Annis's final days: he was "staked to the ground with four pins through a cord, two on his wrists, and two on his ankles, was cut and flogged most unmercifully and afterwards loaded cruelly with irons about his neck." Finally, "kind death released him out of the hands of his tyrants."18

Equiano blamed himself for failing to protect his friend. He wanted to die himself. He thought of going to Turkey and converting to Islam, as his good life in England now seemed empty and meaningless. Feelings of sinfulness overcame him, and he sailed for Spain, reading his Bible, hating all things, and wishing that he had never been born. Thinking himself the unhappiest man who ever lived, he was convinced that God treated him better than he deserved, and wondered what his fate might be. In the Spanish port of Cádiz on October 6, 1774, he began to get a strange feeling that his life was about to change. He spent the evening reading and meditating on the Bible. Then, suddenly,

> the Lord was pleased to break in upon my soul with his bright beams of heavenly light; and in an instant, as it were, removing the veil, and letting light into a dark place, I saw clearly with an eye of faith, the crucified Saviour bleeding on the cross on mount Calvary; the scriptures became an unsealed book; I saw myself a condemned criminal under the law, which came with its full force to my conscience, and when "the commandment came sin revived, and I died." I saw the Lord Jesus Christ in his humiliation, loaded and bearing my reproach, sin, and shame. I then clearly perceived that by the deeds of the law no flesh living could be justified. . . . It was given me at that time to know what it was to be born again.[19]

John Annis's suffering and death seemed taken up in the death and resurrection of Jesus, and both redeemed Equiano. In later years, looking back on his life, Equiano would recall as equally important the date of his freedom from slavery and the date of his spiritual conversion.

Though reborn spiritually, Equiano still found it difficult to cut his ties to slavery. He returned to England to work for Dr. Irving, who now was planning a colony on the Mosquito Coast of Nicaragua. He hired Equiano as his foreman, and the two sailed for Jamaica to buy slaves to work on their plantation. Equiano reconciled himself to his new role by purchasing only Ibos, and as overseer he made sure that the slaves were well clothed and fed and not overworked, and he instructed them in Christianity. Maintaining a spiritual community on a tropical plantation was difficult. Equiano soon grew disgusted at the lack of religious devotion among the Europeans and the wild drinking bouts of the Mosquito Indians. He left Nicaragua in June 1776; and, after nearly being killed en route by an English captain, he reached Jamaica. He found Dr. Irving in Jamaica, where he had gone to buy more slaves. After Equiano had left the plantation, the new European overseer had cut the slaves' food supply and forced them to work harder. They had fled into the jungle and drowned. Dr. Irving's plantation was doomed to failure.

Equiano returned to England with the British fleet, now convoying ships in the first year of the American Revolution. He watched a British vessel destroy an American privateer, a lesson in the consequences of rebelliousness. He petitioned the Anglican Church to send him as a missionary to Africa, but his application was denied. He then settled down to a "more uniform" life, pursuing his religious devotions and working as a personal servant. Equiano might have lived out his days in the quiet role of an English servant, and never have written his book, had he not been called to action in 1783.

In November 1781 disease had broken out on the British slave ship *Zong*. Sixty slaves and seven white crew members died before the ship reached Barbados. The shipowners could collect insurance on slaves who drowned, but not on slaves who died of disease. Consequently, the captain ordered 54 sick Africans brought to the deck, had them chained together, and then thrown overboard. The next day, he had another 42 chained and thrown into the sea; and on the following day, 36 more who showed symptoms of disease were chained and forced over the side. He brought the remaining 248 Africans into port and sold them, then sailed for England to file a claim for 132 drowned slaves.

Equiano learned this story, perhaps from a sailor on the London docks. In early 1783 he told it to Granville Sharp, the British philanthropist who had helped James Somerset win his lawsuit for freedom under British law eleven years earlier. Sharp tried to stop the insurance company from paying the claim. He was unsuccessful, and the shipowners collected insurance on the murdered slaves. But this vivid demonstration of the slave trade's horrors pressed Sharp and other philanthropists to arouse public opinion. In 1784 and 1785, British antislavery advocates, including Sharp, David Ramsay, and college student Thomas Clarkson, published pamphlets attacking the inhumanity of the slave trade and the brutality of West Indian planters.

West Indian planter James Tobin responded with a vigorous defense of slavery. He argued that blacks were inherently inferior to whites and would not be suited for freedom. What would happen to the slaves of the West Indies if they became free? Would they be accepted in England as members of British society? Would they be able to work without the whites forcing them to do so? These were critical arguments, since even whites who believed slavery to be morally repugnant might see blacks as their inferiors and might doubt if the two races could live together in peace.

Equiano recognized the importance of these arguments. He also saw that white philanthropists would not effectively answer the racial charges of black inferiority. Equiano responded to Tobin in a series of letters to the British newspapers, arguing for the full equality of Africans before God and man. Equiano's solution to the supposed problem of innate racial differences was simple: whites and blacks should intermarry, in "open, free, and generous loves upon Nature's own wide and extensive plain, . . . without distinction of color of skin."[20] Intermarriage, and offspring who were neither white nor black, would ultimately make color differences irrelevant.

Equiano resumed his travels, making trips in 1785 and 1786 to New York and Philadelphia, two centers of the American antislavery movement. Both cities had large free-black communities, and Pennsylvania had become in 1780 the first American state to abolish slavery. Quaker Anthony Benezet had long argued against the slave trade and had established a school for free blacks in Philadelphia. New York's Society for Promoting the Manumission of Slaves had been formed in 1785, and a school for free blacks opened there in 1787. Equiano visited Benezet's school, and saw these free schools as models for British philanthropy. He argued that with proper education, blacks could become productive members of society. He saw the color distinction as artificial, and hence one that could be made to fade away.

British philanthropists either were less optimistic or did not see the color line as an artificial one. After the American Revolution, England's black population grew with arrivals of slaves belonging to American Loyalists and blacks who had fought against the rebellious colonists. Although free under British law, economically and socially these blacks were confined to menial positions, where it was feared they would take jobs away from poor whites. A group of philanthropists formed a Committee for the Black Poor, which hoped to improve the lot of both white and black poor people by sending the blacks to West Africa. Although Equiano opposed this proposal, as he believed black men and women could become members of British society, he agreed to serve as the expedition's commissary when the committee invited him. But Equiano discovered corruption and mismanagement in the planned expedition. The agent contracted to supply the expedition overcharged the government and failed to deliver the goods for which he had been paid. Equiano accused the agent of corruption, the agent accused Equiano of mismanagement, and Equiano was fired. He took his case to the public, was cleared of wrongdoing, and was paid for his services. (The expedition did go to West Africa and founded the colony at Sierra Leone.)

In London, Equiano joined with other Africans living in England to form the Sons of Africa. They planned to stay in England and wanted to live as Englishmen. Although they came from many different African nations, they had begun to recognize a common African identity. To improve the lives of all African people, the Sons of Africa launched a campaign against the slave trade, and on

March 21, 1788, Equiano presented an antislavery petition to Queen Charlotte. He began to write his autobiography, which would be a more powerful weapon against slavery and the slave trade. Published just as Parliament began to debate the slave trade, his *Interesting Narrative of the Life of Olaudah Equiano, or Gustavus Vassa, the African* presents the story of a real man, not a distant abstraction, caught in the horrors of slavery. It shows not only that he could endure, but also that once free he had become a valuable member of society. Equiano embarked on a national tour, and for the next eight years he visited all parts of the British Isles, speaking against slavery and the slave trade and selling copies of his book. By 1790 it appeared in its third English edition, and it had been translated into Dutch; in the following year, the first American edition of his book appeared in New York.

In 1792, Equiano married Susan Cullen, who came from a small town near Cambridge, England. They had known one another since at least 1789, when she subscribed to the first edition of the *Interesting Narrative*. Their marriage was an example of the kind of open, free, and generous love that he had recommended in 1785. Their first daughter, Anna Maria Vassa, was born in 1793, and then Johanna in 1795. Susan Vassa died a few months after her second daughter's birth, and Equiano died in April 1797. Anna Maria survived her father by only a few months. Johanna lived into adulthood and collected an inheritance from her parents' estate, £950 earned from the sale of the *Interesting Narrative*.

The story of Equiano's life, recorded in his autobiography, remained a weapon against slavery and the slave trade long after his death. Written as an indictment of slavery, the book serves as testimony to one person's ability to survive and to endure against the brutality of others.

Notes

1. Olaudah Equiano, *The Interesting Narrative of the Life of Olaudah Equiano, or Gustavus Vassa, the African* [first published edition, 1789], ed. Robert J. Allison (Boston, 1995), 47.

2. Ibid., 53–54.

3. Ibid., 54.

4. Ibid., 55.

5. Ibid.

6. Ibid., 58.

7. Ibid.

8. Ibid., 61.

9. Ibid., 64.

10. Ibid., 65–66.

11. Ibid., 78.

12. Ibid., 102–3.

13. Equiano, *Interesting Narrative*, 1st American ed. (New York, 1791), vol. 2, title page.
14. Equiano, *Interesting Narrative* [1789], 116; *Georgia Gazette,* February 21, 1765.
15. Equiano, *Interesting Narrative* [1789], 139.
16. Ibid.
17. Ibid., 141.
18. Ibid., 152.
19. Ibid., 159.
20. Equiano to James Tobin, Esq., quoted in Folarin Shyllon, *Black People in Britain, 1555–1833* (London, 1977), 251.

Suggested Readings

Equiano's autobiography, *The Interesting Narrative of the Life of Olaudah Equiano, or Gustavus Vassa, the African* [first published edition, 1789], ed. Robert J. Allison (Boston, 1995), is the best source for his life. Catherine Acholonu, *The Igbo Roots of Olaudah Equiano* (Owerri, Nigeria, 1989), has fascinating information on both his family, then and now, in the village of Isseke. On slavery and the slave trade, particularly valuable are Joseph E. Inikori and Stanley Engermen, eds., *The Atlantic Slave Trade: Effects on Economies, Societies, and Peoples in Africa, the Americas, and Europe* (Durham, NC, 1992); and Patrick Manning, *Slavery and African Life: Occidental, Oriental, and African Slave Trades* (New York, 1990). Michael Craton, *Sinews of Empire: A Short History of British Slavery* (Garden City, NY, 1974) is an excellent overview. Robin Blackburn's twin volumes, *The Making of New World Slavery: From the Baroque to the Creole* (London, 1997) and T*he Overthrow of Colonial Slavery, 1776–1848* (London, 1988), are compelling syntheses. On the ideology of slavery, Winthrop Jordan, *White over Black: American Attitudes toward the Negro, 1550–1812* (Chapel Hill, NC, 1969); David Brion Davis, *The Problem of Slavery in the Age of Revolution, 1770–1823* (Ithaca, NY, 1975), and his more sweeping *Slavery and Human Progress* (New York, 1984); Orlando Patterson, *Slavery and Social Death: A Comparative Study* (Cambridge, MA, 1982); and Eric Williams, *Capitalism and Slavery* (Chapel Hill, NC, 1944) are well worth reading. Folarin Shyllon, *Black People in Britain, 1555–1833* (London, 1977), looks at the status of Africans and their descendants in English society; and W. Jeffrey Bolster, *Black Jacks: African-American Seamen in the Age of Sail* (Cambridge, MA, 1997), takes a long-overdue look at the world of black sailors like Equiano.

Index

Abbington Iron Furnace, 167–68, 171
Abenaki Indians, 25, 30, 141, 277; Johnson's adoption, 259–62, 265, 268. *See also* Montour, Madame Isabel
Abercromby, James, 210
Abortion, 110
Acadia, 38, 40, 203, 263, 278, 280
Adams, Abigail, 246
Adoption rituals: Indian, 79–80, 143, 148, 261–62
Adultery, 110, 120–21, 288
Affaire du Canada, 213
Africa: slavery in, 292–94, 302; slaves from (*see* Slaves)
Agriculture: in Chesapeake region, 102–4; in England, 105; by Indians, 22, 31, 39, 74; in New England, 239, 276, 278. *See also by crop*
Aix-la-Chapelle, Treaty of, 202–3
Alabama, 16
Albany, 143–44, 148–51, 263; Commissioners of Indian Affairs, 145, 148–50
Alcáraz, Diego de, 15
Alcide (ship), 204, 206
Alexander, James, 192
Algonquian Indians, 39, 76–78; emigration, 250–53; in Great Lakes region, 150–51, 199, 239–40; Montour's relationship, 143–45; music importance, 249–50; trade routes, 143–44, 151
Algonquian-speaking Indians, 73, 84, 239
Algonquin Indians, 143
Allen, John, 120
Alling, James, 130
Allison, Robert J.: *Crescent Obscured,* 291
Allumapees, 153

American Revolution, (Revolutionary War), 214, 244, 252; blacks' experience, 301–2; Montour family role, 156; Morris family and, 194–95; Whitefield's impact, 233–34
Americas: English infiltration, 24–29, 34, 71–72, 99–100, 144 (*see also* British America); French infiltration, 37–47, 143–44 (*see also* Canada); opportunities to sail for, 98, 168, 170, 172, 274–75; Spanish infiltration, 2–3
Amerindians, 208, 211, 258–59, 266
Amherst, Jeffrey, 211–12, 280–81
Andrews, Peter, 174
Angier, Rev. Samuel, 130
Anglicans and Anglicanism, 51–52, 227, 296, 301; Whitefield's relationship, 218–19, 225–27, 231; *Whole Duty of Man,* 225, 227
Anglo-Indian relations, 73, 78, 88–89
Anne, queen of England: and Mohawk alliance, 146
Annis, John, 299–300
Apalachee Indians, 5–7
Argall, Samuel, 85
Arminianism, 223, 225
Aros clan, 292–93
Asunción, 16
Attakapa Indians, 10
Attiwondaronk nation, 45
Aute, 6
Avavares Indians, 12–13
Aztec Indians, 2, 6, 7

Bahamas, 225
Baker, Nicholas, 130
Baker, Richard, 295–96

Baltimore, Lord: authority threats, 108, 111–12; indentures offered by, 99–100; land disputes, 171, 175–76; as Proprietor, 99, 101, 107
Bang's Island, 278
Baptism, 87–88, 126
Baptists, 226
Barbados, 182, 283, 294–95
Barnstable, 126, 128, 134
Bartlett, Rob, 132
Bartram, John, 175
Bay of Fundy, 278, 280
Bearde, John, 164
Beezley, Michael, 191
Beiler, Rosalind J., 161
Belle-Isle, Louis-Charles Auguste Fouquet, Comte de, 207
Benezet, Anthony, 302
Berks County, 171
Bethesda orphanage, 219–20, 226–27, 230, 298
Bible, bilingual, 240
Bigot, François, 213, 265
Bisaillon family, 151
Book of Common Prayer, 219, 225
"Born again" experience, 223–25, 231, 233, 300
Boscawen, Edward, 280
Boscawen (ship), 198
Boston: Board of Commissioners, 243, 247; Cotton's ties, 121, 123, 125, 127, 132–33, 136; General Court, 56, 58–59; Johnson's connections, 263, 267; original colonists, 54, 56; Pope's Day in, 277; Sheehan's experience, 276–77; as transatlantic center, 125, 276; Whitefield's sermon, 224–25
Boston Church, 57–59, 65
Boston's First Church, 121
Bourcet, Pierre-Joseph de, 200–201
Braddock, Edward, 204, 264
Bradford, William, 26
Brant, Joseph, 244
Brent, Margaret, 107, 109
Brent, Mary, 109
Bridgeham, Deacon, 136
Bridgewater, 130
Bristol, 220
British America: Americanization,

218; native-born elite, 182–83, 185–86, 195, 222; settlers (*see* Immigrants); 1700s government structure, 183–85. *See also by colony*
British army, 200, 278; 40th Regiment of Foot, 278–79, 282–83, 285; Provincial, 278–79, 286
British Royal Navy, 146, 149, 204, 292
Brothertown, 237, 252–53
Brown, Kathleen: *Good Wives,* 71
Bucks County, 171–72
Bulfill, Mabel, 98
Burial rituals, Indian, 28, 42
Burnet, William, 183–84
Byrd, William, II, 175

Cabeza de Vaca, Alvar Núñez: as Argentina governor, 16; battles fought, 3; downfall, 16–17; family history, 2; as healer, 11–13, 15; as Indian survivor, 9–17; as La Florida conquistador, 3–9, 13, 15; metamorphosis, 10–12, 15, 17; New World journey, 1–17; *Relación*, 12, 15; as trader, 9–11
Cádiz, 292, 300
Calvert, Charles, 113
Calvert, Leonard, 100–101, 108, 111
Calvert, Philip, 112
Calvin, John, 51, 57
Calvinists and Calvinism, 44, 51, 57, 229; Whitefield's conviction, 223, 226
Cambridge, 125, 127, 303
Cambuslang Revival, 228–29
Campeau, Lucien, 46
Canada: colonist captives in, 261, 264, 268; French and British control fights, 192–94, 199, 203–12, 279–82; French missionaries in, 37–47, 143; fur trade, 38–39, 44–45, 143–46, 150–51; Indian allies, 207–8, 210–12; natives in, 24–25, 142
Cannibalism, 10, 45, 293
Canonicus, 32

Capawack, 26
Cape Breton Island, 203, 232
Cape Breton War, 259
Cape Cod, 22, 24–25, 27, 30–32, 126
Caragouha village, 37, 39–40
Caribbean, 3, 193, 283, 294, 297
Carolinas: Anglicans in, 225; disease in, 135–36. *See also* North Carolina; South Carolina
Carondawanna, 147, 149–53
Carr, Lois Green: *Robert Cole's World,* 97
Casco Bay, 277–79, 285–87
Castillo Maldonado, Alonso del, 12, 14–15, 17
Cataraqui, 204
Catawba Indians, 142, 153
Catholics and Catholicism: German, 165; Irish, 274, 276–77, 279, 289; missionaries, 38, 42, 151; Penal Laws, 274, 276, 287; Puritans' opposition, 51, 289; refuge in Maryland, 97, 100, 108, 111; in Scotland, 246
Cautantowwit (deity), 28
Cayuga Indians, 143–44, 239
Chamberlain, John, 92
Chambly, 261
Champlain, Samuel de, 24, 33, 38–39, 239; *Voyages,* 43
Champlain village, 282
Chandler, Mr., 113
Chapouin, Jacques Garnier de, 38
Charles I, king of England, 53–54, 108, 111
Charles II, king of England, 112
Charleston, 122, 135–36
Charlestown, 251, 258–59, 267–68, 276
Charlotte, queen of England, 292, 303
Chartier family, 151
Chauncy, Charles: *Seasonable Thoughts,* 231
Chesapeake Bay (region): agricultural methods, 102–4; charter protections, 107; disease impact, 100; English attack on, 108; English colonization, 97, 99, 106; husbandry methods, 104–6; Indians in, 73, 100–101; living

conditions, 102–4, 106; Protestant government, 111–12; "time of troubles," 108. *See also* Maryland; Virginia
Chignecto Bay, 280
Child, Lydia Maria, 273
Children's issues, 109–10, 115
Chittenden, Miss, 120
Christians and Christianity: conversions *(see* Indians; Slaves; *specific individuals);* English, 26, 100, 296; freedom of worship, 100, 111; French, 42, 143; Spanish, 2
Churche, John, 132
Churche, Jos., 132
Church of England: Puritans' opposition, 51–54; Roman Catholic influence, 51, 53, 100; Whitefield's association, 217–21, 223–25, 227
Clarke, George, 187, 191
Clark's Freehold, 114, 117
Clarkson, Thomas, 301
Climate, 102, 116, 275–76
Clinton, George, 191–92, 253
Clocker, Bridgid, 98, 114
Clocker, Catheryn, 109
Clocker, Daniel: ancestry, 98; as appraiser, 110, 113; as carpenter, 101, 108–9; debt left, 114–16; descendants, 109, 114, 117; emigration, 97–98, 100–101; as farmer, 101, 104–6, 108–10; freedom choices, 106; government service, 110–14; as guardian, 115–16; household inventory, 114–15; income sources, 109; indenture, 97, 99–102; land owned, 108–9, 114, 117; life overview, 97–98, 114, 116; longevity, 100, 114; marriage, 107–8; as tenant, 106–7; vote proxies, 106–7
Clocker, Daniel, Jr., 109, 114
Clocker, Daniel, III, 117
Clocker, Daniel, IV, 117
Clocker, Elizabeth, 109
Clocker, Gosper, 98
Clocker, Hans, 98, 114
Clocker, Jasper, 98
Clocker, John (Daniel's brother), 98

Clocker, John (Daniel's son), 109
Clocker, Mary (daughter), 109, 114
Clocker, Mary (née Lawne): as dairy maid, 109–10; indenture, 107; as midwife, 110, 113; as mother, 109, 114, 117; personality traits, 112–13; theft indictment, 112–13; as wife, 97, 107–8
Clocker, Rebecca, 114
Coddington, William, 59
Cod fishing, 275–76
Coehoorn, Menno van, 200
Coggeshall, John, 62
Colden, Cadwallader, 147
Cole, Nathan, 222–24
Colorado River, 13
Columbus, Christopher, 1–2
Commissioners for the United Colonies, 125
Committee for the Black Poor, 302
Communion (Lord's Supper, Eucharist), 126, 130, 229
Company of New France, 43
Concord, 252
Conestoga Indians, 151
Congregationalism, 220, 226, 231, 238, 270, 277; New England ministry, 119, 121
Connecticut, 120, 122, 240, 248, 251
Connecticut River, 127, 249, 258
Contraband, 193
Cordelier community, 46
Corn, Indian, 103–5; in Jamestown, 74–75, 82; in La Florida, 5–7, 12; in Maryland, 102; in New England, 22, 25, 31, 33
Cornwaleys, Thomas, 97, 101–2, 104, 106
Coronado, Francisco de, 17
Cortés, Hernándo, 2
Cosby, William, 185–87
Cotton, Elizabeth (Mrs. James Alling, Mrs. Caleb Cushing), 130
Cotton, Joanna (née Rossiter): as healer, 131–32; as midwife, 131, 136; as wife, 119, 123, 131, 134–36
Cotton, John: Hutchinson's views and, 50, 57–58, 66; *Keys to the Kingdom,* 121; Puritan

differences, 57–60; as Puritan pastor, 53, 56–57, 66, 121; support of Hutchinson, 50, 58, 62
Cotton, John (grandson), 130–31
Cotton, John, Jr. (son): apprenticeship, 122; Boston ties, 121, 123, 125, 127, 132–33, 136; Charleston ministry, 122, 135–36; correspondence network, 119, 123, 125, 127–28, 130, 132; as cultural mediator, 122–24; excommunication, 121–22, 133; as father, 119, 130–31; as husband, 120, 123, 131, 134–36; Indian diary, 123; Martha's Vineyard ministry, 122–25, 136; Mayhew power struggle, 124–25; ministerial ancestry, 121–22; missionary work, 126–27; near banishment, 119, 121, 123, 133; Plymouth ministry, 119, 122, 125–34; rituals led by, 124, 126, 129–30; sex scandals, 119–22, 131, 133–34; sons' ministerial careers, 119, 130–32; Wampanoag Indians ministry, 119, 123–26; wartime ministry, 127–29
Cotton, Josiah, 130
Cotton, Rowland, 130–31, 133–35
Cotton, Samuel, 130
Cotton, Sarah (granddaughter), 130
Cotton, Sarah (née Mather), 121
Cotton, Seaborn, 122
Cotton, Theophilus, 130, 136
Cotton plantations, 294
Couc, Isabelle (née Montour), 143, 145–46
Couc, Madeleine (née Montour), 143, 146
Couc, Marguerite, 146
Council of the Indies, 17
Coureurs de bois, 143, 151
Courtney, James, 107
Courtney, Thomas, 107
Cow People, 14
Cratho, John, 166
Croix de St. Louis, 201–2, 207
Cromwell, Oliver, 111
Cromwell, Richard, 112

Crown Point, 211, 268
Cuba, 4, 273, 283–85
Culiacán, 16
Curaçao, 193
Cushing, Caleb, 130
Cushman, Robert, 30
Cutler, Timothy, 231

Dairy products, 105–6, 108–10
Dale, Sir Thomas, 86–87, 89–91
Daniell, Jere, 248
Dartmouth College, 244, 248, 251
Davenport, Rev. John, 120–21,
    229–31; *Confession and
    Retractions,* 230
De Lancey, James, 187, 192
De Lancey, Peter, 192
Delaware Indians, 151–53, 170, 208
Dermer, Thomas, 27–29, 33
De Soto, Hernando, 16
Detroit, 144–47, 210
Dichter, Ursula, 173
Diet: of settlers, 102–4, 108, 260
Diman, Rev. James, 289
Diseases: in Caribbean, 283–84; in
    Carolinas, 135–36; in
    Chesapeake region, 100;
    immigrants' immunity, 99;
    Indian epidemics, 10, 27, 33; in
    New England, 131, 280; from
    settlers, 2, 7, 10, 27, 41;
    pellagra, 103; on slave ships,
    293–94, 301
Dominican Republic, 3
Dorantes, Andrés, 11–12, 15, 17
Dryden, Bridget, 52
Dryden, John, 52
Dudley, Thomas, 61
Du Fay, Polycarp, 41
Dulany, Daniel, 181
Dummer, Shubael, 130
Dunham, Mercy, 134
Dunnigan, Brian L., 197
Duquesne, Ange Duquesne de
    Menneville, Marquis, 262–63
Dutch immigrants, 183
Dutch Reformed Church, 220
Dutch Surinam, 191
Dutch traders, 27, 29, 32, 297; in
    Albany, 143, 145, 148, 151;
    merchant ships, 191, 193–94

Duxbury, 126, 128
Dyer, Mary, 65, 67

Eastham, 128
Edict of Nantes, 44
Edinburgh, 229
Education: Equiano's, 295–96, 298;
    of Indians, 237–38, 240, 243–44,
    246, 251, 254; Johnson's, 258,
    268–69; Morris's, 183; Occom's,
    238, 241–42, 244–48; political
    importance, 111–12. *See also*
    Missionaries; *specific schools*
Edwards, Rev. Jonathan, 220, 226,
    228, 246
Edward VI, king of England, 51
Eeyamquiltoowsuconnuck, 252
Election (doctrine), 57, 66, 223–24
Eliot, John, 124, 240
Elizabeth (ship), 193
Elizabeth I, queen of England, 51,
    77
Elizabeth Islands, 124
Endt, John Theobald, 175
England: common law, 107; fishing
    industry, 275–76; in New World,
    24–29, 34, 71–72, 99–100 (*see
    also* British America); troops of
    (*see* British army; British Royal
    Navy). *See also* Church of
    England
English Civil War, 108, 111
Epenow, 26, 28, 32
Epidemics. *See* Diseases
Equality, racial, 301–2
Equiano, Jacob, 295
Equiano, Olaudah: British naval
    service, 292, 295–97; conversion
    to Christianity, 296–98, 300;
    early life, 291–93; English life,
    292, 296, 299, 301–3; as free
    man, 291–92, 297, 303;
    Interesting Narrative, 291–92,
    298, 303; on interracial
    marriage, 291, 302–3; as
    merchant, 297; in plantation
    management, 291, 300; reading
    abilities, 295–96; sailing skills,
    298; as slave, 291, 293–97; as
    slavery abolitionist, 291–92, 297,
    302–3; as slave trader, 291,

297–98. *See also* Vassa, Gustavus
Estate inventories, 104, 115, 173–74, 267
Esteban (Estevánico), 12, 14–15, 17
Evangelism, 123, 219, 221, 226, 228–29

Farmington, 249–51
Farnsworth, Ebenezer, 259, 262, 264, 269
Fendall, Josias, 112
Fenwick, Robert, 134
Ferdinand, king of Spain, 3
First Church of Boston, 231
Fishing industry, 275–76, 278, 287
Five Nations of Indians, 142–46, 149–51, 153
Florida. *See* La Florida
Forests, virgin, 102, 106
Fornication, 110
Förster, Georg Michael, 163
Fort Beauséjour, 280
Fort Cumberland, 280
Fort Duquesne, 210, 264
Fort Frontenac, 204, 210
Fort James, 71
Fort Lamotte, 143
Fort Lévis, 198, 211–12
Fort Necessity, 263
Fort Niagara, 151, 206–11
Fort Number 4, 258–59. *See also* Charlestown
Fort Oswego, 151, 206–8, 265
Fort Pittsburgh, 211
Fort St. Frédéric, 261, 263
Fort William Henry, 209
Fowler, David, 244, 249–50
Fowler, Hannah Garrett, 244, 250
France: fishing industry, 275; Ministry of War, 200; in New World, 37–47, 143–44 (*see also* Canada; West Indies); troops of (*see* French troops)
Franciscan monks, 42; La Florida expedition, 3–4, 17; Ontario mission, 37–47
Francis of Assisi, Saint, 38, 46
Franklin, Benjamin, 162, 182, 224; *Autobiography,* 222
Freedom dues, 99
Free will, 223

Frelinghuysen, Theodorus, 220–21
French and Indian War, 198, 257, 273, 279
French Canada. *See* Canada
French-Huron dictionary, 41, 43
French-Indian relations, 206, 208–12
French troops: command titles, 198–99, 201–2; Guienne Regiment, 205; *marine,* 199, 203–4, 206–7, 209–10; in New France war, 203–12; Régiment de Béarn, 198, 200–204, 213; tensions between branches, 204, 207, 209–10; *troupes de terre,* 198–99, 203, 206–7, 209–10, 212, 214
Frontier, western, 117
Furnishings, household, 104, 115
Fur trade: French Canadian, 38–39, 44–45, 143–44, 149–51; Iroquois diversion to Albany, 143–44; Montour family, 143–44, 151; by Patuxet, 25, 27, 29

Gabarus Bay, 280
Galveston Island, 9
Garden, Alexander, 225, 230, 232
Gateau, Nicholas, 166
George II, king of England, 203
Georgia, 5, 7, 297–98; Whitefield's mission, 217, 219–20
Georgian Bay, 37, 39
German immigrants: communication center, 175–76; in 1742 election, 176; individuals, 153, 161, 174; influx period, 168, 170, 172; inheritance laws, 166; naturalization petitions, 166–67; political influence, 176–77; as squatters, 170–72; Wistar as leader, 173–78
Germantown, 165, 175
Gill, Joseph-Louis, 261
Glasgow, 228
Gloucester, 218
Gold, 4–5, 73
Gordon, Patrick, 151, 153
Gorges, Ferdinando, 25–28

Gosnold, Bartholomew, 25
Grains, 30, 102–3
Great Awakening: First, 220, 233; Indian impact, 240–41, 247; Second, 233
Great Lakes Basin (region): in French war, 204; fur trade, 39, 143, 151; Indians in, 144, 146, 150–51, 199, 239
Green Bay, 251
Gregory XIV, Pope, 38
Grenada, 283
Grenoble, 213–14
Groton, 242, 251
Guanche servants, 3
Guerin sisters, 296, 298
Gulf of Mexico, 7-8
Gulf of St. Lawrence, 40

Haiti, 3
Halifax, 279–80, 285
Hall, Ebenezer, 289
Hall, Samuel, 289
Hamilton, Andrew, 187
Hamilton, James, 177
Hamor, Ralph: Pocahontas accounts, 72, 85–87, 89–90; *True Discourse,* 85
Hampton Falls, 130, 136
Hanover, 244
Harlow, Will, 132
Harris, Howell, 220, 228
Harris, John, 156
Hartford, 249
Harvard College, 122, 131–32, 224–25, 232
Hastings, John, 268
Hatch, John, 112
Hatton, Richard (father), 115–16
Hatton, Richard (son), 116
Hatton, William, 115–16
Havana, 273, 283–85
Háwikuh Pueblo, 17
Headrights, 100, 106
Hean, Thomas, 171
Helm, Arthur, 191
Henry VIII, king of England, 51, 77
Herbal medicine, 108, 132
Heretics, 58
Hetaquantagechty, 154
Hiacoombes, John, 124

Hiestand, Heinrich, 173
Hispaniola, 3, 193
Hobbamock (deity), 23
Hobbamock (warrior), 32
Hobson, Nicholas, 26
Hodenosaunee Indians, 239
Hollowell, Abiel (Mrs. Benjamin), 288–89
Hollowell, Benjamin (father), 276–77, 280, 288
Hollowell, Benjamin (son), 288
Hölzer, Georg Friedrich, 174
Hominy, 103
Housewifery, 105–6, 108
Housing construction, 104
Huddlestone, Jacob, 174
Hudson River, 211, 239
Huguenots, 40–41, 44
Hunt, Thomas, 26
Hunter, Robert (governor), 146–47, 149–50, 183
Hunter, Robert (Indian). *See* Carondawanna
Hunting: for survival, 22, 25, 84, 103, 239–40, 260
Huron Indians: dialects of, 41, 43; epidemics' effects, 41; in politics and war, 41, 45, 144, 239; religious conversion, 41; societal mores, 42, 44–46; spiritual beliefs, 44–46; trading role, 37, 39–41, 44
Husbandry, animal, 104–6, 127
Hutchinson, Anne (née Marbury): banishment, 50, 60, 65–66, 68; blasphemy charges, 50, 63–64; church trial, 65–67; early life, 50–53, 55; excommunication, 65–66; General Court trial, 50, 60–65, 67–68; as midwife, 56; as mother, 53, 55, 67; Puritan beliefs and, 57–58, 119; as religious leader, 49–50, 53, 55, 57–58, 61, 64, 66, 68; sedition charges, 50, 64, 68; slaying by Indians, 66; Spirit revelation, 58, 63–64, 67; threat to patriarchs, 56, 58–60, 66–68; as wife, 53, 55, 67
Hutchinson, William, 53, 56, 66
Hyde, Edward, Lord Cornbury, 144
Hymnody, 249

Ibo people, 291, 294, 300
Illiteracy, 111–12
Immigrants: adjustment
 challenges, 100, 102, 104, 107–9,
 116; disease immunity, 99; as
 family groups, 109; indenture for
 passage, 99, 102; inheritance
 limitations, 166; lures for,
 98–100; opportunities for,
 116–17.
Indentured servitude, 99, 102,
 116–17
Independent Company, 149
Indians: adoption rituals, 79–80,
 143, 148, 261–62; agriculture,
 22, 31, 39, 74 (*see also* Corn,
 Indian); burial rituals, 28, 42;
 Canadian, 24–25, 142;
 Chesapeake region, 100–101;
 Connecticut, 251; conversion to
 Christianity, 4, 9–15, 26–27,
 123–26, 151, 237–38, 240–42,
 244; disease epidemics, 10, 27;
 French (*see* Huron Indians);
 Great Lakes region, 144, 146,
 150–51, 239; as guides, 25,
 27–28, 31; kidnapping of, 24–26;
 La Florida, 1, 4–17; literacy, 238,
 240, 243–44, 246; marriage
 customs, 83–84; Martha's
 Vineyard, 122–25; nations of (*see*
 Five Nations of Indians; Six
 Nations of Indians); New
 England, 21–22, 25, 29–30,
 239–40; New Jersey, 152; New
 Mexico, 14, 17; New York,
 143–44, 148–50; Ohio Valley,
 156; Pennsylvania, 151, 154;
 Rhode Island, 251; as slaves, 4,
 25–26, 73; survival patterns,
 240; Virginia, 73, 75–78, 81;
 Whitefield's sermons, 226; in
 Wisconsin, 251. *See also by tribe*
Industrious Bee (ship), 295
Infanticide, 110
Ingle, Richard, 108, 111
Ingoldsby, Richard, 145–46
Iopassus, 85
Irish immigrants, 170, 172, 274–75
Iroquoia, 239, 244
Iroquoian language, 37, 41
Iroquois Confederacy, 153

Iroquois Indians: adoption rituals,
 143, 148; Fort Niagara and,
 206–8, 210–11; gender reciprocity,
 148; Grand Council, 149–50, 152,
 154; male public authority, 148;
 matrilineal structure, 147–48;
 Montour's relationship, 141,
 143–50; in Moor's School, 244–46,
 249–50; mourning-war tradition,
 143, 148; as nation (*see* Five
 Nations of Indians; Six Nations of
 Indians); in New England, 39,
 239–40; peace treaties, 144;
 Pennsylvania ties, 151–52,
 154–55; Pouchot's relationship,
 199, 206, 208–11; in
 Revolutionary War, 252; as
 Tuscarora allies, 149–50. *See also*
 Montour, Madame Isabel
Irving, Charles, 299–300
Itinerancy, 217, 219–20, 224,
 230–32, 241

Jaenen, Cornelius J.: *French
 Régime,* 37; *Friend and Foe,* 37
Jamaica, 300
James I, king of England, 31, 79,
 81, 92
James (ship), 198, 212
James River, 79
Jamestown, 72–74, 77–78
Jansen, Catharine, 168
Jansen, Dirk, 168
Jansen, Margaret (née Milan), 168
Jesuit priests: missions, 108, 155,
 262; opposition to Récollets, 38,
 40, 43–44; *Relations,* 43–44
Johnson, Captive, 260–62, 264–69
Johnson, James: Abenaki capture,
 258–62, 269; estate settlement,
 267; as family man, 259–65, 269;
 indenture, 258–59, 262; militia
 service, 259, 262, 265, 267; parole
 issues, 263–64; as prisoner of
 war, 264–65; redemption money,
 263–64, 267; sold to Canadians,
 262–63; as trader, 259
Johnson, Joseph, 249–52
Johnson, Polly, 259–60, 262–63,
 267–68
Johnson, Susannah (daughter),

258–60, 262

Johnson, Susannah (née Willard): Abenaki adoption, 257, 259–62, 266, 268–69; cash donations to, 265, 267; early life, 258, 268; languages of children, 260, 267–68; literacy, 258, 268–69; as mother, 259–65, 268; *Narrative,* 258, 269–70; as prisoner of war, 264–66; redemption of family, 266–68; release journey, 266–67; sold to Canadians, 257, 262–63, 266; as wife, 258, 265–66, 268

Johnson, Sylvanus, 259–61, 267–68

Johnson, Sir William, 211, 245, 251

Joncaire, Louis-Thomas Chabert de, 144

Julius II, Pope, 3

Kaqucka, 145

Karankawa Indians, 9–11

Katarionecha, 147, 153

Kaunoaurohaure, 249–50

Keith, James, 130

Keith, William, 170

Kellow, Margaret, 273

Kennebec River, 278

King, Robert, 297

King George's War, 176, 258, 276

King Philip's War, 119, 127–29, 258

Kingswood, 220

King William's War, 143–44

Kirke brothers, 40

Kirkland, Samuel, 250, 253

Kirkpatrick, John, 299

Kneeland, Rev. Abner, 269–70

Kocoum, 84

Krefeld, 165, 175

Labarree, Peter, 259, 262, 264, 267, 269

La belle-rivière, 203, 210

Labor shortage, 102, 106

La Florida: Indians of, 4–17; Spanish expedition, 1–17

Lake Champlain, 143, 146, 209

Lake George, 208

Lake Huron, 37

Lake Ontario, 204, 206, 209–12

Lake Simcoe, 39

Lake Winnebago, 251

Lalemant, Jérôme, 43

La Madeleine (ship), 39

Lambert, John Peter, 173

Lancaster (Massachusetts), 127, 258

Lancaster (Pennsylvania), 141

Lancaster County, 151, 171–72

Land: asset appraisals, 110; colonists' desire for, 25, 30, 127; development leases, 106; English claims, 73–74, 127; German squatters, 170–72; Indians' regard for, 73–74; inheritance laws, 166; profits from, 169; title disputes, 169–72, 175–76; Walking Purchase, 170; warrants, 99–100

Langdon, 270

La Réalle (ship), 39

Lathrop, Robert, 130

Lauson, Jean de, 43

Laval, François de, 38

Lebanon, 241

Le Caron, Joseph, 39, 43

L'Enfant-Jésus, Esther-Marie-Joseph de, 265

L'Entreprenant (ship), 281

Leominster, 258

Lescarbot, Marc: *Histoire,* 43

Le Tort, James, 151–52

Leverett, Thomas, 62

Lévis, François, 209, 211

Lexington, 252

Literacy. *See* Education

Livestock. *See* Husbandry

Logan, James, 151–52, 154, 170, 172

Long Island, 29, 242

Long Island Sound, 242–43

Lord, Mrs., 135

Loudoun, John Campbell, Earl, 279

Louis XIII, king of France, 38, 43

Louis XV, king of France, 201–3, 208, 214

Louisbourg: British siege, 209–10, 232–33, 279–82, 296; French troops at, 203, 209; Sheehan's involvement, 273, 280–82

Louisiana, 204

Loup Indians, 208

Lush, John, 191

Luther, Martin, 51
Lutherans, 165, 176
Lys (ship), 204

Mackay, Samuel, 279, 282
Magouaouidombaouit, 261
Maine, 217, 239
Maize. *See* Corn, Indian
Málaga, 23, 26
Malden, 134
Maliacones Indians, 13
Manawkyhickon, 152
Mansfield, William, 299
Marblehead, 287
Marbury, Francis, 52
Marcos, Fray, 17
Maritime commerce, 188–89
Maritimes (Maritime Provinces), 239
Marriage: Indian customs, 83–84; interracial, 291, 302–3
Marshe, Witham, 141
Marshfield, 126, 128
Martha's Vineyard, 22, 26, 28, 122–25, 136
Martinique, 273, 283
Mary, queen of England, 51
Maryland: Assembly, 106–7, 111–12; as Catholic refuge, 97, 100, 108, 111; early government, 106–7, 111–12, 141; immigrant settlement, 97–117; land title disputes, 171, 175–76; Proprietor (*see* Baltimore, Lord); "pigmie Rebellion," 112
Mashantucket, 252
Mason, John T., 267
Masques, 81, 92
Massachusett Indians, 22, 33–34
Massachusetts Bay (colony), 122; captive redemptions, 263; colonists, 24 (*see also* Puritans and Puritanism); native wars, 31–32, 127–29; Newfoundland and, 276
Massasoit, 29, 31–33
Mather, Cotton, 130, 133–34, 136
Mather, Increase, 125, 130–31, 133, 230
Mather, Richard: *Cambridge Platform,* 121

Mather, Sarah. *See* Cotton, Sarah
Mather family, 125
Matoaka. *See* Pocahontas
Mayflower (ship), 25, 30
Mayflower Compact, 30
Mayhew, Thomas, 124
Mayhew, Thomas, Jr., 124
McCulloch, Rev. William, 228
McIntyre, Sheila, 119–20
Medfield, 127–28
Medicine: English settlers', 131–32; herbal, 108, 132; medical texts, 132; Spanish, 11–13, 15
Medina Sidonia, Duke of, 3
Mendoza, Antonio de, 16–17
Merrimack River, 127, 263
Metacomet, 127
Methodists and Methodism, 218–19, 226–29
Mexico: Cabeza de Vaca in, 2, 5–8, 12–16; slaves from, 15, 73
Mexico City, 16
Miami Indians, 144, 146, 152
Michigan, 143
Michilimackinac, 143, 145–46
Micmac River, 25
Midwives and midwifery: Clocker as, 110, 113; Cotton as, 131, 136; Hutchinson as, 56; politics of, 55–56
Minerva (ship), 285
Missionaries: Catholic, 38, 42, 151; Cotton as, 126–27; English, 219, 226, 243, 250, 253, 301; Franciscan (*see* Franciscan monks); French, 37–47, 143, 262; Huron, 37, 39–41; Jesuit (*see* Jesuit priests); on Martha's Vineyard, 124–25; Moravian, 155; Native Indian, 243–44; Récollets (*see* Récollets); salary, 243; Whitefield as, 217, 219–20, 226
Mississauga Indians, 145, 206
Mississippi River, 9
Mitchell, William, 110
Mobile Bay, 8
Moctezuma, 6
Mohawk Indians, 143, 146, 148, 239
Mohawk River, 209, 211
Mohegan Indians: emigration, 250–53; English connections,

240–41; land dispute with
Connecticut, 248, 251; lifestyle,
237, 239–40. *See also* Occom,
Samson
Mohegan River, 240
Monckton, Robert, 283
Monomoy, 28, 33–34
Montagnais people, 39
Montauk, 242
Montauk Indians, 237, 239, 242
Montcalm, Louis-Joseph de, 206,
208–11
Montgomerie, John, 184
Montgomery County, 172
Montmorency, Duke of, 44
Montour, Andrew (Sattelihu): as
interpreter, 155–56; as son, 145,
147, 151, 153
Montour, Catherine, 147
Montour, Esther, 147
Montour, Madame Isabel:
Christianity grasp, 155; as
cultural broker, 142, 147–48,
156–57; family network, 141–43,
145–47, 156–57; as free-lance
consultant, 152–56; as
government adviser, 146–50;
Great Lakes contributions, 146,
150–51; as interpreter, 141–42,
146–52; Iroquois adoption,
141–42, 146–47; as Iroquois
matron, 141, 147–50, 155–56;
language fluency, 146, 148; as
mother, 145, 147, 150, 155; New
York contributions, 142, 146–51,
156; as Oneida wife, 147, 150,
156–57; Pennsylvania
contributions, 142, 151–57;
retreat to Ostonwakin, 151, 155;
trading connections, 142, 145
Montour, Isabelle. *See* Couc,
Isabelle
Montour, Jean, 146
Montour, Jean-Baptiste, 146–47
Montour, Joseph, 146
Montour, Lewis, 147
Montour, Louis, 143–46
Montour, Madeleine. *See* Couc,
Madeleine
Montour, Margaret, 147, 151
Montréal: British attack, 273,
282–83; colonist captives sold in,

262–64, 266; significance, 146,
208, 210–12
Montserrat, 297
Moors, 2, 11–12
Moor's Indian Charity School,
243–50
Moravian missionaries, 155
Morris, Anthony, 167
Morris, Anthony, Sr., 167
Morris, Gouverneur, 194
Morris, Katerina (née Staats), 183
Morris, Lewis, Jr.: Dutch ship
decisions, 193–94; early life,
182–83; as politician, 183–85,
191–92; public offices held,
183–84, 187–88; relationship
with father, 187–88; as vice-
admiralty court judge, 181,
188–94
Morris, Lewis, Sr.: censure of
governor, 184–85; as father,
182–83, 187–88; land
inheritance, 182; London trip,
186; as New Jersey governor,
187–88; as politician, 182–87;
public offices held, 182–84,
187–88; suspension from council,
185
Morris, Lewis (grandson), 183, 194
Morris, Richard, 187, 190, 194
Morris, Robert, 186, 188, 192
Morris, Sarah (née Gouverneur), 183
Morris, Staats, 183, 194
Morton, Nathaniel, 31
Morton, Rebekah, 133
Mosquito Coast, 300
Mosquito Indians, 300
Muslims. *See* Moors

Nanamaghemet, 261
Nantucket, 124, 126
Narragansett Bay, 22, 27–28
Narragansett Indians, 239, 251;
epidemic survival, 27–28; as
political force, 29–30, 32–34, 127
Narváez, Pánfilo de, 3–9, 16
Native Americans. *See* Indians
Native-born elite, 182–83, 185–86, 195
Navigation Acts, 188
Neckar River Valley, 173–74
Nemasket, 28

New Birth conversion, 223–25, 231
Newburyport, 233–34
New Castle, 170
New Castle County, 167
New England: agriculture in, 239,
    276, 278; disease outbreaks, 131,
    277; English interests, 24–27,
    29, 34, 198, 203; fishing
    industry, 275–76; French
    interests, 24–25, 27, 198, 203;
    Indians of, 21–22, 25, 123, 127;
    Pilgrims' colonization, 22–34;
    Whitefield's relationship, 220,
    222–23, 225–27, 229–32, 234
New England Company, 243, 247
Newfoundland, 23, 38, 275–76
Newfoundland Company, 27
New France. *See* Canada
New Hampshire, 65, 244, 276;
    Indian raids in, 258–60, 263
New Israel, 53–54
New Jersey, 152, 183–85
Newman, Noah, 127–28
New Mexico, 2, 13–14, 17
New Netherlands, 27, 29
Newspapers, 193, 217, 224, 226,
    292, 301
Newton, 59
New York: Assembly, 149–50,
    184–85; in French and Indian
    War, 198; Indians of, 143–44,
    148–50; Morris family
    contributions, 183–85; plan to
    attack Canada, 145–46, 150;
    political reform, 186
New York City, 181, 183, 189,
    192–93
New-York Weekly Journal, 186–87
Niagara Falls, 205
Niantic Indians, 239, 251
Nicaragua, 292, 300
Nicholson, Francis, 146, 149
Nigeria, 291, 293
Nipmuck Indians, 127, 239
Nitschmann, Anna, 155
Norris, Isaac, 167, 171–72
Northampton, 220, 226
Northampton County, 172
North Carolina, 149–50
Norwich, 246
Nova Scotia, 232, 275, 285

Obadiah, 124
Occom, Mary (née Fowler), 243–44,
    252–53
Occom, Samson: as artisan, 243;
    British fund-raising trip,
    244–48, 253; *Choice Collection of
    Hymns,* 249; conversion to
    Christianity, 237–38, 241; as
    cultural broker, 237–38, 242–45,
    253–54; Dutch contacts, 240;
    early life, 240; English
    relationship, 240, 242, 245–47,
    251; as family man, 243–44,
    252–53; Indian relationship,
    239–40, 242, 245; Johnson's
    relationship, 249–52; language
    fluency, 237–39, 242; literacy,
    238, 241–42, 244–49; migration
    north, 250–54; as minister,
    237–38, 242–43, 246–47, 249,
    251, 253; as schoolmaster, 238,
    242; Scotland trip, 246, 253; as
    tribal councilor, 241–42;
    Wheelock's relationship, 241,
    243–44, 247–48, 250, 253–54;
    Whitefield's association, 237,
    241–42, 246–47; written legacy,
    238–39, 249
Occom, Tabitha, 250
Ockham, Jonathan, 241
Ockham, Joshua (father), 241
Ockham, Joshua (son), 241
Ockham, Lucy, 241
Ockham, Sarah, 241–42
Oglethorpe, James, 298
Ohio River Valley (region), 156,
    203–4, 210, 264, 278
Oklahoma, 10
Old South Church (Boston), 133,
    224
Oneida Indians: emigration,
    151–54, 251; in Iroquois nation,
    143, 147, 239; Montour
    relations, 151–54; tribes
    emigrating into, 250–53
Onondaga Indians, 143, 146, 149,
    239
Ontario, 38, 43
Oonchiarey, 45
Opachisco, 89
Opata Indians, 14
Opechancanough, 80

Orphanages, 115, 219–20, 226–27
Ossassane, 40
Ostonwakin, 151–52
Ousamequin. *See* Massasoit
Overzee, Mrs. Simon, 113
Overzee, Simon, 113
Owen, Evan, 168
Oxford University, 218–19

Palatinate region (Germany),
    161–66, 173
Pánuco, 9, 16
Paoli, Pasquale, 214
Papists. *See* Catholics and
    Catholicism
Paris, Treaty of, 285
Parmenter, Jon, 141
Parsons, Mr., 233
Pascal, Michael, 295, 299
Paskannahommen, 124
Paspahegh Indians, 75–76
Patawomeck Indians, 85
Patuxet village: colonization,
    21–34; epidemic impact, 27–28,
    33; as trading center, 24, 34
Paulmy, Antoine-René de Voyer
    d'Argenson, Marquis de, 202–3, 207
Pawtucket Indians, 22
Paxton, 151
Pays d'en haut, 143–44, 150
Peace of Paris, 252
Peace of Pocahontas, 90
Pecos River, 13
Pemaquid River, 25, 30
Penal Laws, 274, 276, 287
Peñasco River, 13
Penn, John, 154–55, 168–70, 172
Penn, Richard, 168
Penn, Thomas, 168, 175–77
Penn, William, 164, 168–70
Pennsylvania: Commissioners of
    Property, 166, 169, 171; Indians
    in, 151–54; land title disputes,
    169–72, 175–76; Proprietors,
    168–72, 175–78
Penobscot River, 25, 27
Pensacola Bay, 8
People of the Longhouse, 239
Pepperrell, William, 233
Pequot Indians, 59, 239, 242,
    251–52

Peters, Hugh, 62
Peters, Richard, 176
Petun people, 39
Philadelphia: Equiano's connection,
    292, 297; German immigrant
    traffic, 161–62; Indian
    conferences, 151, 153–54;
    Whitefield's sermon, 222, 226
Philadelphia County, 171
Philadelphia Monthly Meeting of
    Friends, 166–67
Pilgrims: New England, 22–34. *See
    also* Puritans and Puritanism
Pima Indians, 14
Pitt, William, 283
Plains of Abraham, 281
Pleasant Harbor, 28
Plymouth (England), 229, 266–67
Plymouth Bay (colony): Cotton's
    ministry, 119, 122, 125–34;
    initial settlers, 22, 24, 29–30;
    political strengthening, 31–34;
    Squanto's plot against, 32–34;
    treaty of, 31
Pnieses, 23–24
Pocahontas: baptism, 87–88;
    brother's involvement, 86, 89;
    conversion to Christianity,
    87–88, 91; as cultural bridge,
    76–78, 83, 88; England journey
    and life, 71, 87–88, 90–93;
    English captivity effects, 86–89;
    Hamor's accounts, 72, 85–87, 89;
    kidnapping of, 85–87; life
    overview, 71–73, 93; marriages,
    83–85, 88–89; as mother, 91–93;
    as "Nonpareil" of Virginia, 72,
    75, 81, 88; personal qualities,
    77–78; as political pawn, 75–76,
    83, 85–87, 89–90; portrait, 92; as
    Powhatan's daughter, 72–78, 87;
    as Rebecca, 88; as Rolfe's wife,
    87–91; Smith's meetings, 75–76,
    92–93; Smith's relationship, 79,
    81–82, 84–85, 88, 92–93; as
    Smith's rescuer, 78–83;
    Strachey's accounts, 76–77,
    84–85; as traitor, 82–83; Virginia
    Company and, 91–92
Pokanoket, 27–29, 32
Ponce de León, Juan, 4
Portland, 277

Portsmouth (England), 198, 267
Portsmouth (New England), 267
Portugal, 275
Potomac River, 100, 239
Pouchot, Pierre: as cartographer,
    197–98, 201, 206, 208–9; as
    commoner, 199; early life,
    199–200; as engineer, 197–98,
    200, 204, 206, 214; European
    battles, 200–202; Fort Lévis role,
    211–12; Fort Niagara role,
    197–98, 205, 207, 209–11; as
    historian, 198–99, 208–9,
    213–14; as Indian envoy,
    198–99, 206–8, 210–12;
    Mémoires, 198–200, 203, 208–9,
    214; military career
    advancement, 197–203, 206–7,
    212–14; New France service,
    197, 199, 204–12; as prisoner of
    war, 197, 199, 211–12; return to
    France, 212; titles held,
    198–202, 204, 207, 213
Powhatan: as chieftain, 71, 74, 80,
    90; as father, 72–78, 84, 86, 89;
    Jamestown ambush plans, 75,
    82; Smith's relationship, 79–82;
    use of Pocahontas, 75–76, 83,
    85–87, 89–90
Powhatan Indians, 73; adoption
    rituals, 79–80; female sexual
    hospitality, 81–82; marriage
    customs, 83–84. *See also*
    Pocahontas
Predestination, 57, 124, 223
Preparationism, 57
Presbyterians and Presbyterianism,
    221, 226, 228, 231, 238, 246
Price, Anne, 115
Price, John, 115
Prisoners of war: from Fort
    Oswego, 265; French, 198;
    Johnson family as, 264–66;
    Pouchot as, 197, 199, 211–12;
    treatment standards, 266
Privateers and privateering, 181,
    189–93, 278, 301; Prize Goods
    Exemption Act, 190
Protestant Reformation, 51, 238, 254
Protestants and Protestantism:
    beliefs, 42, 44, 124; immigration
    role, 100, 111; Indian literacy and,

238, 240, 251, 254; in Ireland,
    274, 276; Puritans' opposition, 51;
    Reformed, 238, 254
Pueblo Indians, 14, 17
Puritans and Puritanism (New
    England): beliefs, 49, 51–52,
    54–55, 67–68, 230; defiant
    history, 49, 51; as flexible,
    119–21, 136; Hutchinson crisis,
    49–50, 54, 59–68; initial
    colonists, 29–30, 53–55;
    opposition to Church of England,
    51–54; rituals, 124, 126, 129–30;
    salvation struggles, 52, 62, 66,
    126; sin list, 129; Whitefield's
    resemblance, 218, 223, 230;
    women's roles, 55–56

Quakers: domination of
    Pennsylvania Assembly, 176–77;
    Germantown settlement, 165,
    168; loyalty to Great Britain,
    166; meeting chapters, 166;
    scruples against war, 176;
    slavery condemnation, 297, 302;
    Wistar's conversion, 161,
    164–166
Québec, 39, 41, 143, 147; Johnsons'
    imprisonment, 265–66, 278;
    Pouchot's association, 203–4,
    210–11
Queen Anne's War, 144–45, 150

Racial differences, 301–2
Ramsay, David, 301
Randolph, John, 181
Rape, 288–89
Rawhunt, 75
Reading (town), 269
Récollets: of Aquitaine, 38; Jesuits'
    opposition, 38, 40, 43–44;
    missions, 37–47; of Saint-Denis,
    37–38
Reconquista, 2
Reformed Church, 165, 176
Rehoboth (Massachusetts), 127–28,
    130
Repentance, 129, 136
Revelation, divine, 58, 63, 221
Revivalism, interdenominational:

Americanization role, 218, 233; beginnings, 220; fundamental power, 224, 233; Indian impact, 240, 242, 249, 251; mass marketing, 226; oppositions, 229–31; political impact, 233; in Scotland, 228–29; Whitefield's role, 217, 220–21, 224, 226, 228–29
Revolutionary War. *See* American Revolution
Rhine River Valley, 165, 173–74
Rhode Island, 65–66, 127, 240, 251
Rhoden, Nancy L.: *Revolutionary Anglicanism,* 217
Richelieu, Cardinal, 43
Richelieu River, 39
Ridgely, Robert, 114
Riehm, Abraham, 162
Ring, Will, 132
Río de la Plata, 16
Río Grande, 2, 13–14, 17
Río Sinaloa, 15
Roanoke, 175
Roebuck (ship), 295
Roger, Robert, 268
Rolfe, John, 71–73, 87–89, 91
Rolfe, Thomas, 71, 91
Rossiter, Bray, 125, 131
Roturiers, 199, 207
Rutter, Thomas, 167

Sabatis, 262, 268
Saco River, 22
Sagard, Gabriel: *Dictionnaire,* 42–43; *Grand voyage,* 37, 42, 44, 46–47; *Histoire du Canada,* 43, 46–47; Huron mission, 40–41; open-mindedness, 44–45; return to France, 41–42; trip to New France, 38–40, 43
Sagogaliax, 153
Saguenay River, 39
Saint-Ange, Louis Charly, 263
Saint-Cercy, Madame, 146
St. Andrews, 109
St. Botolph's Church, 53
St. Clement's Manor, 112
St. Eustatius, 297
St. François, 261, 263, 268
St. François-du-Lac, 143
St. Kitts, 299

St. Lawrence River, 204, 209–12, 233, 239
St. Lucia, 283
St. Mary's City, 98, 108, 113–14
St. Mary's County, 111, 114
St. Mary's River, 100–101, 103
St. Vincent, 283
Ste. Magdalene, 282
Salem, 54, 287–89
Salisbury, 130
Salisbury, Neal: *Manitou and Providence,* 21
Saltonstall family, 125
Salvation, personal, 57, 62, 66, 223, 233
Samoset, 30–31
Sandwich, 128, 130, 134
Saratoga, 149–51
Saristagoa, 153–54
Sassamon, John, 127
Sategariouaen, 208
Sattelihu. *See* Montour, Andrew
Sauer, Christopher, 176
Savannah, 219, 298
Schuyler, Peter, 146, 149–50, 265, 267
Scituate, 128, 130
Scottish Church, 229
Secessionists, 228
Seneca Indians, 143–45, 150, 208, 239
Servants, 102, 116–17, 141; immigrants as (*see* Indentured servitude)
Seven Years' War, 192–94, 197, 199
Sewall, Samuel, 134
Seward, William, 229
Sharp, Granville, 301
Shate, Henry, 174
Shawnee Indians, 151
Sheehan, Bryan: battles fought, 273, 280–85; in British Army, 273, 278–86; as criminal, 287–89; disease survival, 273, 280, 283–84; as drunkard, 277–78; emigration, 273–76; as fisherman, 275–79, 287; indenture, 273, 276–77; marriage, 273, 278, 286; in poverty, 285–87; resentments, 277, 285–86; as sailor, 277–78, 287; sexual impropriety, 278, 287–89
Shickellamy, 152–56

Shinnecock Indians, 239, 242
Shippen, Edward, 181
Shirley, William, 263, 278
Six Nations of Indians, 143, 153, 207–8, 239, 252
Slany, John, 27
Slaves: in Africa, 292–94; Africans as, 291–303; in America, 222, 240, 294–98; brutality toward, 293, 297–98, 303; conversion to Christianity, 296, 298, 300; efforts to free, 292, 302–3; in Europe, 292, 294, 299, 302–3; Indians as, 26, 73; rebellions on ships, 294; revivalism impact, 226, 240, 298; rights of, 292, 299, 301; Spanish expedition, 15–16; volume traded, 294; in West Indies, 291, 294, 297, 299, 301; Whitefield's views, 226, 298; work performed, 294–95. *See also* Equiano, Olaudah
Slave ships, 293–94, 301
Slave trade: African origins, 291–94; efforts to abolish, 292, 302–3; insurance claims, 301; from West Indies to America, 292, 297–98
Slye, Robert, 111
Smith, John, 239; *Generall Historie,* 79–80, 82–83; Jamestown role, 74; *Map of Virginia,* 78; New England explorations, 24–27; Pocahontas accounts, 71–76, 78, 81, 83, 86–88; Pocahontas relationship, 75–76, 79, 81–82, 84–85, 92–93; Pocahontas rescue, 78–82; Powhatan adoption, 79–80, 88, 93; *Proceedings,* 79–80, 84; *True Relation,* 74–76, 79
Smith, Samuel, 128
Society for Promoting the Manumission of Slaves, 302
Society in Scotland for the Propagation of Christian Knowledge (SSPCK), 246, 248
Sodus Bay, 144
Somerset, James, 299, 301
Sonora, 14
Sons of Africa, 291–92, 302
South Carolina, 122, 135–36, 297
Spain, 275; Cuban interests, 283–85; La Florida expedition, 1–17; in slave trade, 15–16
Springfield, 267
Squanto: alienation from Indians, 28, 32; in Europe, 22–23, 26–27, 71; family history, 22; as guide, 27–28, 31; in Pilgrim settlement, 21–34; as *pniese,* 24; political success, 28, 31–33; return to New England, 27–29, 31
Standish, Miles, 30, 33
Staten Island, 283
Stauffer, Jacob, 174
Steel, James, 169
Steele, Ian K.: *Betrayals,* 257; *Warpaths,* 257
Stern, Peter, 1
Stobo, Robert, 263–64, 266
Stockholm syndrome, 86
Stone, Samuel, 120, 122
Stone, William, 111
Stonington, 251
Strachey, William: *Historie,* 76; Pocahontas accounts, 76–77, 84–85
Stroud blankets, 151–53
Stuart, Charles Edward Louis (Bonnie Prince Charlie), 246
Sugar, 190, 283, 294–95, 297
Sunbury, 151
Susquehanna River, 101, 151
Susquehannock Indians, 101
Suwanee River, 6
Szasz, Margaret Connell: *Indian Education,* 237

Tackanash, John, 124
Tadoussac, 39
Tampa Bay, 3, 5
Tantaquidgeon, 241
Taxation, 276
Teganissorens, 149
Tenancy, 106, 117
Tennent, Gilbert, 221, 228–29, 231; *Danger of an Unconverted Ministry,* 231
Texas, 2, 9–10, 16
Thames River, 240
Thayendanegea, 244
Thommen, Durst, 175
Ticonderoga, 210–11, 267

Tillotson, John (archbishop of Canterbury), 225, 227, 230, 232
Timucan Indians, 5
Tisquantum. *See* Squanto
Tobacco, 45, 87; farming methods, 104–5; as Maryland export crop, 99, 105, 108, 110; plantations, 294–95
Tobin, James, 301
Tomockham, 240
Trade laws: maritime, 181, 188; Wistar's petition, 166–67
Trading centers: in Canada, 39, 144; in Great Lakes region, 143–44; in Maryland, 108; in New England, 22, 24–25, 29–30, 277–78, 287; in New York, 144, 189, 192–93, 206–7; in Pennsylvania, 151; in Rhode Island, 192; in South Carolina, 192; in Southwest, 9–11; in Virginia, 73, 108; in West Indies, 297
Trois-Rivières, 143, 282
Tunxis Indians, 239, 250
Tuscarora, 253
Tuscarora Indians, 143, 149–51, 239
Tuscarora War, 149–50

Uncas, Benjamin, 240–41
Universalists, 270
Urban VIII, Pope, 43
Utrecht, Treaty of, 150
Uttamatomakkin, 91–92

Vacuum domicilium, 30–31
Van Braam, Jacob, 263, 266
Vane, Henry, 58–60, 66
Van Sweringen, Garrett, 114
Vassa, Anna Maria, 303
Vassa, Gustavus, 295–96. *See also* Equiano, Olaudah
Vassa, Johanna, 303
Vassa, Susan (née Cullen), 303
Vauban, Sébastien Le Prestre de, 200, 205
Vaudreuil, Philippe de Rigaud, Marquis de, 144–45, 150
Vaudreuil, Pierre de Rigaud, Marquis de, 204–6, 208–13, 264–65, 282

Vaux, Noel Jourda, Comte de, 214
Ventadour, Duke of, 40
Vice-admiralty courts, 181, 188–93
Viel, Nicolas, 39
Virginia: Indians in, 73, 75–78, 81; settlers, 72–74, 175; slaves in, 295. *See also* Chesapeake Bay
Virginia Company, 72–74, 78, 91–92
Voting rights, 106–7

Wager, Sir Charles, 186–88, 192
Walking Purchase, 170
Walpole, 269
Wampanoag Indians: colonist relations, 31, 127; corn trade, 25–26, 33–34; Cotton's ministry, 119, 123–26; epidemic impact, 27–28; hostility rituals, 31; society norms, 21–24, 28; Squanto capture, 28–29; vulnerability, 29–31. *See also* Squanto
Wampum belts, 145, 148
Wanna, John, 124
War of the Austrian Succession, 201–2, 214
War of the Polish Succession, 200
Warren, Ben, 132
Warren, Susan, 110
Washington, George, 252, 263
Watson, Michael, 181
Watts, Mary (daughter), 114
Watts, Mary (mother). *See* Clocker, Mary
Watts, Peter (father), 114
Watts, Peter (son), 114
Weathersfield, 269
The Weekly History (England), 228
Weekly Mercury (Philadelphia), 167
Weiser, Conrad, 153, 155
Weld, Thomas, 67
Wells, Mrs., 120
Wequela, 152
Werowances, 74
Wesley, Charles, 218–19, 223
Wesley, John, 218–20, 223, 230, 233–34
West Africa, 302
Westerkamp, Marilyn: *Triumph of the Laity,* 49
West Indies: British attack, 283;

Cabeza de Vaca's expedition, 3,
16–17; slavery and, 291, 294,
297, 299, 301
Wethersfield, 120, 122
Weymouth, 126–27
Wheat, 102–3
Wheatley, Phillis, 234
Wheelock, Rev. Eleazar: Occom's
relationship, 241, 243–44,
247–48, 250, 253–54; schools
started by, 237, 243–48
Wheelwright, Esther, 265
Wheelwright, John, 57–60, 64
Whitaker, Rev. Alexander, 87, 89
Whitaker, Nathaniel, 246–47
White, Colonel, 258
Whitefield, Elizabeth James,
227–28
Whitefield, George: American
travels, 219–27, 229, 231–33;
attacks on, 225, 229, 231; on
"born again" conversion, 223,
225; as Calvinist, 223, 226;
crossed eyes, 223; crowds at
sermons, 224–25, 227; as
delusional, 225, 230–31; early
life, 218; as emotional, 219,
221–22, 229–30; England
relationship, 217–21, 223–24,
227, 229; as evangelist, 219, 221,
226, 228–29; extemporaneous
style, 219–21, 227; hierarchy
dislike, 230, 233; humble image,
221–22; as husband, 227–28; as
itinerant minister, 217, 219–20,
224, 230–32; Louisbourg role,
232–33; mass-marketing
techniques, 217, 226–27; as
missionary, 217, 219–20, 226;
New England relationship, 220,
222–23, 225–27, 229–32, 234;
Occom's association, 237, 241–42,
246–47; open-air preaching, 220,
224, 227, 230; ordination,
218–20; orphanage post, 219–20,
226–27, 230, 298; political
impact, 233–34; religious beliefs,
218, 221–23, 225; revivalism role,
217, 220–21, 224, 226–30;
Scotland trips, 219, 221, 227–28;
Short Account of God's Dealings,
218; slavery views, 226, 298;

theatrical passion, 217–18, 221;
Wales trips, 219, 227;
youthfulness, 219, 223
Whitefield, John, 228
Wigwams, 240–41, 244, 261–62
Willard, Aaron, 267
Willard, Major, 258
Willard, Miriam, 259–60, 262–65,
267
Willard, Moses, 258, 265, 267
Willard, Samuel, 133
Willard, Susannah (daughter). *See*
Johnson, Susannah
Willard, Susannah (née Hastings),
258
Williams, Mary, 113
Williams, Roger, 49
Wilson, Rev. John, 56–57, 59, 62,
128
Winslow, Edward, 22, 32–33
Winslow, John, 278
Winthrop, John: as governor, 49,
56, 58–59, 66, 121; in
Hutchinson trial, 50, 60–65
Winthrop, Wait, 181
Wisconsin, 251
Wistar, Caspar (father): as business
owner, 161, 167; as button maker,
161, 164, 167; as cultural broker,
162, 173, 177–78; early life,
162–64, 168; emigration, 161, 164;
estate settlement, 173–74; as
financier, 171, 173; as immigrant
benefactor, 172–77; international
networks, 173–75; as investor, 167,
171; as laborer, 164; land
speculation, 166, 168–75; as
merchant, 167, 171;
naturalization, 166–67; New
Jersey glassworks, 173; political
power, 172–74, 176–77;
Proprietors' relationship, 168–72,
175–78; as Quaker convert, 161,
164–66, 176; social status rise,
164, 167–68; squatter resolutions,
171–72; success strategies, 162,
164, 166–68, 172, 178
Wistar, Caspar (son), 174
Wistar, Catherine, 174
Wistar, John, 169, 175–76
Wistar, Margaret, 174
Wistar, Rebecca, 174

Wistar, Richard, 168–69, 174
Wistar, Sarah, 174
Witches and witchcraft, 42, 288
Wolfe, James, 281–82
Women: "traffic in," 83; woman-
  short society, 108
Worcester, 263
Worcester County, 258
Wright, Mrs., 120

Yale College, 122, 183, 224–25, 232

Yamassee Indians, 150
Yaocomico Indians, 100–101
Yarmouth, 128, 130, 134
York, 130, 229

Zenger, John Peter, 187
Zimmerman, Abraham, 173
Zimmerman, Melchior, 173
Zinzendorf, Nicholas Ludwig von, 155
Zong (ship), 301
Zuñi Indians, 17